THE ECONOMICS OF NATURAL AND HUMAN RESOURCES IN AGRICULTURE

THE ECONOMICS OF NATURAL AND HUMAN RESOURCES IN AGRICULTURE

AYAL KIMHI

AND

ISRAEL FINKELSHTAIN

EDITORS

Nova Science Publishers, Inc.

New York

NOTICE TO THE READER

The Publisher has taken reasonable care in the preparation of this book, but makes no expressed or implied warranty of any kind and assumes no responsibility for any errors or omissions. No liability is assumed for incidental or consequential damages in connection with or arising out of information contained in this book. The Publisher shall not be liable for any special, consequential, or exemplary damages resulting, in whole or in part, from the readers' use of, or reliance upon, this material. Any parts of this book based on government reports are so indicated and copyright is claimed for those parts to the extent applicable to compilations of such works.

Independent verification should be sought for any data, advice or recommendations contained in this book. In addition, no responsibility is assumed by the publisher for any injury and/or damage to persons or property arising from any methods, products, instructions, ideas or otherwise contained in this publication.

This publication is designed to provide accurate and authoritative information with regard to the subject matter covered herein. It is sold with the clear understanding that the Publisher is not engaged in rendering legal or any other professional services. If legal or any other expert assistance is required, the services of a competent person should be sought. FROM A DECLARATION OF PARTICIPANTS JOINTLY ADOPTED BY A COMMITTEE OF THE AMERICAN BAR ASSOCIATION AND A COMMITTEE OF PUBLISHERS.

LIBRARY OF CONGRESS CATALOGING-IN-PUBLICATION DATA

Kimhi, Ayal, 1959-
  The economics of natural and human resources in agriculture / Ayal Kimhi and Israel Finkelshtain.
    p. cm.
  Includes index.
  ISBN 978-1-60741-029-4
  1. Agriculture--Economic aspects. 2. Water resources development. 3. Natural resources--Management. 4. Agriculture and state. 5. Farm management. I. Finkelshtain, Israel. II. Title.
  HD1415.K515   2009
  338.1--dc22
                                                                       2008056001

Published by Nova Science Publishers, Inc. ✤ *New York*

CONTENTS

PART A. NATURAL RESOURCES IN AGRICULTURE
SECTION I: MANAGEMENT OF WATER SALINITY

In: The Economics of Natural and Human Resources...   ISBN 978-1-60741-029-4
Editor: Ayal Kimhi and Israel Finkelshtain   © 2009 Nova Science Publishers, Inc.

Chapter 1

INTRODUCTION TO THE ECONOMICS OF NATURAL AND HUMAN RESOURCES IN AGRICULTURE

Ayal Kimhi and Israel Finkelshtain[*]

The theme of this book is the allocation of natural and human resources in the agricultural sector of both developed, developing and transition economies. Extensive search for the ·sources of economic growth have lead economists to comprehend that sustainable growth requires efficient allocation of natural resources, complemented by high levels of human resources, such as knowledge, management and governance. This conception is particularly applicable in the context of agriculture productivity, which has been a major contributor to economic growth, world-wide.

The book brings together various findings of leading international scholars of agricultural economics on the management of natural and human resources. It addresses a variety of problems that are related to the above issues and are common to many countries.

The contribution of this book to the literature stems from the novelty of the reported research and the innovative approach to integrate studies in the areas of natural and human resources and their role in agriculture. The various chapters present original theoretical ideas, applications of up-to-date methods and analyses of unique data sets that together shed light on many issues that are related to resource allocation in agriculture and are part of ongoing public and academic discussions.

The book is aimed at scholars of agricultural and resource economics in universities and research institutes, world-wide. In addition, the volume is expected to be valuable for graduate students who study agricultural and resource economics. Since it presents original studies in the areas of salinity management, water pricing and policy, agricultural policies and agricultural households' labor supply and management, it is useful to any student who takes on advanced research towards a Ph.D. dissertation in one of these areas.

Finally, as many of the chapters in the book conclude with policy implications, it will be useful also for decision makers and policy designers dealing with agricultural and resource issues around the world.

---

[*] Israel Finkelshtain and Ayal Kimhi are Associate Professors at the Department of Agricultural Economics and Management of the Hebrew University, PO Box 12, Rehovot 76100, Israel.

The book is organized in two parts, each composed of three sections. The first part is devoted to natural resources, while the second part is devoted to human resources. Beginning with the first part, section I deals with management of water salinity. Water quality and salinity are becoming significant issues in both developed countries and agrarian societies. The section includes both macro and micro approaches to deal with this issue. In chapter 2, Or Goldfarb and Yoav Kislev present a dynamic and stochastic framework for the characterization of policies that ensure the sustainability of a national aquifer. The sustainability criterion consists of two dimensions: water salinity and water quantity. Management instruments are annual withdrawals, desalinations and dynamic decisions. The framework is applied to identify a sustainable management regime for the costal aquifer in Israel. This aquifer provides 20% of the country's fresh water supply.

In chapter 3, Ernst-August Nuppenau raises the problem of water salinity in small-holder communities in developing countries. Conventional practices to reduce salinity, such as limitation of water dosage and set-aside, reduce current income of the agricultural households, and hence are usually not adopted. The chapter formulates a community-level dynamic model to assess the performance of an innovative remedy for salinity - tree planting. The model accounts for political considerations and bargaining among community members.

Section II deals with management of water resources and offers an economic approach to hydrological policies. Population and income growth have lead to increased water demand around the world. One result of the rising pressures on this scarce resource is the growing interest of policy makers in economic analysis and incentives. In chapter 4, Peter Berck and James Manley identify two distinct phases in the development of water resources. In early phases of economic development, there is a large supply of economically worthwhile projects of water development. Therefore the benefits of these water projects that are built exceed their costs. In latter stages of economic development, economically beneficial water projects are in short supply, but there are increasing needs to subsidize the agrarian sector. This combination leads to overdevelopment of water resources in highly developed economies. The authors sketch a plausible theory and empirical evidence that supports his hypothesis.

The section continues with country-studies of water resources management. An example of a developed economy with increasing water demand is provided in chapter 5 by Steven Renzetti who presents an analysis of the Canadian water economy. Canada is perceived to be a water-abundant country, with sustainable per capita annual water supply of 100,000 m^3 (compared to 400 m^3 in Israel). Despite this abundance, however, it is apparent that Canada's water resources face a number of policy challenges, some of which stem from agriculture. The chapter offers directions for regulative reform, which is based on economic principles. Special attention is devoted to the agricultural and agri-food sectors.

In chapter 6, Cemal Fert and Burhan Ozkan describe the developing water economy in Turkey. Surface and ground water resources of Turkey are 110 billion CM and the average per capita water availability is about 1.735 m^3 per year. Population growth and industrialization increase water demand in nonagricultural sectors of the economy. As a result, there is an increasing awareness among politicians and administrators to the need of efficient, economic-based water management.

Section III portrays alternative perspectives on the role of land resources in the process of development of the agricultural sector and the economy as a whole. In chapter 7, Meir Kohn introduces an innovative explanation to the prevalence of land tenure institutions in developing economies. Traditionally, economic historians viewed land tenure as an arrangement for labor supply. Kohn argues that alternative land tenure arrangements can be best explained as alternative forms of supplying external financing to agricultural households. Empirical support of this theory is provided by a discussion of land-tenure contracts in pre-industrial Europe.

In chapter 8, Ayal Kimhi and Dennis Chiwele investigate factors that limit the ability of Zambian farmers to increase Maize productivity and/or diversify their crop mix. Crop production is modeled as a two stage process. In the first stage, farmers decide on land allocation among the different crops. In the second stage, output is influenced by irrigation, fertilization and general cultivation decisions, in addition to the land allocation decision. The results of the empirical study indicate that crop diversification can be promoted by changing a variety of economic and environmental characteristics, among them increasing the size of landholdings. They also show that the yield of Maize is inversely related to the size of the plot allocated to Maize.

In chapter 9, Zvi Lerman examines the sweeping agrarian reforms in the three Trans-Caucasian states – Armenia, Georgia, and Azerbaijan. Not all the agricultural land resources have been privatized, and yet the author shows that it is the individual sector that generates practically the entire agricultural output in these countries. The chapter reviews the extent of transition from collective to individual farming, discusses the different approaches to privatization and individualization in the three countries, and examines the difficulties associated with the fragmented farm structure. Lerman concludes that in order to reap the full benefits of individualization, land markets must be developed and resources should be devoted to investments in rural infrastructure and farm support services.

We now move to part B which includes three sections dealing with human resources in agriculture, offering perspectives on knowledge, policy and management. Section IV begins with discussions of knowledge, productivity and growth. Human capital and knowledge are essential inputs to the process of improvements in agricultural productivity and production of sufficient food supplies with limited natural resources. Agricultural knowledge is created via RandD. The section commences with chapter 10, in which Robert Evenson proposes a generalization of the Evenson and Kislev (1975) approach of "Research as Search". The model describes the course of advances in the technology frontier as a process of adaptive inventions. The theoretical framework is applied to explain the patterns of plant breeding programs, which have lead to the Green Revolution.

In chapter 11, Yacov Tsur and Amos Zemel study the importance of knowledge spillovers to educational investments, growth and welfare. They find substantial effects of these externalities on all three outcomes. A simple, self-financed education policy that implements the socially optimal outcome is offered.

Section V deals with governance, resources and agricultural policies. Comparative international studies of economic growth have proven that governance characteristics, such as secured property rights, openness, efficient bureaucracy and low levels of protection are key factors in assuring sustainable growth. The three chapters in this section discuss some of these policy issues in relation to agriculture. In chapter 12, Bruce Gardner considers the short- and long-run effects of commodity price support policies on the agricultural sector, with special attention to investment in agriculture and productivity growth. The chapter reviews the details of the 2002 farm bill in the U.S. and policies that preceded it. This recent legislation was originally viewed as a mechanism to phase out commodity support programs while preserving the high support levels of previous programs.

Increasing criticism against the distortion and efficiency losses caused by high levels of agricultural protection have lead to the design of, so-called, "decoupled" farm programs with the premise of separation between income transfer and incentives. In chapter 13, Barry Goodwin and Ashok Mishra assess the extent to which new programs, such as market loss assistance payments, are really decoupled. The authors employ farm-level data and discrete choice econometric techniques to examine the effects of the market loss assistance program and agricultural market transition act on land idling and purchasing decisions. It is found that both programs increase agricultural production, although the effect of the agricultural market transition act is modest.

In recent years the export sector of Israeli agriculture was deregulated. The previously government-controlled marketing and export agencies were dismantled and substituted by private firms. In chapter 14, Israel Finkelshtain and Yael Kachel examine the performance of the citrus industry in the post-reform period. They find that pre-reform concerns regarding harsh competition among Israeli exporters in target markets and the collapse of prices were not realized. However, as a result of privatization, the market for export services in Israel has evolved into an oligopolistic structure that leads to informational imperfections, efficiency losses and reduced revenue to growers.

Section VI, the final section of this book, offers three aspects of labor and management on farm households. Education, efficient allocation of time between farm work and off-farm employment opportunities, and management and entrepreneurial skills, are essential human resources for profitable modern agriculture. The section begins with chapter 15, in which Ayal Kimhi and Eddie Seiler study the labor supply of farm operators and their spouses. The authors employ a discrete choice econometric model and find dependency between participation in the labor market and family composition. In particular, it is shown that both the operator and his spouse reduce off-farm labor supply, as the number of elderly children in the household rises. This outcome seems to be driven by both agricultural production and household production considerations.

In chapter 16, Christoph Weiss and Kevin McNamara study the ability of family-farm operators to diversify and reduce income risk through on-farm crop diversification and off-farm employment. The authors integrate the two strands of the literature that analyze the two types of diversification instruments and construct a unified econometric model to assess their empirical importance. The model is applied to study the diversification decisions of more than 39,000 family farms in Upper Austria. The results demonstrate that diversification decisions are related to both physical resources in the farm and operator's characteristics.

An additional analysis of diversification activities is offered in chapter 17 by Anat Tchechik, Aliza Fleischer and Israel Finkelshtain, who study rural tourism in Israel. It is shown that on-farm inns make an important source of income to agricultural households. The chapter proceeds by investigating the technological interdependencies of farming and rural tourism. The empirical evidence supports the hypothesis of the existence of scope economies in operating a combined business of farming and agro-tourism.

ACKNOWLEDGEMENTS

The chapters of this book are all based on papers presented during the international workshop "The Economics of Water and Agriculture" conducted in Rehovot, Israel in December 2002 in honor of Professor Yoav Kislev upon his retirement. We are deeply indebted to David Zilberman, the co-organizer of the workshop, for his comments and advice on earlier drafts of this volume. We owe a great deal of gratitude to all the participants who contributed to the stimulating and fruitful discussions that emerged during the workshop, to the staff and students of the Department of Agricultural Economics and Management of The Hebrew University, to the University employees who provided perfect logistic support, and to the financial assistance of the United States-Israel Binational Science Foundation, the Authority for Research and Development of The Hebrew University, The Center for Agricultural Economic Research, the Citrus Marketing Board of Israel, The Central Bureau of Statistics in Israel, the Israel Association for Canadian Studies, the Chief Scientist of the Ministry of Agriculture and Rural Development in Israel, The Maurice Falk Institute for Economic Research in Israel, and Mehadrin Ltd.

Above all, we wish to dedicate this book to our long-time teacher, supervisor, mentor, colleague, co-author and friend, Yoav Kislev, who had and still has a pivotal role in shaping our careers as academic economists.

ABOUT THE EDITORS

Israel Finkelshtain is Associate Professor at the Department of Agricultural Economics and Management of the Hebrew University since 2005. He has a Ph.D. in Agricultural and Resource Economics from the University of California, Berkeley (1990). He previously served as the Director of Research of the Center for Agricultural Economic Research. He published more than 20 articles in refereed journals, including *The American Economic Review*, *Journal of Political Economy*, *Journal of Economic Growth*, *American Journal of Agricultural Economics*, *Economics* Letters, *Agricultural Economics*, *Management Science*, and *Journal of Economic Behavior and Organization*. His research spans the fields of Industrial Organization, Agricultural Economics, and Political Economy. His main areas of research are choice under uncertainty, pricing policies, agricultural market structures, and the political economy of public policy. He has also written about productivity and growth, rural tourism, rural municipalities, and markets for water and pollution.

Ayal Kimhi is Associate Professor at the Department of Agricultural Economics and Management of the Hebrew University since 2004. He has a Ph.D. in Economics from the University of Chicago (1991), and has held visiting positions at the University of Maryland, Yale University, the University of Pennsylvania, and Nagoya University. He also serves as the Director of Research of the Center for Agricultural Economic Research, and worked as a consultant for the World Bank on various projects. Since 2006 he serves as Editor-in-Chief of the *Journal of Rural Cooperation*. He published more than 30 articles in refereed journals, including *The Econometrics Journal*, *Journal of Development Economics*, *Economic Development and Cultural Change*, *American Journal of Agricultural Economics, European Review of Agricultural Economics, Agricultural Economics*, and *Journal of Population Economics*. His research spans the fields of Family Economics, Agricultural Economics, and Development Economics. He has studied structural changes in agriculture in both developed, developing and transition countries. His main areas of research are the time allocation decisions in farm households, intergenerational succession on family farms, and the process of farm growth and diversification. He has also written about health and nutrition, poverty and inequality, agricultural policy reforms, and labor supervision.

In: The Economics of Natural and Human Resources...   ISBN 978-1-60741-029-4
Editor: Ayal Kimhi and Israel Finkelshtain   © 2009 Nova Science Publishers, Inc.

Chapter 2

A SUSTAINABLE SALT REGIME IN THE ISRAELI COASTAL AQUIFER

*Or Goldfarb and Yoav Kislev**

ABSTRACT

Water utilization, particularly in dry areas, augments the accumulation of salts in soils and groundwater. This chapter reports a study of the economic aspects of maintaining sustainable salt concentrations in the reservoirs and in water supplied to agriculture and urban consumers. The study has two major purposes, to stress the need to remove salts, an expensive process, and to point to the water sources from which salts should be removed. The analysis is of the Coastal aquifer in Israel and the area above it and on data forecasted for the year 2020. The total amount of salts that can be expected to reach the coastal region in that year is 120,000 tons chlorides; the same quantity has to be removed yearly for a sustainable salt regime to be maintained. A third, perhaps even half, the salts imported to the region will be removed in the natural outflow to the sea or in water exported to other regions, as fresh or recycled water. The rest, tenths of thousands tons per year, will have to be removed actively.

The study is done under simplifying assumptions and it should be taken as a first step. A more detailed analysis will incorporate additional hydrological and engineering considerations and perhaps also other sources of contamination. But it seems that the major conclusions, on the need to remove the salts and the efficient way of doing it, will not be modified significantly.

A. INTRODUCTION

Israel has three major water reservoirs: Lake Kinneret (the Sea of Galilee) in the north, the Coastal aquifer along the shore of the Mediterranean Sea, and the Mountain aquifer further east, partly under the hills of the West Bank.[1] Most regions of the country are covered

---

* Or Goldfarb is with the Water Authority, Israel, and Yoav Kislev is a Professor Emeritus at The Hebrew University, Israel.
[1] For a survey of the water economy of Israel, see Kislev (2006).

by a grid of pipelines connecting water sources with areas of utilization. The major conduit is the National Carrier moving water from Lake Kinneret to the central and the southern regions of the country. The coastal region, the focus our analysis, receives water from all three reservoirs—Kinneret, Mountain, and the Coastal aquifer itself. It is expected that in the future it will also receive desalinated seawater. The water is supplied to the region's urban centers and agriculture.

The reservoirs are replenished yearly by precipitation: rains and some snow in the Kinneret's watershed drain into the lake in rivers and springs and the aquifers are fed with rainwater falling directly on the land surface above them. The replenishing water carries salts to the reservoirs, in Lake Kinneret from salty springs, and in the aquifers from ocean spray. Additional sources of salts are underground brines and seawater intrusion. As a result, the water stored in the reservoirs contains significant quantities of salts. Irrigation with water imported to the coastal region from Lake Kinneret or the Mountain aquifer adds further amounts of salts. [2] Another source is effluent: salts used in households and manufacturing are carried in the sewage and increase the mineral concentration of the effluent. [3] They are added to the groundwater wherever crops are irrigated with effluent. The salts are harmful to soils and crops and also, when their concentration is large, to households and industry. Hence the need to halt their accumulation.

Salts also leave the reservoirs—in water outflows. From Lake Kinneret with the water drained to the Jordan River and pumped into the National Carrier and sent southward. As a result, salt concentration in the lake's water is stable (the stability is stochastic, reflecting fluctuations of the precipitation).

In the past, before the development of intensive agriculture, the concentration of salts in the aquifers was also stable: all the replenishment water left the aquifers, either in springs or under the ground through the seawater-freshwater interface; in this way salts entering the reservoirs were flushed away and minerals did not accumulate. Irrigation modifies this equilibrium: most irrigated water evaporates, either directly or through the plants, and the natural outflow from the aquifer is then reduced. Unlike water, salts do not evaporate; they remain on the surface of the land or in the subsoil and are carried back into the groundwater with rainwater and irrigation return flow. Consequently, minerals accumulate in the aquifer wherever irrigation is practiced. In the coastal aquifer, as indicated above, the accumulation is augmented with salts imported with water from non-coastal sources and salts added to the effluent.

The future will see two parallel but opposing processes in the water economy of Israel. The first will be an increased provision of freshwater and effluent; the added freshwater will be mainly desalinated seawater (the first large scale desalination plant commenced operation in summer 2005) and the quantities of the effluent will grow as the population and urban water use increase.

The second process will be active removal of salts. The increased supply of freshwater answers needs created by expanded population and growing demand; the removal of salts is necessary for the sustainability of the reservoirs.

---

[2] Salts are not the only pollutants of the aquifer. Mercado (1980) discusses nitrates and chlorides and many more pollutants have been found in the water since his writing.

[3] Households include, in the terminology of the water sector, family dwellings and also places of commerce, workshops, hotels and other water users in the urban sector.

Actually, there are two alternative policy options in reaction to the accumulation of salts. One, let salts accumulate in the aquifers and replace gradually water from natural sources with desalinated seawater. The second option is to remove actively the salts and maintain a sustainable water economy of natural water. This article is about the second option but toward its conclusion we also indicate that the first option, neglecting the reservoirs, is not efficient economically.

Our analysis is limited to the Coastal aquifer and we examine alternative salt concentrations and compare the cost of these alternatives and cost of alternative ways of salt removal.

Under the assumptions of the analysis and with the information at our disposal, our main conclusion is that the efficient alternative is to remove the salts by desalination fresh water from natural source (particularly from the Coastal aquifer). However, even if the removal of the salts is conducted efficiently, it will increase significantly the total cost of the water economy of the country.

B. Assumptions

We are not the first to deal with the accumulation of salts and the need to remove them.[4] But earlier studies did not examine alternative ways to treat the salts and did not consider the economic implications of these alternatives. We are expanding the analysis.

The forecast for the area west of the water divide of Israel is that by the year 2020 total water supply will be 2,206 MCM/Y and of those 1,135 MCM/Y from natural sources (fresh and saline), 621 MCM/Y effluent, and 450 MCM/Y desalinated sea water.[5] Salts added are expected to reach 272,000 tons per year from natural sources and effluent and 9,000 tons from desalinated water (the concentration of salts in the desalinated water is 20 ppm of chlorides).[6]

It is expected that 126,000 tons chlorides will be added in 2020 to the Coastal aquifer. The analysis is based on a set of simplifying assumptions to be described below, we shall remark on several of the assumptions at the conclusion of the article.

The movement of water in the coastal aquifer is slow and the reservoir is therefore often visualized as made of separate cells. Still, for simplicity, the aquifer is taken here as if it was a single cell reservoir into which all the salts deposited on the surface of the land are drained with rainwater and irrigation return flow.

We assume complete mixing of the salts with the water in all the active volume of the aquifer. It is reasonable to expect changes in the coastal region after 2020: there will be expansion of the supply of both desalinated water and effluent, and the area covered with buildings will increase; the amount of salts added to the aquifer will therefore also increase. However the additional quantities will be relatively small and therefore, and for simplicity, we are conducting the analysis for constant quantities of water and salts; in other words, the analysis is conducted for a steady state.

---

[4] Hebrew references will not be quoted in the paper; they can be found in Goldfarb and Kislev (2002).
[5] Water units are: CM cubic meter, MCM million CM, and MCM/Y MCM per year.
[6] The most prevalent salt in the water is table salt (sodium chloride). Sodium is the element causing most damage, but it is more convenient to test for chlorides. The unit of measurement is ppm, parts per million. It is useful to remember that one ppm is one ton per MCM.

A steady state is a characterization of a sustainable system and its implication here is that at any time, year in and year out, the same quantities of water and salts are added to the aquifer and identical quantities leave the reservoir.

There is no accumulation, negative or positive, of water or salts. Because of the stochastic nature of the precipitation and other factors, even if a steady state prevails, it will be a stochastic steady state: the quantities entering the aquifer and the quantities leaving it will not be identical every year; the equality will be maintained only for the average. But, at this stage, we are disregarding the between years variations, and conduct the computations as if the years were identical.

C. MODEL I

This section of the chapter opens the conceptual discussion of the study with agriculture as the single water-using sector. Expanded models are introduced below. The models are presented in the chapter as diagrams, in algebraic terms, in equations, and in balanced tables.

In Model I (Figure 2.1) precipitation is added to the groundwater (replenishment), part of the water is withdrawn for irrigation and the rest is outflow to the sea. Irrigated water is evaporated from the surface of the land and through plants and part of it reaches the groundwater as irrigation return flow.

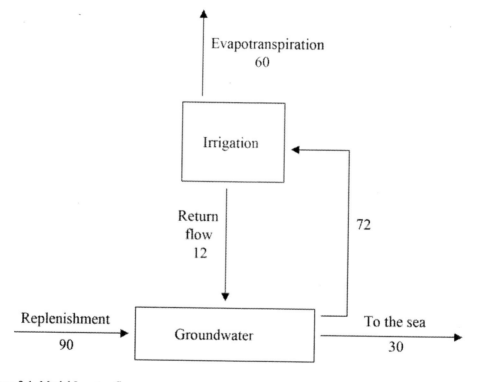

Figure 2.1. Model I, water flows.

C.1. The Algebraic Model

Quantities in the model are flows per year. The variables are

	Water in MCM	Salts, chlorides in tons per year
Replenishment	R	M_R
Irrigation (fresh water)	H	M_H
Irrigation return flow	Z	M_Z
Outflow to sea	Y	M_Y
Evapotranspiration7	E	

The balancing equations are
Water balance

$$R + Z = H + Y \tag{1}$$

Salt balance

$$M_R + M_Z = M_H + M_Y \tag{2}$$

Irrigation return flow

$$Z = 0.17H \tag{3}$$

Irrigation water balance

$$H = E + Z \tag{4}$$

Equations (1) and (2) describe the entry of water and salts into the reservoir and exit away from it. The water supply is augmented with the irrigation return flow. There is some arbitrariness in the division of the salts to the different flows as salts deposited on the surface of the land are drained into the subsoil both with rainwater and with irrigation return flow. For convenience, we combine in M_R salts added with rain (ocean spray), from underground brines, and from other sources. All these quantities are taken as salts coming with the replenishment. Salts deposited on the surface of the land with irrigation we see as if it was all drained to the subsoil with the return flow. Equation (3) defines that the return flow is 17% of the quantity of water in irrigation (an assessment received from hydrologists). The last equation, (4), completes the picture, it separates irrigation water to the part evaporated and the part returning to the reservoir.

To illustrate the model, let us assume (water in MCM/Y; salts, chlorides, in tons per year): replenishment R=90 with salt concentration of 50 ppm; that is, M_R=4,500. Groundwater outflow to the Mediterranean Sea Y=30. As indicated, entering quantities are identical to quantities leaving the aquifer. The balance for water is

$$90 + 0.17H = H + 30$$

hence irrigation $H=72$, return flow $Z=12$, evapotranspiration $E=60$ (Figure 2.1).

We turn now to the calculation of the concentration of salts in the flows of water in the model. In the steady state, all the salts in the irrigation water reach the reservoir; that is $M_H=M_Z$ and therefore $M_R=M_Y$. In words, all the salts reaching the reservoir leave the aquifer in the water drained to the sea (salts in harvested crops are disregarded). Define the concentration of salts in the outflow to the sea as P and write the equality $M_R=M_Y$

$$90 \times 50 = 30P \tag{5}$$

The solution to the equation is $P=150$; that is, the concentration of salts in the outflow to the sea is 150 ppm chlorides. Also, since groundwater is the source the outflow, the concentration of chlorides in the groundwater will be 150 ppm as well, and this will also be the concentration of salts in the irrigation water.

C.2. The Balance Sheet

The balance sheet (Table 1) summarizes inflows and outflows of water and salts and it is ordered in accordance with the construction of equations (1) and (2). However, the quantities in the table are only quantities of water and salts *added* to the aquifer; for example, there is exit of salts in irrigation, this exit is not recorded in Table 1 since, by assumption, all salts leaving the reservoir in water used for irrigation above the aquifer return to the reservoir— they are drained, with rainwater and in the irrigation return flow, back into the groundwater. Still, because of its significance, we do report in the table the concentration of salts in the irrigation water, 150 ppm chlorides.

Table 1. Model I: balance sheet of water and salts

Entry to the reservoir				Exit from the reservoir			
	Water	Salts	Concentration		Water	Salts	Concentration
Replenishment	90	4,500	50	Irrigation	72		150
Irrigation return flow	12			To the sea	30	4,500	150
Total	102	4,500		Total	102	4,500	

C.3. Remarks

1. The total quantities of water in Table 1, 102 MCM/Y on each side of the balance sheet, are sums of flows. These values are larger than the quantity of water utilized in the model economy (72 MCM/Y).
2. The concentration of the replenishment, 50 ppm chlorides, is not rainwater concentration; it is an artificial average, the ratio of salts coming from several sources to the volume of the replenishment.
3. In the model and in the steady state, the flows of water and salts come and go year in and year out. In reality, the salts move through the subsoil slowly and therefore salts

added to the groundwater in a certain year were deposited on the surface of the land several years beforehand. In the steady state, a given quantity of salts is deposited on the land every year (4,500 tons in model I) and an identical quantity is added to the groundwater.

4. The replenishment and the withdrawal determine simultaneously, in the steady state, both the outflow to the sea and the level of the water table in the reservoir. A comprehensive model would therefore have included equations determining the quantity of the outflow to the sea. Here we assume, for simplicity, given quantities of replenishment and withdrawal and hence also a given outflow to the sea.

C.4. Intuition

For an intuitive grasp of the concept of the steady state it is useful to notice that the endogenous variable in the model is the concentration of salts in the groundwater. The following three examples should clarify.

Example 1. Assume that exit of water to the sea is not 30 MCM/Y but 25 MCM/Y. The solution of equation (5) will now be 180 ppm chlorides (not 150). With a smaller quantity flowing to the sea, the concentration of salts in the aquifer is larger; the larger quantity ensures that, even with a smaller outflow, all the salts added with the replenishment are flushed to the sea (180*25=4,500).

Example 2. The calculation of the steady state can be reversed to compute the quantity of salts added to a reservoir. We do it for the entry of salts to Lake Kinneret. Chlorides concentration in the lake has been, for the past several decades, approximately 230 ppm; outflow to the river and the National Water Carrier is 418 MCM/Y. This means that on average 96,140 tons of chlorides exit the lake annually. Assuming a steady state, the annual entry into the lake is also 96,140 tons chlorides.

Example 3. Here we are returning to Model I and its arbitrary data; we shall exhibit dynamics, examine the first stages of the move from a given initial condition to the steady state. Assume that the initial sate is an aquifer with chloride concentration of 100 ppm, the total volume of the aquifer is 300 MCM. All other data are as in Model I.

The quantity of salts entering the aquifer this year (as in any year) is 4,500 tons. The quantity leaving in the outflow is 3,000 tons (30 MCM with a concentration of 100 ppm). Consequently, the net addition to the aquifer in this year is 1,500 tons; this addition increases the chloride concentration to 105 ppm. The quantity of salts entering next year will again be 4,500 tons. Exit will be 3,150 tons (30 MCM *times* 105 ppm). Hence the quantity added to the groundwater will be 1,350 tons chlorides and its concentration will reach 109.5 ppm. In this way the reservoir will converge gradually to the steady state in which chloride concentration in the groundwater is 150 ppm.

The last example demonstrates that the volume of the reservoir (the active volume) determines the *rate of convergence* toward the steady state; it does not affect the steady state itself. This is why the volume of the aquifer did not appear among the variables in Model I and its steady state analysis.

D. MODEL II

Model II is broader than Model I in two aspects: it is real and it deals with magnitudes that will serve for the extension of the analysis to the Coastal aquifer—including water use in the urban sector, desalination and utilization of effluent—and it also incorporates active removal of salts. Figure 2.2 will be explained below; it describes the flows of water and the concentrations of salts in the model. The removal of salts in Model II is by desalinating water from natural sources (Lake Kinneret and the aquifers) other alternatives will be examined in the next section of the chapter. The desalination reduces the quantity of salts in the water, but it also modifies the water balance since 10% of the water to be desalinated is removed to the sea as concentrate. We assume that this amount will be replaced by an identical quantity of desalinated seawater. In this way, there will be in the model (in the year 2020) two factors determining the quantity of seawater desalination; one is the aggregate demand for water in the country that will be, by forecasts, larger than the supply of water from natural sources; part of this desalinated water will reach the coastal region. The second factor will be desalination to replace the concentrate of the desalinated natural water. [7]

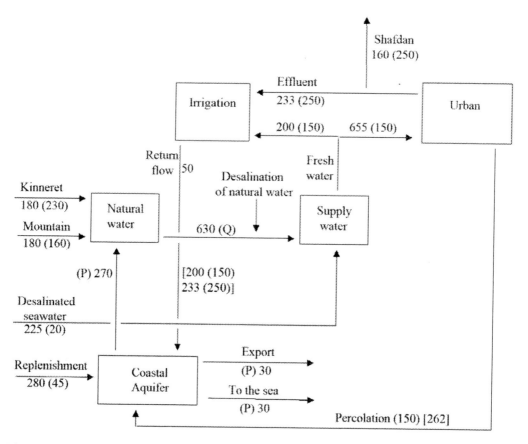

Figure 2.2. Model II, water flows and salt concentration.

---

[7] Perhaps it need not be added that, as seawater for desalination is external to the model, its concentrate is not replaced. It is only the net quantity that is incorporated into the model's computations.

In the circumstances described above, the magnitudes of the steady state—water and salts—will be found in the solution of a system of three equations in three unknowns. We term the magnitudes that vary with the solution *endogenous variables* and those taken as data *exogenous*. The distinction should become clearer once the variables are displayed in tables and equations.

D.1. Exogenous Variables

Table 2 reports water and salt magnitudes for 2020. The table is divided into three parts: natural water is the water from natural sources utilized above the coastal aquifer, in agriculture and in the urban sector; included here is water extracted from the Coastal aquifer itself as well as water imported from the mountain aquifer and Lake Kinneret. This water carries salts that are also recorded in Table 2. Other sources for water used above the coastal region are desalinated seawater and effluent. The third part of the table reports water use, outflow to the sea, and irrigation return flow (30 and 50 MCM/Y, respectively); for simplicity, we assume that these quantities are given. The last two magnitudes in table 2, export (outflow) of fresh water and Shafdan effluent, indicate use of coastal water and effluent in non-coastal regions. [8] The salts carried with this water will not be deposited above the Coastal aquifer and will therefore not return to the reservoir.

Table 2. Exogenous magnitudes in the Coastal aquifer in 2020

	Water	Salts added	Concentration
Natural water			
Coast	280	12,600	
Mountain	180	28,800	160
Lake Kinneret	180	41,400	230
Total natural	640	82,800	
Other sources			
Desalination (seawater)	225	4,500	20
Effluent	393	39,300	100
Other variables			
The urban sector	655		
Irrigation (fresh water)	200		
Outflow, to the sea	30		
Irrigation return flow	50		
Export, fresh water	30		
Export, Shafdan	160		

Remark: water in MCM, salts in tons chlorides per year, concentration in ppm chlorides.

Water imported adds salts to the Coastal aquifer. For example, salts concentration in the water of the mountain aquifer is 160 ppm chlorides; multiplied by 180 MCM, the imported

---

[8] Shafdan is the Dan (Tel Aviv) region wastewater reclamation project. Its effluent is delivered to the Western Negev; 100 km and more south of Tel Aviv.

mass is 28,800 tons chlorides. For the Coastal aquifer, water withdrawal and used in the region is forecasted to be 280 MCM. It is estimated that salts *added* from various sources will be 12,600 tons chlorides. The concentration cell is left empty for the Coast row in the table since the entry of these salts into the aquifer is not a function of the quantity withdrawn. Salt content in the aquifer's water is today close to 200 ppm. This magnitude does not appear in Table 2 either as the use of the aquifer's water above the reservoir does not *add* to the reservoir's mass of salts.

The forecast is that by the year 2020 the use of desalinated seawater in the coastal region will reach 225 MCM/Y and this is the magnitude recorded in Table 2 as an exogenous variable. The quantity of effluent was calculated as 60% of the water utilized in urban sector. The concentration of salts in the desalinated water is 20 ppm and 100 ppm chlorides are added in the effluent (added to the background water, to the water supplied to households and manufacturing). The quantities of salts and their concentrations for the section of Other variables are not recorded in Table 2 since these are endogenous variables and will be determined below.

D.2. The Water Sector of the Coastal Region

As indicated, we are examining in Model II a steady state with desalination of natural water in the coastal region. The *quality goal of the water economy* in the model is that fresh water is supplied in chlorides concentration of 150 ppm to all the users in the region—households, manufacturing, and agriculture. Total supply of water and salts, as reported in Table 2, is summarized below. Out of this, the supply of natural water is 630 MCM/Y (640-30-30+50).

	Water in MCM/Y	Chlorides in tons per year
Natural water	640	82,800
Seawater desalination	225	4,500
Effluent	393	39,300
Outflow of fresh water	-30	
Outflow to the sea	-30	
Irrigation return flow	50	
Total	1,268	126,600

To determine steady state magnitudes under the above constraints, define 3 endogenous variables to be the unknowns in the computation,

The concentration of salts in the natural water, ppm chlorides Q
Concentration of salts in the coastal aquifer, ppm chlorides P
Desalination of natural water, MCM/Y D

Turn now to Figure 2.2. Water flows are marked in the diagram by arrows and salt concentration is indicated in parentheses wherever appropriate. The natural water is, as in Table 2, water from Lake Kinneret, the mountain aquifer and the water withdrawn from the coastal aquifer. (Withdrawal is replenishment *minus* outflow to the sea and to other regions *plus* irrigation return flow.) The concentration of chlorides in the coastal water is marked *P* and it is an endogenous variable to be calculated below. The water supplied for irrigation and the urban sector (households and manufacturing) is natural and desalinated water (the quantity of water desalinated for the removal of salts is not recorded in the diagram, it will be computed below). In accordance with the quality goal of the water economy, the concentration of salts in the water supplied to the urban sector will 150 ppm chlorides. The urban sector produces 393 MCM/Y sewage with salt concentration of 250 ppm chlorides (100 ppm are added to the background water). One hundred and sixty MCM/Y are exported from the region as Shafdan effluent, and 233 MCM/Y of local effluent is utilized for irrigation in the coastal region. Irrigation return flow to the coastal aquifer is 50 MCM/Y, however all the salts in irrigation water, both fresh water and effluent, reach the aquifer. To indicate this, we recorded in Figure 2.2, in brackets by the axis representing irrigation return water, irrigation water of the different kinds and the corresponding salt concentration. We assume that salts reaching households and not leaving in sewage also reach the coastal aquifer. The axis representing these salts is marked as percolation. [The water entering households and not leaving in sewage does not return to the aquifer; its quantity is therefore recorded in brackets (262 is 40% of 655).]

As the diagram indicates, the desalination for salt removal will be of natural water; as if all sources of natural water are mixed to a uniform quality before any part of it is desalinated. Other possibilities will be examined below.

The steady state magnitudes are computed recursively in three equations. In the first equation we calculate the concentration of salts in the coastal aquifer

$$280 \times 45 + 200 \times 150 + 233 \times 250 + 262 \times 150 = (270 + 30 + 30)P \tag{6}$$
$$P = 425$$

The left-hand-side of equation (6) records the salts entering the aquifer: in the replenishment, freshwater irrigation, effluent and percolation. The magnitudes on right-hand-side are the quantities leaving the aquifer: withdrawals, exported to other regions, and outflow to the sea; these quantities are multiplied by the factor *P*, salt concentration of the steady state in the coastal aquifer. By the solution of the equation, the concentration is 425 ppm chlorides.

In the second equation of the model we calculate the concentration of the salts, before their removal, in the natural water

$$Q = (180 \times 230 + 180 \times 160 + 270 \times 425)/630 \tag{7}$$
$$Q = 293$$

In equation (7) we have used the concentration of salts in the coastal aquifer (425 ppm) calculated in equation (6). By the solution, the concentration of the salts in the natural water before desalination is 293 ppm.

We now calculate the quantity of water to be desalinated in the steady state to remove the salts reaching the coastal region

$$160 \times 250 + (30 + 30) \times 425 + (293 - 20)D = 126{,}600$$
$$D = 224 \tag{8}$$

In the steady state, 224 MCM/Y of natural water will be desalinated to maintain the goal of supplying freshwater to households, agriculture, and manufacturing with chloride concentration of 150 ppm and still remove all the salts reaching the coastal region. (Recall that in the wake of this desalination there will be a desalination of additional 22.4 MCM/Y to compensate for the concentrate).

The solution of the three equations was reported here in rounded values, in the following calculations we use exact figures. Table 3 summarizes the quantities involved—exogenous and endogenous, the latter are underlined. Thus, for example, outflow of 30 MCM/Y to the sea flushes 12,741 tons of chlorides. The quantity of salts to exit is determined endogenously as it is the product of the quantity of water (an exogenous variable) by the concentration of the salts; the latter being an endogenous variable determined in the solution of the steady state. In the seawater desalination, the quantity 225 MCM/Y is determined exogenously, but the quantity 22 MCM/Y, against the concentrate, is determined endogenously.

The effluent appears in both sides of Table 3. All the quantity of the effluent produced in the coastal region is recorded on the left-hand-side: 393 MCM/Y. On the right-hand-side we write separately 160 MCM/Y of Shafdan water exported from the coastal region with the salts it carries. The rest, 233 MCM/Y of effluent, will be used for local irrigation. Hence the salts it carries do not exit from the coastal region and are therefore not registered on this side of the table.

Table 3. Salts and water in the steady state in Model II

Entering the reservoirs				Exit from reservoirs			
	Water	Salts	Concen-tration		Water	Salts	Concen-tration
Coast	280	12,600		Urban	655		
Mountain	180	28,800	160	Irrigation, fresh	200		
Kinneret	180	41,400	230	Outflow to sea	30	12,741	425
Seawater desalination	225 (22)	4,500	20	Export fresh	30	12,741	425
Effluent	393	39,300	100	Export Shafdan	160	40,000	250
Irrigation Return	50			Effluent in the coast	233		250
				Desalination of natural water	(224)	61,118	293-20
Total	1,308	126,600		Total	1,308	126,600	

Remarks: a. water in MCM/Y, salts in tons chlorides per year, concentration in ppm chlorides.
b. Underlined, endogenous variables.
c. Values in parenthesis are not included in the column's total.

The natural water to be desalinated, 224 MCM/Y, is closed in parenthesis as it does not leave the coastal region; the salts carried in this water do exit. The sum total for the water columns, 1,308 MCM/Y, is larger than the magnitude registered earlier (1,268 MCM/Y) as it includes here the exported freshwater as well (30 MCM/Y).

E. SELECTION OF A SUSTAINABLE ALTERNATIVE

This section examines the cost of 12 alternatives of the sustainable policy. Four are salt removal alternatives:

Desalination of natural water as in Model II (for average concentration of all natural water);
Desalination from a given source of natural water such as the Coastal aquifer or Lake Kinneret;
Desalination of the effluent (the salt concentration of which is relatively high);
Removal of the effluent to the sea and replacement of the same quantity by desalinated seawater.

Likewise, we examine three alternative salt concentrations in the supplied water (for households, manufacturing, and irrigation): 150, 100, or 50 ppm chlorides. As will be explained below, steady state quantities are maintained in all alternatives. Table 4 reports the cost assumptions (in US dollars) for the alternatives to be examined.

Desalinating the effluent improves the quality of the water supplied to agriculture; replacing effluent removed to the sea with desalinated seawater has a similar effect. To bring the other alternatives to a comparable water quality, we add in the following examination the option of upgrading the effluent; adding tertiary sewage treatment to the secondary treatment usually employed. The cost of the option is recorded in Table 4 as $0.10 per CM.

Table 4. Cost of operations

	Cost (US dollar per CM)
Seawater desalination	0.55
Desalination of natural water	0.20
Desalination of effluent	0.40
Removal of effluent to the sea	0.05
Tertiary treatment	0.10

E.1. The Twelve Alternatives

The endogenous magnitudes, the solution values of the steady state equations, are reported in Table 5. The first alternative is Model II that was calculated for the goal of 150 ppm chlorides in the water supplied and for the removal alternative by desalination natural water. As found above, for this alternative there will be a desalination of 224 MCM/Y of natural water and the average salt concentration in the coastal aquifer will be 425 ppm chlorides. Recall that this alternative also involves additional seawater desalination of 22 MCM/Y against the concentrate from the desalination of the natural water. This desalination comes in addition to the desalination of 225 MCM/Y determined exogenously and reported in

Table 3. (The desalination of 225 MCM/Y is not reported in Table 5 as its cost is not included in the comparisons of the table.)

Table 5. The twelve alternatives—quantities, concentration of salts in coastal water and cost

Removal alternative	Seawater desal	Natural w desal	Coastal w desal	Effluent desal	Effluent removal	Concentration in Coast aquifer	Cost
Quality goal: 150 ppm chlorides							
Natural water desal	22	224	0	0	0	425	80 (57)
Coastal water desal	14	0	151	0	0	425	62 (39)
Effluent desal	35+7	0	71	233	0	262	131
Effluent removal	233+7	0	71	0	233	262	158
Quality goal: 100 ppm chlorides							
Natural water desal	33	330	0	0	0	319	108 (84)
Coastal water desal	24	0	252	0	0	319	88 (64)
Effluent desal	35+24	0	239	233	0	192	173
Effluent removal	233+24	0	239	0	233	192	201
Quality goal: 50 ppm chlorides							
Natural water desal	49	490	0	0	0	214	148 (125)
Coastal water desal	48	213	270	0	0	214	146 (123)
Effluent desal	35+38	360	19	233	0	122	209
Effluent removal	233+38	360	19	0	233	122	236

Remarks: a. Columns 2-5 MCM/Y, concentration in ppm chlorides, cost in million US dollar per year.
b. In parenthesis cost of alternative without upgrading of effluent.
c. The desalination of natural water in the alternatives of effluent desalination and effluent removal for 50 ppm is of the water of Lake Kinneret and the Mountain aquifer.

The cost of removing the salts in Model II is $80 million per year (Table 5 row 1). This sum includes the cost of upgrading the effluent to tertiary treatment. Without upgrading, the cost is $57 million per year (in parenthesis). The alternative of desalination of water withdrawn from the coastal aquifer is examined in the second row of the table (in Figure 2.2, the desalination arrow is now pointing to the axis going from the coastal aquifer to natural water). Since in the steady state, salt concentration in the coastal water will be higher than in the other sources of the natural water, less coastal water will have to be desalinated to remove a given quantity of salts than in the desalination of mixed water; consequently, the cost of this alternative is lower than the cost of the first alternative.

In the third row, still fort the quality goal 150 ppm, we examine the alternative of salts removal by desalination of the effluent. The effluent to be desalinated is that remaining in the coastal area; the Shafdan effluent will not be desalinated. This alternative creates a difficulty: given the 2020 quantities, even if all the quantity of the effluent is desalinated, not enough salt will be removed to maintain a concentration of 150 ppm chlorides in the supplied water. This is the reason for the inclusion, in this alternative of 71 MCM/Y of coastal water desalination. There will be also additional desalination of seawater, 7 MCM/Y against the concentrate from the fresh water and 35 MCM/Y against the concentrate of the desalination of the effluent (15%). The total quantity of desalination in this alternative for the coastal region in the year 2020 will be 571 MCM (225+233+71+35+7) and the cost of salt removal will be $131 million per year.

Desalination is even larger in the fourth row, where the alternative is to remove the effluent to the sea.

Desalinated water replaces in this alternative the effluent removed (this is desalination to maintain the total water quantity of the steady state). The cost of this alternative is $158 million per year.

The interpretation of the entries for the other 8 alternatives in Table 5 is similar to that of the alternatives that have been reviewed and, as can be expected, salt removal becomes more and more expensive as the quality goal tightens.

A Remark

The examination of the removal of salts in the steady state in the data for 2020 raises the issue of the salts that had accumulated in the last 50 years, part of this mass is already in the aquifer's water and part is still in the subsoil in the unsaturated zone above the groundwater table. Will these salts not be removed? The answer to the query depends on the choice of the quality goal for the steady state. A goal of 150 ppm chlorides means that a salt concentration of 425 ppm chlorides in the aquifer's water is acceptable (Table 5). If so, not only that salts accumulated in the past will not be removed, but salts will be allowed to accumulate further until the steady state is reached. If however, the goal is 50 ppm chlorides and salt removal is in desalination of the effluent, the salt concentration in the steady state in the aquifer will be 122 ppm chlorides (as against 200 today) and then, as the salts are removed the aquifer will gradually converge toward the steady state in a similar fashion to the way it did in the example presented in section C. That is, in this case the removal of salts will remove both all the salts that will be added in the future and part of the salt accumulated in the past.

Summary

The principal finding of the analysis is that, for all the alternative quality goals considered for the water economy of the coastal region, desalination of the coastal water is the lowest cost option. The cost differences between the alternatives are large and it is therefore safe to assume that a more detailed examination will not modify our principal finding and conclusion.

F. TIMING AND PRICES

The analysis, conducted for the conditions expected to prevail in 2020, raises two economic questions, the timing of salt removal and the implication for prices in the water economy.

F.1. Timing

Salts accumulate gradually; it takes years and even decades for salts deposit on the surface of the land to reach the aquifer's water. The question is then, when should salt removal commence? Could the expensive activity be postponed and left to future generations?

Here is a simple method for the determination of the activation date of salt removal: choose a water quality goal, it could be one of the goals specified in Table 5. The activation date of salt removal will be when chloride concentration in the aquifer's water reaches for the first time the steady state concentration corresponding to the chosen goal. For example, if the chosen goal is 100 ppm chlorides, removal will first be activated when concentration of salts in the coastal water reaches 319 ppm chlorides. In this way, the aquifer enters the steady state on the day the removal is first activated.

The difficulty is that this simple method ignores two aspects of the problem. One, that the removal of the salts improves the quality of the water, the other aspect is that there are now large quantities of salts doing their way toward the aquifer. This is why experts forecast that salt accumulation will accelerate in the coming years; salt concentration of 266 ppm chlorides is predicted for the year 2015. If this "time bomb" is really ticking on its way to the aquifer, the water economy is already in the salt accumulation rates expected for the future. Taking these two aspects of the accumulation problem into account justifies advancing the desalination to a date earlier than when the concentration in the aquifer reaches the chosen steady state.

F.2. Prices

The derivation of prices is presented in the appendix in a programming model. Here we offer a verbal discussion. Water in the model is supplied from the Coastal aquifer, Lake Kinneret, and seawater desalination. There are two consuming sectors, agriculture and urban. Agricultural production in the model is a function of fresh water and effluent. The effluent is a given ratio of the amount of water supplied to urban uses. Salts are removed by desalination of natural water.

The freshwater cost function is increasing: the lowest cost is coastal water, Lake Kinnert's comes next, and desalinated seawater is the most expensive. By assumption, prices are set equal to marginal cost. The appendix considers two cases that differ by the demand for water.

In the low demand case, the coastal region is supplied with fresh water from the local aquifer and from Lake Kinneret; seawater is not desalinated. Salts are removed by desalination of natural water. The price of fresh water is determined by the marginal product of water in agriculture and it is set, in equilibrium (at maximum net income), to equal the cost of moving water from Lake Kinneret *plus* the cost per CM of removing from the water of the Coastal aquifer the salts imported with the lake's water. The price of the effluent is a fraction of the price of fresh water, the fraction representing the comparative productivity of the recycled water.

In this low demand case, only the coastal water is scarce and has, in the model, a scarcity value. This value, and hence the extraction levy of coastal water, is equal to the price of fresh water *minus* the cost of its withdrawal. No scarcity value is attributed to the water of Lake Kinneret. The urban sector is seen in the program as if selling the effluent to agriculture; hence the net price urban dwellers pay for water equals the opportunity cost, the marginal productivity of water in agriculture, *plus* the cost of treating the sewage *minus* the price farmer pay for the effluent (only part of the water ends as effluent).

In the high demand case, seawater desalination is activated and the marginal productivity of water in agriculture is equal to the cost of desalination *plus* the cost of the removal of the (small amount) of salts left in the desalinated water. Desalinated water is supplied when the other water sources cannot satisfy the demand. Hence, in this case, the withdrawal constraint in Lake Kinneret is binding and the scarcity value of its water is positive; it is equal to the marginal productivity of water at the coast *minus* the cost of moving the water from the lake, and *minus* the cost of removing the salts carried in the Kinneret water. It is interesting to examine the difference in the cost of the lake's water in the two demand cases. In the low demand case, the users of water at the coast pay for the removal of the imported salts; the higher salt concentration, the higher the price of water. In the high demand case, on the other hand, water users pay the same price whatever the salt concentration in Kinneret's water. The fisc, the taxpayers, pay for the removal of the salts: the higher the concentration, the lower the extraction levy. The government sells low quality (salty) water and is paid accordingly.

CONCLUSION

Our calculations were based on simplifying assumptions and they should be taken as first approximations. Still, it can be expected that the two principal conclusions we have reached will not change with more detailed analysis. The first conclusion is that salt removal is an expensive operation. To show this, assume that the cost of delivering water to the coastal region is $0.15 per CM for aquifer water (Coastal or Mountain) and $0.30 per CM for Lake Kinneret water. With these magnitudes, the total cost of supplying 640 MCM/Y is $123 million per year. The cost of removing the salts in the steady state (desalination of coastal water), even if the modest quality goal of 150 ppm chlorides is chosen and the effluent is not upgraded, will be $57 million per year. This is an addition of close to 50% to the cost of the water economy.

The cost of removing the salt is high, but the cost of not doing it will be even higher. For example, if we let the aquifer deteriorate until its water cannot be used any more, water will be supplied from seawater desalination; the cost will be $154 million per year, more than twice the cost of maintaining a sustainable aquifer. Salt removal is a precondition for the maintenance of a sustainable water economy and its cost is part and parcel of the cost of the intensive utilization of the water resources. Just as a household has to remove sewage and garbage, so also one of the tasks of the water economy is to remove the salts and prevent their accumulation in the reservoirs.

The second principal conclusion of the analysis is that the efficient way to remove the salts is desalination of natural water from the saltiest source. The reason being that with this alternative the quantity desalinated is markedly smaller than in the other alternatives.

The computations in the analysis were conducted for the steady state in which, for example with the quality goal of 150 ppm, the concentration of salts in the coastal water is

425 ppm chlorides and then the efficient way to remove salts is by desalination of this source. However, if desalination were to commence today, when the concentration of salts in the coastal water is only 200 ppm, it would be advisable to start by desalinating the water coming from Lake Kinneret until the concentration in the Coastal aquifer exceeds that of the imported water. Another possibility, and even more reasonable, is to start desalination in most salty regions in the coastal aquifer itself.

These comments demonstrate, if a demonstration was necessary, that the analysis was preliminary. The continuing analysis will cover the other aquifers and incorporate engineering considerations. Also, the expected rate of desalination and the optimal date for removing the salts will have to be studied in further detail. Another subject for inquiry is the fate of salts exported from the coastal region; for example, will salts have to be actively removed from areas irrigated by Shafdan water?

APPENDIX: PRICES IN THE WATER ECONOMY

The prices are determined in a mathematical programming model of the coastal region in a steady state. The model is both broader and narrower than the framework of the discussion in the chapter. It incorporates agricultural production, that was not included explicitly in the chapter, but import of mountain water and exit of water and effluent from the region are disregarded in the formulation of the appendix. The objective function of the programming model is the value of agricultural output *minus* the cost of the water economy. The sources of freshwater are the Coastal Aquifer, Lake Kinneret, and seawater desalination; effluent is used in agriculture. There are two consuming sectors in the model—urban and agriculture. The urban sector receives a predetermined quantity of water. A given ratio of the water used in this sector is collected as sewage and, after treatment, provided as effluent. Irrigation deposits salts on the surface of the land and identical quantities are added to the water in the aquifer. Additional salts come from autonomous sources (ocean spray and underground brines). Freshwater desalination is used to remove the salts.

A. Functions and Variables

$F(\ )$	A well-behaved production function in agriculture (NIS per year)
$f(\ )$	Value of marginal product in agriculture (NIS per CM)
b	Constraint or requirement of provision (CM per year)
M	Freshwater (CM per year)
R	Effluent (CM per year)
μ	Salt concentration in water (gram chlorine per CM)
δ	Addition of salt (gram per CM, per year)
Δ	Autonomous addition of salts (grams per year)
λ, ϕ	Lagrange multipliers (shadow prices)
γ	Value of effluent in agriculture relative to freshwater
r	Ratio of effluent in urban water
C	Cost (dollars per CM)

P   Price (dollars per CM)

E   Extraction levy (dollars per CM).

B. Indexes

A   Agriculture
U   Urban
K   Kinneret
H   Coastal region or aquifer
DH   Desalination of coastal water
DK   Desalination of Kinneret water
T   Desalination of seawater
R   Effluent.

C. The Structure of Cost

Average cost is assumed to be constant per source, scale effects are disregarded and the costs rise; the lowest cost is withdrawal of coastal water, next Kinneret's water at the coast, and the most expensive is desalinated seawater.

$$C_H < C_K < C_T$$

D. Resources and Uses, Constraints, and Supply Requirements

D.1. Equality Constraints

Freshwater: provision to agriculture and the urban sector is equal to supply for the coastal aquifer, Kinneret, and seawater desalination

$$M_A + M_U = M_H + M_K + M_T$$

Effluent: supply to agriculture plus removal to the sea is equal to the quantity collected and treated in the urban sector

$$R_A + R_S = rM_U$$

Salt: the quantity added to the coastal region is eliminated by desalination of coastal or Kinneret water (the concentration of chlorides in the desalinated water is 20 ppm)

$$\Delta_H + \mu_K M_K + \delta_R R_A + 20 M_T = (\mu_H - 20) M_{DH} + (\mu_K - 20) M_{DK}$$

Urban water constraint

$$M_U = b_U$$

D.2. Inequalities

Coastal Aquifer, extraction	$M_H \leq b_H$
Kinneret, extraction	$M_K \leq b_K$
Coast, desalination	$M_{DH} \leq M_H$
Kinneret, desalination	$M_{DK} \leq M_K$

D.3. Nonnegativity
All the quantity variables are nonnegative.

E. The Programming Problem

Equation (A.1) is the Kuhn-Tucker Lagrangian of the programming problem. Following Simon and Blume (1994), we write specific multipliers for the constraints: λ for equalities and ϕ for inequalities. In this formulation, the quantities are the primal variables, they are the activities of the program; the Lagrange multipliers are the dual variables.

$$\begin{aligned}
L = &F(M_A + \gamma R_A) - C_H M_H - C_K M_K - C_T M_T \\
&- C_A R_A - C_D(M_{DH} + M_{DK}) \\
&- \lambda_M(M_A + M_U - M_K - M_H - M_T) \\
&- \lambda_R(R_A - rM_U) - \lambda_D[\Delta + \mu_K M_K + 20M_T + \delta_R R_A \\
&- (\mu_H - 20)M_{DH} - (\mu_K - 20)M_{DK}] \\
&- \lambda_U(b_U - M_U) - \phi_H(M_H - b_H) - \phi_K(M_K - b_K)
\end{aligned} \qquad (A.1)$$

We skip the derivation of the first order condition and demonstrate application in two cases; the first corresponds to relatively low demand for water in the coastal region; the second case represents conditions of higher demand.

E.1. Case I
By construction, in the solution of this case, extraction from the coastal aquifer is up to the constraint and additional quantities of water are moved from Kinneret; part of the water extracted in the coast is desalinated; fresh water is supplied to the urban sector and to agriculture; effluent is supplied to agriculture.
Writing formally,

$$\begin{aligned}
&M_A > 0 \\
&R_A = rM_U > 0 \\
&M_H = b_H > 0 \\
&0 < M_K < b_K \\
&M_U = b_U > 0
\end{aligned} \qquad (A.2)$$

The value of the primal variables that do not appear in (A.2) is zero.

Combining the first order derivatives and (A.2), the following multipliers were factored out

$$\lambda_D = C_D/(\mu_H - 20)$$
$$\lambda_M = f(M_A + \gamma R_A) = C_K + C_D \mu_K/(\mu_H - 20)$$
$$\phi_H = f(M_A + \gamma R_A) - C_H$$
$$\lambda_R = \gamma f(M_A + \gamma R_A) - C_A - C_D \delta_R/(\mu_H - 20)$$
$$\lambda_U = \lambda_M - \lambda_R r$$
$$= f(M_A + \gamma R_A)(1 - r\gamma) + r[C_A + C_D \delta_R/(\mu_H - 20)]$$

$$(A.3)$$

The first shadow price in (A.3) is of desalinated coastal water. It is the cost of desalination of one CM divided by the amount of salt removed; that is, λ_D is the cost of salt removal per gram of chloride.

The multiplier in the second equation in (A.3), λ_M, is the Value of the Marginal Productivity of water in the coastal area agriculture and it is also equal to the marginal cost of water provision. The cost of moving water from Lake Kinneret to the coastal region is higher than the cost of local extraction. Hence, if in the solution of (A.1) water is moved, the marginal cost of freshwater, λ_M, is the cost of the lake's water at the coast and this magnitude is equal to the cost of moving the water from the lake *plus* the cost of removing the salts brought by its water.

The third equation defines the scarcity cost of coastal water, ϕ_H; it equals to the VMP of water *minus* cost of extraction; in other words, to the cost of water from Lake Kinneret *minus* extraction.

The value of the effluent in coastal agriculture is λ_R and it is its VMP (water's multiplied by γ) *minus* the cost of sewage treatment and the removal of the salts added in the urban sector. The cost of water to the urban sector is the opportunity cost of freshwater in agriculture *minus* the value of the effluent the town transfers to the farm sector; that is, the program visualizes the urban sector as purchasing water, treating its sewage, and selling the effluent to farmers at a price equal to its VMP.

Given the multipliers of (A.3), the prices and the extraction levy will be

$$P_A = \lambda_M = f(M_A + \gamma R_A) = C_K + C_D \mu_K/(\mu_H - 20)$$
$$P_R = \gamma P_A$$
$$P_U = \lambda_U$$
$$E_H = \phi_H$$

$$(A.4)$$

By the first line in (A.4) farmers (and urban users) pay for the transfer of water from Kinneret and also for the removal of the salts carried by the water from this source. The last attribute will be modified in the next case.

E.2. Case II

This case corresponds to higher profitability in agriculture than in Case I and therefore the solution calls for larger quantities of water, the extraction constraint in the Kinneret is met, and seawater is desalinated. Formally, we add to (A.2)

$$M_K = b_K > 0$$
$$M_T > 0 \tag{A.5}$$

The shadow price of freshwater is now

$$\lambda_M = f(M_A + \gamma R_A) = C_T + 20C_D / (\mu_H - 20) \tag{A.6}$$

The marginal cost of desalinated water is the cost of desalination *plus* the cost of removing the (small amounts of) salts desalinated water adds to the aquiver.

The other multipliers will be in this case

$$\lambda_D = C_D / (\mu_H - 20)$$
$$\phi_H = C_T + 20C_D / (\mu_H - 20) - C_H$$
$$\phi_K = C_T + 20C_D / (\mu_H - 20) - C_K - C_D\mu_K / (\mu_H - 20) \tag{A.7}$$
$$\lambda_R = \gamma\left[C_T + 20C_D / (\mu_H - 20)\right] - C_A - C_D\delta_R / (\mu_H - 20)$$
$$\lambda_U = \left[C_T + 20C_D / (\mu_H - 20)\right](1 - r\gamma) + r[C_A + C_D\delta_R / (\mu_H - 20)]$$

Again, the prices are

$$P_A = \lambda_M$$
$$P_R = \cdot\gamma P_A$$
$$P_U = \lambda_U \tag{A.8}$$
$$E_H = \phi_H$$
$$E_K = \phi_K$$

Here, in Case II, the scarcity value of Lake Kinneret water, ϕ_K, is positive; it was zero in Case I. Unlike in the previous case, now the cost of removing the salts carried from the lake is shouldered by the public at large (the fisc) and not just by the users in the coastal area. To see this, examine the components of ϕ_K: the higher the concentration of salts in the lake's water (μ_K) the lower the scarcity value. The government provides the coastal users with water of low quality (salty) and is paid accordingly.

REFERENCES

Goldfarb, O., and Kislev, Y. (2002). A Sustainable Salt Regime in the Coastal Aquifer. The Center for Agricultural Economic Research, Discussion Paper No. 1.02 (Hebrew) http://departments.agri.huji.ac.il/economics/yoav-hof1.pdf.

Kislev, Y. (2006). The Water Economy of Israel. In K. D. Hambright, F. J. Ragep, and J. Ginat (Eds.), *Water in the Middle East: Cooperation and Technological Solutions in the Jordan Valley* (pp.127-150). Norman, OK: University of Oklahoma Press.

Mercado, A. (1980). The Coastal Aquifer in Israel: Some Quality Aspects of Groundwater Management. In H. I. Shuval (Ed.), *Water quality management under conditions of scarcity: Israel as a case study* (pp. 93-146). New York: Academic Press.

Simon, C. P., and Blume, L. (1994). *Mathematics for Economists*. New York, NY: W.W. Norton.

In: The Economics of Natural and Human Resources...   ISBN 978-1-60741-029-4
Editor: Ayal Kimhi and Israel Finkelshtain   © 2009 Nova Science Publishers, Inc.

Chapter 3

MANAGING SALINITY IN DEGRADED SOILS BY MANDATORY TREE PLANTING: ON THE DYNAMIC AND POLITICAL ECONOMY MODELING OF A COMMON POOL RESOURCE

Ernst-August Nuppenau[*]

ABSTRACT

Many farming areas in the tropics and subtropics are characterized by increasing salinity. These areas include traditional, poorly managed, rain fed dry-land farming areas as well as modern, intensively used irrigation schemes. In particular intensification of agriculture, due to human population pressure, and increased economic incentives for land development, due to commercialization, have contributed to salinity. Salinity nowadays stretches over large landscapes in tropical and subtropical countries. Surface and ground water systems as well as deeper aquifers are heavily infiltrated, i.e. polluted with salt. Being largely an uncontrolled externality of plant production under less appropriate technology, high salt content reduces productivity, noticeable as a common-pool externality. In particular, small-holder communities with low technological levels, short term needs for agricultural produce, and strong capital constraints have the tendency to overexploit water. Moreover, the potential of soils to regenerate from the tendency towards salinity declines with time.

Due to the immanent common property problem of the medium, water, as well as to high transaction costs in soil protection and non-point-pollution problems, salinity is a common feature of poorly, publicly managed irrigation schemes in dry-lands. Salinity levels of small-holder areas are alarmingly high. High salinity levels, for instance, - recognizable as reduced short term resistance to water stress, long term development of high pH-levels, and high water tables - are effecting the food security of small-holders. Concerning causes of pollution, overuse of water subject to high evaporation and no abatement, is regarded as the main cause of continuing problems.

---

[*] Department of Agricultural Policy and Market Research, University of Giessen, Germany Mail Address: Senckenbergstrasse 3, D-35390 Giessen Germany E-mail: Ernst-August.Nuppenau@agrar.uni-giessen.de

Environmental regulations governing water use and farm practices, such as limitations in water dosage, specific plants mixes etc., but also regeneration of soils, by methods such as land set-aside, tree planting etc., are normally not in the direct interest of small-holders, since these measures reduce current income and result in benefits that have to be shared. In particular, tree planting to extract salt and minimize shocks caused by droughts has recently gained the interest of scheme management as a low cost and appropriate technological solution. However, an area covered by trees reduces cropping area. This paper presents a model that accounts for salinity in the short and long run, attributes levels of mandatory tree planting to farmers for salinity reduction as well as recognizes short term income waivers from reduced crop land. A dynamic framework is used to control farm activities and to cater for a reduction of salinity in a community. It models water tables, tree cover and salt content.

The paper applies a combination of a dynamic control model with the optimization of a common property by a manager. He/she seeks to achieve an agreed level of cleanliness or salinity on behalf of the community. A political economy model depicts the bargaining process for the establishment of an objective function which includes the manager's own objective. The manager is a partial manager, not a benevolent dictator, but has the statutory power to regulate tree planting for the extraction of salt. Farmers can cut organic matter from plants grown on land set-aside, and benefit from use or sales. Benefits are derived from better quality soil which helps all members. As institutions, the approach investigates the tragedy of the common and statutory regulations. Financial innovations for compensation are also possible.

A. INTRODUCTION

The salinity of soil is a serious and complex problem in resource, environmental, and ecological economics as well as an issue in the related policy debates (Singh and Singh, 1995 and Wichelns, 1999). Salinity threatens agricultural production in many areas of the tropics and subtropics. These areas are primarily characterized by uneven rainfall patterns combined with necessary irrigation, high evaporation, and notable salinity threats. Particularly and increasingly over the last decades, farmers are criticized for contaminating their soils, since they do not sufficiently invest in the abatement of salinity or do not apply available techniques such as drip irrigation, leaching technologies, etc.; even more pronounced, farmers simultaneously pollute soils of neighbors. Non-point pollution (resource economics), common property management (environmental economics), and ecosystem (ecological economics) problems have emerged and are mostly unsolved in the context of salinization. Since salinity is a feature not confined to a single field, common-pool property management problems and institutional deficits have evolved fairly rapidly and are now widespread. Consequently, farmers are even criticized for contributing to greater regional ecological problems and sometimes to ecological disasters, such as desertification; an extreme case or result of salinization.

The processes of salinization can threaten the livelihood of entire communities that are dependent on fertile soils, irrigation, and eco-system health. The observation is not confined to countries with outdated technology. Instead, the problem also seems to be prevalent in modern irrigation schemes of arid zones in developed countries or countries with more advanced technologies. For instance, salinity poses the threat of degradation of soils and negative impacts on farming in complete irrigation schemes of large watersheds in Australia

(Gretton and Salma,1997). While treatment methods seem to be expensive and go beyond single farm abatement (Qadir et al. 2001); farmers may need help for public management.

Public management includes several aspects. For instance, public management may imply direct control of farm activities on all levels, such as water application levels, tree cutting, leaching, etc., or it may be more indirect, such as verifying land set-aside, water tables, etc. Furthermore, we have to note that the capacity or control of a complex farming system, such as an irrigation system, which is embedded in watershed and which contains numerous farmers, is normally beyond the capability of a small unit of experts. In addition, the property rights structure prevalent in a community is a question that should never be overlooked. Only if we assume that all property rights are with a superior manager who completely pursues public planning to combat salinity in the interest of the community, notably a benevolent dictator, we can perhaps drop the problem of the identification of elements such as participation, command, coordination, trust, etc. Even in that context the question is, will the dictator make profits from the introduction of devises like tree planting and who bears the costs of losses in farm land, etc. In our suggested outline, the manager has an interest function, since farmers will lobby and lobbying means material compensation for doing the job of community work.

It is primarily the objective of this chapter to show how tree planting can be an alternative to economically unsustainable methods. We put an emphasis on the common property management aspect of tree planting in small-holder communities, the necessary stock and flow variables of control, and provide policy recommendations. The method used is a mix of a dynamic and political economy model which serves several small-scale farmers. The chapter is organized into four sub-chapters. Firstly, we will look at the dynamics of salinity. Secondly, we will state farmers' objective functions with regard to waivers on land use. Thirdly, we will use this information to explore the dynamic behavior of tree growth. Fourthly, we will show how the tragedy of the common situation can be modeled and why limited improvement prevails. Fifthly, a political economy model will show how a particular improvement can occur using a given interest and power structure in a community; now a partial manager manages the community. Finally, suggestions for application will provide ideas for empirical research.

B. PROBLEM STATEMENT

B.1. Confronting the Problem

Two major arguments are normally put forward to explain individual behavior resulting in salinization and low interest in abatement. The first argument is that individual rationality in balancing short term and long term benefits is in favor of an increase of salinity. Farmers deliberately accept salinization in exchange for short term profits whereas the creation of salinity only results in a long term decline of soil fertility. Acceptance of higher salinity and productivity decline of soils in future periods is congruent with the private interest argument of those doing so, as long as interest rates are high. Irrespective of sustainability considerations put forward in policy debate, farmers may act rationally when depleting soils and contributing to salinity of watersheds. In particular, this argument includes a positive discount rate as the driving force; "comparatively high discount rates determine the speed of salinization!", so the argument goes. Normatively speaking, the theory of discounting tells farmers to reap short term benefits and disregard long term negative externalities from increase in salinity. This behavior apparently depends on the option to substitute natural soil fertility with other inputs (Knapp and Olsen, 1996). This is especially the case if costs for abatement today compared to yield losses tomorrow are high; then farmers will only make limited efforts to combat salinity.

However, this creates the question whether individual time preference (discount rates) and social time preference (discount rates) are compatible. Even if Pigouvian taxes are involved, for instance, see the similar case of peat (Goetz, 1997 and Goetz and Zilberman, 1995), private and public discount rates become distinct. Note further, time preferences are invariant (Barry et al. 1996).

From observations that poor farmers have higher discount rates it is concluded that soil degradation (as an escalation of reversible damage by low salinity, irreversibility, desertification, abandonment of farming) is a social phenomenon of low income groups and is justified by unequal distribution of resources. It is hoped that in future the discount rate may decrease with increases in welfare acquired by soil exploitation. Nevertheless, improved individual rationality might just extend the time horizon for degradation, not halt it, and sustainability seems also to be a rather weak concept (Conrad, 1999).

Secondly, common-pool property rights problems can create an open access situation (Bromley, 1992) which discourages individuals to move in the direction of soil conservation, and diverges farmers' interests from fighting against salinity as the single, most superior, strategy of soil conservation. This aspect, as a standard argument, means that an individual rationality does not include the behavior of neighbors who are defecting in cooperation (Hanna et al. 1996). As a by-product of intensive cropping, excessive water use and salt penetration accumulates salt due to high evaporation rates and salinity becomes a serious problem for the preservation of fresh water, notably of extended areas (Singh and Singh, 1995).

The increase of salt contents can even go beyond certain thresholds, which make the loss of farming area irreversible or re-cultivation expensive (i.e. desertification). Moreover, salinity is not only threatening the future but also the present. Many ecosystems are already nowadays characterized by high salt loads and have become increasingly negatively affected and endangered in their natural status. Generally, salty water and near surface levels of salt-infiltrated ground water are immediate threats, and successes in improvement can be labeled as a research priority in achieving sustainability, i.e. economic, ecological and social sustainability.

However, there seems to be some type of treatment which is associated with tree planting. Tree planting for the extraction of salt out of contaminated soils has gained considerable attention (Barrett-Lennard, 2002). Many questions appear: 1) Is there a problem in competition between tree planting and agricultural land use (which is foreseeable when land is scarce)? 2) Is there a coordination problem that requires public management? 3) What are objectives? 4) What is the assurance of commitment in small-holder communities? 5) What is the adult life span of a tree and what is the level of remaining salinity in a steady state? 6) How can sustainability be reached? 7) What roles do tree planting and cutting play, as trees do not live forever? 8) What is the commercial and what the common interest? etc.

B.2. Economizing the Problem

However salinity can change, soil improvement is a non-point pollution problem of communities that share a common-pool property, soil. A common property management problem emerges. The reduction of salinity may be a technical problem and tree planting is the measure.

But both, common property and technique should be considered together as a management tool, notably a common one. The task is to extract salt from infected soils so that an improvement occurs and the costs of the improvement are minimized. The management of cleaning an infected area, as understood in this paper, is a co-management problem consisting of benefits from reduced salt inflows, delineated as higher productivity of farm land, and costs from restrictions in land use, detected as strips planted with trees and shrubs (Tanji and Karajeh, 1993).

Costs also include planting and cutting costs of trees and water evaporated by trees. Benefits include fire wood and annual fruits from trees. The questions are how soils improve if a will exists to organize public action, and how to impose public management, where free-riding is a pertinent strategy. Furthermore, what are the ecological prerequisites, the economic incentives and the institutional needs to achieve improvements?

Firstly, we assume that an irrigation scheme, given a certain tree cover, has the potential to reduce salt, though only to a certain extent. Secondly, we assume that farmers have an interest in better soil quality.

Thirdly, we assume that an institutional setting has been agreed upon by which the problem of non-point pollution and common property will be overcome. In principle, we will hand over the task of improving soils to a common-pool property manager, whose task is to reduce the negative externality of salinity. The manager will be given the right to allocate tree planting which is of public interest to individual farmers. However, we will not naively presume that the manager is maximizing social welfare, i.e. being a benevolent dictator. Instead, we presume that he is a partial manager. A partial manager is a manager who reacts to political power.

Common property management may be exposed to political economy influence; i.e. interest and political power of groups will determine the outcome of a negotiated and environmentally motivated measure such as tree planting. Though this situation could be possibly welfare improving, since we have the open access or tragedy of the common situation, it means no benevolent manager, as the reference situation is realistic.

Including the argumentation concerning common-pool property management, we will further follow trails of thought concerning political economy modeling of environmental policy that have been developed in political bargaining models (Harsanyi, 1963). On the basis of the design of statutory regulations in communities of common property users, we will derive rules regarding land use to combat salinity (Rausser and Zusman, 1996). The size of land set-aside for tree strips is under strict rules of planting, but cutting trees is not forbidden. This waiver on the use of certain farm land is specified as the distances in a rectangular field system. Soil improvement aspects are treated dynamically, and a dynamic optimization model is presented. Then dynamic optimization is understood as an optimization task of a manager who is subject to the political pressure of interest groups, i.e. he lives within the farming community!

C. Dynamics of Soil Quality and Land Set-Aside in Small-Holder Agriculture

The soil quality of a watershed or irrigation system will be described by an index that measures negative productivity impacts of salinity. As discussed elsewhere (Gretton and Salma, 1997), a decline in soil quality associated with salinity in irrigation schemes, has several implications for the productivity of soils as a public good. Soils no longer serve different farm types with fresh water, and limitations in the application rates of fertilizer reveal soil stress. As a measurable variable of salinity (an index), concentration of sodium - in principle - is accepted as the major quantitative contributor to soil quality decline. Sodium can change, and is subject to accumulation. The accumulation is stimulated by water use in irrigation, the rise of the water table, and the fertilization of the watershed. Beside natural increases in salinity, artificial or unintended enrichment of salt is the big threat. Mostly imposed by farmers as a non-point pollution phenomenon, salinization is not only a by-product of irrigation, but also a serious problem of its own. There might have been other sources of salt infiltration, historically, and soils find a steady state themselves in the long run, since they have natural processes of enrichment and cleaning; but how can an improvement be obtained?

To present the dynamics of soil salinity in conjunction with farm activities, and the deduction of salty nutrients by explicitly recognizing land allocation for tree and shrub land, which are set-aside by farms, we use a first order differential equation for movements of soil quality such as

$$\dot{S}(t) = -\kappa_0 S(t) + \kappa_1 W(t) + \kappa_2 [\sum_j (A^1 - A_j)] + \kappa_3 [O^0 - O(t)] - \kappa_4 l^1(t) \qquad (1)$$

Equation (1) recognizes the dynamics of salinity S(t) as dependent on the water table, land allocation "A" and organic matter "0", where one part describes farming activity by area under crops (A-ΣA_j), and a second part area under land set-aside A. The water table comes soon.

$$\Leftrightarrow \dot{S}(t) = -\kappa_0 S(t) + \kappa_1 W(t) + \kappa_2 [\sum [A^1 - A_j] + \kappa_3 [F^0 \cdot A^0 - F(t) \cdot A(t)] - \kappa_4 l^1(t) \qquad (1')$$

where:

S(t) : soil quality index (based on salinity) at time t (can also be directly sodium content)
W(t): water table at time t
A^1-A_j(t): polluting acreage of individual farmer under given technology, i.e. irrigation use
O(t): organic matter by growth in organic matter per hectare on communal fallow
A(t): area under fallow
l^1(t): deliberate used water for leaching of water to combat salinity
F(t): organic matter per hectare
A^0: steady state fallow stand to offset salinity

First and foremost, the equation describes a natural system, whereby salinity is reduced by natural leaching of soils due to rainfall, natural water tables, etc. The vegetation on land set-aside is an amplifying measure for salt reduction. But soils show decline in salinity only after years. The equation (1') also models the change in soil quality at given areas under agricultural use in such a way that upper and lower boundaries are specified. Presuming that salinity is associated with an increasing or declining prevalence of trees in the area, a first order differential equation with a coefficient of "κ" below 1 implies that the soil is still capable of improving itself over time, with shrub and tree cover strongly contributing to the improvement. However, the size of "κ" determines the time period needed for improvement; values close to 1 mean very long periods of salinity, while values close to zero mean strong improvement. The size of land set-aside plays a major role. For instance, presuming an approachable constant level of salinity at a certain size of natural vegetation or tree vegetation, the value of "A^0" can specify the steady state situation. Zero salinity, from a modeling point of view, is the steady state under the condition "$\kappa_2(A^0-A(T))/\kappa_0$", apparently, without agricultural use. Hence, if A(T) is approaching A^0 and the improvement took place, S(t) becomes zero. Natural tree cover ,"A^0", serves as a benchmark. It can be used for the calibration of the lower bound of no salinity (upper end of soil quality). The different levels in land set-aside and agricultural area change the steady state and the improvement capacity. Special cases can be distinguished beside the natural situation! In the case of no land set-aside in the model, i.e. "A=0", farm land is maximized, and the second part equals A^0, the model would apparently move to an upper point of salinity ($\kappa_1[\Sigma A^*_j-A^0]+\kappa_2 A^0)/\kappa_0$". On the other extreme lies $A(T)=A^0$. The latter implies an ideal situation without human influence. A^0 is a matter of the definition of S and calibration.

Mainly, equation (1) describes a natural curing system on the level of salt content. However, in equation (1) we have already anticipated that the water table, which is crucial for the prevalence of salt, plays a major role in the dynamics of salt. Primarily by infiltration, soils would show, depending on the local conditions, changes (rises) in water tables after years.

$$\dot{W}(t) = \zeta_0 + \zeta_1 W(t) + \zeta_2[\sum_i (1-z)l_j] + \zeta_3[F^0 \cdot A^0 - F(t) \cdot A(t)] - \zeta_4 F(t) \cdot A(t) + l^l_m(t) - l^p_m(t) \quad (2)$$

where additionally:

l(t): water not used in plant production and retained by soils at farm j in time t
z: technical factor on leaching
l^l(t): leaching water to clean surface soils from salt on a hectare basis
l^p(t): water pumped out of the system with special technical devices
ζ_0: threshold of water table

Equation (2) reckons the change in the water table given new inflows of water from the fields, inflows from leaching activities, extraction of water on the sites of set-aside by trees, and additionally a policy variable such as pumping ground water. Furthermore, we assume a natural outflow given as an autonomous change of the system and we consider the possibility to make the function linear to distinguish between water and land allocation.

$$\dot{W}(t) = \zeta_0 + \zeta_1 W(t) + \zeta_2 (1-z) \sum_j I^{l_0} [A^l - A_j] + [A^l - A_j^0 I]_j] + \zeta_3 [F^0 \cdot A(t) - A^0 \cdot F(t)] - \zeta_4 F(t) \cdot A(t) + I_m^l(t) - I_m^r(t) \quad T \quad (2')$$

This representation of the water table is considered crucial for combating salinity subject to individual farm behavior with respect to irrigation intensity and land provision as well as to public policy interventions. It includes the potential to pump water to lower the water table.

Next, organic matter inventories that catch salt are also dynamic processes. The catching of salt by trees and shrubs shall be associated with the volume of organic matter standing on land set-aside. Organic matter, as a quantity standing ready for extraction, supports desalinization of soils by filtering salt out of water. The filter potential is determined by the size of the organic mass. Hence, bio-mass enters our dynamic function (1'). Vice versa, the water table influences the growth of organic matter. Loss or enrichment (change) of bio-mass $\dot{O}$ (equation 3), primarily due to cutting of trees by farmer j on land set-aside area "$a_j(t)$" and vice versa, building up organic matter on land set-aside "$u_j(t)$" shall also be described by a differential equation, whereas coefficients measure the proportional annual decline due to the cutting of mature shrubs and trees, and the periodical contribution by virgin planting in the first instance:

$$\dot{O}(t) = -\varphi_0 O(t) + \varphi_1 \sum a_j(t) - \varphi_2 \sum u_j(t) + \varphi_3 W(t) \qquad (3)$$

As stated, the organic matter "O" is qualified as land set-aside multiplied by stands of organic matter per hectare "F" and area measured as number of hectare "A", i.e. F·A. Hence, it follows:

$$[F(t) \cdot \dot{A}(t)] = \varphi_0 [F(t) \cdot A(t)] - \varphi_1 \sum a_j(t) + \varphi_2 \sum u_j(t) + \varphi_3 W(t) \quad (3')$$

where additionally: F(t) : organic matter at time t
a_j (t) : individual cutting of bush and tree land set-aside: optimized
u_j (t) : individual new set aside of small-holders to shrub and bush land: mandatory regulated

After some manipulations intended to reduce complexity and to focus on the area in land set-aside, in particular assuming a constant growth of the existing area, we receive

$$F(t) \cdot \dot{A}(t) + \dot{F}(t) \cdot A(t) = -\varphi_0 [F \cdot A(t)] + \varphi_1 \sum a_j(t) - \varphi_2 \sum u_j(t) + \varphi_3 W(t) \qquad (3'')$$

and

$$\dot{A}(t) = [\varphi_0 - \xi] A(t) + \varphi_2 \sum a_j(t) - \varphi_2^* \sum u_j(t) + 1/F_0 e^{-\xi \cdot t} + \varphi_3 W(t) \qquad (3''')$$

Given in equation (3'''), the expression of the dynamic equation (3) depicts the collective action of communities; i.e. collective bush and tree land on set-aside farm land. Equation (3''') shows how the aggregated change of farmers' decisions materializes in a partial restoration of the ecosystem. In the initial equation (3'), the change of tree and bush on land set-aside, i.e. its organic mass "$\dot{O}(t)$", and what is needed hence for remedies, depends on the previous year's level of organic mass O(t) (i.e. $\varphi_0 > 1$ reflects natural growth), individual land $a_j(t)$ of trees cut, and annual intake of land from various farms $u_j(t)$. The total level of individually newly contributed land as a movement of organic matter (Σu_j; sum of all farmers' provisions) is collectively determined; cutting is free. Farmers make decisions - calculating the status of the common-pool property from which the negative externality, i.e. salinity, is derived as a stock variable - on farming modes (setting aside of land, cutting trees, and contributing arable and irrigate land in production to salinity). If the community wants to decrease salinity, tree cover on land set-aside has to be increased, i.e. land planted with trees has to overcome short term interest.

D. THE FARMERS' OBJECTIVE FUNCTION

Allocation of land with different use options has to be seen in conjunction with the overall use of agricultural land and farmers' objective function. The applied micro-theory (Varian, 1994) is similar to the one of Nuppenau and Slangen (1998). It focuses on constrained profit functions. In the case of salinity, we distinguish between farming on a remaining field and afforested land dedicated to the improvement of soils. Given minimum requirements for tree planting, farmers lose profits as negative effects of regulating land use. Positive effects of land set-aside (e.g. higher local humidity on fields adjacent to forests and higher yields due to cooling evaporation) from common property management should be distinguished, as short term public goods "A_j", from long term salinity reduction "S". The adjusted total profit is calculated using crop yields and gross margins on farm "j". Profits are essentially determined by patterns of farmers' location and the dedication of land for recreation (For instance as strips of land, Nuppenau, 1999). The policy variable "u_j" might stretch as strip. Theoretically, the objective function of allocating land corresponds to a constrained profit optimization of farms (Chambers, 1988). In the case of combating salinity, a farmer, j, will recognize salinity in the watershed as a public good given a profit function "$P=P(A_j,a_j,u_j,S)$". Salinity "S" is common property. Land set-aside appears because this land cover already improves the micro-climate on the farm. In addition, individual farmers work with a time horizon "T" and discount "ρ".

$$P_{j,[0,T]} = \int_o^T e^{-\rho t} \{P(A_j(t), a_j(t), u_j(t), S(t))\} dt \qquad (4)$$

where additionally : P(t) : profit at time t

This profit function needs an explicit specification in terms of land allocation, gross margins, waiver on land use, and the recognition of profits from collectively-managed common property. The water table is a system parameter that does not directly relate to costs. The cost function is adjusted to impacts of land set-aside and salinity.

$P_{j,[0,T]}=$

$$\int_0^T e^{-\rho t}\{p_j^a d_j^*[A_j^0 - A_j(t)] + p_j^f a_j(t) - C(d_j[A_j^0 - A_j(t)], a_j(t), r(t), S(t), A_j(t), u_j(t), z_j)\}dt$$

where: increase: "⇑" and decrease "⇓" :   (4')

    $p^a=$ gross margins per ton and hectare according to yields per hectare in agriculture, (profit⇑)

    $p^f=$ gross margins per ton in sales of fallow products from tree cutting, (profit⇑)

    $r^f=$ water price, (cost⇑)

    $d_j=$ yields per hectare including size of the field, (profit⇑)

    $(1-A_j)=$ acreage as area cropped, (profit⇑);

    $A_j=$ acreage under fallow, not cropped, (profit⇓);

    $a_j=$ acreage where trees are cut, newly cropped next period, (profit⇑);

    $C(.)=$ cost function on quantity of q_j at fields with the yield $a=q_{ij}/l_{ij}$, (cost⇑=>profit⇓)

    $(1-A_j)=$ production effect on unit costs (ambiguous)

    $_{aj}=$fallow land, *individual* cost reducing effect by biological activity (cost⇓=>profit⇑)

    $r=$ water costs (cost⇑=>profit⇓)

    $z=$ input costs, farm specific (cost⇑=>profit⇓)

    $S=$ soil quality index (profit⇑), exogenous to farmer

    $F=$ organic matter on fallow per hectare (profit⇑), exogenous to farmer

D.1. Farm Behavior

Assuming that there is homogeneity in land with respect to the cost function, equal time horizons for all farmers, and interaction of profits with land quality, i.e. substitution between other inputs and soil quality, as derived from salinity (2), the specification of profits in (4') can be used for optimization in the traditional sense of an individual farm behavior. Notice: we still have to elaborate on the distinction between the sector approach and a sum of farm approach in management. Equation (3"") qualifies land use in terms of fertility of soil/land and set-aside by having an option to cut trees "a" and plant trees "u":

$$\dot{A}_j(t) = -\varphi_0^* F \cdot A_j(t) - \varphi_1 a_j(t) + \varphi_2 u_j(t) + \varphi_3 W(t) + 1/F_0\, e^{-\xi t} \qquad (3"")$$

Using land allocation as a constraint for farm behavior, the intention of the following intermediate analysis is to explain cutting- and land-clearing-behavior of individual farms. Farms are primarily interested in crop land and not forest land; though considering the taking advantage of firewood if prevalent. The clearing of land for cropping is an instantaneous exercise. It provides land for obtaining farm surpluses. In order to make the analysis operational, we will now introduce a quadratic cost function, i.e. applying the cost function (5a):

$$C(d_j^*(A_j^0 - A_j), S(t), r, a_j, u_j, r_j) = \gamma_{10}A_j + \gamma_{20}S + \gamma_{30}a_j + \gamma_{40}u_j + 0.5\gamma_{11}A_j^2 + 0.5\gamma_{22}S^2 + 0.5\gamma_{33}a_j^2 +$$
$$0.5\gamma_{44}r_j^2 + 0.5\gamma_{55}u_j^2 + \gamma_{12}A_jS + \gamma_{13j}A_ja_j + \gamma_{14j}A_ju_j + \gamma_{23}S u_j +$$
$$\gamma_{24}S a_j + \gamma_{34j}a_ju_j + \gamma_{31}r A_j + \gamma_{32}r S + \gamma_{33j}r a_j + \gamma_{34j}r u_j \tag{5a}$$

In this context we can use Shepherd's Lemma to derive water demand per hectare which is:

$$1_j = \gamma_{44}r_j + \gamma_{31}A_j + \gamma_{32}S + \gamma_{33j}a_j + \gamma_{34j}u_j \tag{5b}$$

Equation (5b) can be inserted in the water table differential equation in order to reveal a dependency of the water table on the demand for water. Furthermore, the production of farmer j is determined by the marginal revenue minus the marginal cost; the farm size is (5c).

$$p_j^a d_j^* - \gamma_{10} + \gamma_{11}A_j + \gamma_{12}S + \gamma_{13j}a_j + \gamma_{14j}u_j + \gamma_{31}r = 0$$
$$\Rightarrow q_j^s = d_j[A_j^0 - A_j] = d_j[A_j^0 - \gamma_{11}^{-1}[\gamma_{10j} - p_j^a d_j + \gamma_{12}S + \gamma_{13j}a_j + \gamma_{14j}u_j + \gamma_{31}r]] \tag{5c}$$

in which yields per hectare are not yet defined, yet; but we can determine them as

$$d_j = \xi_j 1_j = \xi_j[\gamma_{44}r_j + \gamma_{31}A_j + \gamma_{32}S + \gamma_{33j}a_j + \gamma_{34j}u_j] \tag{5d}$$

Finally, note in this context that a determination of production and technology additionally can be the basis for the estimation of behavioral equations of farmers. Next, we can specify the cost function (5a) as determined by state variables of the system by a system of behavioral equations. However, farmers do not only behave statically with respect to water demand, given state variables, etc. Rather they decide on dynamics: tree planting, duration and cutting of trees. Inserting state variables in function (4) and following conditions (6). that reflect dynamic optimization of a Hamilton function, equation (7) is the dynamic criteria (Tu. 1992).

$$H(t)_{A_j(t)} = -\dot{l}(t) \qquad H(t)_{a_j(t)} = 0 \qquad H(t)_{l(t)} = -\dot{A}_j(t) \tag{6}$$

Then we use the Hamilton of the problem (4):

$$H_j(S, A, a, t) = e^{-rt}\{p_j^a d_j[1 - A_j(t)] + p_j^a a_j(t) - [\gamma_{10}A_j + \gamma_{20}S + \gamma_{30}a_j + \gamma_{40}u_j + 0.5\gamma_{11}A_j^2 + 0.5\gamma_{22}S^2 + 0.5\gamma_{33}a_j^2 + 0.5\gamma_{44}r_j^2 + 0.5\gamma_{55}u_j^2$$
$$+ \gamma_{12}A_jS + \gamma_{13j}A_ja_j + \gamma_{14j}A_ju_j + \gamma_{23}S u_j + \gamma_{24}S a_j + \gamma_{34j}a_ju_j + \gamma_{31}r A_j + \gamma_{32}r S + \gamma_{33j}r a_j + \gamma_{34j}r u_j]\}$$
$$+ L_1(t)[\varphi_0 A(t) - \varphi_1 a(t) + \varphi_2 u(t) + \varphi_3 W(t)] \tag{7}$$

Applying (6) to (7) provides us with 3 conditions of dynamic behavior on arable land set-aside:

$$+ \gamma_{11} A_j(t) + \gamma_{13} a_j(t) + [\beta - \rho] \cdot L(t) = -\dot{L}(t) + \gamma_{10} - d_j^* p_j^a + \gamma_{12} S(t) + \gamma_{14j} u_j(t) + \gamma_{31} r \quad (8a)$$

$$\gamma_{13} A_j(t) + \gamma_{33} a_j(t) - \varphi_1 L(t) = p_j^f + \gamma_{24} S(t) + \gamma_{34j} u_j + \gamma_{33j} r \quad (8b)$$

$$\varphi_0 A_j(t) + \varphi_1 a_j(t) - \varphi_2 u_j(t) + \varphi_3 W(t) + 1/F_0 \, e^{-\xi t} = -\dot{A}_j(t) \quad (8c)$$

Conditions (8) express the dynamic behavior of farms with regard to the use of land for inter-temporal use as Hamilton function (7, Tu, 1992). We encounter an individual rationality. It is intended to optimize the Hamilton function as immediate cash (to derive short term benefits) or investment into land set-aside for salinity control (to derive long term benefits). Comparable to incentive constraints, conditions (8) depict farm behavior given "S". The interesting feature of the equations in (8) is the dependency between land set-aside and salinity. Given different stages of salinity – guaranteed by an authority - the farmer has different incentives to invest in land set-aside; vice versa.

Simplifying (8) by eliminating the instrument variable – cutting - of trees which is "a", we also get a dynamic constraint for the manager as additional differential equations:

$$\dot{L}_j(t) = v_{10}^* + v_{11}^* L_j(t) + v_{12}^* A_j(t) + v_{13}^* S(t) + v_{14}^* W(t) + v_{15j}^* u_j(t) + v_{16}^* r + v_{17}^* e^{\rho t} \quad (9a)$$

where L(t) is the shadow price and "A" is the area under land set-aside (opposite to cropping)

$$\dot{A}_j(t) = v_{20}^* + v_{21}^* l_j(t) + v_{22}^* A_j(t) + v_{23}^* S(t) + v_{24}^* W(t) + v_{25}^* u_j(t) + v_{26}^* r + v_{27}^* e^{\rho t} \quad (9b)$$

These equations apply to all farmers, which means summing up, whereas A=Σa_j.

$$\dot{A}(t) = v_{20}^* + v_{21}^* L(t) + v_{22}^* A(t) + v_{23}^* S(t) + v_{24}^* W(t) + \sum_j v_{25j}^* u_j(t) + \sum_j v_{26j}^* e^{\rho t} \quad (10a)$$

Simultaneously, a vertical summing up of shadow prices gives a second conditions: L=ΣL_j

$$\dot{L}(t) = v_{10}^* + v_{11}^* L(t) + v_{12}^* A(t) + v_{13}^* S(t) + v_{14}^* W(t) + \sum_j v_{15j}^* u_j(t) + \sum_j v_{16j}^* e^{\rho t} \quad (10b)$$

Equations (10) are derived and aggregated positions for public good managers who want to infer the tendency to cut wood and convert land set-aside back into arable land.

D.2. System Behavior

By solving the system of dynamics (10) as the private behavior of farmers, i.e. eliminating the result for the shadow price and tree cutting, we receive a movement of area under tree cover

$$\dot{A}(t) = v_{20} + v_{22}A(t) + v_{23}S(t) + v_{24}W(t) + \sum_j v_{25j}u_j(t) + \sum_j v_{26j}e^{\rho t} \quad (11a)$$

Next, for the condition of soil quality we use again our treatable linear differential equation which we simplify condensing coefficients into a representation of the system

$$\dot{S}(t) = v_{10} + v_{11}S(t) + v_{12}W(t) + v_{13}A(t)_2 + v_{14}l^l(t) + v_{15}e^{\rho t} \quad (11b)$$

These two differential equations have to be supplemented with the water table development. We have to reconsider that the individual water use is dependent on farm behavior and that cutting is a behavioral function depending on prices and structural variables. We start with

$$\dot{W}(t) = \zeta_0^* + \zeta_1^* W(t) + \zeta_2^* A(t) + \zeta_3^* \sum_i l_j + \zeta_{14}e^{\rho t} + l_m^l(t) - l_m^p(t) \quad (11c')$$

and as a sequence of further determining we use our water demand function from previous (5b):

$$l_j = \gamma_{44}r_j + \gamma_{31}A_j + \gamma_{32}S + \gamma_{33j}a_j + \gamma_{34j}u_j \quad (5b)$$

As an argument we further recognize that water demand is a function of trees and other variables. See:

$$a_j = \frac{1}{\gamma_{33}}[p_j^f + \gamma_{24}S(t) + \gamma_{34j}u_j(t) + \gamma_{43j}r_j(t) + \varphi_1 L_j(t) + \gamma_{13}A_j(t)] \quad (11c'')$$

and we receive

$$l_j = \gamma_{44}r_j + \gamma_{31}A_j + \gamma_{32}S + \gamma_{33j}\frac{1}{\gamma_{33}}[p_j^f + \gamma_{24}S(t) + \gamma_{34j}u_j(t) + \gamma_{43j}r_j(t) + \varphi_1 L_j(t) + \gamma_{13}A_j(t)] + \gamma_{34j}u_j$$

$$(5b')$$

which is a function of state variables A and S, controlling variable u, plus exogenous variables.

Note water applied in fields as provided by farmers also delivers an estimation of water used in plant production. This can be important for a calculation of water available for leaching.

$$l_m^1 = \sum_j l_j = \sum_j [\gamma_{44}r_j + \gamma_{31}A_j + \gamma_{32}S + \gamma_{33j}\frac{1}{\gamma_{33}}[p_j^f + \gamma_{24}S(t) + \gamma_{34j}u_j(t) + \gamma_{43j}r_j(t) + \varphi_1 L_j(t) + \gamma_{13}A_j(t)] + \gamma_{34j}u_j]$$

$$(5e)$$

Then the internal optimization of water use in a farm behavior model can be specified as

$$\dot{W}(t) = v_{30} + v_{31}W(t) + v_{32}A(t) + v_{33}S(t) + \sum_j v_{34j}u_j + v_3 r(t) + \zeta_{35}e^{\rho t} + l_m^1(t) - l_m^p(t)$$

$$(11c'')$$

Note the water table movement is no longer a pure physically driven process, rather the inclusion of explanatory equations of water demand functions determines endogenous variables. The procedure results in a deliberately modifiable behavior of water tables.

At this stage we have to contemplate on the model design and especially, with respect to the management capabilities in a watershed, on control variables. If we want to improve soil quality by combating salinity by tree planting, a certain set of control variables becomes necessary. One aim of the previous sessions was to get effective management tools and to reduce the number of management instruments on the side of the community. Apparently, by describing the system through 3 differential equations we have depicted three processes that interdependently determine a humanly modified soil quality, water table, and phyto-mass in the system. The result of that process is a dynamic of salinity which is manageable. So far, we have intuitively included options for mandatory tree planting, pumping water in and out of the system, and leaching as instrument or control variables. This provided us already with a necessary set of tools and dynamics in equation (12).

$$\dot{S}(t) = v_{10} + v_{13}A(t) + v_{11}S(t) + v_{12}W(t) \qquad + v_{14}l_m^1(t) \qquad + v_{15}e^{\rho t}$$

$$\dot{A}(t) = v_{20} + v_{21}A(t) + v_{22}S(t) + \qquad \sum_j v_{14j}u_j \qquad + v_{25}e^{\rho t} \qquad (12)$$

$$\dot{W}(t) = v_{30} + v_{32}A(t) + v_{33}S(t) + v_{31}W(t) + \sum_j v_{34j}u_j + l_m^1(t) - l_m^p(t) + \zeta_{35}e^{\rho t} + v_3 r(t)$$

The system (12) offers a foundation for the management decisions of a public unit that has sufficient influence to control salinity. However, before we enter into the debate on the establishment of a public objective function which will redirect the decision making, some remarks on the economic background are to be made. First, the system considers water pricing as happening on a competitive market. There is no water constraint in the system. Second, the system is land use oriented and we pursue the idea of profit maximizing farmers. Third, the model is considering the farming system model on the aggregated level. Next, in its initial version, the model focuses on mandatory tree planting to regulate salt inflows caused by farmers. Institutional amendments to other rights, and eventual payments for special improvement services, could be analyzed.

D.3. Social Welfare Function and Optimization

In the case of a benevolent manager who maximizes social welfare, social welfare is the sum of individual welfare (Bentham's utilitarian perspective). A benevolent manager should look for long term profitability (sustainability), i.e. optimal utility of clients who depend on water quality. He should seek to maximize benefits for his/her clients, regardless of distribution consequences; not only maximize short term benefits, but balance them with long term impacts of sustaining soil quality (apparently, a norm to be justified). From the perspective of the management of soil quality, the task is to create a temporal welfare function which includes all members of a community (and time preferences). We represent the problem of a socially oriented manager:

$$W_{[0,T]} = \sum_j P_{j,[0,T]} \tag{13}$$

Drawing on the above representation of individual profit functions, we can again establish the problem as a temporal optimization problem, but now of the manager. It is easiest if we start with identical farmers and later extend the problem to a bargaining model. Presuming "n" farmers and optimizing over a time horizon from 0 to T, we get the objective function (13').

Using similar arguments, as given above for gross margins and cost functions (5a), and given an agreed time horizon ("T") in terms of integrating long term welfare arguments, uniform time preference ("$e^{-\rho t}$"), and recognizing the temporal development of soil quality from equation (1), we would write the optimal control problem for a benevolent dictator as:

$$W = e^{-\rho t} \int_0^T \{\sum_j \{\gamma_{20} + \gamma_{10}S(t) + \gamma_{20}W(t) + \gamma_{30j}u_j(t) + 0.5\gamma_{11}S^2(t) + 0.5\gamma_{22}W^2(t) + \gamma_{12}S(t)W(t) + \gamma_{31j}S(t)u_j(t)$$
$$+ \gamma_{32j}W(t)u_j(t) + \gamma_{41j}u_j(t)x(t) + \gamma_{42}W(t)x(t) + \gamma_{43}S(t)x(t)\}\}dt$$

c.t. $\dot{S}(t) = \kappa_0 + \kappa_1 S(t) + \kappa_2 W(t) + \sum_j \kappa_{3j}u_j^0 - \kappa_4 l^l(t)$

and $\dot{W}(t) = v_0 + v_1 W(t) + v_2 S(t) + \sum_j v_{3j}u_j(t) + v_5 e^{-\zeta t} + l_m^l(t) - l_m^p(t)$

$$\tag{13}$$

and $a_j = \dfrac{1}{\gamma_{33}}[p_j^f + \gamma_{24}S(t) + \gamma_{34j}u_j(t) + \gamma_{43j}r_j(t) + \varphi_1 L_j(t) + \gamma_{13}A_j(t)]$ $\tag{11c'''}$

where L(t) is practically given by an internal determination of the shadow price as discussed previously before including a further determination by S(t):

$$L(t) = v_{40}^* + v_{41}^* A(t) + v_{42}^* S(t) + v_{43}^* W(t) + \sum_j v_{44j}^* u_j(t) + \sum_j v_{45j}^* e^{\rho t} + v_{46}^* r(t) \tag{13''}$$

This specification of the temporal management problem of a benevolent dictator includes area of land in non-agricultural use "A" (land "A" is under land set-aside and "A^0-A" as cropped land) as state variable. Furthermore, state variables are salinity "S" *and* the water table "W". Newly assigned land to be set-aside "$\Sigma v_j u_j$", is the prime control variable. Note also "u_j" is in the above profit delineation. This means we included costs for planting. From an institutional point of view, some rights on land set-aside are still with farmers; so they can cut trees and bring land set-aside into cultivation after some years. This is crucial for individual, agricultural practices. But note, trees are only cut after a certain amount of salt has been extracted.

Moreover, the problem is incomplete in so far as the costs of the control variables are not recognized, because they impose extra costs of the management and the utilization of control variables,. In concrete terms, opportunity costs of the water that is used for leaching have to be deducted on the basis of an equilibrium price for fresh water in the region. We take a given water price of p^w for fresh water that is used from a source outside the system. In addition, we have to include the pumping costs and the potential external costs from salty water p^w to outsiders. Then, the management problem is technically solved by control theory (Tu, 1991) as function (14):

$$H(A,S,W,u_j,I_m,I_p,t) = e^{-rt}\{\sum_j P_j^*[\gamma_{4j}r_j + \gamma_{3j}A_j + \gamma_{32}S + \gamma_{33}[\gamma_{00}^*A(t)+\gamma_{02}^*S(t)+\gamma_{03}^*W(t)+\sum_j\gamma_{04j}^*u_j(t)+\gamma_{05}^*r(t)]$$

$$+\gamma_{34j}][1-A(t)]-[[\gamma_{10}^*-P_j^*][\gamma_{00}^*A(t)+\gamma_{02}^*S(t)+\gamma_{03}^*W(t)+\sum_j\gamma_{04j}^*u_j(t)+\gamma_{05}^*r(t)]-0.5\gamma_{11}^*A^2(t)$$

$$-0.5\gamma_{11}^*S^2(t)-0.5\sum_j\gamma_{44j}^*u_j^2(t)-\gamma_{12}^*A(t)S(t)-\sum_j\gamma_{14j}^*A(t)u_j(t)-\sum_j\gamma_{24j}^*S(t)u_j(t)-P_j^*I_m^p-P_j^*I_m^p\}dt$$

$$\Lambda_1(t)[v_{10}+v_{11}A(t)+v_{11}S(t)+v_{11}W(t)+v_{14}^jI_m^j(t)+v_{15}e^{rt}]+$$

$$\Lambda_2(t)[v_{20}+v_{21}A(t)+v_{22}S(t)+v_{23}W(t)+\sum_jv_{24j}u_j+v_{25}e^{rt}]$$

$$\Lambda_3(t)[v_{30}+v_{32}A(t)+v_{32}S(t)+v_{31}W(t)+\sum_jv_{34j}u_j+I_m^p(t)-I_m^p(t)+\zeta_{35}e^{rt}+v_3r(t)] \tag{14}$$

Using standard mathematical approaches to solve dynamic optimization problems (Tu, 1992), a control theory problem has to fulfill three conditions for a maximum: (14a to 14i)

$$H(t)_{A(t)} = -\dot{\Lambda}_1(t), H(t)_{S(t)} = -\dot{\Lambda}_2(t), H(t)_{W(t)} = -\dot{\Lambda}_3(t), H(t)_{u_j(t)} = 0, H(t)_{I_m(t)} = 0, H(t)_{I_p(t)} = 0,$$

$$H(t)_{\Lambda_1(t)} = -\dot{A}(t), H(t)_{\Lambda_2(t)} = -\dot{S}(t), H(t)_{\Lambda_3(t)} = -\dot{W}(t) \tag{14a to 14i}$$

Conditions (14) are applied to the stated function (14); again, we resume a non-varying cost function (A quadratic function provides linear derivatives, with similar coefficients see Nuppenau and Slangen, 1998), and the cost function of (9) rechecks cross effects (note: the size of land set-aside in the community improves the micro-climate).Then the Hamilton is:

$$H(A,S,W,u_j,l_m,l_p,t)=e^{-rt}\{P^*[\gamma_{44}^*r_j+\gamma_{31}^*A(t)+\gamma_{32}^*S(t)+\gamma_{33}^*[\gamma_{00}^*A(t)+\gamma_{02}^*S(t)+\gamma_{03}^*W(t)+\gamma_{04}^*u(t)+\gamma_{05}^*r]$$

$$+\gamma_{34}^*u(t)][1-A(t)]-[[\gamma_{10}^*-P_j^f][\gamma_{00}^*A(t)+\gamma_{02}^*S(t)+\gamma_{03}^*W(t)+\gamma_{04}^*u(t)+\gamma_{05}^*r]-0.5\gamma_{11}^*A^2(t)$$

$$-0.5\gamma_{11}^*S^2(t)-0.5\gamma_{44}^*u^2(t)+\gamma_{12}^*A(t)S(t)+\gamma_{14}^*A(t)u(t)+\gamma_{23}^*S(t)u(t)-P_j^{f}l_m^l-P^{f}l_m^p\}dt+$$

$$\Lambda_1(t)[v_{10}+v_{13}A(t)+v_{11}S(t)+v_{11}W(t)+v_{14}l_m^l(t)+v_{15}e^{rt}]+$$

$$\Lambda_2(t)[v_{20}+v_{21}A(t)+v_{22}S(t)+v_{23}W(t)+v_{14}u+v_{25}e^{rt}]$$

$$\Lambda_3(t)[v_{30}+v_{32}A(t)+v_{33}S(t)+v_{31}W(t)+v_{34}u+l_m^l(t)-l_m^p(t)+\zeta_{35}e^{rt}+v_3r(t)] \qquad (15)$$

Formulation (15) includes all behavioral components of the farm sector expressed in incentives to cut and collect organic matter from land set-aside, convert land into cropping area, etc. The manager controls afforestation, he uses land planning in terms of system effects. Applying the optimality criteria to the Hamilton equation (14a to 14i), the three equations comprising two differential equations appear, $A(t)$, $S(t)$, $L(t)$, $u(t)$, and $\Lambda_i(t)$ are endogenous.

$$P_a^*\gamma_{31}^*-[\gamma_{10}^*-P^f]\gamma_{00}^*+[P_a^*\gamma_{33}^*\gamma_{00}^*+\gamma_{00}^*]A(t)+\gamma_{12}^*S(t)+v_{14}^*u(t)+v_{13}^*\Lambda_1(t)+v_{21}^*\Lambda_2(t)+v_{32}^*\Lambda_3(t)=\dot{\Lambda}_1(t)-\rho\Lambda_1(t)$$

$$\qquad (16a)$$

$$P_j^f\gamma_{32}^*+[\gamma_{10}^*-P^f]\gamma_{02}^*-[\gamma_{33}^*\gamma_{02}^*P_j^f+\gamma_{12}^*]A(t)-\gamma_{11}^*S(t)-\gamma_{14}^*u(t)+v_{11}^*\Lambda_1(t)+v_{22}^*\Lambda_2(t)+v_{10}^*\Lambda_3(t)=\dot{\Lambda}_2(t)-\rho\Lambda_2(t)$$

$$\qquad (16b)$$

$$[\gamma_{10}^*-P^f]\gamma_{03}^*-\gamma_{33}^*\gamma_{03}^*P_j^f A(t)+v_{12}^*\Lambda_1(t)+v_{23}^*\Lambda_1(t)+v_{31}^*\Lambda_3(t)=\dot{\Lambda}_3(t)-\rho\Lambda_3(t) \qquad (16c)$$

$$[\gamma_{40j}^*-p_j^f]+\gamma_{00}\gamma_{04}A(t)+\gamma_{44}u(t)+\gamma_{14}^*A(t)m\gamma_{23}S(t)+v_{24n}^*\Lambda_2(t)+v_{34}^*\Lambda_3(t)=0 \qquad (16d)$$

$$p^w+v_{14n}^*\Lambda_1(t)+\Lambda_3(t)=0 \qquad (16e)$$

$$p^e+\Lambda_3(t)=0 \qquad (16f)$$

$$v_{10}+v_{13}A(t)+v_{11}S(t)+v_{12}W(t)+v_{14}l_m^l(t)+v_{15}e^{\rho t}=\dot{S}(t) \qquad (16g)$$

$$v_{20}+v_{21}A(t)+v_{22}S(t)+v_{23}W(t)+v_{14}u+v_{25}e^{\rho t}=\dot{A}(t) \qquad (16h)$$

$$v_{30}+v_{32}A(t)+v_{33}S(t)+v_{31}W(t)+v_{34}u+l_m^l(t)-l_m^p(t)+\zeta_{35}e^{\rho t}+v_3r=\dot{W}(t) \qquad (16i)$$

The system (16) can be solved for time dependent paths on stage variables: Firstly on "soil quality" as an index for salinity: "$S(t)$"; secondly, on "land set-aside", hence, agricultural area: "$A(t)$"; and thirdly, on the "water table" "$W(t)$" (Tu, 1991). For pathways to reach envisaged states, control variable $u(t)$ provides necessary annual changes on the tree cover, afforestation. Furthermore, we established leaching $l_p(t)$ and pumping $l_p(t)$ of water as control variables. Note, simultaneously the model provides a solution for the cutting of trees on farm land. Results are watershed related. They are dependent on the composition of the farm sector; i.e. the system (16a to i). This aspect becomes even more pronounced when the prime objective of the exercise of a public management, the control of salinity, becomes reconsidered. In the framework, "lowest salinity" could be stated as <u>the</u> final goal or a future state. Deliberations that involve discounting and resource depletion must take place; certainly some salinity in future is "optimal", dependent on different rates of discounting. Minimal salinity or a hundred percent improvement, depending on current salinity, is never optimal involving discounting. In such a case no simple transversality condition occurs! But what is it? Other questions emerge: How can a benevolent planner be institutionalized? Why should he pursue public interest or adopt a minimal discount rate? Why should farmers follow him? etc. Even more pronounced and interesting is the question how we can explain what happens further if no planner is equipped with the coercion to enforce mandatory tree planting? Do we really have a rationale for common-pool property management on the basis of a benevolent dictator?

E. POLITICAL ECONOMY BARGAINING MODEL AND GAME SOLUTION

In the previous chapters we have assumed that a benevolent or impartial manager intertemporally optimizes the set-aside regime for trees as biodrainage. In runs for comparison, we could also model the tragedy of the common looking at the long run impacts of water quality to demonstrate the severity and contingency of the problem. In reality, the community has the choice between the tragedy of the common or a manager that is a partial manager, but how can we equip a manager with political power for statutory regulations? Note, a benevolent manager is fictional, and a partial manger is subject to political influence. A situation with a partial manager coincides with a political bargain. Our model of bargaining centers around Harsanyi's (1963) multiple agent model.

$$L = [\prod_j (I_j - I_j^0)](I_m - I_m^0) \tag{17}$$

This mathematical presentation of a bargaining solution refers to a situation with lobbying and interest functions. Technically, it maximizes the product of the differences between the cooperative value of each participant in a game and their possible disagreement value (Rausser and Zusman, 1992). The manager "m" is subject to a lobbying "s" that increases his welfare, while farmers use resources to lobby "c"; in traditional societies one speaks of gifts. Taking the logarithm of the above specification, and recognizing the sum of lobbying activities $s_j = s(c_j, \alpha_j)$ as a function, the bargaining can be more explicitly expressed as a joint function:

$$\ln W = \ln[W_m + \sum_j s_j(c_j, \alpha) - I_m] + \sum_j \ln[W_j - c_j - I_j] \tag{18}$$

where: W_m: is the welfare of the community as anticipated by the manager and
W_j: are individual welfare functions of farmers.

s_j : "political gifts" by j to the manager
c_j : "costs of lobbying" of j

Moreover, an interior solution can be derived that is similar to the one prescribed by Rausser and Zusman (1992), resulting in a weighted objective function. In that function, individual weights correspond to the power of a pressure group (farmer). It has to be noticed that bargaining solutions differ from a policy preference function approach. Instead, the authors show that weights reflect the analytic properties of both aspects: the "production function" aspect and the "resources devotion" aspect in political bargaining. "Production function" means that political power is built up according to efficiency and technologies in bargaining, and "resource devotion" means that clients have to use resources, "money, bribes, gifts, etc."

However, the summing up of farmers and integrating over time gives an objective function that includes "social" welfare only as one part of the objective function of a manager. He/she also follows his/her own objectives. A "social" manager is partial and deviates from social welfare by giving weights to different farmers, or, on a more aggregated level, to interest groups. Interest groups may represent farmers with homogeneous interests. In order to capture the argument of bargaining in the interest function, one has to decide on elements of bargaining, specific bribing, procedures and eventually on rules, institutions and external forces for regulation, i.e. the institutional economics framework. A detailed analysis on local constellations in watersheds may reveal complex behavioral patterns of bargaining. For simplification and in order to keep the model treatable, our analysis is confined 7o a pattern of bargaining that entitles the manager of a watershed the right to regulate land brought into land set-aside, i.e. u_j. The manager is charged with power to allocate land to be set-aside for controlling salinity. As a departing institution from free leasehold, farmers are no longer free in allocating land. The manager bargains with farmers on land set-aside. Consequently, bargaining elements affect the elements of the manager's objective function. He charges farmers with obligations to plant trees on newly set aside land. In doing so, we get the following new objective function. Note weights that reflect bargaining are with u_j elements in the objective function (19)

$$H(A,S,W,u_j,t)=e^{-rt}\{\sum_j P_j^*[\gamma_{4j}r_j+\gamma_{3j}A_j+\gamma_{52}S+\gamma_{53}[\gamma_{00}^*A(t)+\gamma_{02}^*S(t)+\gamma_{03}^*W(t)+\sum_j(1+\omega_j)\gamma_{04}^*u_j(t)+\gamma_{05}^*r(t)]$$

$$+\gamma_{34}u_j][1-A(t)]-[[\gamma_{10}^*-P_j^*][\gamma_{00}^*A(t)+\gamma_{02}^*S(t)+\gamma_{03}^*W(t)+\sum_j(1+\omega_j)\gamma_{04}^*u_j(t)+\gamma_{05}^*r(t)]-0.5\gamma_{1F}^*A^2(t)$$

$$-0.5\gamma_{1S}^*S^2(t)-0.5\sum_j(1+\omega_j)\gamma_{4u}^*u_j^2(t)\ \gamma_{12}^*A(t)S(t)-\sum_j(1+\omega_j)\gamma_{14}^*A(t)u_j(t)-\sum_j(1+\omega_j)\gamma_{23}^*S(t)u_j(t)$$

$$-P_j^ml_m^r-P_j^pl_m^p-\tau_j\frac{1}{n}[\sum_j u_j^2(t)-[\sum_j u_j(t)]^2]dt+$$

$$\Lambda_1(t)[\nu_{10}+\nu_{13}A(t)+\nu_{11}S(t)+\nu_{12}W(t)+\nu_{14}l_m^r(t)+\nu_{15}e^{rt}]+$$

$$\Lambda_2(t)[\nu_{20}+\nu_{21}A(t)+\nu_{22}S(t)+\nu_{23}W(t)+\sum_j\nu_{24}u_j+\nu_{25}e^{rt}]$$

$$\Lambda_3(t)[\nu_{30}+\nu_{32}A(t)+\nu_{33}S(t)+\nu_{31}W(t)+\sum_j\nu_{34}u_j+l_m^r(t)-l_m^p(t)+\zeta_{33}e^{rt}+\nu_3r(t)]$$

$$(19)$$

Here weights $[1+\omega_j]$ reflect the recognition of farmer "j" in the objective function of a partial manager (his weight is 1 a reference numeraire); The size, "plus"-weights $(\omega_1,..., \omega_m)$, give the corresponding strength in achievements of farmers in bargaining. The two final parts reflect transaction costs associated with a variability of regulations (Transaction costs increase with size and complexity (variance). Weights (20) are calculated as first derivatives of the strength (attributed to a threat strategy) minus a reference interest in political bargaining: Formally:

$$\omega_1 ...; \omega_j = \frac{(I_C^{opt} - I_C^0)]}{(I_j^{opt} - I_j^0)]} = \frac{\partial s(c_j, \delta_j)}{\partial c_j} ;...; \omega_n \tag{20}$$

Weights in equation (20) can be interpreted as a notification of political power which can also be inferred using the model for experiments. Vice versa, given weights in underlying profit functions, i.e. of the manager, he controls the allocation of land. In order to proceed, we re-specify the dynamic Hamilton problem of equation (8) making use of multiple control variables $u_j(t)$.

The application of the model has to involve a participatory planning process. Technically, the model provides solutions simulating impacts of different patterns of power structure of farmers. An interaction of modeling system impacts and income effects of power patterns as well as a negotiation on commitments and community management can be perceived; in it an iterative process of adjusting power coefficients and regulations gives a solution. In (21)

$$
\begin{aligned}
H(A,S,W,u_j,t) = e^{-rt} &\{\sum_j P_j^c [\gamma_{44} r_j + \gamma_{31} A_j + \gamma_{32} S + \gamma_{35}[\gamma_{00}^* A(t) + \gamma_{02}^* S(t) + \gamma_{03}^* W(t) + \sum_j (1+\omega_j) \gamma_{04j}^* u_j(t) + \gamma_{05}^* r(t)] \\
&+ \gamma_{36} u_j][1-A(t)] - [[\gamma_{10}^* - P_j^c][\gamma_{00}^* A(t) + \gamma_{02}^* S(t) + \gamma_{03}^* W(t) + \sum_j (1+\omega_j) \gamma_{04j}^* u_j(t) + \gamma_{05}^* r(t)] - 0.5\gamma_{11}^* A^2(t) \\
&- 0.5\gamma_{13}^* S^2(t) - 0.5\sum_j (1+\omega_j) \gamma_{44}^* u_j^2(t) - \gamma_{12}^* A(t)S(t) - \sum_j (1+\omega_j) \gamma_{14j}^* A(t)u_j(t) - \sum_j (1+\omega_j) \gamma_{23}^* S(t)u_j(t) \\
&- P_j^s I_m^l - P_j^e I_m^p - \tau_j \frac{1}{n}[\sum_j u_j^2(t) - [\sum_j u_j(t)]^2]\}dt + \\
&\Lambda_1(t)[v_{10} + v_{13} A(t) + v_{11} S(t) + v_{12} W(t) + v_{14} I_m^l(t) + v_{15} e^{rt}] + \\
&\Lambda_2(t)[v_{20} + v_{21} A(t) + v_{22} S(t) + v_{23} W(t) + \sum_j v_{14j} u_j + v_{35} e^{rt}] \\
&\Lambda_3(t)[v_{36} + v_{32} A(t) + v_{33} S(t) + v_{31} W(t) + \sum_j v_{34j} u_j + I_m^l(t) - I_m^p(t) + \zeta_{35} e^{rt} + v_1 r(t)]
\end{aligned}
\tag{21}
$$

Formally it means to calculate derivatives of "$u_j(t)$", $I_m^l(t)$, $I_m^p(t)$ and "$A_j(t)$", "$W_j(t)$" as well as "$S(t)$", the core variable of the dynamic system. It provides a bargaining solution, if the coefficients including the bargaining power ones are "known". Mathematically, because linear supply and factor demand functions correspond to quadratic functions, we get a treatable analytical expression of bargaining problems, solvable for u_j's that are embedded in dynamics of land set-aside $A(t)$, water table $W(t)$, and salinity $S(t)$. The optimal function for (21) which is equation system (22) provides an extension of equations (16a to g). It recognizes individual contributions instead of normalized provision of land set-aside in watersheds.

$$
\begin{bmatrix}
-(1+w_1^{*})\gamma_{441}^{*}+u_1 & \cdots & u_1 & 0 & [1+w_1^{*}]\gamma_{141}^{*} & 0 & 0 & v_{241}^{*} & v_{141}^{*} \\
\cdots & \cdots & \cdots & \cdots & \cdots & \cdots & \cdots \\
u_1 & \cdots & -(1+w_n^{*})\gamma_{44n}^{*}+u_1 & 0 & [1+w_n^{*}]\gamma_{14n}^{*} & 0 & 0 & v_{24n}^{*} & v_{14n}^{*} \\
0 & \cdots & 0 & 0 & 0 & 0 & \kappa_0+\rho & 0 & 0 \\
v_{241}^{*} & \cdots & v_{24n}^{*} & 0 & 0 & 0 & \kappa_1-\kappa_2 & v_{22}^{*} & v_{21}^{*} \\
v_{141}^{*} & \cdots & v_{14n}^{*} & 0 & 0 & 0 & v_{23}^{*} & v_{23}^{*} & v_{11}^{*} \\
0 & \cdots & 0 & \kappa_0 & \kappa_1-\kappa_2 & 0 & 0 & 0 & 0 \\
v_{241}^{*} & \cdots & v_{24n}^{*} & v_{23}^{*} & v_{22}^{*} & v_{21}^{*} & 0 & 0 & 0 \\
v_{141}^{*}0 & & v_{14n}^{*} & v_{13n}^{*} & v_{12n}^{*} & v_{11}^{*} & 0 & 0 & 0
\end{bmatrix}
\begin{bmatrix}
u_1^{b}(t) \\
\cdots \\
u_n^{b}(t) \\
S(t) \\
A(t) \\
W(t) \\
\Lambda_1(t) \\
\Lambda_2(t) \\
\Lambda_3(t) \\
l_m^{l} \\
l_m^{p}
\end{bmatrix}
$$

$$
=
\begin{bmatrix}
[\gamma_{10} - p^{f}](1+\omega_1)\gamma_{401} - \upsilon_0 \\
\cdots \\
[\gamma_{10} - p^{f}](1+\omega_n)\gamma_{40\,n} - \upsilon_0 \\
-\dot{\Lambda}_1(t) + [\gamma_{10} - p^{f}]\gamma_{02} \\
-\dot{\Lambda}_2(t) + p^{*}D + [\gamma_{10} - p^{f}]\gamma_{01}^{*} \\
-\dot{\Lambda}_3(t) + [\gamma_{10} - p^{f}]\gamma_{03}^{*} \\
\dot{S}(t) \\
\dot{A}(t) + \gamma e^{rt} \\
\dot{L}_w(t) + \gamma e^{rt} \\
p \\
p^{e}
\end{bmatrix}
\qquad (22)
$$

Technically, conditions for (22) are similar to (16), but with new coefficients and the explicit recognition of individual regulations in the interests on set-aside $u_j(t)$. I.e. embedded in the dynamics of the salt index "S", actions occur community-wise and individually executed. Also, "A" provides shadow prices for "L". The manager can optimize the function (21) with targeted controls "u_j" which gives us a matrix representation of the derivatives. The system (22) is dynamic and mathematically it can be solved by firstly eliminating all instrument variables u_j^{b}, $l_m^{l}(t)$, $l_m^{p}(t)$, and secondly solving the dynamic differential equations.

Graphically, solutions can be expressed, for instance, as opposing poor, powerless farmers and powerful farmers. Figure 2.1 demonstrates short term commitments of interest groups. The institutional set is given as the following one: a common property of soil quality, a compulsory newly set-aside of land, a controlled water table, and a reduction of salt contents by leaching and costs for leaching taken by the community, handed over to a manager. The land vector $u^{b'}=[u_1^{b},\ldots,u_n^{b}]$ is the control instrument that is negotiated and conducted with farmers. In such solutions, we explicitly represent economic and political components of soil quality as a bargaining. The solution in equation (22) sketches an economically, ecologically and politically feasible dynamic equilibrium.

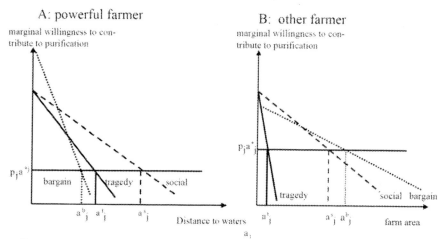

$A(T) = A^{fix}$, we can derive the constants of integration in four differential equation (Tu, 1992).

Figure 2.1. Bargaining solution and modified willingness to contribute after bargaining.

For numerical solutions, the system again needs transitory conditions. In case of an agreement on a well specified salt content that is given at the final time of "planning" $S(T) = S^{fix}$ and that has to correspond to a steady state of forest land.

CONCLUSION

The analysis, presented, puts its main emphasis on a theoretical model that describes a political economy oriented model of common property management. The ecological context of soil quality and farmers' waivers on land for trees is firstly depicted by a multiple stage model of salinity and land set-aside. The corresponding parameters of the model can be gained from ordinary salt dynamics, water tables, and detection of links between forest stands and salinity. Quantified examples of the ecosystem behavior of watersheds will be the support basis for empirical analysis. Empirical analysis should include social science experiments to find power coefficients for interest groups. Natural science can quantify self improvement of soil quality indices with reduced salt inflows, water tables, and tree cover on percentages of farm land. Any analysis of dynamics has to be supplemented with the corresponding inflow measurement from agriculture, depending on the intensity of farming, strips of trees, etc.

The last aspect will also be reflected in the economic modeling of interest functions. Surveys on particular "homogenous" interest groups can be the basis for the estimation of loss functions due to land waivers and practice restrictions. Much attention has to be devoted to clarifying the interest in land use and trees as part of intensity in farming. It can be assumed that large land holdings imply low costs while intensive farming of small-scale farms is the major problem.

However, vice versa, the problem of strong non-point pollution of watersheds will be most prominent in intensively farmed areas of many small-holders. Therefore, the specification of loss functions is most crucial since farmers mostly object if their income is considerably reduced, and no alternatives to land markets exist. However, such cases can be handled with comparative ease within the given theory. Furthermore, the economics of water management and water pricing could be an amendment of the model, perhaps by internal pricing.

REFERENCES

Barbier, E. B., Burgess, J.C., and Folke, C. (1995). *Paradise Lost: The Ecological Economics of Bio-diversity.* London, EN: Earthscan.

Barrett-Lennard, E.G. (2002). Restoration of saline land through revegetation. *Agricultural Water Management, Vol.53* (issues 1-3), 213-226.

Barry, P.J., Rpboson, L.J., and Nartea, G.V. (1996). Changing Time Attitudes in Temporal Anaylsis. *American Journal of Agriclutural Economics, Vol. 78*, 972-981.

Bromley, D.W. (Ed.). (1992).*Making the Commons work: Theory, Practice and Policy.* San Francisco: ICS Press.

Chambers, R. (1988). *Production Economics.* New York: Cambridge University Press.

Conrad, J.M. (1999). *Resource Economics.* New York: Cambridge University Press.

Hanna, S.S., Golke, C., and Mäler, K.G. (Eds.) (1996). *Rights to Nature: Ecological, Economic Cultural and Political Principles of Institutions for the Environment.* Washington, CA: Island Press.

Harsanyi, J. C. (1963). A simplified bargaining model for the n-person cooperative game. *International Economic Review, Vol. 4, No. 2*, 194-220.

Knapp, K. C, and Olsen, L.J. (1996). Dynamic Resource Management: Intertemporal Subsitution and Risk aversion. *AJAE, Vol. 78*, 1004-1014.

Goetz, R., and Zilberman, D. (1995). Mining the Soil-Agricultural Production Systems on Peatland. *Environment and Resource Economics, Vol.30*, 119-38.

Goetz, R. (1997). Land Development and Pigouvian Taxes: The case of Peatland. *American Journal of Agricultural Economics. Vol.79*, 227-234.

Gretton, P., and Salma, U. (1997). Land degradation: links to agricultural output and profitability. *Australian Journal of Agricultural and Resource Economics, Vol. 41, No.2*, 209-225.

Nuppenau, E.A., and Slangen, L.H.G. (1998). Principal Agent Framework: How to Achieve Environmental Improvements in Agriculture through Improved Payment Schemes. Reports on Current Research in Agricultural Economics and Agribusiness Management: Forum No.24, Kiel.

Qadir, M., Schubert, S., Ghafoor, A., and Murtaza, G (2001). Amelioration strategies for sodic soils: A review. *Land Degradation Development, Vol.12* (issue 4), 357-386.

Rausser, G. C., and Zusman, P. (1992). Public Policy and Constitutional Prescription. *American Journal of Agricultural Economics. Vol. 74, No. 2*, 247-257.

Singh, J., and Singh, J.P.(1995). Land degradation and economic sustainability. *Ecological Economics Vol. 15*, 77-86.

Tanji, K.K., and Karajeh, F.F. (1993). Saline Drain Water Reuse, in Agroforestry Systems. *Journal of Irrigation and Drainage Engineering. Vol. 119, no.1*, 170-180.

Tu., P.N.V. (1992). *Introductory Optimization Dynamics: Optimal Control with Economics and Management Science Application.* Berlin: Springer-Verlag.

Varian, H.L. (1992). *Microeconomic Analysis.* New York, NY: W.W. Norton.

Wichelns, D. (1999). An Economic model of waterlogging and salinization in arid regions. *Ecological Economics, vol. 30,* 475-491.

SECTION II: MANAGEMENT OF WATER RESOURCES

In: The Economics of Natural and Human Resources...   ISBN 978-1-60741-029-4
Editor: Ayal Kimhi and Israel Finkelshtain   © 2009 Nova Science Publishers, Inc.

Chapter 4

THE OVERDEVELOPMENT OF WATER RESOURCES

*Peter Berck and James Manley**

ABSTRACT

Inefficient water projects are regularly constructed. In the context of a model of optimal taxation we show that the inability to tax some netputs can disrupt the standard efficiency results and lead to the building of inefficient projects as a second best. If water projects were efficient, then, at least among drier countries, one would expect welfare to increase with rainfall. That turns out to be true only among the poorer countries. Middle and upper income countries, even dry ones, have little change in welfare as a function of precipitation.

A. INTRODUCTION

Agricultural development has been linked to overall economic growth, and the development of economies has been described as a process of reducing the share of GNP comprised by agricultural value added (van Rooyen and Sigwele 1998). In early stages, rain fed agriculture dominates employment and productivity and forms the tax base. Later, with sufficient investment in infrastructure and technology, irrigation improves agricultural efficiency while the productivity of other sectors increases.

As linkages and multipliers emerge and increase, factor and financial markets organize the more diverse economy, reallocating labor from relatively inefficient uses in agriculture to more productive sectors. The proportion of the labor force involved in agriculture declines, as does the proportion of urban household expenditures dedicated to food. This process of economic osmosis continues until political forces intervene and policy is created to prop up the agricultural sector, usually protectionism, subsidies, or price controls.

The development of water resources follows a similar trajectory. Early investments in agriculture have benefits greater than their costs, but as the number of available projects

* Peter Berck is Professor at the University of California, Berkeley, and James Manley is Assistant Professor at Towson University

declines and the perceived need to use water projects to achieve distributional goals increases, the possibility of the overdevelopment of water resources emerges. The purpose of this paper is to sketch a plausible theory of water project development and to seek empirical verification for it.

Developing countries' dependence on rainfall is both intuitive and empirically verifiable. For countries in which agricultural value added represents a relatively large share of GDP and in which little has been invested in infrastructure, the economy remains essentially dependent on the caprice of weather. Many developing African nations are to a large degree economically dependent on agriculture.[1] We can even quantify that Zimbabwe's real GDP growth is strongly correlated with annual rainfall (Grey 2002). In 2002, low rainfall lowered predictions for India's GDP growth rate by one half of one percent (Rediff.com 2002).

As countries develop and diversify economically, their dependence on agriculture and hence on weather decreases dramatically. The example of Great Britain in the late 19th and early 20th centuries is instructive. In 1870 the agricultural sector employed 22 percent of the labor force and comprised 15% of GDP, but by the 1900's these numbers had decreased to 12 percent and 7%, respectively (Khatri et al. 1998). With this decrease came a degree of independence from the weather. In the late 1870's, excess rain led to a supply-side shock of a *minimum* of 1.5% of GDP (measuring effect on GDP solely via agriculture), while a drought in the 1890's had a *maximum* estimated effect of about 0.14% of GDP (again considering only effects on agriculture), a shift of about an order of magnitude (ibid.). While part of this is due to the nature of the particular shocks that the country suffered, much of the decrease can be attributed to the reduced role of agriculture in the economy as a whole.

As agriculture ceases to play a central role in the economy, the abundance or lack of rainfall loses significance. However, in many cases water resources continue to be developed, sometimes to the point of being counterproductive. It is a staple of water project evaluation that projects are built whose costs are greater than their benefits, to whomever they may accrue (Caves, Bain, and Margolis). In the extreme case considered here, a large project may in fact have operating costs in excess of benefits. That is, a government may have built water projects to the point where each additional cubic meter of water pumped through the project causes a net loss to the economy. Although this extreme state of affairs sounds somewhat preposterous, this shutdown test may be relevant both in the US and in Israel (Committee on Sustainable Water Supplies for the Middle East 1999, p. 113).

A series of studies, by Kislev (1990), UC Cooperative Extension (1992), and Dinar and Letey (1991), imply that a cubic meter of water has a marginal value product in growing cotton of approximately ten cents. A study by the World Bank gives a cost of 50 cents per cubic meter as the cost of irrigating in the Negev with Mekorot water (World Bank 1990). Our own estimates for California suggest that when cotton is taken at world price and power from the Central Valley project is priced at market, growing cotton in the Westlands water district is a money-losing proposition. In late 2002 (New York Times) the US Bureau of Reclamation agreed to settle a lawsuit by buying and shutting down 34,000 acres of Central Valley farms. Thus it is at least plausible that water use decreases value added in agriculture.

---

[1] See, e.g. the following web pages, all accessed Jan. 9, 2003: http://sudaniharare.org.zw/about_sudan1.html, http://www.melissa.org/english/publications/Proceedings1998/gambia98.htm, http://www.kenyaweb.com/economy/sectoral/domestic.html.

It is also possible that there is profligate use of water in other sectors of the economy, though agriculture is often the predominant user of water.

To examine the state of water resource development empirically, we examine the relationship between precipitation and various measures of output in a set of countries over approximately forty years. We generate the precipitation elasticity on output for each country over the time period in question, and note that interpretation depends a great deal upon whether the country is in a dry climate and on whether greater water availability actually lowers the output measure. The clearest case of overdevelopment would be for additional precipitation to lower aggregate measures of output in a dry country. However, even this case is not as strong as one would like. The precipitation could be out of season, and therefore damage crops, or it could have the effect of discouraging some other industry, such as tourism.

B. EFFECTS OF PROJECTS

Water projects have two purposes, the prevention of floods and the storage of water.[2] In climates with ample rainfall throughout the year, like the American Southeast, the prime purpose of projects is flood control. Where excess rainfall would have a deleterious effect on income, projects mitigate this effect. Thus high rainfall countries where additional rainfall has little effect or actually increases income would be countries that are candidates for the category of overdeveloped work projects.

On the other side of the coin, in dry climates (or climates with dry growing seasons) like the San Joaquin Valley or Israel, water projects are largely for storage—either between seasons or years. Additional water increases agricultural output and also contributes to recreation—lawns, pools, etc.

Without storage, additional water may be valuable in a dry year or nearly worthless in a wet year. In California, with a favorable overall water balance (though highly variable), extensive development leads to low water prices (farmers in the Imperial Valley in southern California pay about $15.50 per acre foot of water (Vogel, 2002)) and low expected increases in income from additional rain. In Israel, which is more globally water short, water projects are also likely to reduce the value of water, because the marginal benefit curve is expected to be concave.

However, there should always be a substantial value for raw water. The expected outcome is that in water short countries, projects should decrease the value of precipitation. As pointed out above, it is possible to overbuild these projects to the extent that additional precipitation leads to irrigation that actually decreases value added. In this extreme case, the value of precipitation in a water short country would be negative.

Although it is clear that a government could build water projects beyond what the cost/benefit rule or even the shutdown point would require, the economic conditions for such actions are not obvious and will be examined in the next section.

---

[2] More generally, they move water across time or space to areas that have good growing conditions.

C. A THEORETICAL FRAMEWORK FOR OVERDEVELOPMENT

The Diamond Mirrlees (DM) optimal taxation model provides a framework for discussing when a government will elect a project that is not efficient.[3] The conclusion of that paper is that the government produces efficiently. Surprisingly, that result is not altered by assuming that the government wishes to show favoritism to its supporters, as described by Tullock (1980). A plausible case for a government to overbuild a water project requires both a desire to favor one group over another and a lack of other instruments to accomplish the favoritism.

The DM framework is an economy with consumers, producers, and possibly a productive government sector. The government levies taxes on consumers both to finance its projects and for distributional purposes. The prices paid by consumers for netputs are q and the prices paid by producers are p, with the difference being the commodity tax.[4] The allocation of netputs to the m consumers is x,[5] production is y, and government activity is z. Consumers supply labor and other factors of production and demand goods and services, hence x has positive elements for their supplies and negative elements for their demands. The consumers' offer curves are x(q) and X(q) is the total over consumers of the n vectors of consumer netputs as a function of the consumer prices q. Government is supposed to maximize a function W(x(q)) over q,y, and z. The constraint on the maximization is that consumption must be on or under the production possibility frontier.

Since lowering the price of a strictly consumed good makes consumers better off, the solution to this optimal tax problem is to choose commodity prices low enough so that the constraint that the aggregate offer curve is on the PPF is binding. Apart from the issue of allocation feasibility (on or under the PPF), the set of achievable consumer allocations is determined by the choice of prices q. In this setup, driving the PPF inwards by implementing inefficient projects makes fewer allocations achievable and cannot increase the value of W. This is the productive efficiency result of DM.

The DM result of productive efficiency is not sensitive to whether the government has an individual social welfare function or operates in the mode suggested by Tullock. In the latter case the government might wish to choose commodity prices to favor agents likely to make monetary contributions to the government rather than to favor agents for the purpose of promoting social equity.[6] So long as the form of the function W respects individuals, the arguments in the original article are unchanged.

Tullock discusses unproductive activity, the use of resources to influence income distribution. While this is a form of inefficiency, it is not the productive inefficiency of inefficient projects.

One of the conclusions of the DM model is that intermediate netputs are not taxed. This conclusion is not borne out in practice, and a simple example makes it plain why it is not. In economies with absolute power or corruption, lump sum taxes and subsidies are possible, and these are known to be first best instruments. Thus it is only economies where overt favoritism

---

[3] Diamond, P. A, and Mirrlees, J. (1971). Optimal Taxation and Public Production I: Production Efficiency. American Economic Review, Vol. 61 (No. 1), 8-27.

[4] p,q,t are n-vectors.

[5] x is a mxn-vector; n netputs for each of m consumers.

[6] The algebraic model of DM can include endowments, so consumers could sell labor of different types and the government could subsidize the price of the labor of those who contribute.

is consequential to the government that resorts to commodity taxes or other means to transfer income. If a government wished to favor the owners of a cement plant, it would, in theory, subsidize the provision of the plant's services by the agent who owned the plant, thus subsidizing a transaction between a consumer (in their role of shareholder) and an industry. However, this is precisely the type of transaction that draws opprobrium and apparently more opprobrium than the transfer of an equal amount of funds by the steering of contracts to the favored agent at more than the market price. The latter transaction is a tax on intermediate netputs, cement, and in the DM theory ought not be observed. Thus social mores, incomplete power, and corruption combine to defeat the predictions of the DM model.

In more theoretical terms, the DM model assumes the government can choose any point on the PPF by the selection of prices p and can set the utility of individuals by the choice of consumer prices q. Politics may limit the use of these instruments. Consider the ways a government might favor a particular consumer (or group of consumers.) Subsidizing a factor sold by the group is an obvious mechanism (and if this factor is inelastically supplied, it is also an efficient mechanism.) However, suppose that this is not a politically feasible mechanism. Then the choice might be to set a high price for the output of the firm that uses the factor that they supply. This choice leads to the need to either subsidize the good or endure the wrath of other consumers for the high price of the good. In the case of agricultural goods, subsidy is almost the rule—US support prices, Common Agricultural Policy of the EU, etc. However these policies may not be targeted enough for the garnering of political contributions. When these possibilities are blocked by political considerations, the remaining method is to undertake a project that increases the value of the factor owned by the favored group, even when that project is inefficient. Water projects might fall into this category.

D. Productive Efficiency in a Pure Household Model

Our interest is in less corrupt situations and we produce an illustration with just two agents, with labels A and C, who each produce netputs from endowments e^A and e^C. The simple example of productive inefficiency begins with a household model. The production functions for the two agents are F and G and they produce the same good from their endowment and a government provided good, z, that is in fixed supply, K. Productive efficiency requires that $F_z = G_z$. However the government maximizes

$$W(U^A(F(e, z), U^C(G(e, K-z)))$$

with the result that

$$W_A U^{A'}F_z = W_C U^{C'}G_z$$

This outcome is not entirely theoretically satisfactory because it posits that the government itself begins with an endowment of K units of some good. A fuller model can be constructed by having the government purchase z from the C-agent by taxing both agents equally on their produced food at rate t.

E. THE DM MODEL

In contrast, the DM framework permits the C-agent to be paid q (an optimally chosen consumer price with implicit tax $G_z - q$ for the units of K that are purchased.) In this case, the government problem is to maximize

$$W(U^A(Q^A), U^C(Q^C))$$

$$\text{s.t. } Q^A = (1-t) \, e^A$$

$$Q^C = (1-t) \, (\, e^C + q_z \, K)$$

$$Q^A + Q^C = F(e,z) + G(e,K-z)$$

There is no need to write the government budget constraint explicitly in this model because the assumption of constant returns to scale, the budget constraints of the consumers and the requirement that production equal consumption jointly force the government to have a balanced budget.

Because the distribution of available income can be completely controlled by choosing t and q, there is no need to use the government project for this purpose. The first order conditions of the maximization problem set out above include productive efficiency. Thus projects will only be inefficient when the tax system is not sufficient to redistribute income.

In fact, in this contrived example, the allocation achievable using the commodity taxes is first best. This follows from the ability to tax perfectly inelastically supplied factors of production.

F. THE CONSTRAINED DM MODEL

What is needed to disrupt the efficiency result is that the government cannot choose the price, q_z, that it pays to the C agents for the z purchased. Law may require that the factor be purchased at fair market value, which is G_K. With the addition of the constraint that $q_z = G_K$, the first order conditions for maximization with respect to z now involve terms in $G_{KK} \, K$, rather than just the efficiency criteria, $G_z = F_z$.

G. SUMMARY

Rent seeking alone is not sufficient to drive a country to productive inefficiency. It is helpful in that it creates a large incentive for the transfer of resources to an identified group. However, it is the lack of the ability to tax all consumer netputs that makes inefficiency plausible.

In this line of reasoning, it is economies operating in a Tullockian framework, with governments that depend upon interest groups yet have insufficient power to favor these groups more directly that would opt for production inefficiencies.

Thus the political economic argument is that richer countries should be the candidates for overbuilt projects. The physical arguments—that poorer countries have not exhausted sites that yield efficient projects—work in the same direction. For both of these reasons, we should expect to see richer countries less influenced by precipitation.

H. EMPIRICAL EVIDENCE

In this section we examine the empirical evidence of water on output. There are two major determinants of water's effect on output. One is simply climate. In wet climates, additional water may be bad rather than good. Flooding, injury to tourism and lack of sunlight during the growing season are three reasons why additional water may be detrimental to output. The second determinant is the building of water projects, which is of interest.

In order to determine the effect of precipitation on an output measure, we regress household consumption expenditure on its lag and measures of climate. This methodology has strong justification.

Hall's version of the permanent income hypothesis is that, to a good approximation, household personal income is best predicted by its lag times a constant (1978). Hall reasoned as follows: Consumers have the opportunity to save money. If they save a dollar their utility will decrease by marginal utility. If they spend that dollar in the next period their utility will increase by marginal utility divided by the time preference rate, which accounts for utility in the future being less valuable than current utility, times the number of additional dollars available, which is one plus the interest rate. This leads Hall to regress transformations, to represent marginal utility, of personal consumption expenditure on its lag. In Hall's examination of aggregate American personal consumption, expenditure itself was an adequate proxy for marginal utility. As predicted by theory, Hall also found that adding other variables (dated in t-1) to the regression didn't result in statistically significant coefficients on those variables. In contrast to Hall's finding that this period's consumption is sufficient for the purpose of predicting consumption in the next period, Hansen and Singleton (1983) found that utility functions would need to have considerable curvature in order to explain the premium that equities enjoy over bonds. I believe that the source of the apparent contradiction between these two observations lies in the use of aggregate data which masks the risks that individuals face. Thus the empirical evidence for the US does not settle the proper transformation that one should use in Hall's regressions. Below we have chosen to report logarithmic transformations, but we have also tried linear with very similar results.

The theory thus predicts that only variables dated in period t can add to the predictive power of lagged consumption. Weather is such a variable, with the additional property that innovations in weather are not dependent (at least in the short run) on innovations in economic conditions. Further, other studies imply the necessity of including weather as an independent variable in estimating agricultural production or derivative figures (Hayes and Decker, 1998). Thus including them as independent variables while omitting relevant economic variables does not result in biased coefficients on weather variables.

The result of this argument is a second order polynomial regression of log(hce) on its lag, precipitation, and temperature. (If we had logged temperature and precipitation this would be a translog.) To check for interactive effects, we included all second order terms as well.[7]

The sample was chosen to include a maximal number of countries for which there were data on both weather and household consumption expenditure. Temperature and precipitation were taken as the deviation from their mean values country by country. 88 countries[8] met our criteria of having at least 22 observations available on household consumption expenditure between the years 1960 and 1998, a time period chosen for availability of both weather and expenditure data.

The regression of household consumption expenditure on its own lag fits extremely well, so the R^2 from all the regressions are quite high. In the case of some countries, particularly countries with lower household consumption expenditure (HCE) per capita, the Durbin Watson statistics indicated residual autocorrelation, which we would take as evidence that there were omitted variables. We used an AR(1) regression in these cases. The Hall theory predicts that there would be no omitted variables. Table 1 presents the summary statistics for the data as well as goodness of fit and the DW statistics for the regressions.

Table 1. Data summary and regression diagnostic statistics

	Mean	Median	Max	Min
HCE*	1.12×10^{11}	1.54×10^{10}	3.21×10^{12}	1.91×10^{8}
Temperature	19.2	22.1	28.4	-5.2
Precipitation	1242	1150	3116	50
# observations per country	36.8	38	39	23
R^2	0.948	0.985	0.999	0.478
final DW	1.94	1.94	2.49	1.08

* HCE= Household final Consumption Expenditures, in constant 1995 US dollars.
Temperature= average annual temperature in country.
Precipitation= average annual precipitation in country.
The AR(1) regression was performed in 36 of the 89 cases.
Sources: Mitchell for temperature and precipitation (in mm and degrees Celsius), World Bank, World Development Indicators 2001 for household consumption expenditure, and the authors' computations for the regression results.

We did try to embed these countries in a single estimation and found the results to be less than satisfactory. Small changes in specification inverted the effect of the weather variables.

[7] Independent variables were: lag, lag squared, lag*temperature, precipitation, lag * precipitation, precipitation squared, temperature * precipitation, and temperature squared.
[8] Algeria, Argentina, Australia, Austria, Bangladesh, Belgium, Benin, Brazil, Burkina Faso, Burundi, Cameroon, Canada, Chile, China, Colombia, Congo, Costa Rica, Denmark, Dominican Republic, Ecuador, Egypt, El Salvador, Finland, France, Gabon, Gambia, Ghana, Great Britain, Greece, Guatemala, Guinea-Bissau, Guyana, Haiti, Honduras, Hong Kong, Hungary, India, Indonesia, Iran, Ireland, Israel, Italy, Ivory Coast, Jamaica, Japan, Kenya, Lesotho, Luxembourg, Madagascar, Malawi, Malaysia, Mali, Mauritania, Mexico, Morocco, Nepal, Netherlands, New Zealand, Nicaragua, Niger, Nigeria, Norway, Pakistan, Papua New Guinea, Paraguay, Peru, Philippines, Portugal, Rwanda, Senegal, Singapore, South Africa, South Korea, Spain, Sri Lanka, Sweden, Switzerland, Syria, Thailand, Togo, Trinidad and Tobago, Tunisia, Uruguay, USA, Venezuela, Zaire, Zambia, and Zimbabwe

Test statistics did not favor uniformity of coefficients over countries, either in per capita or expenditure form.

To determine the overall effect of precipitation and temperature variables on the household consumption expenditures, we computed and tested for the significance of each country's elasticity of HCE with respect to precipitation[9]. 54 of the 89 countries had elasticities significant at the .05 level, and 45 of these were significant at the .01 level.

CONCLUSION

To begin with, we anticipated that wetter countries would have lower precipitation elasticities of HCE than drier countries. Figure 4.1a shows elasticity compared with precipitation. Although there is substantial diversity, the overall trend is as predicted. However, as we noted above, considering all countries together makes for a complex picture in which the object of our study can become lost. To gain a bit more focus we look at the effects of increasing HCE on precipitation elasticity in countries with low rainfall in Figure 4.1b.

The chart shows that drier countries tend to have positive or only slightly negative responses to added rainfall, while those with precipitation levels above 1000 cm are less uniform in their responses. Overall, we see that the benefit of additional precipitation decreases as the average rainfall of a country rises, which fits our intuition. However, the trend line is perhaps not as sloped as we might expect; the result is not a strong one, and the regression describing the trend line does not indicate that rainfall is a predictor of elasticity of precipitation at any conventional level of significance.

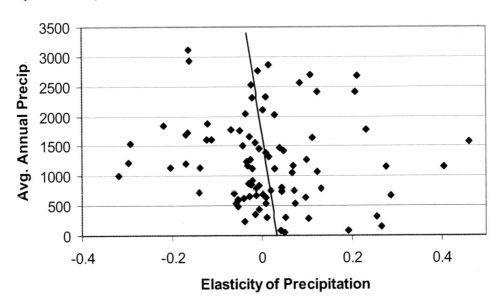

Figure 4.1. Elasticity by Rainfall.

---

[9] elast of precipitation = mean precip * [coeff. of precip. + 2*(coeff. of precip^2)*(precip.)+ (coeff. of interaction between temperature and precipitation) * temperature + (coeff. of interaction between lag and precipitation)* (ln(lag))]

Another possible explanation is the relative importance of agriculture in a country's GDP. A higher percentage of agriculture usually implies that other industries are not very developed, as we saw above in the case of late 19th century Britain.[10] Less developed countries are likely to also have less developed water resources. In Figure 4.2 agricultural value added as a percentage of GDP is compared with precipitation elasticity. Figure 4.2a shows the case of the dry countries, and 2b the wet countries.

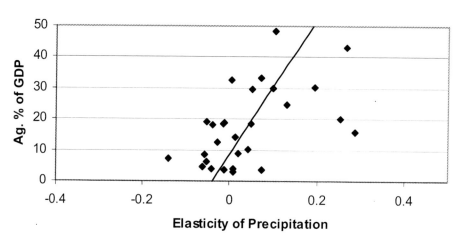

Figure 4.2a. Agriculture as % of GDP and Precipitation Elasticity: Dry Countries.

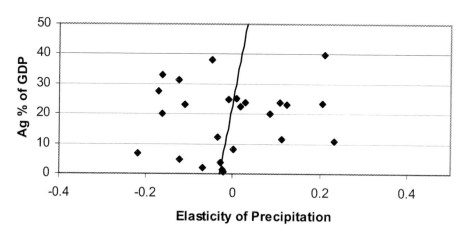

Figure 4.2b. Agriculture as % of GDP and Precipitation Elasticity: Wet Countries.

---

[10] We also verified this finding within our own data set: we noted a correlation of –0.84 between an ordinal ranking of countries' per capita HCE and agricultural value added as a percentage of GDP. Note that our main regressions were based not on per capita HCE but on raw HCE.

Countries that are to a large degree dependent on agriculture tend to benefit from additional precipitation, regardless of the country's baseline of average rainfall. However, again we see that wet countries' response is weaker overall and much less uniform. Additionally, increased rain in dry countries has a positive effect on output when agricultural value added reaches a threshold of about 10% of GDP, while in wet countries the threshold is above the 20% level. In other words, countries that are not reliant on agriculture tend to suffer losses from increased rain, while countries more dependent on agriculture benefit from it, particularly if they typically receive little rainfall. Countries with higher levels of rainfall exhibit a variety of responses to additional precipitation.

Finally we consider the direct role of HCE on elasticity of precipitation. We would hypothesize that greater HCE would dampen elasticities, since as countries develop their water resources they become less susceptible to the effects of increased or decreased precipitation, at least in the short run. Figure 4.3 compares HCE with elasticity of precipitation first for all countries and then for just the exceptionally wet and dry countries.

Figure 4.3 tends to confirm the (loose) inferences from theory described above, with the variance in elasticity tending to decrease with HCE. The "triangle" shape of the countries in the first graph is the effect we had anticipated, namely the dampening of elasticities as HCE increases. Note that due to heterogeneity within the sample we were forced to compress the graph using a log scale on the vertical axis; a more precise graph would show a more gradual tapering effect. On the bottom chart we can see that in drier countries, those with the lowest incomes are those with the strongest positive response to rainfall. All countries with less than 800 mm of precipitation per year and HCE under $10 billion (1995 US$) have positive elasticities of HCE with respect to rainfall (except one, Senegal, with an elasticity of –0.01). Wet countries show the opposite effect, though less clearly. Under a certain level of HCE, excepting the very poorest countries, lower income "wet" countries tend to have negative responses to increased precipitation. Middle and upper income countries of both varieties tend to be closer to an elasticity of zero.

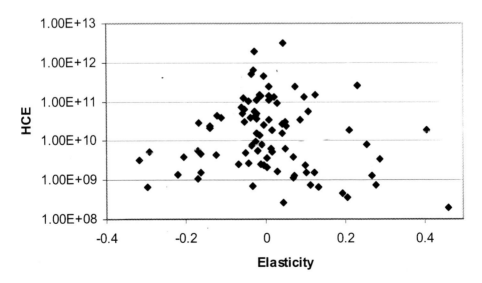

Figure 4.3a. Elasticity by HCE.

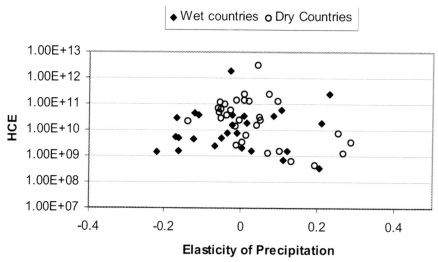

("Wet" countries average more than 1600mm of precipitation per year, while "dry" countries average less than 800mm.).

Figure 4.3b. Elasticity by HCE, wet and dry countries only.

Finally, to see if our results held for per capita HCE, another index of development, we mathematically evaluated the relationship between per capita HCE and the absolute value of the precipitation elasticity statistic. The results were positive, with the coefficient significant at the 0.001 level (Table 2).

Table 2. The absolute value of the elasticity of precipitation regressed on per capita HCE

R Square	0.13579		# Obs:	83
Coefficient	Value	Standard Error	t Statistic	p(t)
Per Capita HCE	-8.7317 E-06	2.4475 E-06	-3.5675	0.0006
Intercept	0.1213	0.0126	9.6556	4.0344 E-15

Note that the number of observations dropped as all statistics were not available for all countries.

The empirical evidence presented here is suggestive of countries with higher HCE moderating the effects of the weather on their economies and there may be evidence that some dry countries have indeed overdone this modification. Further research might include comparing the response of different countries to different levels of meteorological variability, since a relative immunity to the effects of climatic variation would also demonstrate the presence of adequate (or excessive) water resources.

REFERENCES

Caves, R.E., Bain, J.S., and Margolis, J. (1966). Northern California's water industry; the comparative efficiency of public enterprise in developing a scarce natural resource. Baltimore, Maryland : The Johns Hopkins University Press.

Committee on Sustainable Water Supplies for the Middle East (1999). Water for the Future: The West Bank and Gaza Strip, Israel, and Jordan. Washington, D.C.: The National Academy Press.

Diamond, P.A., and Mirrlees, J. (1971). Optimal Taxation and Public Production. 1. Production Efficiency. *American Economic Review*, Vol.61, 8-27.

Dinar, A., and Letey, J. (1991). Agricultural Water Marketing, Allocative Efficiency, and Drainage Reduction. *Journal of Environmental Economics and Management*, Vol. 20:3 , 210 – 223.

Grey, D. (2002). Water Resource and Poverty in Africa: Breaking the Vicious Circle. Presentation at African Ministerial Conference on Water, 30 April 2002, Abuja, Nigeria. www.thewaterpage.com/Documents/amcow_wb_speech.pdf accessed Jan. 6, 2003.

Hall, R. (1978). Stochastic Implications of the Life Cycle-Permanent Income Hypothesis: Theory and Evidence. *Journal-of-Political-Economy*; Vol. 86, 971-87.

Hansen, L.P., and Singleton, K. (1983). Stochastic Consumption, Risk Aversion, and the Temporal Behavior of Asset Returns. *Journal of Political Economy*, Vol 91:2, 249-65.

Hayes, M.J., and Decker, W. L. (1998). Using Satellite and Real-time Weather Data to Predict Maize Production. *International Journal of Biometeorology*, Vol 42, 10-15.

Khatri, Y., S. Solomou, and W. Wu. "Weather and Fluctuations in Agricultural Output 1867 – 1913." *Research in Economic History* 18 (1998): 83-102.

Kislev, Y. (1990). Meshek haMayim beYisrael. unpublished manuscript. *The Center for Agricultural Economic Research*, Rehovot, Israel.

Mitchell, T. D. , Hulme, M., and New, M. (2002). Climate Data for Political Areas. Area Vol. 34, 109-112.

Murphy, D.E. (2002). $100 Million Deal Proposed for Central Valley Farmers. New York Times. December 12.

Tullock, G. (1980). Efficient rent-seeking. In Buchanan, J.M., Tollison, R.D., and Tullock, G. (Eds). Toward a theory of the rent-seeking society (pp. 97-112). College Station, Texas: AandM University Press.

University of California Cooperative Extension Service (1992). Cost of production. University of California, Berkeley, Working Paper.

Vogel, N. (2002). Farmers' Water May Be Sent to San Diego: Deal Would Delay Cut From Colorado River. San Francisco Chronicle, October 17.

World Bank (1990). Israel water sector study: Past achievements, current problems, and future options, Draft. Tel Aviv, Israel.

In: The Economics of Natural and Human Resources...   ISBN 978-1-60741-029-4
Editor: Ayal Kimhi and Israel Finkelshtain   © 2009 Nova Science Publishers, Inc.

Chapter 5

CANADIAN AGRICULTURAL WATER USE AND MANAGEMENT

Steven Renzetti[*]

ABSTRACT

This chapter provides an overview of a number of issues and past economic research related to water-use by the Canadian agricultural sector. While this sector is responsible for only 10-15% of national water withdrawals, it is an important water consumer in a number of regions and is responsible for significant levels of nonpoint source emissions of nutrients, animal wastes and pesticides. The sector's water-use also faces a number of challenges stemming from urbanization, climate change, population growth and increasingly stringent water quality regulations. The chapter concludes with an examination of the implications and appropriate policy responses to these challenges.

A. INTRODUCTION

Canada is widely considered to be a water-rich country. Indeed, it has approximately 10% of the Earth's stock of fresh surface water and 7% of its sustainable flows (Natural Resources Canada, 2002). This perception of Canada as a country with plentiful water supplies, however, is somewhat misleading. One reason is that approximately ninety percent of Canada's population lives within 100 kilometres of its southern border while two-thirds of its rivers' sustainable flows empty into the Artic Ocean. Another reason is that there are already a number of agriculturally-important regions in Canada where water-use conflicts have arisen such as in southern British Columbia and southern Alberta. Furthermore, a number of areas such as southwestern Ontario, where agricultural operations have grown in intensity and scale in the last decade, have observed significant declines in water quality.

[*] Brock University, Canada. This chapter was begun while the author was a Visiting Scholar at CSERGE, University of East Anglia. The author thanks Diane Dupont, Chandra Madramootoo and conference participants for constructive comments. The usual disclaimer applies.

Canada's agricultural sector is a dynamic and important part of the Canadian economy. Despite declining in importance relative to other sectors, it is still a significant source of export earnings and is a dominant sector for a number of the country's regions such as the Prairie provinces (Alberta, Saskatchewan and Manitoba). For example, employment in the agricultural sector is approximately 450,000 or 3% of the Canadian labour force. Similarly, agricultural exports were worth approximately $22 billion in 2000 or 7% of aggregate Canadian exports. Canada's share of the global agricultural export market has remained in the range of 3% to 4% since the 1960's (Agriculture and Agri-Food Canada, 2000).

This chapter explores a number of issues related to the economic features of water-use by the Canadian agricultural sector. The next section provides a brief overview of the Canadian agricultural sector. Section 3 discusses water-use by this sector. Of particular importance is the growing competition for water faced by agricultural operations from in-stream, urban and industrial demands and the need to reform the regulatory frameworks in many Canadian provinces in order to promote the efficient allocation of water. Section 4 examines nonpoint source water pollution emanating from Canadian agricultural operations. In parallel with the discussion regarding water-use, an important finding in this section is that rapid growth in the agricultural sector has pushed governments to re-examine their methods to protect water quality. The chapter concludes by examining some of the trends and challenges facing the Canadian agricultural sector.

B. The Canadian Agricultural Sector

The agricultural sector has played an important role in shaping Canada's economic evolution. However, as Table 1 demonstrates, the last several decades have seen a decline in the relative importance in this industry despite evidence of its ability to innovate and adapt. For example, at the turn of the century, approximately 1 in every 6 dollars of GDP was generated by a farming operation. Today, fewer than 1 in 40 dollars are generated in this way (Leacy, 1999; Agriculture and Agri-Food Canada, 2000). It is interesting to note that this decline in relative importance has occurred despite significant increases in the levels of production and livestock populations (see Table 2). In addition, the decline in relative importance has occurred despite continued innovation in the sector. Evidence of innovation in the Canadian agricultural sector includes adoption of new crops and varieties and farming practices (such as conservation tillage) and shifting patterns in livestock populations in response to changing consumer preferences. Furthermore, the sector has maintained its share in world markets despite intense pressure from foreign competitors who have often been supported by much higher levels of subsidies and support from home governments.

Agricultural operations are found in every province with the majority of farms found in southern parts of Prairie provinces as well as the southern portions of central provinces (Ontario and Quebec). Close to 80% of all farm land is located in the Prairie provinces with Ontario and Quebec having 8.5% and 5%, respectively. The distribution of farm receipts also varies across provinces but it does not follow the distribution of farm land. The provincial shares in the value of the national agricultural sector's output are the following: Ontario (26%), Alberta (23%), Quebec (18%), Saskatchewan (15%), British Columbia (8%) and Manitoba (6%) (Agriculture and Agri-Food Canada, 2000).

Table 1. Trends in the Canadian Agricultural Sector, 1961-1996

	1961	1981	1996
Real Output (Million Canadian $)	18,769	31,424	34,638
% Share in GDP	8.5	5.7	4.5
% Share in Exports	17.0	10.7	6.6
% Share in National Employment	14.1	7.1	5.5

(source: Statistics Canada, 2002b).

Table 2. Trends in Major Crops and Livestock Populations in Canadian Agriculture

Crop (M tonnes)	1970	1990	2000
Grains	25,811	36,313	35,970
Corn	12,665	12,949	14,262
Legume	335	2103	4077
Livestock^2 (1,000)			
Poultry	91,300	94,872	126,159
Cattle	15,063	12,560	14,640
Pigs	5,885	10,146	12,883
Sheep	577	874	1041

Notes to Table 2:
1. Source for figures is Statistics Canada (2002b)
2. The data in the first column for livestock populations are for 1976, not 1970.

Like most OECD countries, the Canadian agricultural sector and Canadian federal and provincial governments have developed a close and multifaceted relationship. This relationship includes many forms of regulation, support for RandD, export promotion, direct and indirect support and lobbying. The levels of these support programs have been substantial but were never as high as other major agriculture-exporting nations (with the exception of Australia) and have declined rapidly over the last decade. For example, in 1999/00, total support provided to farmers as a percentage of GDP is estimated to range from 1.2-1.4% in the EU, Japan and the U.S while in Canada the figure is 0.7% and in Australia, 0.45% (Agriculture and Agri-Food Canada, 2000). Furthermore, from 1990-2000, Canadian government subsidies to the agricultural sector declined in nominal terms from $9 billion to $4.2 billion. As Canada moves further to comply with recent WTO rulings on agricultural subsidies and other trade barriers, these subsidies are expected to decline even further.

In addition to anticipated changes in international treaties governing agricultural production and exports, the Canadian agricultural sector faces a number of pressing issues. One of the most important of these concerns the potential impacts of climate change. While there is still significant uncertainty regarding climate change, a number of large scale studies recently have suggested that it may have overall positive effects for the Canadian agricultural sector by raising mean temperatures, extending growing seasons, extending geographic regions for farming and increasing atmospheric CO_2 levels (Standing Senate Committee on Agriculture and Forestry, 2003). For example, Reinsborough (2003) employs a Ricardian model approach to estimate the economic impact of climate change on agriculture in Canada.

Reinsborough states that a Ricardian approach is the preferred method over crop yield studies as it implicitly includes adaptation while crop yield studies do not. On the other hand, the Ricardian approach may be biased towards providing an upper bound on the benefits of climate change as it assumes that adaptation is perfect and costless. Furthermore, it does not take into consideration a potential increase in extreme weather events or the potential introduction of new pests and diseases. Despite these concerns, the estimated benefits of climate change on agriculture in Canada in the short term are found to be small and positive: approximately $1.5 million per year. There is, however, a relatively large margin of error associated with this point estimate.

C. AGRICULTURAL WATER-USE

There are two fundamental ways in which farming operations interact with water resources. The first occurs when a farmer withdraws water from the natural environment in order to irrigate her crops or provide water for her livestock[1]. The second way in which farming operations interact with water arises from off-farm deposition of fertilizers, pesticides, herbicides, agricultural pharmaceuticals, topsoil and other substances into neighbouring ground and surface water bodies. This section of the chapter considers water withdrawals by the Canadian agricultural sector. I first present data regarding the magnitude of sectoral water withdrawals in Canada including the agricultural sector. I then turn to assessing the regulation of these withdrawals and, finally, the state of research regarding their economic characteristics.

C.1. Canadian Water Supply and Demand

Canada is a country blessed with abundant water resources. It has approximately 10% of the Earth's stock of freshwater and 7% of its sustainable flows. Because of Canada's relatively small population (approximately 31.6 million), these figures imply an annual per capita sustainable supply of approximately 100,000 m^3-one of the highest levels on the planet. Despite these figures, water availability is a growing concern for many Canadians and regions of Canada. This is primarily due to two reasons. First, water is distributed unevenly across Canada. Two-thirds of Canada's water flows north to the Arctic while 90% of population lives close to its southern border. Second, rising population, food production and energy production are leading to increasing water demands. In addition, parts of Canada receive less than 30 cm/yr of precipitation (including important grain-growing regions of southern Alberta and Saskatchewan).

Table 3 provides data on aggregate water withdrawals and consumption by the major water-using sectors of the Canadian economy. Unlike many other countries, the Canadian agricultural sector represents a relatively small portion of total water withdrawals-never exceeding 10% of national withdrawals.

---

[1] Farmers also withdraw water for domestic uses such as washing and cooking. This type of water-use is not considered here.

Table 3. Sectoral Water Withdrawals and Consumption in Canada (Million m^3)

Sector	1981	1986	1991	1996
Agriculture	3125 (2412)	3559 (2752)	3991 (3089)	4098 (3036)
Mining	624 (3)	544 (2)	489 (1)	681 (9)
Manufacturing	10,153 (610)	8381 (439)	7410 (547)	6397 (598)
Electricity Production	18,166 (82)	24,964 (261)	28,289 (105)	28,664 (481)
Other Industries	890 (126)	915 (138)	999 (157)	880 (84)
Municipal and Government	3760 (397)	3719 (381)	3802 (428)	3922 (440)
Total	36,717 (3629)	42,083 (3973)	44,979 (4320)	44,874 (4740)

Notes to Table 3:
1. Source: Statistics Canada (2002a).
2. Withdrawals and consumption are measured in millions of cubic metres per year.
3. Annual Consumption (the difference between withdrawal and discharge) is reported in parentheses for each sector.

This is due, in part, to the heavy dominance of thermal electric power generation and the water-intensive nature of the Canadian manufacturing sector. Nonetheless, the agricultural sector exhibits the fastest rate of growth of all major water-using sectors in Canada. Indeed, by 1996-the most recent year for which there are data- withdrawals by the agricultural sector exceeded those of the municipal and government sector. What is particularly important about the growth in the agricultural sector's level of water withdrawals is the attendant level of water consumption (that is, withdrawals net of return flows). As the data in the table indicate, water-use in agriculture is characterized by the highest consumption rates of any sector.

Agricultural water-use is often difficult to measure. Unlike the manufacturing, mining, energy production and municipal sectors which are directly surveyed for their water-use in Canada, the agricultural sector's water-use is estimated by using data from several sources. In British Columbia and the Prairie provinces, water provided to large scale irrigation districts is recorded and makes up the bulk of agricultural water-use. These data form the basis for estimating agricultural withdrawals in those provinces. In other provinces, where large-scale irrigation projects are not in place, estimates of aggregate agricultural withdrawals must be derived by combining water-use coefficients with data on crop production and livestock populations (Statistics Canada, 2003). This is because many agricultural operations are exempted from the requirement to possess a permit to withdraw water and those which do hold a withdrawal permit are typically not required to meter their water withdrawals (de Loë, Kreutzwiser and Ivey, 2001). It is likely that these imputation methods provide an accurate estimate of agricultural water-use at the aggregate national and provincial levels. What is of concern is the accuracy of these estimation methods at the river basin or sub basin levels where variations in temperature, soil type and farming practices can be significant and lead to deviations in water-use from the norms reflected in industry-wide water-use coefficients.

The growth in the aggregate agricultural water withdrawals seen in Table 3 may be explained by the growth in irrigated acreage and the expansion in livestock herds in Canada. In aggregate, irrigation accounts for approximately 80-85% of all agricultural water withdrawals, livestock water accounts for 10-15% and domestic uses make up the remainder (Agriculture and Agri-Food Canada, 2000). As Table 4 indicates, the percentage of cropland in Canada for which natural rainfall is augmented by irrigation has increased rapidly in recent years. For Canada as a whole, the proportion of cropland that is irrigated has risen by almost 20% in the period 1991-1996. The rather large percentage increases in Table 4 are, in part, explained by the quite small initial irrigated areas such as in Ontario, Quebec, Saskatchewan and Manitoba.

Table 4. Irrigation Water-use and Irrigated Acreage by Province

Prov.	Water-use for Irrigation (M m³)	Total Crop Area (M ha)	% of Cropped Area that is Irrigated, 1996	% change in Cropped Area that is Irrigated, 1991-1996
B.C.	1301.0	1.375	20.7	21.5
Alberta	2609.0	23.59	54.1	12.8
Saskatchewan	271.3	35.58	1.0	32.0
Manitoba	24.6	11.61	*	68.0
Ontario	114.0	9.76	1.7	25.5
Quebec	58.3	4.29	1.6	52.7
New Brunswick	1.4	0.33	*	34.1
Nova Scotia	2.3	0.28	2.0	2.6
P.E.I.	1.7	0.42	6.3	182.8
Newfoundland	0.1	0.02	2.0	39.4
CANADA	4384.1	87.26	2.5	19.0

Notes to Table 4:
1. Sources: Water-use for Irrigation is from Statistics Canada, 2003; all other data from Statistics Canada, 2002a.
2. * denotes a value less than 1.0.

However, it is particularly interesting to note that in provinces such as B.C. and Alberta where a significant portion of cropland is already irrigated, the rates of growth are also high.

It is also interesting to note that the rates of application of irrigation water to crops vary significantly across provinces due largely to differences in cropping patterns. In Alberta, for example, the annual average rate of application of water onto land that is irrigated is approximately 12.7 m^3/ha while in Ontario it is over 600 m^3/ha. The latter figure is explained through reference to the large number of greenhouses, orchards and golf courses in Ontario (until recently, water use by golf courses was recorded as agricultural water use).

There are several potential reasons explaining the rapid increases in irrigated acreage observed recently in Canada. In traditional farming areas such as the Prairies, there recently has been substitution away from grain crops due to low market prices. The introduction of irrigation has followed from the planting of crops such as soybeans. In provinces such as Ontario and Quebec, the growth in irrigation appears to be driven by concerns regarding the potential impacts of climate change and by the potential returns to achieving greater consistency in product quality made possible through irrigation. Finally, historically low real interest rates in Canada over the last decade have spurred investments in many sectors. Despite these possibilities, the motivations behind the observed trends in irrigation investments have not yet been adequately investigated.

C.2. Regulation of Water Withdrawals

Under the Canadian Constitution, regulation of the commercial exploitation of natural resources is a provincial responsibility (Field and Olewiler, 2002). As a result, the provincial governments regulate the withdrawal of surface and ground water. In general, a firm or farming operation may withdraw water only after receiving a permit that specifies, *inter alia*, the maximum quantity that may be withdrawn and the duration of the permit. There are a number of features of these permits to withdraw. First, in many provinces, withdrawals below a specified volume are exempted from requiring a permit. In Ontario, for example, any withdrawal less than 50 m^3/day is exempt from requiring a permit. Furthermore, Alberta exempts "traditional agricultural uses" from requiring a permit so long as withdrawals remain less than 6250 m^3/year. Second, permits are provided at little or no cost to many users. In Ontario, British Columbia, Quebec and Alberta a permit to take water is provided at no cost to the user. In Canada's other major agricultural provinces, the price charged for water withdrawals is very low. In a recent study of groundwater permitting and pricing, Nowlan (2005) estimates the price of privately withdrawn water in Saskatchewan to be $0.0015 to $0.038/m^3/year and in Manitoba to be $0.0001/m^3/year. Third, once issued, permits are not transferable or tradeable. Finally, the permits do not provide compete property rights. In times of drought, provincial legislation allows the government to reduce permitted withdrawals-in some cases according to a pre-specified order of priority or in reverse order of seniority of the permit holding. All of these features of the provincial water permitting systems strongly indicate that water is seriously undervalued in Canada and that the permitting system does little to promote the efficient allocation of water (Dupont and Renzetti, 1999).

A contrast to the above situation relates to water purchased by farmers from irrigation districts. In Alberta and Saskatchewan, most farms with irrigation systems acquire their water from these irrigation districts and face higher prices than if they were self-supplied. In Alberta, for example, irrigation rates are based on "assessed acres". For non-pressurized service, annual rates vary between $8 and $14/assessed acre (Alberta Ministry of Agriculture,

Food and Rural Development, 2005). Irrigation rates in Saskatchewan are comparable. Furthermore, as the following textbox indicates, one province at least has demonstrated an interest in improving the efficiency of its water allocations by implementing a more market-orientated regulatory structure.

Alberta's move towards market-based water allocation

Alberta, Canada's leading agricultural province, is contemplating reforming its water allocation regulations. Under the existing system of water allocation, most self-supplied agricultural operations are granted free access to surface and groundwater supplies. Furthermore, once granted, permits for water withdrawals can not be traded or transferred. Unfortunately, the combination of growth in the water-intensive oil and gas industry, rapid urbanization and inter-provincial water allocation agreements mean that withdrawals from the largest rivers in southern Alberta are reaching sustainable limits.

It is expected that the efficiency of water allocation will be improved significantly if Alberta moves to liberalize trading in water permits. Horbulyk and Lo (1998) and Mahan, Horbulyk and Rowse (2002) consider the welfare effects of these types of reforms. In order to do this, the authors develop a programming model that simulates the optimal water allocation. Demand curves are calibrated using data for the entire province although the emphasis is placed on a set of river basins in southern Alberta where competition for water is increasing. The demand curves employ published elasticity estimates for irrigation, municipal and industrial water-uses. The program seeks a static allocation of water that maximizes the sum of producer and consumer surpluses while meeting any exogenous hydrologic, instream and inter-provincial transfer constraints. A valuable feature of the work is that the authors use net consumption (withdrawal minus return flow) as the unit of measure for allocations and trades.

The simulations indicate that the broadest definition of allowable trades yields significant intersectoral shifts in water consumption and welfare gains. Specifically, 23% of irrigation water consumption is shifted to municipal and industrial uses and this represents almost a doubling of the latter's water-use. The aggregate welfare gain from this shift is approximately $530 million (Canadian). A more limited market arrangement that allows trades only within a sub-basin achieves more than 85% of the welfare gains and 75% of the volume of trades. This may be due to the fact that the model assumes that all of the farms and cities are basically the same in terms of their water demands aside from their scale.

C.3. Economic Research on Canadian Agricultural Water Withdrawals

There is relatively little known about the economic characteristics of Canadian agricultural water-use. This contrasts to the attention paid to the relationship between water and other inputs and to decision-making surrounding the adoption and usage of irrigation systems in American farming (cf. Renzetti, 2002, ch. 5). A large part of the reason for this gap is the lack of data on farm-level water-use. Indeed, there are no data collected by the Census of Agriculture on farm-level water-use. Furthermore, while a number of Canadian farms hold permits to withdraw water from groundwater and rivers and lakes, these permits only specify the maximum volume of water that may be withdrawn in a specified time period.

There have been a limited number of studies that examine the value of irrigation water in Canadian farming operations. Kulshrestha and Brown (1990) compare crop returns under dryland and irrigated farming in the South Saskatchewan River Basin during the period 1968 to 1986. The authors estimate the short-run value of irrigation water to be $0.061/m^3$ and the long-run value to be $0.020/m^3$ (1986 Can$). Long run estimates subtracted both variable and fixed costs, while short run estimates accounted only for variable costs. In a similar study, Kulshrestha (1994) estimates the value of groundwater in Manitoba by measuring the additional returns to producers for irrigating a given crop. The estimated values of the groundwater are $0.615/m^3$ for potatoes and $0.198/m^3$ for all other crops (1990 Can$). More recently, researchers have employed alternative methods to assess the value of irrigation water. Veeman et. al (1997) apply a hedonic price model to agricultural land in southern Alberta in order to estimate the market's valuation of access to irrigation water. The hedonic price equation provides an estimate of the value of access to the irrigation network of $0.102/m^3$ (1993 Can$). Finally, Dachraoui and Harchaoui (2003) estimate an aggregate cost function for the Canadian agricultural sector that includes the quantity of irrigation water as a quasi-fixed factor. The estimated cost function yields a shadow price of the quantity of irrigation water which, in turn, provides an estimate of the sector's average willingness to pay for water of $0.46/m^3$. Despite the commonly held view that agricultural use of water is a relatively low-value application, this estimated value compares favourably with the "all industries" estimated value of water of $0.73/m^3$ (1996 Can$).

D. CANADIAN AGRICULTURE AND NONPOINT SOURCE WATER POLLUTION

The second aspect of the relationship between agricultural activity and water resources concerns the loss of nutrients, fertilizers, pesticides, animal wastes and other potentially harmful substances from farm sites and the subsequent re-emergence of those substances in Canadian water bodies. For many years, it was believed that the sheer size of Canada's land mass and volume of water resources was sufficient to assimilate whatever byproducts were released from agricultural operations. In recent years, however, a growing body of scientific evidence demonstrates that growth in the scale of agriculture, intensification of agricultural operations, and inadequate monitoring of water quality have all combined with lax land use and water quality regulations to cause a number of local water quality problems. In this section, I first describe the types of nonpoint source pollutants that may arise from agricultural operations. Next, I briefly discuss current Canadian efforts to regulate this type of pollution and, finally, I discuss the limited amount of economic research conducted in Canada regarding agricultural nonpoint source water pollution.

Soil erosion is a natural process that may be accelerated by some farming practices. Soil erosion is a concern not only because it represents the loss of a valuable asset to the farmer but also because it may impose costs on the rest of Canadian society by increasing water turbidity and by serving as a mechanism for the off-farm transportation of other harmful substances. Chambers, Dupont, Schaefer and Bielak (2002) report that provinces varied significantly with respect to the percentage of cropland that exceeded a "tolerable" level of risk of water erosion with the lowest being Saskatchewan (10%) and Quebec (12%) and the highest being Ontario (42%), B.C. (44%) and Prince Edward Island (41%).

The scale of modern farming would not be possible in Canada without the intensive use of artificial nutrients such as nitrogen and phosphorous. Excess nutrient levels originate in over use of fertilizers and inappropriate manure management. The available scientific evidence suggests that this is a problem in areas of intensive agricultural operation. Chambers, Dupont, Schaefer and Bielak (2002) indicate that "20% of surface water samples from the Great Lakes basin were high enough to cause developmental anomalies and 3% were high enough to kill amphibians" (p. 5). Another source of nitrogen and phosphorous comes from the application of sewage biosolids (the residue remaining after municipal wastewater treatment) to fields. Almost half of the total Canadian production of biosolids (667,000 tonnes annually) is applied to agricultural lands. Despite the fact that these biosolids may contain trace metals, pathogens, nutrients and organic materials, the authors argue that there is relatively little risk in its application as observed surplus levels of nitrogen (approximately 15 kg/ha in southern Ontario) are still low compared to levels observed in the U.S. and Europe (30-100 kg/ha).

The growth in intensive feedlots and its implications for water quality.

One of most important trends in Canadian agriculture is the growth in average farm size. Statistics Canada (2002) indicates that the average farm increased from 510 acres to 610 acres during the period 1980 to 1990. In addition, with growing size have come increased livestock populations. Between 1996 and 2001, the average livestock populations per reporting farm have increased as follows: cattle: 104.7 to 127.4; pigs: 523.1 to 902.2; and poultry: 3620.9 to 4763.6 (Census of Agriculture, 2001). Furthermore, intensive feedlot operations tend to be geographically concentrated in southern Alberta and south-western Ontario, as well as south-eastern Quebec. In parts of these regions, annual manure production is estimated to exceed 6,000 kg/hectare (Statistics Canada, 2001).

This intensification of feedlot operations has raised concerns about the potential for negative impacts on local water quality resulting from off-farm transport of pathogens and veterinary pharmaceuticals in animal wastes. These concerns come at a time when rural water supplies are already under threat. As indicated above, a significant number of rural wells exhibit significantly high levels of coliform. Nonetheless, establishing a link between the intensification of feedlot operations and deteriorating rural water quality remains controversial. Goss et al. (2002) point out that, while intensification generates increased waste management challenges, there is evidence of scale economies and greater sophistication in waste management approaches in large scale farms. For example, Statistics Canada (2003) reports that larger pig operations tend to have proportionately more on-farm storage than smaller farms although cattle farms' waste storage methods are largely independent of farm size.

Pesticides represent another source of nonpoint source pollution from agricultural operations. There is a growing body of evidence that Canadian surface and ground waters are contaminated with pesticide run-off (Coote and Gregorich, 2000). For example, surveys have found that 48%, 63% and 100% of sampled farm dugouts to be contaminated with pesticides in Alberta, Ontario and Saskatchewan, respectively. Rates of pesticide contamination in wells range from 2% in B.C., 11.5% in Ontario to 38% in Nova Scotia and 55% in Quebec.

Another form of agricultural nonpoint source pollution results from pathogenic organisms such as bacteria, protozoa and viruses that reside in animal wastes. There is a risk that the application of animal wastes and biosolids to agricultural land could result in these pathogens being transported off-farm to surface and ground waters. A number of recent studies have demonstrated that 10-46% of rural wells in any province violate water quality guidelines regarding these substances (CCME, 2001).

D.1. Regulation of Agricultural Nonpoint Source Water Pollution

Provincial water management has tended to be fragmented because the regulation of the water allocation and the protection of water quality have been historically the responsibility of separate agencies. However, there is increasingly an awareness of the interconnectedness of water quality and quantity issues and provincial governments have worked to integrate their regulatory approaches. For example, in many provinces today, applicants for water withdrawals permits must document any ecological impacts related to their water withdrawals. Furthermore, water quality has traditionally been protected by regulations that set out maximum quantities (or in some cases concentrations) of substances that may be deposited into water bodies. With the growing recognition of the challenges posed by nonpoint sources of water pollution, some provinces have extended their water quality protection efforts in the direction of regulating land uses.

A number of provincial governments have acted recently to confront the growing challenges to water quality posed by agricultural runoff and other forms of non-point pollution (Goss et. al, 2002). Given the difficulties presented by the costs of observation and enforcement, most provincial governments continue to rely primarily upon voluntary measures or command and control style regulations that proscribe allowed appropriate technologies and production processes (Chambers, Dupont, Schaefer and Bielak, 2002).

The province of Ontario's efforts to reform its nutrient management regulations provide a good example of the evolution underway. In May, 2000 the water supply of Walkerton, Ontario was compromised when a well was contaminated with E. coli bacteria. Consumption of the contaminated water killed seven people and sickened thousands others. Subsequent research established that heavy rains had washed manure spread on a farmer's field into a malfunctioning well from which Walkerton drew its water (O'Connor, 2002a, 2002b). These tragic events and widespread growing concerns about the environmental impacts of the intensification of feedlot operations prompted the Ontario government to revise its regulations governing the application of animal and artificial fertilizers on agricultural lands.

Prior to the events of Walkerton, the Ontario government relied upon voluntary guidelines that set out Best Management Practices for nutrient management (Goss et. al, 2001). These BMP's did not require that farmers have a manure management plan nor did they provide for penalties if a farm operation did not meet BMP. The growing size of feedlot operations has led to increasing quantities of animal wastes. By 1996, 3 of the 4 sub-river basins in south-western Ontario recorded annual manure production in excess of 6,000 kg/hectare (Statistics Canada, 2001). In 2002, the government of Ontario introduced its Nutrient Management regulations (Ontario Ministry of Agriculture and Food, 2003). Perhaps the most important feature of these regulations is that they replace the previous reliance on voluntary guidelines with mandatory regulations. These regulations specify requirements for the handling, storage and application of animal wastes and there are fines set out for non-compliance. From an economic perspective, it is unclear if these regulations will achieve an efficient or even a cost-effective level of nutrient production. This is primarily because of the absence of information regarding the relative benefits of risk reduction associated with alternative output levels. Nonetheless, it can be expected that the regulations will lead to reduced off-site transport of excess nutrients compared to the past voluntary regime.

Another interesting development is seen in the tradeable emissions credit program being carried out on the South Nation River in Ontario (O'Grady and Wilson, 2004). As a result of this river's heavy phosphorous (P) loadings, regulators required new potential polluters to adopt a zero discharge approach. When this proved infeasible, new polluters were ordered to adopt a 'no net increase' approach whereby any new emissions would be offset by purchased reductions in existing sources of phosphorous (largely local farming operations). Due to the uncertainty regarding the link between changes in farming operations and river phosphorous levels, regulators required new polluters to purchase 4 kg P credits for every 1 kg P emissions planned. The average cost of the 4 kg reduction is approximately $1200 which compares favourably with the current average cost of emission controls for new sources of $2000.

D.2. Economic Research on Canadian Agricultural Nonpoint Source Water Pollution

Agricultural non point source water pollution exhibits several characteristics which present daunting challenges to regulators. These include uncertainty regarding the source of emissions, the quantity of emissions from each source, the relationship between actions of polluters and emissions and between emissions and ambient environmental quality. In addition, because of the crucial importance in physical conditions (such as local soil types, groundwater-surface water interactions and weather conditions), the analysis of nonpoint source pollution and the design of policies aimed at controlling it in a least-cost fashion are likely to be quite case-specific. As is the case with most other forms of pollution, policies can be broadly divided into regulations and economic instruments. As described in the previous section, regulatory approaches include design standards such as specifications of the types of pollution control equipment (such as methods for manure storage) and performance standards (such as limiting the number of livestock per hectare). Economic instruments include taxes, subsidies and tradable permits.

The preference of Canadian governments for regulatory (or in some cases voluntary) approaches to controlling nonpoint source agricultural pollution stands in contrast to prescriptions from economists who have generally favoured economic instruments over regulatory approaches. It has been argued that regulations do not account for differences across polluters (such as their respective costs of abatement or the relative impact of a given quantity of emissions on different parts of a water body) and do not provide polluters with an ongoing incentive to innovate and reduce pollution beyond the mandated standard (Ribaudo, Horan and Smith, 1999).

The main difficulty with the use of economic instruments to address agricultural nonpoint water pollution is the information required to implement them. For example, input-based taxes and subsidies exploit the fact that increasing the use of some inputs (such as fertilizers) increases emissions while increasing the use of other inputs (such as using climate data to improve the timing of fertilizer applications) decreases emissions. In order to make use of these relationships, the regulator must know not only the relationship between each polluter's emissions and ambient water quality but also have complete information regarding the polluters' production technologies. In addition to the interest in taxes and subsidies, economists have considered the application of tradable permits to the control of nonpoint source pollution. For example, farmers within a watershed could be allotted (or sold) permits for the application of phosphorous or nitrogen on their crops. The challenge in implementing trading schemes for nonpoint pollution is two-fold. First, the damage caused by a given quantity of emissions will depend on a variety of factors. As a result, regulators will not, in general, be indifferent to the time, location and manner that the nitrogen is applied. These concerns will necessarily narrow the range of possible trades and, as a result, restrict the potential efficiency gains from trading. Second, it must be possible for regulators to monitor and measure nitrogen use to ensure that farmers are not employing more than they are allotted.

Because of these types of concerns, researchers have turned their attention to the design of second-best instruments. In a second best environment, the goal may be either to find the policy instrument that achieves a given improvement of ambient water quality at least cost ("cost-effectiveness") or to the design of policy instruments under a specific constraint (such as a tax that is common across all firms in a given region). While these types of policy instruments do not yield the same potential efficiency gain as first-best instruments, they potentially have lower informational requirements.

Weersink and Livernois (1996) survey the literature concerned with Canadian agricultural water pollution and use this information to assess the potential efficacy of alternative economic instruments. The instruments considered include performance-based instruments (charges on emissions, charges/subsidies based on ambient water quality, performance bonds and liability rules) and design-based instruments (input charges/subsidies, tradable permits, charges/subsidies on output). Furthermore, the authors consider the environmental effectiveness, cost effectiveness, cost of enforcement and political feasibility of the alternative instruments. Unfortunately, most of the authors' assessments of the potential for economic instruments are negative. They conclude, "Most residuals from agricultural production are insidious and diffuse in nature. The costs of observing and monitoring stochastic emissions generally render any instruments applied to the emissions infeasible." (p. 349). Furthermore, they assert that while charges on input use (e.g. nitrogen) are a logical alternative, "Since charges necessary to induce the required changes in behaviour are so high, such fees are generally used as a source of revenue to fund other environmental programs" (p. 351).

On a positive note, the authors do suggest "Focusing on improving the profitability of environmentally-friendly practices may thus be the most effective way to resolve diffuse water quality problems." (p. 351). Furthermore, despite the difficulty of inducing the changes in agricultural practices needed to reduce off-farm deposition, achieving these changes can yield positive net benefits to Canada. Giraldez and Fox (1995) simulate the costs and benefits of altering farming practices in order to reduce local groundwater levels of nitrates in southern Ontario. The reduction in nitrate emissions primarily considered was from 147 kg/ha to 140 kg/ha. This reduction was said to be sufficient to reduce nitrate levels to the acceptable water standard of 10mg/L. The estimated per capita annual benefits of improved ground water quality range from less than $1000 to more than $30,000 in neighbouring towns. The costs of a reduction in nitrogen application necessary to bring nitrate levels to the acceptable levels were estimated to be $1.81/ha, or $284.31 for the 158 ha of affected farmland area.

The importance of agricultural nonpoint source water pollution and the paucity of economic studies relating to this topic have prompted the federal government to undertake a research program entitled Watershed-based Evaluation of BMP's (Agriculture and Agri-Food Canada, 2005). The objective of the WEBs project is to quantify on a watershed scale the relative environmental and economic performance of selected beneficial management practices. A valuable feature of this research effort is that it will measure both the economic returns to farm operators and to society of any BMP's that are adopted.

CONCLUSION

This chapter has examined water-use in the Canadian agricultural sector. In doing so, it has highlighted a number of trends and has identified several challenges facing the industry. These are summarized here.

Perhaps the most important trend is the observed increase (in absolute terms and relative to other major user groups) in water withdrawals by the Canadian agricultural sector. This increase was traced to the growth in irrigation water demands and also growth in livestock populations. Another important trend is the intensification of feedlot operations. There is already evidence that this development is leading to diminished water quality in sub-watersheds where livestock concentrations are highest. The last trend concerns regulators responses to changes in agricultural water-use. Here, something of a contradictory picture emerges. On the one hand, provincial governments have been relatively slow to reform their permit to take water programs and they continue to inhibit efficient water allocation. On the other hand, there has been a significant amount of attention paid by provincial governments to reforming water quality regulations. It remains to be seen, however, whether the continued reliance on command and control regulations for agricultural nonpoint source pollutants will yield cost-effective improvements in local water quality.

The Canadian agricultural sector and the government agencies responsible for its regulation face a number of challenges and some of these are related to the sector's water-use. The first concerns the potential impacts of climate change. While a number of studies (Standing Senate Committee on Agriculture and Forestry (2003) have suggested that there may be positive aggregate impacts for the agricultural sector, these have to be interpreted in light of constraints such as water supplies and soil fertility. Further, what is likely to be much more important to farmers' adaptive strategies is not the small change in mean annual temperatures or precipitation but rather the changes in the frequency, severity and duration of extreme weather events such as droughts and flooding. The second challenge is related to changes in the regulatory and fiscal environment facing the sector. Canadian farmers have proven quite resilient and adaptive in the past. The industry has seen remarkable changes in international market conditions, changes to tariff and non-tariff barriers and domestic environmental and waste management regulations. It can be expected that the future will seen a combination of decreasing international barriers to trade and increasing regulatory scrutiny relating to agricultural nonpoint source water pollution. This is a particularly challenging combination as the former will likely lead to decreasing revenues while the latter will likely lead to increased costs. The final challenge concerns the agricultural sector's ability to secure access to sufficient water supplies to meet its growing demands. A number of regions where irrigation and stock-watering demands are climbing also have witnessed growing water demands for households, industry and recreation. Once again, it remains to be seen if provincial governments are able to develop water allocation regimes that satisfy the agricultural sector's demands for water while simultaneously promoting efficient and sustainable water use amongst all water users.

REFERENCES

Agriculture and Agri-Food Canada (2000). A Portrait of the Canadian Agri-Food System. http://www.agr.gc.ca/policy/epad (March 3, 2003).

Agriculture and Agri-Food Canada (2005). Watershed Evaluation of BMPs (WEBs). http://www.agr.gc.ca/env/greencover-verdir/webs_abstract_e.phtml (January 11, 2005).

Alberta Ministry of Agriculture, Food and Rural Development (2005). Irrigation District Annual Water Rates. http://www1.agric.gov.ab.ca/$department/deptdocs.nsf/all/irr8780?opendocument (January 13, 2005).

Chambers, P., Dupont, J., Schaefer, K., and Bielak, A. (2002). *Effects of Agricultural Activities on Water Quality*. CCME Linking Water Science to Policy Workshop Series Report no. 1. Winnipeg, Manitoba: Canadian Council of Ministers of the Environment. http://www.ccme.ca (November 6, 2003).

Coote, D.R., and Gregorich, L.J. (Eds.) (2000). *The Health of Our Water: Toward Sustainable Agriculture in Canada* Ottawa. Canada: Agriculture and Agri-Food Canada. http://www.agr.gc.ca/nlwis/pub/hw_se/pdf/intro_e.pdf (September 1, 2008).

Dachraoui, K., and Harchaoui, T.M. (2003). Water-use, Shadow Prices and the Canadian Business Sector Productivity Performance. Microeconomic Analysis Division, Statistics Canada.

de Loë, R., Kreutzwiser, R., and Ivey, J. (2001). Agricultural Water-use in Ontario. *Canadian Water Resources Journal, Vol.26* (issue 1), 17-42.

Dupont, D. and Renzetti, S. (1999). An Assessment of the Impact of a Provincial Water Charge. *Canadian Public Policy Vol* 25 (issue 3), 361-378.

Field, B., and Olewiler, N. (2002). *Environmental Economics: Second Canadian edition*. Toronto, CA: McGraw-Hill Ryerson.

Giraldez, C., and Fox, G. (1995). An Economic Analysis of Groundwater Contamination from Agricultural Nitrate Emissions in Southern Ontario. *Canadian Journal of Agricultural Economics, Vol 43*, 387-402.

Goss, M., Rollins, K., McEwan, K., Shaw, J., and Lammers-Helpo, H. (2002). The Management of Manure in Ontario With Respect to Water Quality. Commissioned Issue Paper #6, The Walkerton Inquiry, Toronto: The Queen's Printer of Ontario.

Horbulyk, T., and Lo, L. (1998). Welfare gains from potential water markets in Alberta, Canada. In Easter, K., Rosegrant, M., and Dinar, A. (Eds), *Markets for water: potential and performance* (pp. 241-257). Boston, Massachusetts: Kluwer Academic Press.

Kreutzwiser, R.D., de Loë, R.C., Durley, J., and Priddle, C. (2004). Water Allocation and the Permit to Take Water Program in Ontario: Challenges and Opportunities, *Canadian Water Resources Journal*, Vol. 29 (issue 2), 135-146.

Kulshreshtha, S.N. (1994). Economic Value of Groundwater in the Assiniboine Delta Aquifer in Manitoba. Social Science Series No.29, Environment Conservation Service, Ottawa. Environment Canada.

Kulshreshtha, S.N., and Brown, W.J. (1990). The Economic Value of Water for Irrigation: An Historical Perspective. *Canadian Water Resources Journal, Vol.15* (issue 3), 201-215.

Leacy, F.H. (Ed.) (1999). *Historical statistics of Canada* (2nd ed.). Catalogue number: 11-516-XIE, Ottawa, Canada: Statistics Canada.

Mahan, R., Horbulyk, T. and Rowse, J. (2002). Market mechanisms and the efficient allocation of surface water resources in southern Alberta *Socio-Economic Planning Sciences, Vol. 36* (issue 1), 25-49.

Natural Resources Canada (2002). *The Atlas of Canada*, Ottawa: Natural Resources Canada. http://atlas.gc.ca/site/english/index.html.

Nowlan, L. (2005). *Buried Treasure: Groundwater Permitting and Pricing in Canada*. Report prepared for the Walter and Duncan Gordon Foundation, Toronto. www.gordon.org (January 31, 2005).

O'Connor, D.R. (2002). *Part One. Report of the Walkerton Inquiry: The Events of May, 2000 and Related Issues*. Ontario: Ontario Ministry of the Attorney General Queen's Printer for Ontario.

O'Connor, D.R. (2002). *Part Two. Report of the Walkerton Inquiry: A Strategy for Safe Drinking Water*. Ontario: Ontario Ministry of the Attorney General Queen's Printer for Ontario.

O'Grady, D., and Wilson, M.A. (2004). Phosphorus Trading in the South Nation River Watershed, Ontario, Canada. www.envtn.org (May 11, 2004).

Ontario Ministry of Agriculture and Food (2003). Nutrient Management. http://www.gov.on.ca/OMAFRA/english/agops/index.html (November 10, 2003).

Reinsborough, M.J. (2003). A Ricardian model of climate change in Canada. *Canadian Journal of Economics, Vol.36* (issue1), 21-40.

Renzetti, S. (2002). *The Economics of Water Demands*. Norwell: Kluwer Academic Press.

Ribaudo, M., Horan, R., and Smith, M. (1999). *Economics of Water Quality Protection from Nonpoint Sources: Theory and Practice*. Economic Research Service Agricultural Research Report 782. Washington, D.C.: United States Department of Agriculture.

Standing Senate Committee on Agriculture and Forestry (2003). *Climate Change: We are at Risk*. Ottawa: Senate of Canada.

Statistics Canada (2001). *A Geographical Profile of Manure Production in Canada*. Catalogue number: 16F0025XIB. Ottawa: Statistics Canada.

Statistics Canada (2002a). *Human activity and the environment*. Catalogue number: 16201XIE. Ottawa: Statistics Canada.

Statistics Canada (2002b). *Census of Agriculture*. Catalogue number: 95F0301XIE. Ottawa: Statistics Canada.

Statistics Canada (2003). *Methodology Used to Determine Water-use in the Agricultural Sector, Census Year 1996*. Internal working document, Environmental Accounts and Statistics Division, Ottawa.

Veeman, T.S., Veeman, M.M., Adamowics, W.L., Royer, S., Viney, B., Freeman, R., and Baggs, J. (1997). Conserving Water in Irrigated Agriculture: The Economics and Valuation of Water Rights. Rural Economy Project Report #97-01. Department of Rural Economy, University of Alberta.

Weersink, A., and Livernois, J. (1996). The Use of Economic Instruments to Resolve Water Quality Problems from Agriculture. *Canadian Journal of Agricultural Economics, Vol.44*, 345-353.

In: The Economics of Natural and Human Resources... ISBN 978-1-60741-029-4
Editor: Ayal Kimhi and Israel Finkelshtain © 2009 Nova Science Publishers, Inc.

Chapter 6

WATER RESOURCES AND IRRIGATION MANAGEMENT IN TURKEY

Cemal Fert and Burhan Ozkan[*]

ABSTRACT

Surface and ground water resources of Turkey are 110 billion m^3. The average per capita water availability in Turkey is about 1,735 m^3 per year which is considerably less than the world average that is nearly 7,000 m^3. By 2025, the water availability is projected to have decreased to 1,300 m^3/person/year. As of 2000, the total water consumption is 42,000 million m^3; 75 % of this amount is used for irrigation, 15 % for domestic consumption and 10 % for industrial purposes.

Although agricultural irrigation is important in terms of increasing productivity in Turkish arable lands, accelerating economic growth and reducing migration from rural to urban areas, it is clear that in the near future, if the population continues to grow at the same rate, the need for water not only for irrigation but also for domestic consumption and industrial use will increase, causing an allocation problem. Until the 1980s, the concept of water management was only considered in terms of investments, today it is regarded as a significant actor in development as a whole.

A. INTRODUCTION

Due to the rapid increase in the world's population, urbanization, income and consumption choices, the increase in the demand for water and the deterioration of its quality, many countries today are faced with significant water problems. The major problems associated with water can be summarized in three main categories, namely the increase in population, financial problems and environmental problems.

Land and water resources are of great importance for countries. Ensuring socio-economic development and increasing income can be achieved by the efficient use of natural resources.

---

[*] Cemal Fert and Burhan Ozkan are Research Assistant and Professor, respectively, in the Department of Agricultural Economics at Akdeniz University, Antalya, Turkey.

In parallel to this purpose, Turkey has abandoned the mentality of only developing water resources and planning of systems for protection of hazards caused by water, and in the 1980s adopted the belief that natural factors have started to be effective because of rapid urbanization and industrialization resulting in low water quality. It is expected that for the future one of the most important factors will become the protection of water resources. Over the last few decades, because of the increased demand for water and deterioration of its quality, there is a need to develop new water resources. And these facts have caused new approaches to emerge in the development and management of water resources. Regarded from this perspective, the economic potential of surface and ground water resources must be managed in a sustainable way. This becomes possible through the development of resources, institutional regulations and participation, training, and education of the water consumers.

Today, the average per capita water availability in Turkey is about 1,735 m^3 per year, which is considerably less than the world's average that is close to 7,000 m^3 per year. The population of Turkey is expected to reach 80 million in the year 2025 and 110 million in 2050. Thus, per capita water availability will be 1,300 and 945 m^3 respectively. As of 2000, the sectoral water use in Turkey is 75% for irrigation, 15% for domestic consumption, and 10% for industrial use. At this point the share of irrigation is rather high; however, water per se is essential for all aspects of life and is a key element for agricultural production.

Agriculture is still an important industry in Turkey, both socially and economically. The contribution of agriculture to Gross Domestic Product (GDP) was about 7.7 % in 2007, although its share had diminished over time as a result of transformation of the economy into industry and service sectors. Agriculture contributes 9.1% of the total exports and about 29.1 % of the total population of the country, which is 71 million according to the 2007 census, is engaged in agriculture, operating about 3 million farm holdings.

In the agricultural industry, transition to irrigated production has showed its result as yield increases. Since the agricultural land has reached its maximum point, the production increase can be provided by the application of new technologies, use of irrigated production and increase in the yield per unit of land. Therefore, Turkey is spending 65% of its agricultural investment budget for irrigated agriculture projects. Irrigated areas have reached 53 % of the total economically irrigable areas which constitute nearly 4.5 million ha.

Irrigation facilities in Turkey are mostly public irrigation facilities built by the government, accompanied by small-scale facilities built by the producers with their own sources. In the verification of investments made in irrigation, the General Directorate of State Hydraulic Works and Directorate of Rural Services are assigned. The management of public irrigation facilities is realized in two ways: government management and management done by the local administration.

On the other hand, as irrigated production spreads further in order to meet the increased demand for food due to the rapid population growth of Turkey and as a result of socio-economic developments, the need for water for agricultural and industrial purposes is continuously climbing. For this end, the planning and management of water resources, and participation of users, are important.

This paper discusses the current situation of water resources, irrigation systems and irrigation management and makes some suggestions as to water usage and management.

B. General Situation and Potential of Water Resources

Due to the geographical, ecological and climatic conditions, Turkey has a great agricultural production potential. Climatic conditions in Turkey are quite temperate and the precipitation regime of Turkey shows great differences from one region to the other and ranges between 200 and 3000 mm. The annual average precipitation fall is 643 mm, which is equal to 501 billion m^3 of water. 54.7% of this amount evaporates, 8.2% is infiltrated water, 46.7% is surface runoff water, and 1.4% is in rivers coming from other countries (Table 1).

The lack of precipitation during the crop production period in Turkey negatively affects agricultural production. Therefore, it is essential to use irrigation in order to gain high yields. As can be seen in Table 2, Turkey is divided into 26 hydrologic basins, and the Euphrates and Tigris basins together constitute 28% of the country's total potential. The potential of underground water is found to be 12.3 km^3, and 3.51 million m^3 of this reservoir is used for irrigation made by the state, 4.42 billion m^3 of it is used for drinking and meeting industry needs, and 1.72 billion m^3 is used for special irrigation by DSI.

Table 1. Water Resources of Turkey (DSI, 2002)

Mean (arithmetic) Annual Precipitation: 643 mm			
Mean Annual Volume of Precipitation: 501 km^3			
Surface Water		Ground Water	
Annual Surface Runoff	186.05 km^3	(Annual Safe Yield)	12.3 km^3
Annual Surface / Rainfall Ratio	0.37	Annual Volume Allocated by DSI	9.0 km^3
Annual Depletible Volume	95.00 km^3	Actual Annual Utilization	6.0 km^3
Actual Annual Utilization	33.30 km^3		

The total area of Turkey is 77.95 million hectares, and the total arable land is 28.05 million hectares (nearly 36%). 25.85 million hectares of this amount can be irrigated but the economically irrigated area is 8.5 million hectares (Table 3). In other words, 33% of the total irrigable land is economically important. When developments in irrigation technology are considered, it is possible to increase this amount. 473 dams in various sizes are under construction right now to serve this purpose. In addition to these, there are some projects such as in-field development, flood control, drainage and drying. Expansion of irrigated lands in Turkey will increase the yield.

Table 2. Annual Average Runoff 26 River Basins in Turkey (DSI, 2002)

Basin Name	Annual Runoff (km^3)	% of the Potential	**Mean Annual Yield (1/sec/km^2)
Euphrates Basin (*)	31.61	17.0	8.3
Tigris Basin (**)	21.33	11.5	13.1
East Black Sea Basin	14.90	8.0	19.5
East Mediterranean Basin	11.07	6.0	15.6
Antalya Basin	11.06	5.9	24.2
West Black Sea Basin	9.93	5.3	10.6
West Mediterranean Basin	8.93	4.8	12.4

Table 2. (Continued)

Basin Name	Annual Runoff (km³)	% of the Potential	**Mean Annual Yield (1/sec/km²)
Marmara Basin	8.33	4.5	11.0
Seyhan Basin	8.01	4.3	12.3
Ceyhan Basin	7.18	3.9	10.7
Kizilirmak Basin	6.48	3.5	2.6
Sakarya Basin	6.40	3.4	3.6
Coruh Basin	6.30	3.4	10.1
Yesilirmak Basin	5.80	3.1	5.1
Susurluk Basin	5.43	2.9	7.2
Aras Basin	4.63	2.5	5.3
Konya Closed Basin	4.52	2.4	2.5
Buyuk Menderes Basin	3.03	1.6	3.9
Lake Van Basin	2.39	1.3	5.0
North Aegean Basin	2.09	1.1	7.4
Gediz Basin	1.95	1.1	3.6
Meric - Ergene Basin	1.33	0.7	2.9
Kucuk Menderes Basin	1.19	0.6	5.3
Orontes Basin	1.17	0.6	3.4
Burdur Lakes Basin	0.50	0.3	1.8
Akarcay Basin	0.49	0.3	1.9
Total	186.05	100.0	

Table 3. Land Resources (DSI, 2002)

Land Resources	Area, Mha
Area of Turkey (projection area)	77.95
Agricultural Land	28.05
Irrigable Land	25.85
Economically	8.5
Irrigation Land Developed by DSI (net area as of 2001)	2.292

1 km³ = 1 billion m³.

C. WATER RESOURCE MANAGEMENT

According to the World Bank definition, "Water Resource Management is the integrating concept for a number of water sub-sectors such as hydropower, water supply and sanitation, irrigation and drainage. An integrated water resources perspective ensures that social, economic, environmental and technical dimensions are taken into account in the management and development of water resources."

Contrary to this definition, in the first years of the establishment of the Republic of Turkey, the main aim was to improve wetlands, followed by small scale irrigation investments until the 1950s. After the 1950s, through the establishment of DSI and TOPRAKSU, the development of irrigation projects gained a new momentum, and Turkey reached its arable land limit in the 1970s. After this period, the increase in yield was enabled by the development of modern irrigation projects. In the operation and maintenance of these projects, a large number of organizations, both governmental and non-governmental, have direct and indirect interests.

On the public side, a complicated institutional structure is responsible for the use and conservation of water resources. The major institution is the Ministry of Environment, being in charge of the conservation and rehabilitation of the environment, rural and urban areas, natural plant and animal availability. According to the Environment Law No: 2872 and in accordance with some regulations, the Ministry of Environment has the function of the controller. Another institution is the General Directorate of State Hydraulic Works (DSI; the Turkish acronym). The main objective of DSI is to develop all water and land resources in Turkey. DSI was established by the Law 6200 dated December 18, 1953, and is empowered to plan, design, construct and operate dams and hydroelectric power plants, and perform some functions such as irrigation, and domestic and industrial water supplies for large cities.

The other institution is GDRS which is now a union of three governmental Directorates: TOPRAKSU (General Directorate of Soil and Irrigation Works), YSE (General Directorate of Rural Road, Potable Water and Electricity Affairs) and TOPRAK ISKAN (General Directorate for Land and Settlement). GDRS is responsible for delivering agricultural services and social infrastructure to rural areas.

After 1963, investments in irrigation facilities to increase the net area opened for irrigation by these two institutions gained momentum. The net area that was 275,449 ha till 1963 increased to 3,094,334 ha at the end of 1998. The shares of DSI and GDRS in these investments are 69.6 % and 30.4 % respectively. By the end of 1998, public irrigation was realized as net 3,094,334 ha of which 2,688,053 ha were irrigated by surface water and the remaining 406,281 ha by ground water.

The major assessment on water is in the Turkish Constitution of 1982, and it states that water resources are the natural wealth of the country, being within the power of the state to be used for the benefit of the public, and that the development of water resources is the responsibility of the government. Large scale irrigation investments within the scope of investment programs are made by the government. As of 1998, irrigated areas reached 53.4 % of the total economically irrigable areas which constitute nearly 4.5 million ha. 4 million ha is irrigated by surface waters and the rest 0.5 million ha is irrigated by underground waters. The area opened for irrigation by the state is nearly 2 million ha by DSI and 1.4 million ha by GDRS.

In 1998, net 4.09 million ha area was opened for irrigation and 2.15 million ha of which constitutes the share opened for irrigation by DSI, 0.94 million by GDRS, and 1.00 million ha by public irrigations (Table 4).

Table 4. Share of Areas Opened to Irrigation According to Enterprise (DSI, 2002)

	Area opened for irrigation	
	Million ha (net)	%
DSI	2.15	53
GDRS	0.94	23
Farmers	1.00	24
Total	4.09	100

In Turkey, the government is spending most of its budget on constructing irrigation facilities. As the number of facilities operated by public institutions increases, funds spent on investment are decreasing. Although administration by the state is the preferred method, today, for most of the irrigation facilities, operation and maintenance activities are transferred to user organizations. Thus, lowering the repair and management costs can increase the budget for researching and developing new irrigation techniques. In Turkey, the user organizations which are responsible for operation and maintenance of irrigation facilities transferred to them by an agreement are irrigation unions, irrigation cooperatives, water user associations, village legal entities and municipalities.

Among the villages, municipalities, irrigation unions and universities to which the operation of irrigation facilities is transferred, irrigation unions are ranked first in terms of the size of the irrigated area they are responsible for. As of the end of 1997, the number of enterprises left to villages is 213, and this figure is 130 for municipalities, 250 for irrigation unions, 33 for cooperatives, and 3 for universities. The total area left constitutes 1,279,039 hectare, and the share of these institutions in the total area transferred is 2% for villages, 4% for municipalities, 3% for cooperatives, less than 1% for universities, and the remaining 91% is managed by irrigation unions. At the beginning of the 1980s, DSI was responsible for 25% of the total area.

In 1998, 406,281 ha constructed and opened for irrigation by DSI was irrigated by ground water. 400,481 ha out of these were operated by cooperatives and other organizations. Today, 1,428,681 ha of the net 1,748,637 ha irrigated by surface water are transferred to irrigation unions or to constructer enterprises in order to pay its construction costs. The area irrigated by DSI is 319,956 hectares.

D. MAJOR PROBLEMS

Today there are some problems associated with the development of water resources. They can be summarized as financial, technical, institutional and legislative problems. The fact that the Turkish population will have risen to 80 million by the year 2025 will result in a significant water scarcity. Increasing irrigation efficiency through investments in regions having less or irregular precipitation regimes will gain importance when it is considered that agriculture constitutes 73 % of the water use in the total general water consumption.

The government can not reserve money for investment because of the limited budget.

Irrigation facilities were suspended at the start up and took excessively long time to complete causing low economic returns on irrigation investments. Therefore, the participation of farmers must be encouraged so that they take responsibility on the operation of irrigation facilities.

Total irrigable land in Turkey was 25.85 million hectares but it has reached 28.06 million ha. This indicates that nonproductive areas are used for production. Since there is no planning for the use of lands, the unconscious use has risen and reached significant levels.

Although the total economically irrigable land of Turkey is 8.5 million hectares, only 53% of this amount can be irrigated. 33% of the surface water potential and nearly 49% of the underground water potential cannot be used.

But much of the problem lies in the inefficient use of water in agriculture. The public sector must consider this problem as a whole. Financial and technical assistance including public education, direct assistance, grants and loans must be given to farmers. Although this practice is applied in the GAP region, there are apparently some problems arising from the excessive use of water due to production technologies. The quantity of water needed by a crop during its growth period is significant, so there is a need to adopt new irrigation systems in these regions to eradicate problems such as Stalinization, erosion etc. associated with water use.

The only way to make farmers change their behavior is to educate them to adopt efficient irrigation practices. Besides, the structure of farm holdings in Turkey is small. Therefore, agricultural land drops the economic usage level.

There are some coordination problems among several organizations in the same area. Lack of coordination results in a significant number of unfinished irrigation and drainage schemes.

The current legislation cannot prevent the deterioration of water resources. Institutions are operating well enough in their own fields of expertise, but when it comes to collaboration with other organizations, there seems to be a confusion arising from laws and the distribution of responsibility. The responsibility for the operation and maintenance of irrigation facilities built by DSI is transferred to user organizations by agreement. However, the support and control of these organizations must be in accordance with legislation, and this must be solved as soon as possible.

E. SOUTH EAST ANATOLIA PROJECT (GAP)

Turkey has general problems in managing water resources. Therefore, Turkey started a water resources development program in the 1950s in order to ensure control and protection of water resources in a sustainable way. The investment in GAP is the most important example for this.

The main goal of the South East Anatolia Project is to increase income, standards of living, and efficiency and employment opportunities in rural areas in an integrated development project. The project area covers the Euphrates and Tigris Basins and 9 provinces, including Adiyaman, Batman, Diyarbakir, Gaziantep, Kilis, Mardin, Siirt, Sanliurfa and Sirnak (Figure 7.1). The total area of this region is 75,358 km^2 and it constitutes 9.7% of the total area of Turkey. GAP region encompasses 20% of the total 8.5 million ha of irrigable area in Turkey, and the large plains in the lower Euphrates and Tigris Basins. With the completion of this project, it is expected that a desert-like area bigger than Belgium, Denmark, Netherlands, Ireland and Luxemburg, 3 times bigger than Israel, half of Greece, 1/3 of England and ¼ of Italy, will change completely.

The GAP region has less precipitation fall compared to other regions of the country. Therefore, at the beginning it is planned that the project benefits from the potential of the Euphrates and Tigris rivers for irrigation and electricity production. However with the GAP Master Plan, it has turned into an integrated regional development project.

The cost of the project is 32 billion dollars, of which 12.5 billion dollars have been spent so far. GAP is composed of several sub projects such as the construction of 22 high dams and

19 hydroelectric generators. As of 2020, 1.7 million ha agricultural land will be opened for irrigated agriculture. This project is expected to become one of the nine biggest projects in the world. The GAP Project is expected to serve the Turkish economy significantly, not only in the agricultural industry, but also in the industry, construction and service sectors.

Figure 6.1. The GAP Region.

CONCLUSION

Water resources must be managed in a sustainable way so as to be secured for future generations, and ensure their development. In the scope of investments for developing land and water resources, a well planned system is also necessary. Not only must the demand for irrigation, but also wider aspects of water use be taken into account while about water resources.

For the rehabilitation of the irrigation network, which is old or has ended its economical life, new projects must be prepared and the participation of farmers must be ensured. The distribution of water must be realized in an efficient way and regions that have low precipitation regimes should be given priority in the provision of water. Quality controls must be utilized systematically, and data obtained on using recent technology must be examined and included in the projects. For this end, the conditions of the infrastructure should be improved.

In order to provide sustainable development, efficient production techniques must be developed, and the implementation of this technology at the farm level must be ensured so as to gain higher yields. Use of irrigable land for other purposes rather than agriculture must be prevented and necessary legislations must be brought into force. It should not be ignored that the development of land and water resources will result in new job areas.

SECTION III: LAND AND AGRICULTURE

In: The Economics of Natural and Human Resources…
Editor: Ayal Kimhi and Israel Finkelshtain

ISBN 978-1-60741-029-4
© 2009 Nova Science Publishers, Inc.

Chapter 7

A FINANCE APPROACH TO UNDERSTANDING PATTERNS OF LAND TENURE

Meir Kohn[*]

ABSTRACT

Economists and economic historians have generally understood different forms of land tenure as arrangements for the supply of labor. This paper suggests a different interpretation—that land-tenure arrangements be understood rather as arrangements for the supply of financing. The cost and availability of financing depend on the arrangements available to ensure the providers of the financing a fair return on their investment. The paper argues that the different forms of land tenure may best be understood in the context of such arrangements—as alternative ways of providing the family farm with the external financing that it requires. The discussion focuses on land-tenure arrangements in pre-industrial Europe, but the conclusions hold quite generally.

A. INTRODUCTION

Economists and economic historians have generally understood different forms of land tenure as arrangements for the supply of labor. They have interpreted them either in Marxist terms of power and class struggle between landowners and peasants or, more recently, in terms of a principal-agent problem with the landlord-employer as principal and the tenant-employee as agent (Dasgupta, Knight et al., 1999). I will suggest a different interpretation—that land-tenure arrangements be understood rather as arrangements for the supply of financing. Since my interest in the subject stems from my work on pre-industrial agriculture, the discussion will focus on land-tenure arrangements in Europe between the twelfth and eighteenth centuries. However, I believe that the conclusions hold quite generally.

---

[*] Dartmouth College, U.S.A.

The farmer, even when he did not own the land, was not an employee but rather the owner of an economic enterprise. He was an owner because he managed the enterprise—often employing hired labor himself—and because he received the residual income from the enterprise once all other payments had been made. The sole proprietorship or family firm was the typical form of economic enterprise in the pre-industrial economy—in industry and commerce as well as in agriculture. This was so because the incentive advantage of having the decision-maker bear fully the consequences of his own decisions generally outweighed any potential economies of scale that might have favored a larger or more complex form of organization.

Economic enterprises mostly finance themselves out of their own internal funds—the profits they themselves generate (Mayer, 1990). Sometimes, however, their need for funds is such that they are forced to turn to external sources of financing. The cost and the availability of external financing depend on the arrangements that can be found to ensure the providers of the financing with a fair return on their investment. I shall argue that the different forms of land tenure may best be understood in the context of such arrangements—as alternative ways of providing the family farm with the external financing that it required.

External financing, its difficulties, and the ways of addressing them are the subject matter of corporate finance. As its name suggests, this discipline concerns itself with the financing of the modern corporation. However its principles apply more generally and, as we shall see, its insights can be quite helpful in understanding the financing of preindustrial agriculture.

B. Financing Medieval Agriculture

Beginning in the twelfth century, and as a consequence of expanding trade and widening markets, European agriculture underwent a profound transformation. Access to markets created a strong incentive for the more efficient use of resources, and this induced a transition from manorial agriculture to an agriculture of family farms (Kohn, 2001). The family farm emerged as the most efficient form of organization because of the overwhelming incentive advantages of owner-management.[1]

Compared to contemporary enterprises in commerce and industry, enterprises in agriculture employed much larger amounts of fixed capital—especially, but not exclusively, land. In some cases, family farmers were able to finance the fixed capital they needed themselves. Most, however, required some form of external financing.

The external financing of fixed capital is usually long-term to match the income stream from the asset in question. Long-term financing is particularly subject to default, so it is normally secured—typically with the asset being financed. There are two ways to do this—the secured loan and the lease. With a secured loan, the asset is collateral for the loan: it belongs to the borrower but becomes the property of the lender in case of default. In contrast, with a lease the asset is and remains the property of the lender/lessor, who provides it to the borrower/lessee together with the financing in a single package. Both secured loans and leases were common in pre-industrial European agriculture.

---

[1] Hayami and Otsuka (1993) "This problem of incentives is considered a key to understanding the dominance of small-scale family farms in agriculture." p 5.

The principal form of secured loan was initially the mortgage. However, by the end of the twelfth century, legal and religious problems led to its displacement by the rente or census. With this instrument, an investor handed over a capital sum in exchange for the promise of an annuity, either for life or perpetual and heritable. Because the rente was considered a sale rather than a loan, it did not run afoul of the prohibition against usury. Moreover, as a sale, it was easier in case of default to seize the land posted as collateral (Kohn, 1999).

Rentes were used initially to finance the consumption of the landed classes and as an instrument of municipal finance. However, especially from the fifteenth century, they were used increasingly to finance investment in agriculture. They were widely employed for this purpose in the Low Countries, in Northern France, in Germany, and in Spain (Tracy, 1985).

The introduction of the lease was part of the restructuring of feudal agriculture into an agriculture of family farms. While a farmer leasing his land and a peasant holding his land under feudal tenure are both called 'tenants', the two situations were entirely different. Under feudal tenure, land was held in perpetuity, and was heritable subject to a quit-rent. In exchange, the tenant was obliged to provide labor and other servitudes as well as rent. In contrast, a lease had a limited term, it was a purely commercial contract, and it required the payment of a rent only. The limited-term lease first appeared in the twelfth century, and it was quite common in most parts of Western Europe by the thirteenth.

There were two types of lease. There were leases that called for a fixed rent (*bail à ferme* or *fitti*) and there were those that called for a share of the harvest (*bail à part de fruits* or, according to the size of the share, *métayage* or *mezzadria*). Initially, both fixed- rent and share leases were to be found wherever the limited-term lease appeared, but in most regions one or the other eventually came to predominate. The fixed-rent lease was the more common form in Northern France, the Low Countries, Western Germany, and the Po Valley. The share lease predominated in Western and Southern France and in Tuscany (Ganshof and Verhulst, 1966).

There were, then, three methods of providing external financing to the family farm— the secured loan (annuity), the fixed-rent lease, and the share lease. While all three methods saw use, one method rather than another would predominate in any particular time or place. To understand why, we need to understand the relative costs and benefits of the different forms of financing. The literature of corporate finance offers us some insights.

C. INSIGHTS FROM CORPORATE FINANCE

Two parts of that literature are of particular relevance—the part that examines the decision to lease or buy and the part that explores the relative merits of debt and equity financing.

C.1. Lease or Buy?

In considering the decision to lease or buy, let us begin by comparing a fixed-rent lease with a purchase financed with a secured loan (Smith and Wakeman, 1985, Krishnan and Moyer, 1994). Both are forms of debt, since each requires a series of fixed payments set in advance. What is characteristic of debt financing in general is that there is no upside: the best that can happen is that the debt is paid as promised. So the focus of lenders is naturally on the downside. What is the probability of default? What is its likely cost?

The cost of default is not only the unpaid debt, but also significant bother (transactions costs). First of all, what is to be done? Should the lender enforce the terms of the contract by forcing liquidation or seizing collateral? Or is it better to allow the borrower some slack in the hope of ultimately recovering more. If enforcement is the course chosen, there are the costs of gaining possession of assets and of liquidating them.

Comparing a lease and a secured loan, if the maturity of each is the same as the life of the asset being financed, then the only difference between them is in the nature of the security. In the case of the lease, because the asset belongs to the creditor rather than to the debtor, the cost of repossession is lower. Moreover, if the asset in question is in general demand and can easily be transferred to another lessee, the cost of default can be made quite low.[2]

So leasing will be preferred when the probability of default is relatively high. Firms that are more likely to suffer financial distress and those that are highly leveraged are the ones most likely to lease. In deciding whether to grant a lease, the lessor will focus on the ability of the asset to generate the cash flow needed to service the lease payments rather than on the credit history, assets, or capital of the potential lessee (International Finance Corporation, 1996).

In contrast, with a secured loan, the cost of default is relatively high even though it is secured. The lender will consequently look for potential borrowers that are less likely to default—those with a good credit history and adequate capital. In addition, the lender will usually demand 'overcollateralization' of the loan, requiring the borrower to finance a significant fraction of the asset out of his own funds.

If the life of the asset is longer than the maturity of the loan or lease, then there is an additional difference between the two forms of financing. When a loan matures, the residual value of the asset belongs to the borrower. When a lease matures, the residual value belongs to the lender/lessor. This difference has several implications.

With a loan, the borrower gains the use of the asset, just as he does with a lease of the same maturity. However, he receives in addition at the end of the loan the residual value of the asset. Since he must pay for this additional value over the life of the loan, his payments will be higher than they would be for an equivalent lease.[3] The lower payments on a leases effectively reduce leverage, reinforcing its suitability for less creditworthy borrowers.

If the useful life of an asset is significantly longer than the period over which a particular firm expects to employ it, and if the costs of transferring ownership are large, then leasing makes it easier to gain use of the asset and to dispose of it afterwards (Smith and Wakeman, 1985). The greater flexibility can be important, for example, when the amount of the asset a firm wishes to employ changes relatively frequently. A relatively short lease also provides the lessor with flexibility, making it easier to change the terms of the lease as market conditions change or to terminate a relationship with an unsatisfactory lessee.

A lease has one important disadvantage compared to secured lending when the useful life of the asset exceeds the maturity of the financing-a potentially serious moral hazard problem. Because the residual value of the asset does not accrue to him, as it does with a secured loan,

[2] While leasing is rare for assets that are highly firm-specific, specificity of the asset can actually benefit secured lending. See Mann (1997). The ability to switch the asset relatively easily from one lessee to another converts the risk of default from 'principal risk' to 'replacement risk'.

[3] The lower payments are the main reason why automobile leasing has become so popular in recent years.

the lessor has an incentive to plunder the residual value to his own benefit. Since the benefits of maintenance accrue largely to someone else, the lessee will tend to under-invest in maintenance. If it is possible to increase the current income from the asset at the expense of its residual value, the lessee will have an incentive to do so.[4] Mechanisms to deal with this problem, which I will call 'asset-stripping', may include detailed contractual constraints on the lessee, requiring the lessor rather than the lessee to be responsible for maintenance, and reputational constraints on the lessee when there is considerable repeat business.

C.2. Debt Versus Equity

Debt financing works best when there is little chance of default: whatever the security and the safeguards, default is costly. When the cost of default makes debt financing problematic, equity financing can be a solution.[5] With equity financing, the provider of financing receives a share of the residual income or profits of the enterprise rather than a set payment fixed in advance as with debt. There are two reasons why this arrangement may be preferable when the risk of default on debt would be significant. First, equity offers the provider of financing an upside to balance his downside risk: if the enterprise does well, he shares in the good fortune. Second, because of its built-in flexibility, equity avoids the dilemmas and the costs of default. The payment to the provider of the financing, rather than being fixed in advance, varies automatically according to the success of the enterprise.

Naturally, these benefits do not come without a cost. The built-in flexibility creates incentive problems. Because the recipient of equity financing has to share the residual income of the enterprise, he may slack. He may also increase the 'costs' of the enterprise to benefit himself at the expense of profits. There may be a serious problem, too, in measuring the profits that are to be shared.

To mitigate these incentive problems, the provider of equity financing generally obtains a degree of control over the ongoing management of the enterprise, something a provider of debt financing does not have. The combination of a claim to residual income and control over management makes the provider of equity financing a part owner of the enterprise.

Of course, exercising control is itself costly and it is unlikely to be entirely effective. Since the provider of equity financing must be compensated both for the cost of exercising control and for the consequences of its ineffectiveness, equity financing is typically expensive relative to debt. Consequently, enterprises generally seek equity financing only when debt financing is either very expensive or unavailable.

In comparing an equity (share) lease with a debt (fixed-payment) lease, the same advantages and disadvantages apply. In addition, the equity lease may offer an advantage with respect to the problem of asset-stripping. The degree of control over current management that goes along with equity financing provides the lessor with better means to defend his interests. Moreover, if asset-stripping takes the form of excessive current output at the expense of residual value, equity financing may mitigate the problem. If such 'over-production' requires greater effort on the part of the lessee, then the effort- reducing effect of

---

[4] "The more sensitive the value of asset to use and maintenance decisions, the higher the probability that the asset will be purchase rather than leased." Smith and Wakeman (1985)

[5] For example, the U.S. equity market emerged in the late nineteenth century as a response to the repeated defaults on railroad debt. See Baskin (1988).

equity may partly correct the distortion induced by the lease. Of course, boosting current output at the expense of residual value may involve different effort rather than more effort, and in this case equity financing will have no mitigating effect. But even here there is a silver lining: because the lessor receives a share of current profit, there is at least some compensation for the loss of residual value.

Let us now apply these ideas to understanding the pattern of financing of preindustrial agriculture. We begin with secured lending.

D. LEASE OR BUY IN PREINDUSTRIAL AGRICULTURE

Secured lending, mostly in the form of *rentes*, seems to have been used principally to finance improvements to land rather than for the purchase of land by family farmers. This may have been because of the significant overcollateralization that would have been required for such a loan. Since land is a very long-lived asset, its value is high relative to the current income that it generates. Consequently, financing the purchase of land would involve very high leverage with a correspondingly high risk of default unless there was significant overcollateralization. Family farmers who did not already own land may have lacked the equity capital for such a loan, or they may have preferred to lease land and put their equity into working capital.[6]

There is evidence of the use of secured lending to finance agricultural development and improvements in Flanders and Brabant from the thirteenth century, in Sicily from the fourteenth, and in France, Germany and Spain from the fifteenth.[7] Land developers, either reclaiming land or restructuring it into family farms, financed their projects by borrowing from urban investors against the future rents the new farms would generate. Individual farmers used well-developed local credit markets to finance improvements to their land such as drainage, buildings, or plantings of vines or fruit trees.

The market for rentes or censos, seems to have been particularly extensive in Spain: "...there is no reason to doubt Valle de la Cerda's statement in 1618 that there were in Spain over a hundred million ducats lent in ducados a censos." (Braudel, 1972) The sixteenth century transformation of Southern Spain from a producer of wheat to a producer of wine and olive oil was largely financed in this way. The borrowers in this case seem to have been substantial landowners rather than family farmers. The lenders were mainly urban investors.

E. DEBT VERSUS EQUITY IN THE LEASING OF LAND

As we have seen, the predominant form of land lease varied from region to region. In some, most leases were for fixed rent; in others, most were for a share of output. Historians have noted some regularities. The share lease was associated with certain kinds of lessee—

---

[6] In the United States in 1997, 79% of commercially farmed land was leased by the farmer rather than owned.

[7] On Flanders, see Thoen (1993) and Nicholas (1971); on Brabant, Germany, France and Spain Van der Wee (1993); on Sicily, Epstein (1998). The rente does not seem to have spread to Italy or to England.

those with relatively little capital.[8] It was associated with certain kinds of crop—vines, olives, and fruit trees.[9] And it was associated with certain kind of landlord—absentee urban landowners.[10] The insights of corporate finance can shed some light on these associations.

E.1. Leverage

While a fixed-rent lease reduced the likelihood and the cost of default compared to purchasing land with a secured loan, default remained an issue. Default was most probable when the farmer was highly leveraged—that is, when his capital was small relative to his contractual obligations. Then, any significant drop in income could leave him unable to pay his creditors.

To some extent, fixed-rent leases were designed to accommodate this possibility—especially if the cause of default was outside the control of the tenant. Landlords would, for example, assume the risks of damage due to invading armies or natural disasters.[11] However, when default was the result of a bad harvest, the landlord faced the familiar dilemma of how to proceed. This was especially true when it was hard to differentiate between bad luck and bad farming.[12] When the probability of default was high and it was difficult to attribute the cause, a fixed-rent lease was not a good solution.

Consequently, fixed-rent leases were generally offered only to tenants who had adequate capital of their own that would enable them to pay their rent even if the harvest was a poor one. On the whole, farmers in the North of Europe were wealthier, and this may explain the predominance of the fixed-rent lease there.[13] However, there were regions in the South too where prosperous farmers leased land for a fixed rent. For example, fixed rents seem to have been common from the fifteenth century in the vicinity of Milan where well-capitalized rural entrepreneurs engaged in intensive mixed agriculture (Epstein, 1998). They also seem to have been common in Sicily during the fifteenth century under similar circumstances (Epstein, 1991).

Where the rural population was relatively poor, often as a result of heavy taxation, the share lease predominated.[14] Not all share tenants, however, were poor: some owned substantial landed property of their own.[15] Nonetheless, such tenants may have been poor

---

[8] See, for example, Duby (1968), Galassi (1992), Hoffman (1984), Epstein (1994), Carmona and Simpson (1999), and Ackerberg and Botticini (2000).

[9] See, for example, on Tuscany Ackerberg and Botticini (2000), on Germany (Toch (1986)), on Catalonia Carmona and Simpson (1999), and on France (Hoffman (1984)).

[10] See, for example, Toch (1986), Jones (1966), Jones (1968), Galassi (1992).

[11] Nicholas (1971). Basu (1992) notes that in developing countries today, leases often allow for reduced rent if the weather fails or if the harvest is sufficiently poor.

[12] In early fifteenth century Tuscany there was a form of 'mixed contract' that allowed for the automatic conversion of fixed rents into shares in the event of a bad harvest. (Galassi (2000)). This obviously created a moral hazard problem, granting the tenant a 'put option' on his enterprise. Compared to a straightforward share lease, this arrangement deprived the lessor of the potential upside.

[13] "While the 'farmer' of the northern lands lived in affluence, most of the métayers of the Midi seemed to be wretched individuals settling on the lords' lands empty-handed and expecting immediate help in the shape of an advance of seed, provision of tools and even sometimes of food for their families during the first year." Duby (1968) p 327.

[14] On the role of taxation, see Epstein (1994) on Tuscany and Hoffman (1984) on France. For another example of the connection between poor tenants and sharecropping see Carmona and Simpson (1999).

[15] Galassi (2000). Share leases are not always associated with poverty. The share lease predominates in the modern U.S. Midwest, and the farmers concerned are by no means poor: see Allen and Lueck (1992).

candidates for a fixed-rent lease because their wealth was small relative to their obligations—that is, they were highly leveraged.

An indication that share tenants were, in fact, more highly leveraged than fixed-rent tenants is the difference between the two in the source of financing of non-land capital. Fixed-rent tenants generally financed their working capital either out of their own funds or by borrowing in the open market.[16] They often also themselves financed investment in non-land fixed capital such as livestock and buildings.[17] In contrast, it was usually the landlord who financed the non-land fixed capital of share tenants.[18] Landlords often financed working capital too. They might even offer a cash or grain advance to support the tenant and his family until harvest time (Touch, 1986). In some cases, lending by the landlord was secured by the tenant's share of the output.[19]

The degree to which leverage increased the risk of default depended on the variability of farm income. For some crops, such variability was particularly great. This could be a consequence both of variability in output and of volatility in market prices. Fluctuations in the output of wine of 60% were common and wine prices were notoriously volatile.[20] This may have been one reason why viticulture was associated with share leases. But wheat harvests were no less variable and wheat prices, too, were volatile. However, wheat does not seem to have had any particular association with sharecropping.

E.2. Asset-Stripping

Another reason that has been offered for the association of viticulture with sharecropping is the problem of asset-stripping. We have seen that if a lease is short relative to the life of the asset, the lessee has an incentive to increase current income at the expense of residual value.

Limited-term leases, when they were first introduced in the late twelfth century, were of relatively long duration—10, 20, or even 30 years. Over time, however, the typical duration seems to have fallen to something like five to seven years.[21] The reason for the shortening of duration may have been the greater ease of adjusting the rent.[22] Shorter leases also made it easier for landlords to rid themselves of bad tenants (Ganshof and Verhulst, 1966 and Galassi, 2000). Leases, although short, were typically renewed repeatedly with the same tenants, sometimes for decades or even generations (de Vries and van der Woude, 1997). Shortening

---

[16] For example, the farmers around Milan and in Sicily themselves financed the wages of their hired workers (Epstein (1998), Epstein (1991)).

[17] When the life of such assets exceeded the term of the lease, and if the lease was not renewed, the landlord was required to compensate them for their investment (de Vries and van der Woude (1997) Ch 5; Laven (1966) Ch. 1; Clay (1984)).

[18] Ganshof and Verhulst (1966), Jones (1968) "...the problem was not that credit was unavailable, but that it was largely unavailable to (poor) *sharecroppers*, who therefore had to resort to credit from their landlord." Epstein (1994) p 116 (italics in original)

[19] Epstein (1998) "the combined burden of debt and rent could also cause tenants to throw up their holdings, abscond, or default on their obligations." p 225.

[20] Galassi (2000) and Toch (1986) have argued this.

[21] This has been suggested, for example, by Jones (1968), Ganshof and Verhulst (1966).

[22] It is sometimes suggested that the frequent inflations of the period were why frequent adjustment was needed (e.g., Ganshof and Verhulst (1966)). However, payment of rents in kind was a more appropriate response to this particular problem: both fixed-rent leases and annuities (for which the problem was even more acute) were frequently paid in this way (Epstein (1994), Nicholas (1971)). Short leases were more useful as a way of adjusting to changing real prices.

the duration of the lease potentially exacerbated the asset-stripping problem. However, the customary renewal of the lease mitigated it, as did the threat of non-renewal. Reputational considerations constrained both tenants and landlords (Carmona and Simpson, 1999). Moreover, leases—fixed-rent and share alike—typically provided the landlord with safeguards. A lease is not only a financial contract: it is also an agreement that specifies the rights and responsibilities of the two parties with respect to the use of the asset (Smith and Wakeman, 1985 and Krishman and Moyer, 1994). Leases often specified permissible crops— excluding those that would exhaust the land as well as changes (such as conversion to arable) that would lower long-term productivity (Nicholas, 1971 and de Vries and van der Woude, 1997). Leases also specified the responsibilities of the tenant with respect to maintenance of non-land fixed capital. In some cases, it was the landlord who provided the maintenance (Nicholas, 1971 and Jones, 1968). To ensure compliance with the terms of the lease, the contract included penalty clauses and tenants were sometimes required to provide security in the form of collateral or third-party guarantees (Ganshof and Verhulst, 1966).

It has been suggested that an important reason for the adoption of the share lease was the superior protection it provided against asset-stripping, and that this explains its association with vineyards and orchards, which were particularly susceptible to this problem (Galassi, 1992 and Galassi, 2000). As we saw earlier, the superiority of the share lease (equity financing) in this respect comes from the greater right of intervention that it provides the landlord, compared to fixed rent (debt financing). It also comes, to some extent, from a closer alignment of interests between lessor and lessee. There are grounds, however, for doubting that this is the main reason for the connection between the share lease and viticulture.

First, it is not clear to what extent landlords exercised the enhanced right of intervention that a share lease offered them. The landlords in question were typically urban investors, for whom direct intervention would have been costly and not particularly effective. In the modern American Midwest, where share leases are also common in the leasing of land by absentee landlords, landlords do little or no monitoring (Allen and Lueck, 1992). Second, the share lease was the preferred form of lease in commercial viticulture in Catalonia from the late seventeenth century. There, however, the vines were planted and owned by the tenant and the leases were essentially perpetual, so the issue of asset-stripping did not arise (Carmona and Simpson, 1999). Third, share leases were especially common, not only in the leasing of vineyards, but also in the leasing of livestock (Jones, 1968 and Toch, 1986). In this case, too, because the duration of the lease is the same as the life of the asset, there is no asset-stripping problem.

E.3. The Difficulty of Measuring Output

As we saw earlier, one of the problems of equity financing is in measuring the profits that are to be shared with the provider of the financing. With a share lease, the tenant has an incentive to underreport the size and quality of output and, when dividing it, to keep the best for himself. Consequently, the share lease is better suited to crops that are more easily measured. Ease of measurement seems to be an important factor in explaining the use of fixed-rent versus share leases in the modern U.S. Midwest (Allen and Lueck, 1992). The share lease is common for land under wheat: wheat is sold at local elevators where quality and quantity are measured independently. The fixed-rent lease is more common for land under hay crops: the quality of hay is hard to assess and hay is usually sold by the farmer privately to individual buyers.

The problem of measuring output was no less important in preindustrial times if the many contemporary complaints about 'thieving sharecroppers' are to be believed (Galassi, 2000). It is notable that share leases were associated not only with the production of wine, but also with the cultivation of olives and mulberry trees and the raising of livestock (Hoffman, 1984). For these, as with wine, the output was sold commercially, making measurement easier. In the cultivation of grain, on the other hand, much was, or could be, consumed by the farmer and his family or sold quietly on the side.

E.4. The Role of Urban Investors

Let us turn now to the association of share leases with absentee urban landlords (Kohn, 2001). To understand this, it is important to realize that the commercialization of medieval agriculture was largely an urban phenomenon. It happened first in regions with good access to urban markets—those that neighbored cities and those with good transportation links to them, usually by water. And commercialization was often driven by urban entrepreneurs and investors, who bought up land and reorganized agricultural production.

Partly, the urban purchase of land was simply the exploitation of a significant economic opportunity. Agriculture was by far the most important sector in the economy, accounting for perhaps 80% of output and producing industrial raw materials and fuel as well as food. At the same time, in its manorial form, agriculture was highly inefficient. The potential profits from raising productivity were huge.[23] But there was another reason for the urban population to invest in land: it was an attractive asset. For a merchant seeking to diversify out of commerce or to provide for his retirement or for his family should he die, land was the best available choice. Compared to investments in commerce, it was safe and easy to manage. Investment in financial assets was often risky, and few such assets were available.[24] The importance of real estate as an asset is suggested by the Florentine *catasto* (tax assessment of wealth) of 1427. It found that the citizens of Florence, a financial center, held over half their wealth in real estate, compared to about a third in movable and commercial capital and a sixth in municipal debt (the principal financial asset available to them).[25] So, urban investors all over Europe, from the twelfth century, bought land. And, even when they did so principally as an investment, they could rarely resist seeking ways to increase their income from it. This meant reorganizing production.

Reorganizing production to raise productivity involved two fundamental changes in feudal arrangements. The first was a change in the terms of employment of labor. Land proved to be most productive when farmed, not by serfs, but by independent contractors— that is, by family farmers. The second change was the creation of units of land of a size

---

[23] "On many properties innovation of farm practice, the arrangement of holdings and the forms of peasant tenure, was the work not of landlords but of enterprising middlemen on the make." Jones (1966) p 418

[24] One financial asset that was attractive and that competed with land itself in the portfolios of urban investors was the *rente* secured by land.

[25] The catasto did not count a citizen's primary residence and furnishings since these were exempt from tax, so the proportion of real estate and movables was certainly higher than the numbers suggest. Neither did it count coin or bullion, presumably because these were easy to conceal, and these certainly made up a significant fraction of people's wealth.

suitable for a family farm. This was the size that would support a farmer—a specialized agricultural producer—at a level of income that would meet his opportunity cost: in regions close to cities, that meant the urban wage. When urban wages rose, the size of the farm had to grow. Urban investors created units of the right size either through consolidation of small holdings or the breaking up of large ones.[26]

As we have seen, family farmers generally required external financing of their fixed capital. Urban landowners and investors met this need with a number of financial innovations and adaptations. It was urban landowners who first introduced the limited-term lease. It was largely urban investors who purchased the rentes used to finance agricultural investment. And it was urban landowners who pioneered the use of share leases.

The share lease was, in fact, an adaptation of an existing equity contract well known to townsmen—the venture partnership or *commenda*. The *commenda* had been used to finance seaborne commerce since the twelfth century. Under this arrangement, one partner (the *stans*) financed the venture and the other (the *tractator*) traveled with the goods and traded them. The two then divided the profits.[27] The share lease was an adaptation of this contract to agriculture, with the urban landlord as *stans* and the farmer as *tractator*.

E.5. The Complete Story

Putting all these elements together, we have a possible explanation for the association of share leases with (a) farmers who possessed relatively little capital (b) the cultivation of vines and other commercial crops and (c) absentee urban landlords.

The reorganization of agriculture required the consolidation of land holdings into relatively large units—units large enough to meet the opportunity cost of the family farmer. The share lease made it possible for farmers with relatively little capital to take control of farms of this size without the impossibly high leverage that would have been implied by a fixed-rent lease.[28] Hence the association of the share lease with relatively poor tenants. The share lease was feasible, however, only if output could be measured at reasonable cost and with some reliability. Hence the association with commercial crops. It was urban investors who led the way in the reorganization of feudal agriculture into family farms. Hence the association with urban landlords.

This story is specific to a particular historical context and it does not necessarily fit all cases of sharecropping everywhere and at every time. However, one would expect two of its elements to be important in every case. The first is that the capital of the farmer is small relative to the value of the land in question—a fixed-rent lease in such a case involving excessive leverage.

The second element is that the crop is relatively easy to measure and divide. These two elements reflect the principal advantage of equity financing and its principal problem

---

[26] Kislev and Peterson (1982) explain the increasing size and mechanization of U.S. farms in the twentieth century as a consequence of the need to meet the opportunity cost of the farmer's labor as urban incomes rise. de Vries and van der Woude (1997) and Allen (1998) apply the same idea to preindustrial agriculture, arguing that the restructuring of land use was necessary to provide farmers with an income that would match high urban wages.

[27] For more on the commenda, see Kohn (1999).

[28] In northern Italy, and Tuscany in particular, mezzadria was associated with the growth of large, consolidated farms known as *poderi*. (Jones (1968), Epstein (1998)).

CONCLUSION

The literature on land tenure has generally viewed it in the context of a choice among three types of contract for the supply of labor—a wage contract, tenancy under a fixed rent, and sharecropping. In choosing among these alternatives, landlords are seen as facing a tradeoff between risk and monitoring costs. For example, one strand of the literature sees share-cropping as a way for wealthy, and so less risk-averse, landlords to attract poor, and so more risk-averse, workers by offering them a form of 'insurance' against income risk. Sharecropping offers lower monitoring cost than a wage contract and greater risk-sharing than a fixed rent.

Here, I have suggested a different context for the analysis of land tenure: still a choice among three types of contract, but this time not for the supply of labor but rather for the supply of external financing. The third alternative, to which fixed-rent and share leases are to be compared, is not a wage contract but a secured loan. Risk is important in the choice of contract, but it is not the income risk of the tenant that is the issue. Rather it is the risk of default.

Several authors have preceded me in rejecting the accepted approach and in setting tenure choice in the context of financing. Hoffman, in a study of land tenure in early modern France, cites a contemporary writer on agriculture, de Serres:

> "It was hard to find a reliable tenant who, while paying a fixed rent, would remain solvent, shoulder all the work and absorb 'at his own loss or profit' all the risks of the farm year. Given the difficulties of finding dependable tenants, de Serres recommended sharecropping for most absentee landlords. It would be easier to find a trustworthy share tenant, for he did not 'risk everything in advance,' and he was less likely to go bankrupt."[29]

In his more recent work, Hoffman has continued to stress the importance of credit in the rural economy and the role of sharecropping in mitigating the risk of default (Hoffman, 1996).[30] Another author who has set tenure choice in the context of financing is Epstein.[31] In his work on Sicily, he compared share contracts with other methods of financing agricultural production. In his work on Tuscany, he has argued for default risk in the presence of an impoverished peasantry as the explanation for sharecropping.[32] Allen, in his theoretical work on share contracts, has argued that they should be seen as a form of financing and that their principal advantage lies in reducing the probability of default (Allen, 1985).

I have attempted to develop these ideas a little further, bringing in the third alternative of a secured loan as a counterpoint to the two types of land tenure, and turning to corporate finance to illuminate the choice of alternative methods of financing. I hope that I have strengthened the case for thinking about forms of land tenure not as arrangements for the

---

[29] Hoffman (1984) p 312 citing Olivier de Serres, *Le Théâtre de l'agriculture* (Paris, 1600).
[30] pp. 68-9
[31] See Epstein (1991) on Sicily; Epstein (1994) on Tuscany.
[32] Another author who has rejected the standard approach is Reid (e.g., Reid (1987)). In his work on the U.S. South, he has placed less emphasis on financing, arguing that the principal virtue of sharecropping was that it assured the continuing cooperation of landlord and the farmer to assure a successful harvest. It was particularly important when the landlord was more knowledgeable than the tenant and could offer technical assistance as well as financing. This argument, too, has its echoes in corporate finance. The virtues that Reid attributes to

employment of labor but rather as arrangements for the provision of financing. The tenant-farmer, even if he did not own the land, was the owner of the agricultural *enterprise*. The landlord was not his employer but rather an investor who financed the agricultural enterprise while simultaneously supplying it with its major capital asset—the land.

REFERENCES

Ackerberg, D. A., and Botticini, M. (2000). The choice of agrarian contracts in Early Renaissance Tuscany: risk sharing, moral hazard, or capital market imperfections. *Explorations in Economic History, 37*, 241-257.

Ackerberg, D. A., and Botticini, M. (2000). Endogenous matching and the empirical determinants of contract form. Economics Department, Boston University, May.

Allen, D., and Lueck, D. (1992). Contract choice in modern agriculture: cash rent versus cropshare. *Journal of Law and Economics, 35* (2)(October), 397-426.

Allen, F. (1985). On the fixed nature of sharecropping contracts. *Economic Journal 95* (March), 30-48.

Allen, R. C. (1998). Urban development and agrarian change in early modern Europe. Department of Economics, University of British .

Baskin, J. B. (1988). The development of corporate financial markets in Britain and the United States 1600-1914: Overcoming asymmetric information. *Business History Review, 62* (Summer), 199-237.

Basu, K. (1992). Limited Liability and the Existence of Share Tenancy. *Journal of Development Economics, vol. 38* (no. 1) (January), 203-220.

Braudel, F. (1972). *The Mediterranean and the Mediterranean world in the age of Philip II.* New York: Harper and Row, p 425.

Carmona, J., and Simpson, J. (1999). The "Rabassa Morta" in Catalan Viticulture: The Rise and Decline of a Long-Term Sharecropping Contract, 1670s-1920s. *Journal of Economic History, vol. 59* (no. 2) (June), 290-315.

Clay, C. G. A. (1984). *Economic expansion and social change: England 1500-1700.* Cambridge: Cambridge University Press.

Dasgupta, S., et al. (1999). Evolution of Agricultural Land Leasing Models: A Survey of the Literature. *Review of Agricultural Economics, vol. 21* (no. 1) (Spring-Summer), 148-76.

de Vries, J., and van der Woude, A. (1997). *The First Modern Economy: Success, Failure, and Perseverance of the Dutch Economy, 1500-1815.* Cambridge, UK: Cambridge University Press.

Duby, G. (1968). *Rural economy and country life in the medieval West.* Columbia, University of South Carolina Press.

Epstein, S. R. (1991). *An island for itself : economic development and social change in late medieval Sicily.* Cambridge [England] ; New York, Cambridge University Press.

Epstein, S. R. (1994). Tuscans and their farms. *Revista di Storia Economica, Vol. 11*, 111-123.

Epstein, S. R. (1998). The peasantries of Italy, 1350-1750. In T. Scott (Ed.). *The Peasantries of Europe from the Fourteenth to the Eighteenth Centuries.* London: Longman.

---

sharecropping are very much like those of private equity—venture capital, for example. There, too, the provider of equity financing provides more than just funds.

Galassi, F. L. (1992). Tuscans and Their Farms: The Economics of Share Tenancy in Fifteenth Century Florence. *Rivista di Storia Economica, S.S. 9* (1-2), 77-94.

Galassi, F. L. (2000). Moral hazard and asset specificity in the Renaissance: the economics of sharecropping in 1427 Florence. *Advances in Agricultural Economic History, Vol 1*, 177-206.

Ganshof, F. L., and Verhulst, A. (1966). Medieval agrarian society in its prime: France, the Low Countries and Western Germany. In Postan, M. M., and Habakkuk, H. J. (Eds.) *The Cambridge economic history of Europe 2nd ed.. v. 1. The agrarian life of the Middle Ages.* Cambridge, UK: Cambridge University Press.

Hayami, Y., and Otsuka, K. (1993). *The economics of contract choice : an agrarian perspective.* Oxford, EN: Clarendon Press.

Hoffman, P. T. (1984). The Economic Theory of Sharecropping in Early Modern France. *Journal of Economic History, Vol.* 44 (June), 309-19.

Hoffman, P. T. (1996). *Growth in a traditional society : the French countryside, 1450-1815.* Princeton: Princeton University Press.

International Finance Corporation (1996). *Leasing in Emerging Markets.* Washington, DC: IFC.

Jones, P. (1966). Medieval agrarian society in its prime: Italy. *The Cambridge economic history of Europe 2nd ed.. v. 1. The agrarian life of the Middle Ages.* M. M. Postan and H. J. Habakkuk, eds. Cambridge, Cambridge U. P.

Jones, P. J. (1968). From manor to mezzadria: A Tuscan case study in the medieval origins of modern agrarian society. In Rubinstein N. (Ed.), *Florentine studies: politics and society in Renaissance Florence.* London: Faber.

Kislev, Y., and Peterson, W. (1982). Prices, Technology, and Farm Size. *Journal of Political Economy, Vol 90* (No. 3) (June), 578-95.

Kohn, M. (1999). The capital market before 1600. Department of Economics, Dartmouth College.

Kohn, M. (2001). The Expansion of Trade and the Transformation of Agriculture in Pre-Industrial Europe. Department of Economics, Dartmouth College, January.

Krishnan, V. S., and Moyer, R. C. (1994). Bankruptcy Costs and the Financial Leasing Decision. *Financial Management, vol. 23* (No. 2) (Summer), 31-42.

Laven, P. (1966). *Renaissance Italy, 1464-1534.* London: Batsford.

Mann, R. J. (1997). Explaining the pattern of secured credit. *Harvard Law Review, Vol.* 625, 639.

Mayer, C. (1990). Financial systems, corporate finance, and economic development. In Hubbard, R.G. (Ed.), *symmetric Information, Corporate Finance, and Investment.* Chicago: University of Chicago Press, 307-332.

Nicholas, D. (1971). *Town and countryside: social, economic and political tensions in fourteenth-century Flanders.* Brugge: De Tempel.

Reid, J. D., Jr. (1987). The Theory of Sharecropping: Occam's Razor and Economic Analysis. *History of Political Economy, Vol. 19* (No.4) (Winter), 551-69.

Smith, C. W., Jr., and Wakeman, L. M. (1985). Determinants of Corporate Leasing Policy. *Journal of Finance, Vol. 40,* (No. 3) (Jul.), 895-908.

Thoen, E. (1993). The Count, the countryside and the economic development of the towns of Flanders from the eleventh to the thirteenth century: some provisional remarks and hypotheses. In Aerts et al (Eds.), *Studia historica oeconomica: liber amicorum.* Leuven, Belgium, Universitaire Pers Leuven.

Toch, M. (1986). Lords and peasants: A reappraisal of the medieval economic relationships. *The Journal of European Economic History, Vol. 15*, 163-82.

Tracy, J. D. (1985). *A Financial Revolution in the Hapsburg Netherlands: Renten and Renteniers in the County of Holland, 1515-1565*. Berkeley : University of California Press.

Van der Wee, H. (1993). *The Low Countries in the Early Modern World*. Aldershot: Variorum.

In: The Economics of Natural and Human Resources...　　ISBN 978-1-60741-029-4
Editor: Ayal Kimhi and Israel Finkelshtain　　© 2009 Nova Science Publishers, Inc.

Chapter 8

LAND ALLOCATION AND MAIZE PRODUCTIVITY IN ZAMBIAN SMALL-AND MEDIUM-SIZE FARMS: EVIDENCE FROM MICRO-DATA

Ayal Kimhi and Dennis Chiwele[*]

ABSTRACT

The objective of this paper is to identify factors which limit the ability of Zambian farmers to increase Maize productivity and/or diversify their crop mix. Both may enable wealth accumulation, investments, and further expansion. Specifically, we link variations in agricultural decisions, practices, and outcomes, to variations in the tightness of the different constraints. We model crop production decisions as having recursive structure. Initially, farmers decide on land allocation among the different crops, based on their information set at planting time. Then, as new information (weather, market conditions) is revealed, farmers can change output by influencing the yield. This recursive structure enables to separate the effects of the constraints on the different stages of production.

We therefore conduct estimation in two stages: we first estimate the fraction of land allocated to Maize as a dependent variable that is censored from below and from above, so that its predicted value is necessarily between zero and one. The yield of Maize is estimated in the second stage as a linear function of calculated land allotment (to avoid simultaneity bias) and the other state variables. Environmental and demographic variables also serve as explanatory variables in each stage. The first-stage results indicate that crop diversification can be promoted by rural road construction, developing markets for agricultural products, increasing the availability of seeds, draught animals, and farm machines, increasing women's farm work participation, and increasing the size of landholdings. Specialization in Maize can be promoted by increasing the availability of credit, fertilizers, hired permanent workers, and irrigation knowledge, and improving the timeliness of input delivery. The second-stage results show that the yield of Maize is inversely related to the area of Maize cultivated and to the operator's age, and is lower in female-headed farm households. Maize productivity can be improved by increasing the availability of seeds, fertilizers, labor, draught animals, machines, and credit.

---

[*] Ayal Kimhi is with the Agricultural Economics Department, The Hebrew University, Rehovot, Israel. Dennis Chiwele is with the Economic and Social Research Unit, University of Zambia, Lusaka, Zambia. This research was financed in part by GIFRID, the German-Israeli Fund for Research and International Development.

A. INTRODUCTION

Zambia has vast natural and land resources that make her well positioned for agricultural development. Only 16% of an estimated 9 million hectares suitable for agriculture are regularly cultivated while only 6% of 2.5 to 3 million hectares of irrigable land are actually irrigated (Chipembe, 1990). Most parts of the country receive adequate rainfall for the production of arable crops despite reoccurrence of droughts in recent years. And yet Zambian agriculture suffers from constraints that make it fail to utilize its potential. This is shown in agriculture's low contribution to GDP (about 20%) despite employing 60% of the labor force; in the sector's growth rate averaging less than the population growth rate; and in the high food imports which make up as much as 11% of total imports during drought years. At the same time, agriculture's contribution to exports has been far lower than its potential although significant improvements have occurred in the 1990s.

Since the early 1980's, there has been no evidence of increase in national average crop yields per hectare (Institute for African Studies, 1996). Yields have noticeably reduced in the 1990s due to exceptionally low levels of precipitation. The problem has been worsened by the sharp fall in the use of modern farm inputs such as fertilizer and hybrid seeds. These declined slightly between the early 1980's and the late 1980's. The decline was very marked thereafter and has been attributed to macroeconomic and agricultural sector policy changes, particularly the removal of subsidies on farm inputs which resulted in a sharp increase in their prices. A cut back on cheap credit made it difficult for farmers to purchase inputs as before. As a result of reliance on simple farm implements and poor farming practices by small and medium farmers, labor productivity is very low with only 0.52 hectares per farm worker being cultivated on average between 1983/84 and 1995/96 agricultural seasons. The situation in the 1990s has been worsened by the major declines in cattle (and hence oxen) population with the total number in 1993/94 at 0.74 million, less than half the 1983/84 peak of 1.88 million. Only 13% of farm households owned cattle in 1993/94, down from 20% in 1991/92.

There have been two main consequences of these declining and stagnating trends. First, farm incomes have declined, thereby worsening rural poverty. Farm incomes showed some signs of improvement in the 1980s as a result of price and subsidy policies but declined rapidly since the removal of these policies. Second, due to year-to-year variations in output for both maize and other food crops, the food security situation has deteriorated. It is clear, therefore, that a technological revolution in Zambian agriculture is required in order achieve two goals: (a) expand the land brought under cultivation and thereby maximize Zambia's advantage as a land surplus country; and (b) raise land and labor productivity.

In order to achieve these goals, it is crucial to identify the major constraints facing Zambian farmers. Previous studies have analyzed several different constraints. For example, Holden (1993) cites the highly imperfect labor markets as the main problem in Zambian agriculture, while in the study of Jha and Hojjati (1993), credit seems to be the most limiting factor. Foster and Mwanaumo (1995) claim that "more emphasis is needed on support systems such as extension education, agricultural research, infrastructure, and marketing." They are all probably right, since all these limitations are interrelated. Modern inputs such as chemical fertilizers, hybrid seed varieties, and irrigation equipment, which are necessary for increasing labor productivity, require credit for their purchase, rural roads for their transport, and extension services for their implementation. The labor shortage can be overcome in part by increasing farm incomes so as to pull labor from other sectors, by changing the crop mix, or by shifting cropping activities to off-peak seasons (which in turn can only be achieved through irrigation).

The question is what are the most important constraints and how does each constraint affect production decisions, which in turn affect the area brought under cultivation and the yield levels that farmers obtain. In the 1995 Crop Forecast Survey conducted by the Central Statistical Office in Zambia, farmers were asked to indicate the major constraint for increasing production. 55% indicated shortage of funds for buying inputs, 27% indicated shortage of fertilizers, 14% indicated shortage of labor, 9% indicated shortage of improved seed varieties and 10% indicated late delivery of inputs.[1] It seems that farmers view shortage of credit as the major constraint, but it is not at all clear that its alleviation will have the greatest impact on production and productivity. It could be that many farmers are not even aware of the potential benefits of irrigation or improved seed varieties, for example. Therefore, a quantitative study of the impact of these and other constraints is needed.

The purpose of this study is to identify factors which could be influenced by policy makers in order to improve the situation of Zambian farmers on two fronts: diversifying the crop mix and increasing crop yields. Improvements in these fronts will naturally increase labor productivity and will lead to increasing land under cultivation. Our approach is to link variations in agricultural decisions, practices, and outcomes, to variations in the tightness of the different constraints. We specifically differentiate between the effect on planting decisions and the effect on the final outcome (yield). This is because of the high uncertainty prevailing in large parts of rural Zambia not only with regard to input availability and prices, but also with regard to rainfall. As more information is collected during the growing season, farmers may still change their cultivation practices accordingly.

Our analytical framework is based on the McGuirk and Mundlak (1992) framework, which relies on the recursive nature of decisions on a farm: "...Initially, farmers decide, given information at planting time, how to allocate land among different crops. Farmers then can change output only by influencing yield" (pp. 133). This recursive structure of crop production decisions is used to solve a common problem in standard estimation of production functions, that inputs of production cannot serve as explanatory variables in a yield regression. In our case, land allocation is instrumented by its determinants, given appropriate exclusion restrictions. The recursive structure also enables us to separate the effects of the various constraints on the different stages of production. For example, availability of improved seeds will likely affect the decision how much land to allocate to a certain crop, while availability of fertilizer, if not known in advance, will likely affect the yield.

Specifically, estimation will be conducted in two stages: we will first estimate equations describing the land allocated to each crop as a function of the state variables known to farmers at planting time. Between planting and harvest, farmers choose the levels of other inputs given the land allocation and perhaps other state variables that are revealed only after planting. Therefore, the yield of each crop will be estimated in the second stage as a function of calculated land allocations (to avoid the simultaneity bias) and the new vector of state variables. The estimated coefficients of the model can be used to evaluate the changes in the land allocation patterns and crop yields that can be attained by relaxing each of the constraints. Thereby the most important constraints can be identified. We start in the next

---

[1] Note that farmers were allowed to indicate more than one major constraint.

section with a more detailed description of the structure of Zambian agriculture, which is important for understanding our choice of data and methods. The analytical framework is described in the subsequent section, followed by a description of the data and empirical specification, results, and conclusions.

B. THE STRUCTURE OF AGRICULTURE IN ZAMBIA

Crops account for more than 60% of the total agricultural output in Zambia. The proportion of cultivated area devoted to different crops has varied little in the last decade, and is dominated by maize cultivation, which accounts for about 54.3%. Cereals other than maize (millet, sorghum and rice) account for 12.7%, oilseeds (groundnuts, sunflower and soybeans) - 13%, cassava - 13.1%, and other crops, mostly cash crops, 6.6%. The changed policies of recent years (removal of production and marketing subsidies) and the introduction of seasonal and regional pricing policy have made maize relatively unprofitable, particularly for farmers in remote areas. In addition, the climatic conditions have shown the susceptibility of maize to droughts. Hence, a challenge facing Zambian agriculture is the diversification into cash (preferably high value) crops and other food crops which tend to be more drought resistant.

Zambia's agricultural sector is divided into three categories, the commercial, medium-, and small-scale sub-sectors, on the basis of the technologies applied (Government Republic of Zambia, 1994). Commercial farmers are characterized by extensive mechanization, use of modern technology and management, rear mostly exotic breeds of livestock and rely heavily on hired labor. They number less than 1,500 and are concentrated in the narrow corridor of the line-of-rail. Small-scale farmers, on the other hand, depend mostly on hand-hoe cultivation and unpaid family labor, and use little of modern farm inputs which, when used, consist mostly of chemical fertilizer and hybrid seeds on maize cultivation. There are about 600,000 farm households classified as small-scale farmers. Medium-scale farmers, also called emergent farmers, who number about 100,000 farm households, fall in between these two categories but are mostly distinguished by their use of animal power. This is a transitional phase prior to commercial farming.

Small- and medium-scale farmers contribute between 40% and 60% of agricultural output. Crops constitute about 80% of their production, while livestock, which contributed around 30% in the mid-eighties, has significantly declined due to the animal losses of the 1990s. They produce most of the food crops, i.e. maize, sorghum, millet, cassava, groundnuts, and mixed beans. The commercial sub-sector produces almost all of the wheat, 80%-85% of the soybeans, up to 75% of the Virginia tobacco, almost all of the coffee and all the horticultural crops for export. The crop yields in the small- and medium-scale sub-sectors are low and usually about half of those in the commercial sub-sector. As a result of the differences in the crop mix and yields, the difference in the value of output between commercial and small- and medium-scale farmers is remarkable.

The farming systems applied in the small- and medium-scale farming vary from location to location and have been historically shaped by agro-ecological zones grouped into three main ones with 36 sub-zones. Zone I includes the main valleys of Zambia such as the Luangwa in the east and the Gwembe in the south. It is characterized by low rainfall, short growing season, high temperatures during the growing season, and a high risk of drought.

Zone II, whose climatic conditions fall in between Zones I and III, covers the central parts of the country. Zone III is in the north and encompasses Northern, Luapula, Copperbelt and Northwestern Provinces. It is a high-rainfall area with a long growing season, low probability of drought, and cooler temperatures during the growing season. There are great variations in the agronomic features within and between the three zones which makes it possible to grow a wide range of crops.

Variation in rainfall from one year to another has been an important determinant of the year-to-year changes in output. In the 1990s, there has been a reoccurrence of droughts, more than in any other decade this century, which has devastated harvests in some years and exposed the vulnerability of small- and medium-scale farmers to variations in rainfall patterns. During the 1991/92 season, which had the worst drought in many decades, rainfall averaged 375.5 millimeters and 615.3 millimeters in Zones I and II respectively. Zone III recorded 971.5 millimeters. If this pattern persists into the future, Zone III, which includes the majority of agricultural land reserves in Zambia, will become the most reliable for agricultural production. However, soils in Zone III tend to be highly acidic and hence less fertile than in Zone II. This problem can be rectified by the use of lime, but this requires an expenditure which few small farmers are able to meet. Unless an aggressive liming program is introduced, the relatively better performance of Zone III cannot be sustained.

C. ANALYTICAL FRAMEWORK

Assume that the production function for the j'th crop is $y_j = F_j(x_j, k_j, e)$, where y is quantity of output, x is a vector of quantities of variable inputs, k is a vector of quantities of quasi-fixed inputs, and e is a vector of environmental variables (constraints, policy, weather, soil type, location, etc.). The farmer's objective in the short run is to maximize the farm's net cash flow: $R = \sum p_j y_j - w \sum x_j$, over choices of x_j and k_j, subject to the constraints on the availability of the quasi-fixed inputs $\sum k_j = K$, where p is the vector of output prices, w is a vector of variable input prices, and K is a vector of total farm-level quantities of quasi-fixed inputs. "Short run" means that K is given in a certain year. If all relevant information is known prior to planting, the results of farmer's optimization are vectors of input demands $x_j(p,w,e,K)$, $k_j(p,w,e,K)$ and output supplies $y_j(p,w,e,K)$.

Alternatively, assume that at the time of planting, the farmer has a partial information set s_1, including last year's prices, early weather conditions and forecasts, other environment variables, and K or parts of it. Hence, planting decisions, i.e. land allocated to each crop (land is assumed to be one of the quasi-fixed inputs), are made according to this information set only, and the land allocated to crop j can be specified as $a_j(s_1)$. After planting, more information is revealed, such as current prices and weather, additional elements of e and K, and of course the vector of land shares a. All these in addition to the previous information, are included in the new information set, s_2. Based on the new information set, farmers choose levels of other inputs: $x_j(s_2)$, $k_j(s_2)$.

If production exhibits constant returns to scale in all inputs, then output can be expressed as a product of land input and yield: $y_j = a_j Y_j(x_j, k_j)$, where Y (yield) is crop output per unit of land. Since the allocation of inputs to crops is not observed, we can substitute optimal inputs into the yield functions: $Y_j(s_2) = Y_j[x_j(s_2), k_j(s_2)]$. This specification leads to the following two-stage estimation procedure. In the first stage one estimates the land allocation equations $a_j(s_1)$. The yield equations $Y_j(s_2)$ are estimated in the second stage, after substituting the calculated value (from the first stage) of a_j in s_2, to avoid simultaneity bias. We will return to the empirical specification of these equations after the presentation of the available data in the next section.

D. DATA AND DESCRIPTIVE STATISTICS

In the survey mentioned in section 1 above, farmers were asked to indicate the major constraint for increasing production. They were also asked about their access to particular services such as extension, credit and marketing channels, and about their irrigation practices. The data set includes 7269 observations, 87% of which are defined as "small-scale farmers" and the other 13% are defined as "medium-scale farmers." The survey was matched to the 1993/4 post-harvest survey in which input-output data were collected in detail, and from which knowledge of and access to modern production techniques such as improved seed varieties and chemical fertilizers can be inferred. The post-harvest survey included 6469 farms. This data set was checked for consistency of the cropping information by checking whether a farmer who indicated that he grows a certain crop also reports a positive amount of land allocated to that crop. 5903 farms (91%) passed this test for all crops reported. The two data sets were then merged, resulting in 5329 matched observations (90% of the consistent observations in the post-harvest survey). Some other observations were excluded due to missing explanatory variables. The estimation procedure eventually used 5280 observations. Table 1 includes definitions of variables used in the analysis and their sample means.

The major crop in these farms is maize, which is grown by 84% of the farmers in the merged data set, and accounts for 78% of the cultivated land in the farms that do grow maize, and 65% overall. Hence, we have decided to concentrate on maize. We have tried to repeat the analysis for several other crops, but the results were not satisfactory and will not be reported here.

Quantitative variables include age, land used for field crops and for maize, yield of maize, number of permanent farm workers, number of male and female family members employed on the farm, number of draught animals, fraction of loans approved and received, total credit received, amount of chemical fertilizer and seeds, total wages paid to hired workers, and number of animal-drawn implements. The amounts of land, credit, fertilizer, seeds, implements, and family and hired workers are considered as quasi-fixed inputs, whose quantity is given in the short run. Fraction of loans approved and received serve as proxies for credit constraints.[2] Indexes of maize suitability and land acidity, average annual rainfall, monthly rainfall as a fraction of the average amount of rainfall in each month of the planting season, and actual monthly rainfall in the months following the planting season are also included. All these are district-level variables.[3]

---

[2] The problem is that loan applications may depend on credit constraints if farmers are aware of those in advance.
[3] Rainfall data were not available for all districts. Especially problematic were the 1993/94 rainfall statistics, which were available for about 57% of the farms only. We used dummy variables to control, at least in part, for the missing data.

Qualitative variables include sex and levels of schooling, distance to nearest road, access and distance to output market, exposure to extension services through direct and indirect channels, major constraints on increasing farm production, an irrigation dummy and the reasons for not irrigating, dummies for loan applications from agricultural financial institutions or other sources, and land accessibility. The distance variables enable us to measure the effect of infrastructure.

Table 1. Variables used in the estimation

Name	Description	Mean
land	total land used for seasonal field crops (Hectares)	1.780
maizelan	fraction of land used for maize	0.654
maizeyld[a]	yield of maize (100 kg/Hectare)	1.420
sex	1=female head of household	0.212
age	age of head of household (years)	44.89
primary	1=head of household has primary education	0.600
higher	1=head of household with higher than primary education	0.188
distrd5	1=nearest road is more than 5 kilometers away	0.179
outputd	1=household has access to output markets	0.726
output20+	1=distance to nearest output market is more than 20 kilometers	0.116
advice (Q8)	1=received advice directly from an extension worker	0.271
group (Q9)	1=member of a village extension group	0.135
demonstA	1=attended an extension demonstration as a participant	0.064
demonstB	1=attended an extension demonstration as an observer	0.067
radio	1=listen to agricultural programs on the radio	0.412
consfund[b]	1=major constraint on farm production is lack of funds	0.566
consseed[b]	1=major constraint on farm production is inavailability of seeds	0.083
consfert[b]	1=major constraint on farm production is inavailability of fertilizer	0.257
conslab[b]	1=major constraint on farm production is inavailability of labor	0.129
constinp[b]	1=major constraint on farm production is late delivery of inputs	0.135
consoth[b]	1=major constraint on farm production is "other"	0.208
irrigat	1=some of the land is irrigated	0.117
noirknow	1=not irrigating more due to lack of knowledge	0.294
noirfund	1=not irrigating more due to lack of funds for equipment	0.263
noirwatr	1=not irrigating more due to lack of water sources	0.277
hired[c]	number of permanent hired workers	0.032
familyM	number of male family members employed on the farm	1.770
familyF	number of female family members employed on the farm	1.890
draught	number of draught animals used on the farm	0.544
loans2a	1=applied for loans from agricultural financial institutions	0.182
loans2b+	1=applied for loans from non-agricultural financial institutions	0.040
approv%	fraction of loans approved	0.167
receiv%[a]	fraction of loans received	0.203
credit[a]	amount of credit received (10000 Kwacha)	3.410
tchem[a]	total amount of chemical fertilizers used (100 kg)	2.550
tseed[a]	total amount of seeds used (100 kg)	0.200

Table 1. (continued)

Name	Description	Mean
tvwage[a]	total amount of wages paid (1000 Kwacha)	6.020
machines	number of animal-drawn implements	0.596
access2	1=land accessibility is at degree 2 (second highest)	0.119
access34	1=land accessibility is at lowest degrees	0.063
msuit	maize suitability index	2.980
acidity	land acidity level	3.630
totrain	average annual rainfall (in mm, last six years)	889.0
missrain	1=missing average annual rainfall data	0.171
rrain7	rainfall in July 1993 relative to average July rainfall	0.067
rrain8	rainfall in August 1993 relative to average August rainfall	0.450
rrain9	rainfall in September 1993 relative to average September rainfall	0.936
rrain10	rainfall in October 1993 relative to average October rainfall	0.108
rrain11	rainfall in November 1993 relative to average November rainfall	1.540
rrain12	rainfall in December 1993 relative to average December rainfall	0.748
rain1	rainfall in January 1994	245.0
rain2	rainfall in February 1994	149.0
rain3	rainfall in March 1994	46.70
rain4	rainfall in April 1994	27.90
rain5	rainfall in May 1994	0.300
missr93/4	1=missing 1993/94 rainfall data	0.427

a. based on the 3973 "clean" observations who reported maize output.
b. farmers could indicate more than one major constraint on farm production.
c. only 76 farms had permanent hired farm workers, among them the average was 1.64.

The extension variables show that 41% of the farmers listen to agricultural programs on the radio, 27% received advice directly from an extension worker, 13% are members of a village extension group, and another 13% attended an extension demonstration, either as participants or as observers. The importance of extension services to farm productivity can be examined by looking at the effects of these variables on the yield of maize. The single most quoted constraint on increasing production is lack of funds, and only second comes inavailability of fertilizer. The third place is shared by late delivery of inputs and inavailability of labor, and last comes inavailability of seeds. Many farmers indicated that there is a different major constraint but did not indicate what it was. These variables tell us which farmers can benefit from the alleviation of each constraint. The irrigation variables show that less than 12% of the farmers irrigate their fields. There is no single major reason for not irrigating, but the reasons can tell us which farmers can benefit from increased knowledge, increased loan availability, or water projects in general.

E. EMPIRICAL SPECIFICATION AND ESTIMATION PROCEDURE

The share of land devoted to maize out of the total land used for seasonal field crops is used as the dependent variable in the first stage regression. As any share variable, it is restricted to be between zero and one. Figure 8.1 shows the distribution of this variable. We see that many observations are concentrated in the limits of the distributions. These are farms which do not grow maize at all, and those who do not grow any field crops other than maize. As a result, we cannot treat the dependent variable as a continuous variable. Alternatively, we assume the existence of a latent continuous variable describing the amount of land that the farmer would have liked to devote for maize, divided by the total land which is available for field crops. Denote this unobserved variable as S^*, and denote the observed dependent variable as S. Then S is derived from S^* as a double-censored transformation according to

$$S = S^* - S^* \, 1(S^* < 0) + (1 - S^*) \, 1(S^* > 1) \qquad (1)$$

where 1() is the indicator function. Assuming that S^* is distributed normally conditional on a set of explanatory variables enables to use the double-censored Tobit model for estimation. Assuming further that $E(S^*) = X\beta$ where X is the matrix of explanatory variables and β is a corresponding vector of coefficients, the likelihood function of the model is

$$\mathrm{p}[1 - F(X\beta/s_s)] \quad \mathrm{p}f[(Y - X\beta)/s_s]/s_s \quad \mathrm{p}[1 - F[(1 - X\beta)/s_s]] \qquad (2)$$

$$\quad S=0 \qquad\qquad 0<S<1 \qquad\quad S=1$$

where F and f are the cumulative distribution function and the probability density function, respectively, of a standard normal random variable, and s_s is the conditional standard deviation of S^*.

An alternative to the estimation procedure above would be to use a nonlinear regression specification that will force the calculated values to be between zero and one. Such an alternative was proposed by Papke and Wooldridge (1996). They suggest that the expectation of the fractional dependent variable S, conditional on the vector of explanatory variables X, be specified as a nonlinear function $G(X\beta)$, where β is a vector of coefficients. As natural candidates for the function G they suggest simple cumulative distribution functions such as the logistic function $G(X\beta)=\exp(X\beta)/[1+\exp(X\beta)]$. Whereas the nonlinear least squares method seems to be the obvious estimation procedure for this case, it could be problematic in the likely case of heteroscedasticity. As an alternative, they propose a quasi-likelihood method, in which the log-likelihood function is

$$S\cdot\log[G(X\beta)]+(1-S)\log[1-G(X\beta)]. \qquad (3)$$

The resulting quasi maximum likelihood estimator is consistent and asymptotically normal regardless of the true distribution function of S conditional on X. The two likelihood functions (2) and (3) were maximized using procedures included in the Gauss software package. The results are reported in the next section.

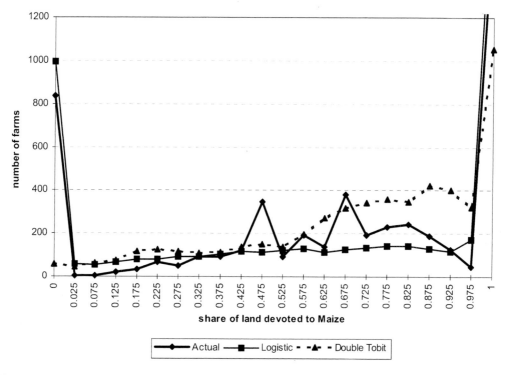

Figure 8.1. Distributions of Actual and Predicted Values.

In the second stage we want to estimate an equation describing the yield of Maize. Clearly, we can only use observations on households who were actually involved in Maize cultivation.

To the extent that the decision to grow Maize and the yield of Maize are correlated due to, say, unobserved farm characteristics, one cannot estimate the yield equation without correcting for selectivity.

We correct for selectivity using the Heckman (1979) procedure. First we specify the expected value of the yield Y as a linear function of land and other explanatory variables Z, $E(Y) = SL + W\alpha$ where L is the total land devoted to field crops, and α is a vector of coefficients.

Then we assume that Y and S^* are jointly normally distributed, conditional on the explanatory variables. As a result, it can be shown that conditional on S>0, the expected value of the yield is

$$E(Y) = SL + W\alpha + s_{sy}/s_y \lambda \qquad (4)$$

where s_{sy} is the covariance between Y and S^*, s_y is the standard deviation of Y, and λ is equal to the Inverse Mill's Ratio $\phi(Z)/[1-\Phi(Z)]$, where $Z = X\beta/s_s$. Equation (4) can be estimated by Ordinary Least Squares in the sub-sample including observations in which S>0, after S and Z are calculated using the first-stage coefficients of the double-Tobit model.

F. RESULTS OF THE SHARE OF LAND DEVOTED TO MAIZE

The results of the Maize share equation are reported in Table 2. We compare the distributions of the predicted values of the two alternative estimation procedures to that of the actual values in order to asses the quality of the fit.

Table 2. Results of land share of Maize

Variable	Double Tobit		Logistic Transformation	
	Coefficient	T-Value	Coefficient	T-Value
intercept	0.6709	6.857	0.6791	2.694
land	-0.0163	-3.405	-0.0143	-1.218
sex	-0.0508	-2.179	-0.1306	-2.152
age	0.1500	2.325	0.3552	2.112
primary	0.0232	0.973	0.0511	0.850
higher	0.1747	5.591	0.4592	5.646
distrd5	-0.0596	-2.634	-0.1580	-2.734
outputd	-0.0743	-3.236	-0.1664	-2.825
output20+	-0.1143	-4.057	-0.2693	-3.723
advice	-0.0193	-0.834	-0.0544	-0.921
group	-0.0365	-1.168	-0.1157	-1.473
demonstA	0.0662	1.643	0.1575	1.590
demonstB	-0.0890	-2.423	-0.1961	-2.089
radio	0.0258	1.348	0.0698	1.399
consfund	0.0160	0.770	0.0729	1.350
consseed	-0.0760	-2.307	-0.2549	-2.995
consfert	0.0635	2.737	0.1914	3.227
conslab	-0.0178	-0.653	-0.0017	-0.024
constinp	0.0498	1.814	0.2117	2.976
consoth	0.0153	0.612	0.0885	1.415
irrigat	-0.0426	-1.522	-0.0958	-1.327
noirknow	-0.0465	-2.089	-0.1210	-2.120
noirfund	0.0353	1.574	0.0585	1.025
hired	0.0601	2.175	0.2088	2.206
familyM	0.0004	0.058	0.0056	0.285
familyF	-0.0162	-2.178	-0.0339	-1.829
draught	-0.0127	-1.613	-0.0355	-2.013
loans2a	0.0962	2.374	0.2595	2.549
loans2b+	-0.0994	-1.784	-0.3837	-2.786
approv%	0.1319	2.953	0.5572	4.882
machines	-0.0162	-1.896	-0.0289	-1.545
access2	-0.0598	-1.921	-0.1254	-1.579
access34	-0.1630	-4.178	-0.4279	-4.179
msuit	-0.0720	-7.800	-0.1838	-7.832

Table 2. (continued)

	Double Tobit		Logistic Transformation	
Variable	Coefficient	T-Value	Coefficient	T-Value
acidity	0.0052	0.607	0.0240	1.006
totrain	-0.1900	-2.122	-0.6796	-2.855
missrain	-0.0754	-2.373	-0.2149	-2.521
rrain7	0.0706	3.466	0.1258	2.408
rrain8	-0.0345	-5.269	-0.0664	-4.006
rrain9	0.0094	1.793	0.0204	1.485
rrain10	0.0037	0.082	-0.1785	-1.457
rrain11	0.0808	5.132	0.0748	1.833
rrain12	0.4909	12.656	1.3188	12.893
missr93/4	-0.0706	-2.754	-0.1626	-2.372
sigma	0.5666a			
# of cases		5280		5280
log-likelihood		-4498		-3081

a. The standard deviation coefficient was transformed in the estimation, so the standard error of the untransformed estimate is not reported.

We can see that the double-Tobit model is not able to correctly predict the concentration of observations in the extremes of the distribution, while the logistic transformation does so in a satisfactory way. On the other hand, the logistic transformation does not account for the peaks on the right hand side of the distribution, while the double-Tobit model does so to some extent. Hence, although the logistic transformation seems to do a somewhat better predictive job, the comparison does not result in an absolute advantage to one of the methods. Also, Table 2 reveals that the statistical significance of the coefficients of the two methods is not extremely different. Therefore, we present both sets of results and focus on signs of coefficients and their statistical significance rather than on magnitudes.[4]

Maize share of the land is decreasing in the total amount of land used for field crops. It seems like diversification into other crops has fixed costs, so the tendency to diversify is positively related to the amount of land. Maize share in smaller in female-headed households, and is positively related to the age of the farmer and his/her level of schooling. Maize share of land is lower in farms which are more than 5 kilometers from the nearest road. It is lower in farms which have access to markets, but is negatively related to the distance from the market. These two effects contradict each other and we do not have a satisfactory explanation for that.

Extension services do not seem to have significant impacts on the share of land devoted to Maize. The only significant extension variable (at the 5% level) is the dummy for attending an extension demonstration as an observer, which has a negative effect. Maize share of the land is lower in farms in which the major constraint is inavailability of seeds, and higher in farms in which the major constraint is inavailability of fertilizer or late delivery of inputs. Irrigation variables are not significant at the 5% level except for the dummy for not irrigating

---

[4] The magnitudes of coefficients are not comparable across the two estimation procedures anyway.

due to lack of knowledge, which is negative. Therefore knowledge of irrigation methods will likely increase the share of land devoted to Maize.

The number of permanent hired farm workers has a positive effect on the share of land devoted to Maize, while the number of female household members has a negative effect, and the number of male household members does not have a significant effect. The number of draught animals as well as the number of farm machines have negative coefficients. The share of land devoted to Maize is higher among farmers who applied for loans from agricultural financial institutions and lower among farmers who applied for loans from other sources. The percent of loans approved, which proxies for lack of credit constraints, has a positive coefficient. Hence credit constraints tend to decrease the share of land devoted to Maize.

The coefficients of land accessibility imply a positive effect of accessibility on the share of land devoted to Maize. The same is true for Maize suitability. Land acidity did not have a significant effect. The average annual rainfall has a negative effect on the share of land devoted to Maize. Actual rainfall in the early months of the season has a mixed effect - rainfall in July and September has a positive effect while rainfall in August has a negative effect - on the share of land devoted to Maize. Rainfall in November and December has a positive effect, with a much larger coefficient in December than in all other months combined.

G. Results of the Yield Equation

Two versions of the results of the yield regression are reported in Table 3.[5] The one on the left includes the district-specific explanatory variables. In the second version, district dummy variables replace the district-specific explanatory variables. The reason for estimating the second version is that the district-specific explanatory variables do not capture all the variation in Maize yield across districts, and to the extent that this variation is correlated with other explanatory variables, other estimated coefficients might be inconsistent.[6]

Not many coefficients of the yield equation turned out statistically significant. Some of the statistically significant coefficients are sensitive to the inclusion of district-specific explanatory variables (version 1) or district dummies (version 2). These cases will be indicated in the following discussion. We first observe that the yield of maize is inversely related to the area of maize cultivated, which implies that small Maize growers are more efficient or employ more intensive cultivation techniques, other things equal. The yield also declines with the age of the household head (version 1 only). Farms in which lack of funds or lack of seeds is the major constraint are associated with lower yields of Maize. The same is true in farms in which there exists a major constraint different than those specified explicitly (version 1 only). Farms in which late delivery of inputs is the major constraint are associated with higher yields of Maize (version 2 only). Farmers who do not irrigate due to lack of knowledge enjoy higher yields of Maize, surprisingly (version 1 only). The number of male

---

[5] We had to exclude a number of observations which apparently devoted land to Maize but did not report the yield.

[6] There is also a way to find the effects of district-specific variables on the yield when estimating the model with district dummies. This is accomplished by running a linear regression of the estimated district dummies on the set of district-specific variables. The use of this method was suggested by Borjas and Sueyoshi (1995). We were not able to get interesting results from this last regression and hence it is not reported here. The reason is that we had very few observations due to the missing rainfall data.

family workers increases the yield of Maize, and the same is true for the number of hired workers (significant at the 5% level only in version 2). The amount of credit received and the amount of chemical fertilizer used by the household have positive effects on yield, and the same is true for the number of draught animals (version 2 only).

Table 3. Results of Maize yield

Variable	Without District Dummies		With District Dummies	
	Coefficient	T-Value	Coefficient	T-Value
intercept	16.9952	12.4251	14.0025	9.9411
landmaiz	-0.7881	-6.2890	-0.8982	-6.5936
sex	-0.3319	-0.7226	-0.7578	-1.6015
age	-3.0566	-2.4267	-1.5072	-1.1440
primary	-0.4912	-1.0555	-0.1362	-0.2910
higher	0.0143	0.0228	1.5214	1.9938
distrd5	0.3076	0.6727	-0.5666	-1.1495
outputd	0.3345	0.7482	-0.4560	-0.9291
output20+	0.7401	1.1584	-0.1430	-0.1995
advice	0.5809	1.3029	0.2771	0.6116
group	-0.2318	-0.3796	-0.6885	-1.1247
demonstA	0.5453	0.7095	1.0507	1.3524
demonstB	0.8914	1.1666	0.3196	0.4005
radio	0.3467	0.9354	0.6666	1.7666
consfund	-0.9826	-2.3909	-0.8579	-2.0130
consseed	-2.4491	-3.7140	-2.2156	-3.1314
consfert	-0.0097	-0.0214	0.2185	0.4469
conslab	0.4759	0.8863	0.7169	1.2974
constinp	0.6613	1.2129	0.9153	1.6101
consoth	-1.3415	-2.7354	-0.7333	-1.4695
irrigat	0.6374	0.9389	-0.5407	-0.7700
noirknow	0.9839	2.2242	-0.2028	-0.4204
noirfund	-0.1152	-0.2672	-0.2383	-0.5275
hired	0.8157	1.3011	1.1282	1.7718
familyM	0.7972	5.4241	0.7570	5.1815
familyF	0.0152	0.1067	-0.0875	-0.5859
draught	0.3106	2.1401	0.2055	1.3835
loans2a	-0.9111	-1.1197	-0.1665	-0.1943
loans2b+	-2.0575	-1.9041	-2.7423	-2.4630
approv%	1.2057	0.8574	2.0651	1.4419
receiv%	0.3978	0.2902	0.6240	0.4583
credit	0.0928	5.9384	0.0828	5.3234
tchem	0.0561	3.0894	0.0534	2.9677
tseed	0.0887	0.4740	0.1358	0.7352
tvwage	0.0093	1.1555	0.0077	0.9733

Table 3. (Continued)

	Without District Dummies		With District Dummies	
Variable	Coefficient	T-Value	Coefficient	T-Value
machines	0.2375	1.5057	0.2045	1.2516
access2	-3.3481	-5.5267		
access34	-2.3585	-3.1852		
msuit	-0.6853	-4.5589		
acidity	0.6744	3.6078		
rain712	-4.0582	-1.3737		
rain1	-2.6009	-0.7972		
rain2	1.4240	0.3987		
rain3	26.5902	7.4384		
rain4	0.9311	0.2510		
rain5	370.723	-1.4136		
missr93/4	-0.1676	-0.3754		
lambda	-7.6646	-3.1847	6.4220	1.1389
sigma	10.30		10.13	
r-squared adjusted R2	0.130 0.120		0.167 0.148	
# of cases	3973		3973	
F (47,3925)	12.52		8.828	

Farmers who applied for loans from sources other than agricultural financial institutions had lower yields of Maize. The model with district-specific variables (version 1) shows that better land accessibility improves the yield of Maize, and the same is true for Maize suitability and land acidity. Among the rainfall variables, only March rainfall has a significantly positive effect on the yield. The statistically significant coefficient of lambda indicates a negative correlation between Maize share of land and the yield of Maize, so the correction for selectivity is indeed important. In version 2, however, selectivity does not seem to be important.[7]

CONCLUSION

In this paper we have used an empirical framework designed for estimating production relationships in two stages, to identify the factors which affect land allocation among Maize and other crops in Zambia, and those which affect the yield of Maize. The results could be useful for the planning authorities for designing policies that could either promote farmers to diversify their crop mix or simply help them to increase the yield of Maize.

For example, according to the results, rural road construction is likely to increase field-crop diversification, and the same is true for developing markets for agricultural products, and

---

[7] Selectivity correction terms were calculated using the results of the double-tobit maize share model. The Heckman (1979) procedure is known to be vulnerable to collinearity between W and λ, yet informal tests revealed little if any collinearity in this case

promoting an increase of average farm land-holdings. Increasing availability of seeds will also have a similar effect. On the other hand, increased availability of fertilizers, a more timely delivery of inputs, and advancement of irrigation knowledge are likely to decrease field-crop diversification. Changes in the availability of labor, draught animals, and machinery, are also likely to affect the crop mix. Increased availability of hired permanent workers may decrease diversification, while increased availability of draught animals and machines may increase it. Crop-mix diversification may also be achieved by increasing the participation of women in farm work. Relaxing credit constraints is likely to increase specialization in Maize. Extension services seem to affect crop diversification to some extent, but the direction of the effect is not clear.

The yield of Maize can be increased by improving the availability of seeds, fertilizers, labor, draught animals, machines, and credit. Roads, markets, extension services, and irrigation, do not seem to have significant effects on the yield of Maize.

REFERENCES

Chipeleme, A. C. (1990). Potential for Irrigation Development in Zambia, in: Proceedings of an International Seminar on Policies for Irrigation Development in Zambia. Ministry of Agriculture, Lusaka.

Borjas, G.J., and Sueyoshi, G.T. (1994). A Two-Stage Estimator for Probit Models with Structural Group Effects. *Journal of Econometrics, Vol. 64*, 165-182.

Foster, K.A., and Mwanaumo, A. (1995). Estimation of Dynamic Maize Supply Response in Zambia. *Agricultural Economics, Vol. 12*, 99-107.

Government Republic of Zambia (1994). National Census of Agriculture (1990/92): Census Report Part 1. Central Statistical Office, Lusaka.

Heckman, J.J. (1979). Sample Selection Bias as a Specification Error. *Econometrica, Vol. 47*, 153-161.

Holden, S.T. (1993). Peasant Household Modelling: Farming Systems Evolution and Sustainability in Northern Zambia. *Agricultural Economics Vol. 9*, 241-267.

Institute for African Studies (1996). *Agricultural Sector Performance Analysis, Vol. 1*. Lusaka: University of Zambia.

Jha, D., and Hojjati, B. (1993). Fertilizer Use on Smallholder Farms in Eastern Province, Zambia. Research Perort 94, IFPRI, Washington, DC.

McGuirk, A., and Mundlak, Y. (1992). The Transformation of Punjab Agriculture: A Choice of Technique Approach. *American Journal of Agricultural Economics Vol. 74*, 132-143.

Papke, L.E., and Wooldridge, J.M. (1996). Econometric Methods for Fractional Response Variables with an Application to 401(K) Plan Participation Rates. *Journal of Applied Econometrics Vol. 11*, 619-632.

In: The Economics of Natural and Human Resources...   ISBN 978-1-60741-029-4
Editor: Ayal Kimhi and Israel Finkelshtain   © 2009 Nova Science Publishers, Inc.

Chapter 9

THE IMPACT OF LAND REFORM ON RURAL HOUSEHOLD INCOMES IN TRANSCAUCASIA AND CENTRAL ASIA

Zvi Lerman[*]

ABSTRACT

The three Trans-Caucasian states – Armenia, Georgia, and Azerbaijan – are unique among the former Soviet republics in having accomplished a sweeping transition from collective to individual agriculture. Not all the agricultural land resources have been privatized, and yet it is the individual sector that generates practically the entire agricultural output in these countries. This chapter reviews the extent of transition from collective to individual farming, discusses the different approaches to privatization and individualization in the three countries, and examines the difficulties associated with the fragmented farm structure. To reap the full benefits of individualization, the Trans-Caucasian countries should aim to increase the level of commercialization of their smallholder farms. The institutional tools necessary for achieving this aim include development of land markets, emphasis on rural infrastructure and farm support services, as well as creation of off-farm job opportunities for the rural population.

A. INTRODUCTION

The former socialist countries embarked on a transition from plan to market with the objective of increasing the productivity and efficiency of their economies. In a way, this was a new strategy to achieve the old dream of "catching up" with the economically more successful Western world (not to say "overtaking" it, as in Khrushchev's days). But behind the macroeconomic and sectoral arguments of improved productivity there always lurks (so we hope) the human objective of improving the standard of living of the common people. In this article we focus on the changes in land use and their impact on rural incomes in a group

---

[*] Professor of Agricultural Economics, The Hebrew University, Israel.

of particularly agrarian transition countries with relatively large rural populations – the three Transcaucasian states (Armenia, Georgia, and Azerbaijan) and the five Central Asian states (Kazakhstan, Kyrgyzstan, Tajikistan, Turkmenistan, and Uzbekistan).

The paper starts with a brief profile of rural Transcaucasia and Central Asia in comparison with the core CIS countries (Russia and Ukraine). Then we describe the three distinct modes of land reform in these regions and present sectoral evidence suggesting that agricultural growth and hence higher well-being of the rural population may be positively linked to individualization of farming structure. The last section discusses survey results indicating that increase of farm size leads to higher rural incomes and greater readiness to engage in sale of the farm products, while commercialization of farm activity in turn generates higher household incomes. We conclude with some policy implications.

The data for our analysis derive from official country statistics as reported in CIS (2005) or national statistical yearbooks, and various farm surveys conducted in Transcaucasia and Central Asia by the World Bank and by the Hebrew University of Jerusalem (HUJ) with financial support from USAID/CDR. Literature references are given in cases when the survey findings have been published; in other cases only the survey sponsor and date are indicated, while further details can be obtained from the author.

B. A PROFILE OF TRANSCAUCASIA AND CENTRAL ASIA

Armenia, Georgia, and Azerbaijan are mountainous countries, with a large part of agricultural land in green mountain pastures and about 40% suitable for cultivation. The climate ranges from warm, almost Mediterranean, in the coastal plains and in the valleys, to severe in the snow-bound mountains. In the Central Asian countries, on the other hand, the climate is arid, most of the agricultural land is in desert pastures, and arable agriculture is confined to a mere 20% of land.

Table 1 presents the aggregated profiles of Transcaucasia and Central Asia compared to the core of CIS – Russia and Ukraine. Georgia, Armenia, and Azerbaijan are small countries, with total population of only 16 million. The rural population in these countries is around 40%, which is less than in Central Asia, where nearly 60% live in rural areas, but substantially higher than the rural percentage in Russia and Ukraine (30%). The large size of the rural population and the relative scarcity of cultivable land combine to produce a high population density per hectare of good productive land in both Transcaucasia and Central Asia.

Transcaucasia and Central Asia are much more agrarian than Russia and Ukraine by the share of agriculture in GDP and in total employment. In Azerbaijan and Kazakhstan, with their well-developed oil and gas sectors, agriculture is relatively less important to the economy than throughout the rest of the region (14% of GDP in Azerbaijan, 8% in Kazakhstan), but nevertheless nearly half the population in these countries is rural. The Transcaucasian states with per-capita GNP at around $850 are slightly better off than Central Asia, where the per-capita GNP is below $800. Yet both regions are poor compared to Russia and Ukraine, not to mention western Europe.

Table 1. Profiles of Transcaucasia and Central Asia (1999-2004)

	Transcaucasia	Central Asia	Russia, Ukraine
Population, millions	16	56	193
Rural population, %	44	60	30
Agricultural land, million hectares	8.9	154	234
Cultivable land, %	40	20	67
Cultivable land per rural resident, ha	0.5	0.9	2.7
Agriculture in GDP, %	19	23	9
Agriculture in total employment, %	42	45	18
GNP per capita	$847	$774	$1,790

Source: CIS (2005); GNP per capita from World Development Indicators 2005 database.

C. THE PROCESS OF LAND REFORM[1]

During the Soviet era, agriculture was characterized by two salient features: absolute state ownership of all agricultural land and concentration of production in large-scale collective farms. These two features are generally counted among the main reasons for the inefficiency of socialist agriculture, because in market economies land is typically in private ownership and production is dominated by relatively small family-operated units. Land reform programs in all transition countries were designed to correct these deviations from the market pattern, and their achievements are usually assessed by examining the extent of privatization of land ownership and (perhaps more importantly) the extent of individualization, i.e., transition from traditional large-scale collectives to smaller family farms.

The former socialist countries in transition – there are about 25 of them in Central Eastern Europe and the former Soviet Union – have made different land reform choices from the start. It is therefore not surprising that Transcaucasia and Central Asia also follow distinctly different land reform paths, and there are furthermore clear differences in implementation among countries within each region. A distinctive feature of the three small Transcaucasian countries is the full acceptance of private land ownership and the total transition to individual farming, accompanied by the virtually complete elimination of large-scale corporate farms. Central Asia, on the other hand, pursues much more conservative land policies. Tajikistan, Uzbekistan, and in a certain sense Turkmenistan do not recognize private land ownership to this day: all agricultural land in these countries remains state owned and non-transferable. Kyrgyzstan and Kazakhstan recognized private land ownership quite recently (1999-2000 in Kyrgyzstan, 2003 in Kazakhstan), after prolonged and sometimes agonizing legal debates. In all five Central Asian countries the creation of individual farms has been minimal, and the bulk of agricultural land is still controlled by large corporate farms that succeeded the former kolkhozes and sovkhozes.

While the Transcaucasian states resolutely individualized their agriculture during the early years of transition by distributing most of the arable land in the form of physical plots to rural households, Kazakhstan and Kyrgyzstan adopted the "share-based distribution" strategy

---

[1] This section draws on Lerman, Csaki, and Feder (2004), Lerman (2004), and Lerman and Stanchin (2004).

favored by Russia and Ukraine. While the distribution of land and asset shares to the rural population allowed creation of independent family farms and augmentation of existing household plots, the share privatization mechanism definitely favored the preservation of large-scale corporate farms. As a result, these successors of former kolkhozes and sovkhozes continue to control most of the agricultural land in all former Soviet countries that opted for share distribution mechanisms (Russia and Ukraine, as well as Kazakhstan and Kyrgyzstan).

Land reform in Turkmenistan and Uzbekistan occupies an intermediate position between the share-based distribution in Kazakhstan and Kyrgyzstan, on the one hand, and the total individualization of land use in Transcaucasia.

Although family farms remain a marginal phenomenon in these countries, there has definitely been a kind of a shift from traditional collective farming to more individualized agriculture. Around 1998, the traditional large-scale farms were transformed into "associations" (*daikhan berleshik* in Turkmenistan, *shirkat* in Uzbekistan) that began to distribute land to their population in leasehold. Former employees of collective farms thus became leaseholders on state-owned land and gained a certain measure of limited independence in their production decisions. The "associations" themselves stopped producing: they act as the guardians or administrators of state-owned agricultural land that is distributed to leaseholders for cultivation; they are the municipal authority responsible for maintaining rural infrastructure in the villages; and most problematic of all, they are the conduit for transmitting state orders for production of strategic commodities to the leaseholders and enforcing compliance.

The countries of Transcaucasia and Central Asia thus fall into three groups by their land reform choices. The first group includes the three Transcaucasian states that have privatized their agricultural land and switched to fully individual agriculture. Armenia and Georgia completely individualized their farm structure as early as 1992-93, whereas Azerbaijan delayed its land reform until about 1995-96, when it recognized private land ownership and began to distribute paper certificates of entitlement ("land shares"), not actual land plots, to the rural population.

The conversion of land shares to physical plots came in 1997-98, and since 2001 the farm structure in Azerbaijan is similar to that in Armenia and Georgia. The second group consists of Turkmenistan and Uzbekistan that have retained state ownership of land but are moving toward increased individualization through leasehold arrangements within peasant associations (this also seems to apply to Tajikistan to a certain extent). Finally, Kazakhstan and Kyrgyzstan have privatized their land but have chosen to maintain an agriculture that continues to be dominated by large-scale corporate farms, as it is in Russia and Ukraine.

The individual sector in Transcaucasia currently produces almost 100% of agricultural output, up from 30%-40% before 1990 (Table 2). The share of individual production in Transcaucasia is substantially higher than in Russia, Ukraine, and Kazakhstan, where the individual sector accounts for 60%-70% of agricultural output, up from 25%-30% before the transition.

The shift of production to the individual sector is a reflection of the dramatic increase in the land holdings of rural households. Prior to 1990, only 4% of agricultural land was on average in individual use in the Soviet republics. A decade later, in 2000, more than one-third of agricultural land is in individual use in Transcaucasia, compared to about 15%-20% in Russia, Ukraine, and Kazakhstan.

Table 2. Land in Individual Use in Transcaucasia and the Rest of CIS

	1990		1999-2000		
	Land in individual use, %	Share of ag output, %	Land in individual use, %	Share of ag output, %	Relative productivity of land in individual use*
Armenia	4	35	33	98	3.0
Georgia	7	48	37	94	2.5
Azerbaijan	3	35	34	96	2.8
Kazakhstan	0.2	28	21	75	3.6
Russia	2	24	13	57	4.4
Ukraine	7	27	18	60	3.3

* The ratio of share of agricultural output to share of land in individual use. This value is 1 for agriculture as a whole. Values greater than 1 imply greater productivity than the average for the entire sector.

Source: Lerman, Csaki, and Feder (2004).

The creation of leaseholder-based associations in Turkmenistan and Uzbekistan may be regarded as a highly significant – if not the most significant – step of the land reform program in these countries because of its scope. The reforms aimed at household plots and private farms, however important, were marginal by the amount of land that they encompassed. The transition to leasehold contracts in Turkmenistan alone involved more than 350,000 rural family units and 1.5 million hectares of arable land, i.e., practically the entire rural population and 90% of arable land in the country. The current structure of the farm sector in Turkmenistan is presented schematically in Table 3.

Table 3. Structure of the Farm Sector in Turkmenistan: 2002

	Number	Land, ha	Average size, ha
Associations	587	33,900,000 (incl. pastures)	
Leaseholders	357,000	1,500,000 (arable)	4
Peasant farms	5,200	81,000	16
Household plots	616,000	133,000	0.2

Source: Stanchin and Lerman (2003).

D. AGRICULTURAL PERFORMANCE

The numbers in Table 2 suggest that the individual sector is much more productive on average than agriculture as a whole. The share of individual farms in agricultural output is roughly three times its share in cultivated land. This phenomenon, however, is not an outcome of the new land policies during transition, as is clear from the pre-transition data for 1990 in the same table. Are there any indications that the unique land policies in Transcaucasia have had a positive impact on agriculture? Has the leasehold system in Turkmenistan produced a measurable result? To answer these questions, we will start by looking at the changes in agricultural performance in Transcaucasia and compare them to the corresponding changes in Kazakhstan, Russia, and Ukraine.

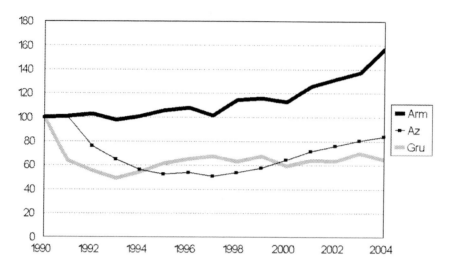

Figure 9.1. Gross agricultural output in Transcaucasia 1990-2004 (1990=100). Source: CIS (2005).

Figure 9.1 shows the changes in agricultural output in Transcaucasia since 1990. Armenia individualized its agriculture swiftly and comprehensively starting March 1991, and there was practically no decrease in agricultural production following the disintegration of the Soviet system, despite the war with Azerbaijan and the aftermath of the 1989 earthquake. Armenian agriculture shows a clear upward trend over the entire period since 1992-93.

Georgian agriculture collapsed in 1991, when the entire country was in total disarray facing a bitter civil war. Land was then quickly distributed to rural households in an attempt to avoid famine. This desperate goal was achieved as Georgian agriculture quickly recovered in 1993-95. The recovery raised the volume of agricultural production in recent years by 25%-30% above its lowest level in 1993, yet the initial collapse was so dramatic that the agricultural output today is still 40% below what it was in 1990.

Azerbaijan also experienced an initial decline of agriculture. The decline continued until 1995, a couple of years longer than in Georgia, and recovery came only in 1997, just as Azerbaijan embarked on mass conversion of paper land shares into physical plots for rural households. Between 1997 and 2004, the index of agricultural output in Azerbaijan rose by 65%, matching and even exceeding the growth in Armenia.

Agricultural performance in Kazakhstan, similarly to that in Russia and Ukraine, presents an entirely different pattern (Figure 9.2). In these countries, the agricultural output showed a steady downward trend throughout most of the 1990s. First signs of modest agricultural recovery appeared only in 1998-99. Without any war, civil upheavals, or natural disasters, the agricultural output in Kazakhstan, Russia, and Ukraine in 2004 is 40% below the 1990 level, comparable to Georgia and much less than in Azerbaijan, both of which had to recover from a traumatic initial collapse. In other words, Kazakhstan, like Russia and Ukraine, reached the present low level of agricultural production along a downward path of continuing decline, whereas Georgia and Azerbaijan are now moving along an upward path from a deeper abyss.

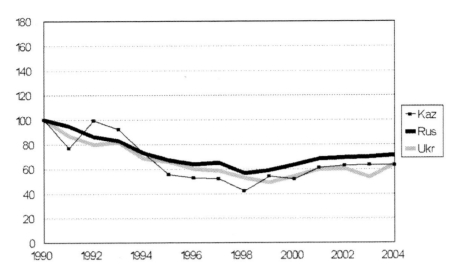

Figure 9.2. Gross agricultural output in Kazakhstan, Russia, and Ukraine 1990-2004 (1990=100). Source: CIS (2005).

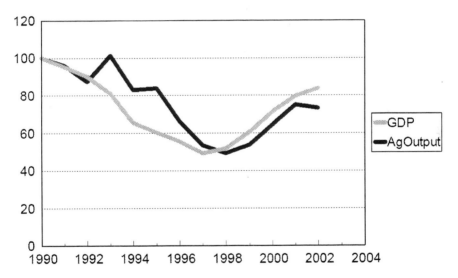

Figure 9.3. Gross agricultural output and GDP in Turkmenistan 1990-2002 (1990=100). Source: Lerman and Stanchin (2004).

In Turkmenistan, both agricultural output and GDP declined sharply after 1990, but signs of recovery appeared in 1997-98 – coincidentally with the introduction of individual leasehold arrangements in agriculture (Figure 9.3). We would like to hope that the incipient recovery is indeed linked with the impact of agricultural reforms, but the data for Turkmenistan are incomplete and only the future will show if this is so.

The data in all countries are still insufficient to establish rigorously a causal relationship between individualization of land and agricultural growth. However, we cannot ignore the strong evidence of Figures 10.1-10.3: in Transcaucasia agriculture recovered roughly in sync with the sweeping individualization of land, in Turkmenistan recovery coincided with the introduction of the individual leasehold system, whereas in Russia, Ukraine, and Kazakhstan, where large-scale corporate farms still dominate agriculture, agricultural output continued to decline until very recently. This conclusion is borne out by an analysis of all 23 transition countries, which shows a strong association between agricultural growth since 1992 and the share of land in individual use (Lerman, Csaki, and Feder, 2004). On an anecdotal level, Ministry of Agriculture officials in Azerbaijan report significant increases in crop yields in 2001, which they proudly attribute to the new land policy.

E. FARM SIZES AND COMMERCIALIZATION OF INDIVIDUAL FARMING

While individualization appears to encourage agricultural growth in transition countries, this process has a downside in that it inevitably produces fragmentation of land holdings – especially in situations where land allocation is based on universal and equitable principles. In Transcaucasia (similarly to Albania, for instance) land was distributed free of charge to the entire rural population. The universality of the process necessarily imposed size limits on the amount of land that an individual or a household could receive. In Armenia, land was allocated in fixed units calculated by dividing the total available land in the village by the total population. In Georgia, rural families actually engaged in agriculture (i.e., families of collective-farm workers – the majority of the population in the villages) were entitled to receive up to 1.25 hectares, while the actual allocation was determined by local availability of land. In Azerbaijan, the land held by local collective or state farm in each village (or cluster of villages) was equally distributed among all rural residents, regardless of occupation or age. The universal process of land distribution, coupled with scarcity of cultivable land, naturally created a large number of small individual farms in Transcaucasia. The average individual holding is between 1-2 hectares (Table 4). In Armenia, only 12% of individual farms use more than 2 hectares; in Georgia, this category accounts for less than 5% (Table 5). The Transcaucasian individualized agriculture is thus essentially an agriculture of smallholders.

Table 4. Number and Size of Individual Farms in Transcaucasia (2000)

	Number of farms, '000	Land used, '000 ha	Average size, ha
Armenia	332.6	458.6	1.38
Georgia	1,015.7	977.7	0.96
Azerbaijan	869.8	1,614.9	1.86

Source: Official country statistics.

Table 5. Size Distribution of Individual Farms in Armenia and Georgia (percent of individual farms)

Size category	Armenia	Georgia
Up to 0.5 ha	–	22.1
0.5-1 ha	30.9	29.7
1-2 ha	56.8	43.6
Over 2 ha	12.3	4.6

Source: Official country statistics.

The pattern of farm sizes is not much different in Turkmenistan, where in principle every family in the village is entitled to a leasehold. In a large survey conducted in 2002 by HUJ with USAID/CDR support, the average leasehold was 5.6 hectares with 3.8 working-age adults in the family, or less than 1.5 hectares per family worker (Stanchin and Lerman, 2003). In countries that do not follow the principle of universal distribution of land for the creation of new peasant farms and land is allocated by application against paper shares, the average farm sizes are much larger (about 50 hectares in Russia, Ukraine, and Kyrgyzstan, and as much as 200 hectares in land-rich Kazakhstan).

Small farms typically generate small incomes. Although they provide a reliable source of food and possibly cash in times of adversity, they may trap the rural population in chronic poverty. Analysis of survey results in all transition countries clearly shows that family income (including both farm and off-farm components) rapidly increases with the increase of land holdings. This effect is demonstrated in Figure 9.4 using the results of a 2003 survey of farm households in Georgia. The level of income reported by families with 5-10 hectares of farmland is double that reported by families with 1-2 hectares. It is mainly the farm component of family income that increases with farm size, while the off-farm components (outside salaries, pensions, etc.) remains fairly stable. Land markets and readiness to engage in land transactions are standard mechanisms for achieving larger farm sizes and thus increasing family incomes.

In agriculture, smallness is usually interpreted as being synonymous with subsistence farming (see, e.g., Abele and Frohberg (2003)). Yet the small individual farms in Transcaucasia are far from being pure subsistence operations. In recent farm-level surveys, a high percentage of respondents (64% in Georgia, 80% in Armenia, 87% in Azerbaijan) report that they sell at least some of their products, and the average individual farm in these countries sells 40% of its output (Table 6). Moreover, as we see from Table 6, this phenomenon is not restricted to Transcaucasia, and even the small household plots in CIS – so often brushed off by local experts and officials as irrelevant for "true" commercial agriculture – are characterized by significant commercialization levels.

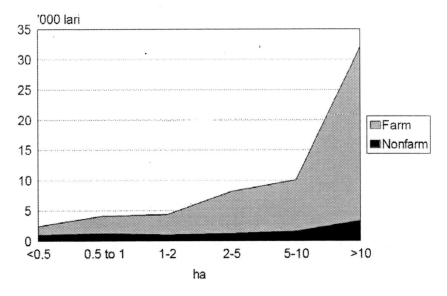

Figure 9.4. Family income versus farm size in Georgia. Source: HUJ 2003 survey.

Table 6. Level of Commercialization in the Individual Sector

	Percent of "sellers"	Percent of output sold by "sellers"
Armenia	80	40
Georgia	64	40
Azerbaijan	87	46
Moldova – small private farms	83	48
– household plots	60	31
Ukraine– household plots	60	50
Belarus– household plots	76	22

Source: World Bank surveys, 1996-2003.

Table 7. Armenia: Comparative Characteristics of Sellers and Non-Sellers

	Sellers (1,104)	Non-sellers (264)
Land, ha	2.3	1.4
Irrigated land, ha	0.44	0.24
Animals, standard head	2.2	1.0
Family size	5	4
Number of farm workers	4	3
Full time occupation on farm	63%	45%
Annual cost of mechanical field services	19,500 dram/ha	8,900 dram/ha
Product mix	60% crops	59% crops
Educational endowment of head of household	13% higher	12% higher
	59% secondary	62% secondary
Household cash income	$430	$210

Source: Lerman and Mirzakhanian (2001), except for household cash income, which has been calculated separately from the same 1998 rural household survey as the other data in the table.

Although individual farms in transition countries are certainly far from the level of commercial operation as we understand it in market economies, we must acknowledge that their commercial activities are not negligible and that on the whole the picture that emerges from Table 6 is definitely different from the traditional view of subsistence agriculture.

Agricultural policies obviously should strive to avoid the "subsistence trap" and encourage commercialization of individual farms. Sales of farm products keep the urban population supplied with food and thus extend the benefits of farming outside the rural communities. It is therefore important to identify the determinants of the decision to sell among individual farmers. Table 7 presents the comparative profiles of "seller" and "non-seller" farms in Armenia. The sellers are characterized by larger land holdings, a larger amount of fertile irrigated land, and more animals. Sellers also command a larger pool of potential family labor, and the head of the household works full time on the family farm in a significantly higher percentage of cases. Finally, sellers allocate much greater sums of money to payment for mechanical field services (both in absolute terms and per hectare). Interestingly, some variables that a priori would appear relevant to the decision to sell are not significantly different between the two categories of households. For example, the average distances to the main delivery location or point of sale and the average road conditions are virtually identical for sellers and non-sellers. The product mix is practically the same. The educational endowment is not different. The picture emerging from the profiles of Table 7 is confirmed by logistic regression: the probability that a household is a "seller" increases with the increase of its land endowment, the number of animals, the number of family members, and the number of farm workers per hectare.

In a broader regional analysis, the specific profile components and regression results vary from country to country because of local differences and also because of different availability of particular variables. Yet farm size as measured by land emerges clearly and consistently in all countries as the major determinant of the decision to engage in sale of farm products. This has been shown by the author's studies of CIS countries and by a recent analysis of Mathijs and Noev (2002) for individual farmers in four transition countries in Central Eastern Europe. Seller farms are larger and use greater inputs of productive resources. They accordingly produce more output and have a greater saleable surplus after satisfying the family's consumption needs. Small farms produce just enough to satisfy family consumption and do not trade. To have saleable surplus output, the farm must be larger than some minimum size.

In transition countries, the level of commercialization is generally observed to increase with farm size. This effect clearly emerges in Georgia from the results of two World Bank surveys (1996 and 1998). The 1996 survey was based on a representative sample of 2,000 individual farms, with average size of 0.75 hectares. The 1998 survey focused on 1,200 relatively large individual farms with 62 hectares on average (of which 61 hectares was leased land). The small individual farms reported selling 40% of their output (this is the number shown in Table 7), while the large individual farms were selling 70% of their output. Among small individual farms about two-thirds had any sales, whereas among the large individual farms virtually all reported commercial sales of products (Table 8). In the HUJ 2003 survey in Georgia, the probability of being a "seller", i.e., of selling at least some of the farm output, was observed to increase with farm size. Figure 9.5 shows the behavior of this probability as a function of farm size, estimated by logistic regression. The probability of engaging in commercial activity is about 0.7 for very small farms of up to 1 hectare and approaches 1 for relatively large farms of 50 hectares and more.

The very fact that sellers engage in additional income-generating commercial activities leads to a striking difference in the level of family income. According to previously unpublished results of the World Bank 1998 survey of rural households in Armenia, "sellers" report an average cash income of 216,000 dram ($430 per year), while "non-seller" households earn less than half this amount (103,000 dram or $210; see Table 7).

The entire difference is attributable to sale of farm products, as off-farm income and unearned income (pensions, transfers, etc.) are on average equal for the two categories of rural households.

Table 8. Effect of Farm Size on Commercialization Level in Georgia

	Small individual farms (1996 survey)	Large individual farms (1998 survey)
Average size, ha	0.75	62
Percent of "sellers"	64	98
Percent of output sold	40	70

Source: World Bank surveys, 1996-98.

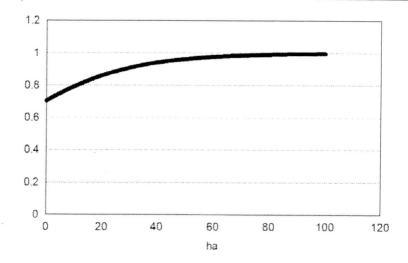

Figure 9. 5. Probability of being a "seller" versus farm size in. Estimated by logistic regression on the basis of the HUJ 2003 survey in Georgia.

If the household incomes are adjusted for the value of own consumption of farm products (estimated at 445,000 dram or $890 for the average household; see Lerman and Mirzakhanian (2001)), the percentage gap shrinks to 20%, but the absolute difference (over $200) is preserved. Recent household surveys in Azerbaijan indicate that "seller" households earn incomes that are 8% higher than the incomes of "non-sellers" (Sedik et al., 2002). This figure is based on household income that includes the value of own consumption of family-produced food and derives from a regression analysis that controls for many additional factors not considered for Armenia. The findings of the HUJ 2003 survey in Georgia presented in Figure 9.6 show that "commercial" households (i.e., households selling some of their farm products) earn incomes that are double the income of "subsistence" households (i.e., households where the entire farm output is consumed by the family). Most of the difference in household incomes between "sellers" and "non-sellers" is attributable to cash revenue from the sale of farm products. The same pattern is observed consistently in all transition countries. Figure 9.6 also highlights the fact that the "seller" farms (averaging 2 hectares in the survey) are significantly larger than the "non-seller" farms (1 hectare only). Survey results for other transition countries also indicate that sellers enjoy higher total incomes, and the difference is basically attributable to cash earned from sales of farm products.

The importance of the farm for the family welfare thus increases markedly with the increase in the level of commercialization, which is observed to rise for larger farms. Individual farmers apparently recognize the advantages of operating a larger farm, as our surveys in transition countries reveal a clear pattern of willingness to increase the farm size. In Armenia, 20% of individual farmers expressed a desire to double their land holdings from 2 hectares to 4 hectares. In Georgia, half the respondents (in the World Bank1996 survey) indicated that they would like to treble the size of their farm from 0.9 hectares to 2.7 hectares. In Turkmenistan, 55% of leaseholders in the HUJ 2002 survey wanted to increase their farm by 6.6 hectares, to more than double the average size. Moreover, half of the respondents seeking to enlarge their farm argued in justification that "a small farm produces insufficient income" and "small farms are unprofitable".

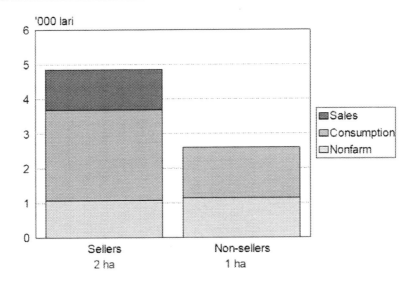

Figure 9.6. Family income for "sellers" and "non-sellers" in Georgia. Source: HUJ 2003 survey.

CONCLUSION

We have tried to demonstrate two main points. First, the transition to individual (as opposed to corporate) farms is conducive to agricultural growth and thus potentially increases the well-being of the rural population. Second, larger holdings lead to greater commercialization and thus to higher family incomes – both directly due to increased production, and indirectly due to additional revenue from sales.

The policy implications for rural poverty are clear. Land should be distributed to the rural population, and not hoarded in large corporate farms in the imaginary interests of efficiency. In parallel, policies should be implemented to overcome the obstacles of fragmentation and smallness that are an inevitable concomitant of the universality of land distribution in rural areas. Poverty alleviation requires overcoming the "subsistence trap" of small-scale farming and developing a stronger commercial orientation than today. This can be achieved by encouraging the development of land markets and investing in rural infrastructure and services, including farmer-owned service cooperatives. In a way, the two directions are interrelated, because investment in rural infrastructure and services, in addition to enabling farmers to sell more, will also have an indirect effect: it will create off-farm employment opportunities in rural areas, thus enabling some people to stop farming for subsistence and put their land on the market – either for sale or for lease. The governments also should support the supply side of land markets by unblocking the large state reserves of land, and the 2001 Land Code of Armenia definitely points in the right direction. Off-farm job opportunities and land markets will encourage the enlargement of family farms; larger farms will generate saleable surpluses; infrastructure and service channels – including agroprocessing – will enable farmers to convert their surpluses into cash; and cash revenues will ultimately increase household incomes and family welfare.

An additional policy-oriented observation is suggested by the analysis of the leasehold-based reforms in Central Asia. Although the transition to leasehold arrangements in

Turkmenistan and Uzbekistan is definitely a move toward greater individualization of farming, survey results show that the productivity of leaseholds is substantially lower than the productivity achieved by the same families on their household plots (Lerman and Stanchin, 2004; Stanchin and Lerman, 2003). The only possible explanation, in our view, lies in the different incentives attributable to the sharp differences in the institutional production and marketing arrangements between the household plots and the leasehold sector. Leaseholders are strictly bound by state orders, and there is not much room for true private initiative in their production and marketing decisions. The household plots, on the other hand, are not subject to these restrictions and they are flourishing thanks to private initiative. To enable the rural population to reap the full benefits of individualization, agricultural policies should ensure freedom of production and marketing decisions at the farm level and thus create incentives for maximizing private initiative.

REFERENCES

Abele, S., and Frohberg, K. (2003). *Subsistence Agriculture in Central and Eastern Europe: How to Break the Vicious Circle?* Halle, GR: Studies on the Agricultural and Food Sector in Central and Eastern Europe, Vol. 22, IAMO.

CIS (2005). *Official Statistics of the Countries of the Commonwealth of Independent States*, CD-ROM 2005-10, Goskomstat SNG, Moscow.

Lerman, Z. (2004). Successful Land Individualization in Trans-Caucasia: Armenia, Azerbaijan, Georgia. In Macey, D., Pyle, W., and Wergen, S. (Eds.), *Building Market Institutions in Post-Communist Agriculture: Land, Credit, and Assistance*. (pp. 53-75). Lanham, MD: Lexington Books.

Lerman, Z. and Stanchin, I. (2004). Institutional Changes in Turkmenistan's Agriculture: Impacts on Productivity and Rural Incomes. *Eurasian Geography and Economics, Vol. 45* (No. 1), 60-72.

Lerman, Z., and Mirzakhanian, A. (2001). *Private Agriculture in Armenia*. Lanham, MD: Lexington Books.

Lerman, Z., Csaki, C., and Feder, G. (2004). *Agriculture in Transition: Land Policies and Evolving Farm Structures in Post-Soviet Countries*. Lanham, MD: Lexington Books.

Mathijs, E., and Noev, N. (2002). Commercialization and Subsistence in Transition Agriculture: Empirical Evidence from Albania, Bulgaria, Hungary and Romania. World Bank Annual Conference on Development Economics, World Bank, Washington, DC, April.

Sedik, D., Fock, K., Davis, B., Trento, S., and Molinari, B. (2002). *Azerbaijan Rural Poverty Assessment* (Working draft). Washington, DC: World Bank.

Stanchin, I., and Lerman, Z. (2003). *Agrarian Reform in Turkmenistan*. Rehovot, Israel: Center for Agricultural Economic Research, The Hebrew University of Jerusalem [in Russian].

PART B. HUMAN RESOURCES IN AGRICULTURE
SECTION IV: KNOWLEDGE, PRODUCTIVITY AND GROWTH

In: The Economics of Natural and Human Resources...   ISBN 978-1-60741-029-4
Editor: Ayal Kimhi and Israel Finkelshtain   © 2009 Nova Science Publishers, Inc.

Chapter 10

RESEARCH AS SEARCH: EVENSON-KISLEV AND THE GREEN REVOLUTION

*Robert E. Evenson**

ABSTRACT

This paper provides a test of the Evenson-Kislev "Research as Search" model utilizing data from plant breeding programs in developing countries conducted both in National Agricultural Research Systems (NARS) and International Agricultural Research Centers (IARC). Data for five crops – the dominant Green Revolution crops – were analyzed. It was shown, for example, that there are implicit scale economies affecting NARS investments. The analysis also showed that population densities stimulate NARS investments. The IARC germplasm effect on NARS investments was related to both size of program (hectares planted) and population density. A significant implication of the study is that recharge of knowledge comes from dedicated programs; these were mostly conducted in the IARCs and not in NARS institutions.

A. INTRODUCTION

Studies of productivity change in the agricultural sector distinguish between changes in the productivity of farmers relative to the technological frontier for a given location and changes in the technology frontier itself. Changes in the technology frontier are produced by a process of adaptive invention/innovation (commercialization of the invention) and diffusion or adoption by farmers. In this paper a model of adaptive invention/innovation is developed as an extension of the "research as search" model of Evenson and Kislev (1976). This model is then evaluated with data on the production of "modern varieties" (MVs) by National Agricultural Research System (NARS) plant breeding programs.

* Yale University, USA.

B. THE ADAPTIVE INNOVATION MODEL

The term "induced innovation" was introduced to the economics literature many years ago. Its most thorough development and empirical testing was reported in Binswanger and Ruttan (1978). The original development of the model was by Kennedy (1964) and Samuelson (1966), with further development by Ahmad (1966). Nordhaus (1973) criticized the model on several grounds, noting first that a convincing case for the representation of the Innovation Possibilities Frontier (IPF) was not put forth. Nordhaus noted that in the absence of evidence for the "inducement" mechanism and its multi-period nature, the induced innovation model was a version of the exogenous technical change models employed in the growth literature at that time.

Evenson and Kislev (1976) employed the search model developed by Stigler (1961) as a representation of the research process. The original work was applied to search for a single "trait" or characteristic, but the extension to multiple traits was relatively straightforward. In this paper these developments are reviewed and further developments regarding the "adaptive" or "recharge" features of the model are reported. Tests of the model are then undertaken.

B.1. The Single Period-Single Trait Model

The model stresses plant traits sought by plant breeders. These plant traits can be given economic values. Plant breeders have two alternative search strategies in their research programs. The first of these is the search for "quantitative" plant traits governing yields. Quantitative traits are controlled by multiple genes (or genetic alleles) and require complex strategies for crossing parental materials and selecting improved cultivars. The second is the search for "qualitative" traits such as host plant resistance (HPR) to the tungro virus in rice. Qualitative traits typically are controlled by a single gene. Conventional breeding programs use "back crossing" strategies to incorporate these traits (modern biotechnology methods are used to genetically engineer these traits).

Both breeding strategies rely on searching for genetically controlled traits in collections of crop genetic resources (CGRs) which include landraces of the cultivated species (distinct types selected by farmers over centuries from the earliest dates of cultivation and diffused across different ecosystems), "wild" species (in the same genus) and related plants that might be combined.[1] CGR collections also include "combined" landraces including varieties (officially recognized uniform populations of combined landraces often with many generations of combinations). The systematic combining of landraces into breeding lines is termed "pre-breeding."[2]

Consider the original Evenson-Kislev model: Existing breeders' techniques and breeders' CGR collections determine a distribution of potential varieties indexed by their economic value, x. Following Evenson and Kislev (1976), suppose this distribution to be an exponential distribution:

---

[1] Wide crossing methods can be used to achieve this. Modern biotechnology methods can also be used.
[2] In Part III, the pre-breeding activities of the International Agricultural Research Center will be an important part of the recharge mechanism.

$$f(x) = \lambda e^{-\lambda(x-\theta)}, \theta \le x \tag{1}$$

The cumulative distribution is:

$$F(x) = 1 - e^{-\lambda(x-\theta)} \tag{2}$$

with mean and variance

$$E(x) = \theta + 1/\lambda \tag{3}$$

$$Var(x) = 1/\lambda^2 \tag{4}$$

The cumulative distribution of the largest value of x, z, from a sample of size n is the "order statistic" (Evenson and Kislev, 1976):

$$H_n(z) = \left[1 - e^{-\lambda(z-\theta)}\right]^n \tag{5}$$

and the probability density function for z is:

$$h_n(z) = \lambda n \left[1 - e^{-\lambda(z-\theta)}\right]^{n-1} e^{-\lambda(z-\theta)} \tag{6}$$

The expected value and variance of $h_n(z)$ are

$$E_n(z) = \theta + \frac{1}{\lambda} \sum_{i=1}^{n} \frac{1}{i} \tag{7}$$

$$Var_n(z) = \frac{1}{\lambda^2} \sum_{i=1}^{n} \frac{1}{i^2} \tag{8}$$

Evenson and Kislev discuss the applicability of expression (7) to plant breeding research. Basically (7) can be thought of as the breeding production function. Equation (9) is a reasonable approximation for any symmetric distribution $f(x)$ including the uniform distribution (Kortum, 1997) and the normal distribution.

$$E_n(z) \approx \theta + B \ln(n) \tag{9}$$

with this approximation, the marginal product of breeding effort is simply:

$$\frac{\partial E_n(z)}{\partial n} = \frac{\lambda}{n} \tag{10}$$

when a measure, V, of the economic units over which z applies, is defined (e.g., the areas in a specific ecosystem) the value of the marginal product can be computed and set equal to the marginal cost of search to solve for optimal n:

$$\lambda V / n = MC(n) \tag{11}$$

B.2. Multiple Traits

For two or more traits, each can be characterized by (8) with different parameters:

$$
\begin{aligned}
E_n(z_1) &= \theta_1 + \lambda_1 \ln(n_1) \\
E_n(z_2) &= \theta_2 + \lambda_2 \ln(n_2) \\
E_n(z_3) &= \theta_3 + \lambda_3 \ln(n_3)
\end{aligned}
\tag{12}
$$

when these traits are qualitative traits, breeders typically search for them independently because there are techniques enabling the breeders to incorporate only the single trait in a cultivar (i.e., by back crossing and other methods, unwanted traits can be discarded). Thus, even if traits are highly correlated, the breeder will typically search independently for them.[3]

Set $n_1 + n_2....n_m = n*$

For a given n*, this defines a transformation curve (in expected value terms). This can be regarded as a single period IPF, with prices for z_1, z_2, etc. The standard induced innovation model predicts optimal trait choice as a function of prices or values [see Figure 11.1 where the Innovation Possibility Frontier (IPF) for n* is depicted]. The Technical Determination (TD) point is also shown. This is the point where full exhaustion of the potential is realized.

B.3. Periodicity without Recharge

In practice, we observe multiple period research and plant breeding programs. There are two reasons for this. The first is that experiments have a natural phasing and evaluation property. In plant breeding programs this entails "selection under pressure." The breeder makes n crosses in each period. Then the F_1 generation from each cross must be evaluated. For some crosses this evaluation may call for termination. For other crosses, further selection is justified. This selection is typically undertaken under pressure to better identify several traits. For example, F_1 plants may be inoculated with plant disease organisms to better select for host plant resistance to the disease.

---

[3] This independent search for traits is dictated by the fact that traits have different genetic sources.

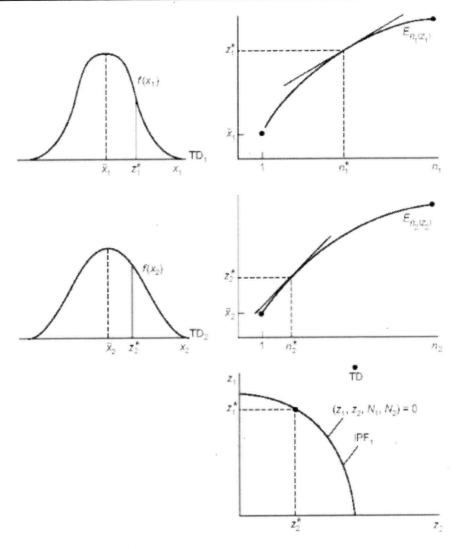

Figure 10.1. The Single Period IPF.

This process of selection is sequence dependent and proceeds for several generations. each requiring an evaluation before the next generation strategy can be developed. As these processes proceed, more lines are dropped as unpromising and more potential crosses are revealed to be unpromising.

Figure 10.2 depicts the nature of the multi-period IPFs in this case. Note that while some early evaluations may produce a pattern of increasing returns to multi-period search. decreasing returns must set in as long as the right hand tails of the distribution (TD) remains fixed. These decreasing returns affect the multi-period IPFs in two ways. First the curve of IPF in the 2nd period will move in the direction of the TD point and its slope will change. This is because a first period search will exhaust more of the distribution favoring the trait selected for in period one than it will for another trait. Second, the R&D process will eventually grind to a halt before the TD (technological determination) point is reached. But the "bending" of the optimal search path in the direction of the TD point effectively steals most of the thunder from the induced innovation model.

Induced Adaptive Invention/Innovation

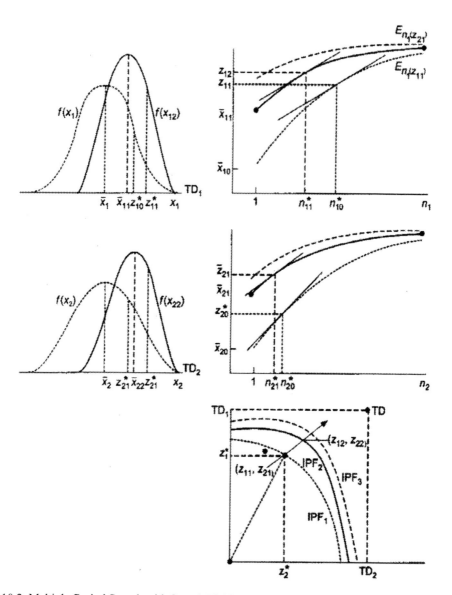

Figure 10.2. Multiple-Period Search with Search Field Narrowing.

B.4. Periodicity with Recharge

The second type of invention distribution shift is associated with several types of recharge mechanisms.[4] These include:

---

[4] Note that for inventors receiving recharge the recharge elements shift the invention distribution linearly. The diminishing returns to pre-invention or recharge activities itself are not incorporated into the recharge recipients invention functions. This implication is tested empirically below.

1. Genetic resource collection and evaluation programs. These programs are designed to discover uncollected materials and make them available to breeders.
2. Pre-breeding programs where landrace materials are systematically combined into potential breeding lines by specialized research programs. These programs do not seek to develop "final products", i.e., new cultivars. Instead they seek to evaluate and produce "advanced lines" that are then used by final product inventors.
3. Wide-crossing programs where techniques for inter-specific combinations of genetic resources (between related species) are made possible. This expands the size and scope of the original materials that can be utilized in breeding programs.

Transgenic breeding programs where DNA insertion techniques allow traits associated with alien genes (i.e., from unrelated species) to be incorporated into cultivated plants.

These programs are "pre-invention science" or applied science programs. They provide recharge to the invention distributions by shifting both the mean and the right-hand tail of the invention search distribution to the right. The actual mechanism of recharge, however, is often in the form of biological invention or varieties that serve as parents in the recharged invention distribution.

Suppose that the shifter of the varietal discovery function (9) is germplasm G_F, delivered from foreign sources. Then the germplasm enhanced varietal discovery function will be:

$$E_n(z) = \theta \, G_F + \lambda \, G_F \, ln(n) \tag{13}$$

Equation (13) could then be considered to be the adaptive invention function for a follower inventor. But adaptive invention programs also produce their own germplasm. A more general expression is:

$$I_F = a_1 + a_2 \ln(R_F) + a_3 \ln(R_F)G_I + a_4 \ln(R_F)G_F \tag{14}$$

where I_F: Follower Inventions (by a developing country)

R_F: Adaptive R&D (by a developing country)

G_I: Cumulated domestic germplasm at the beginning of the period

G_F: Cumulated foreign germplasm relevant to follower inventors in the country during the period.

Figure 10.3 depicts the nature of these recharge processes. Note that with recharge the TD point itself moves. With unbiased recharge the TD path will be parallel to the optimal path thus restoring the meaning of the induced innovation concept.

B.5. Location Specificity and Recharge

Foreign germplasm, G_F, may take the form of varieties suited to direct release in the recipient country. In this case they could be directly substitutable for domestic innovations (varieties).

Induced Adaptive Invention/Innovation

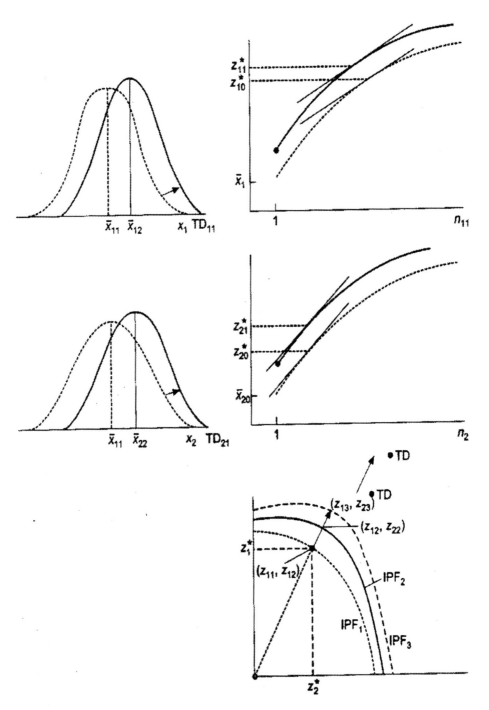

Figure 10.3. Multiple Search with Recharge.

In the empirical section below, a subset of the varieties crossed in an International Agricultural Research Center (IARC) program are treated as germplasm for National

Agricultural research Systems (NARS) programs. If there were no geo-climate barriers to the value of IARC-crossed MVs, i.e., if these MVs were of equal value in all countries, we would observe little or no NARS breeding activities. But geo-climate barriers do exist and thus an IARC-crossed MV has different values in different countries. Potential recharge value is measured by whether the IARC MV was released in a given country.

Gollin and Evenson (1997) report data for rice varieties by country of origin of the cross underlying the variety and by country of release of the varieties. The authors note that of 1,709 varietal releases in their data base, 294 were crossed at the International Rice Research Institute (IRRI) and 1,415 were crossed in a National Agricultural Research System (NARS) program. Virtually all of the IRRI- crossed varieties were released in other countries (25 were released in the Philippines). Release boards in each country determine whether a variety is suited to conditions in the country. The ratio of national releases to origin releases for IARC-crossed MVs was approximately 8 (of a possible 40). However, for the NARS-crossed varieties, the ratio of national releases to origin releases to origin releases was 1.1. Thus, only ten percent of the NARS-crossed releases were actually released in another country. This is a very low rate of international transfer of technology.

Gollin and Evenson also analyzed the parents of the 1,709 varieties. Of the 3,418 parents, 1,022 were based on an IRRI cross and 1,396 on NARS crosses. The ratio of National releases to origin releases for IRRI-crossed parents was 25. The ratio of national releases to origin releases for NARS-crossed parents was 1.37. Thus, many more parents crossed international boundaries than was the case for varieties themselves.

C. Testing the Induced Invention/Innovation Model for the Green Revolution

The model sketched out in Part I shows how recharge research is important to induced innovation. The model does not address the matter of incentives for undertaking R&D. Nor does it address direct inter-industry or geographic spillovers from one region to another. Indirect spillovers in the form of invention recharge from IARCs to NARS breeders are addressed in the model.

As the discussion of the Green Revolution below will show, both problems are central for agriculture. Consider the incentives problem. Public sector agricultural research systems have been built in most countries of the world. These systems were among the earliest cases where governments recognized that incentive systems, chiefly Intellectual Property Rights (IPRs) systems, were not sufficient to bring forth adequate invention from the private sector In response, public sector colleges of agriculture and mechanics (A&Ms) were designed to train agricultural and engineering practitioners, and a system of public experiment stations was established to undertake biological invention in many countries.

During the first half of the 20th century, plant breeding programs were established in most developed countries. Agricultural experiment stations were located in U.S. states and the public competition between states to serve farmers in their constituencies had emerged as the motivating force for investment.

For the developing countries, agricultural research programs were less well developed in the early part of the century. Most developing country systems were guided by colonial politics. This did produce effective research programs for crops destined for export to the mother country (tea, coffee, sugar, spices) but, for most crops, little real research capacity was in place. Many small developing countries could not expect to develop research specializations of the type emerging in the U.S.

During the 1950s, considerable emphasis was given to extension programs providing farmers with technical advice. These programs were motivated by the "easy mimicry" model that also guided industrial policy. By the end of the 1950s, however, the broad outlines of the population expansion in developing countries were becoming clear. Most countries were faced with the prospect of a doubling and in some cases, a tripling of populations in the next four decades. This called for an expansion of food production that was historically unprecedented. The "easy mimicry" model was deemed to be incapable of meeting this challenge.

The response of development agencies, both bilateral and multilateral, was to support National Agricultural Research System (NARS) development and to further support NARS programs by developing a system of commodity-focused International Agricultural Research Centers (IARCs). The IARC system (supported by a consortium of donors – the Consultative Group for International Agricultural Research) design was based on two predecessor projects, each which facilitated early Green Revolution achievements.

The first of these was a Special Project of the Rockefeller Foundation in Mexico. Beginning in the early 1940s, Norman Borlaug instituted a wheat breeding program designed to incorporate genetic improvements in temperate zone wheats into wheat varieties suited to the sub-tropical wheat regions in developing countries. By the early 1960s, this program had achieved considerable success and, by the late 1960s, wheat varieties from this program were credited with creating a Green Revolution in Asia.

The second program was the FAO supported program for Japonica-Indica rice development. This program was also dedicated to incorporating features of temperate zone Japonica rice improvements into tropical zone Indica rice cultivars. While this program was discontinued at the end of the 1960s, it did lead to the development of several important rice varieties and established the foundations for the early development of semi-dwarf plant type rice varieties in the 1960s at the first IARC, the International Rice Research Institute. This development was also credited with creating a Green Revolution.

The design of the IARCs was guided by past experience with agricultural experiment stations. The features of recharge science and the provision of germplasm to NARS in the crop-focused IARCs were guided by induced innovation perspectives. In a sense, the IARCs were built as a remedy for the lack of pre-invention science capacity in developing country NARS programs.

C.1. MV Releases

A picture of the Green Revolution is reported in Table 1 where a summary of the production of modern improved crop varieties for ten food crops is presented. These ten crops account for 85 to 90 percent of food crop production in the developing world. (Rice is the most important crop, followed by wheat and maize).

IARC content in released varieties is summarized by crop and region as well. For all crop varieties, 36 percent were produced in an IARC breeding program where the cross leading to the varietal release was made in the IARC program (IX).

Table 1. Average Annual Varietal Releases by Crop and Region 1965-1998

Average Annual Releases								1965-1998 IARC Content**			
Crop	1965-70	1971-75	1976-80	1981-85	1986-90	1991-95	1996-98*	IX	IP	IA	IN
Wheat	40.8	54.2	58.0	75.6	81.2	79.3	(79.3)	.49	.29	.08	.14
Rice	19.2	35.2	43.8	50.8	57.8	54.8	58.5	.20	.25	.07	.48
Maize	13.4	16.6	21.6	43.4	52.7	108.3	71.3	.28	.15	.04	.53
Sorghum	6.9	7.2	9.6	10.6	12.2	17.6	14.3	.16	.07	.06	.71
Millets	0.8	0.4	1.8	5.0	4.8	6.0	9.7	.15	.41	.09	.35
Barley	0.0	0.0	0.0	2.8	8.2	5.6	7.3	.49	.20	.01	.30
Lentils	0.0	0.0	0.0	1.8	1.8	3.9	(3.9)	.54	.05	.01	.40
Beans	4.0	7.0	12.0	18.5	18.0	43.0	(43.0)	.72	.05	.01	.19
Cassava	0.0	1.0	2.0	15.8	9.8	13.6	(13.6)	.53	.15	.01	.31
Potatoes	2.0	10.4	13.0	15.9	18.9	19.6	(19.6)	.17	.06	.02	.75
All Crops											
Latin America	37.8	55.9	65.9	92.5	116.2	177.3	139.2	.39	.14	.04	.43
Asia	27.2	59.6	66.8	86.3	76.7	81.2	79.9	.18	.29	.10	.43
Middle East North Africa	4.4	8.0	10.2	12.2	28.4	30.5	82.2	.62	.22	.04	.12
Sub-Saharan Africa	17.7	18.0	23.0	43.2	46.2	50.1	55.2	45	.21	.07	.27
All Regions	87.1	132.0	161.8	240.2	265.8	351.7	320.5	.36	.20	.06	.42

* Numbers in parentheses are simple repetition of 1991-95 rates because of insufficient data.

**IX: Variety based on IARC Cross; IA, Variety based on NARS cross with at least one non-Parent IARC ancestor.
IP: Variety based on NARS cross with at least one IARC parent; IN: Variety based on NARS cross with no IARC ancestors.

The remaining varieties were based on crosses made in a NARS program (IARC-crossed MVs accounted for 35 percent of the area planted to MVs in 1998).

NARS-crossed releases can be further classified according to whether one or both parents in the cross was an IARC release. For all NARS-crossed varieties, roughly 17 percent had at least one IARC-crossed parent (IP). (These varieties accounted for 25 percent of MV acreage in 1998.) This attests to a strong germplasmic recharge effect, since NARS breeders found success in using IARC parental material. When grandparents and other ancestors of NARS-crossed varieties are considered, (IA), IARC-crossed germplasm, appears in 23 percent of all NARS-crossed varieties. This IARC germplasm proportion is also rising over time.

Table 1 also reports release data for all crops by region. These data show that the highest rate of increase in varietal production in the 1980s and 1990s occurred in the Middle East-North Africa and Sub-Saharan African regions. These regions were also the most dependent on IARC crosses and germplasm.

Total varietal releases for all crops show a steady increase over time. Annual varietal releases in the 1990s were more than double the releases during the 1970s.

C.2. Testing the Research as Search Model

The induced innovation model outlined earlier provides a basis for testing for a germplasm impact on NARS breeding programs. The "breeding with recharge" function actually imposes a specific functional form for the germplasm impact and this form can be tested against a more general form. This test is carried out using NARS data for three periods, 1965-75, 1976-85 and 1986-96, for varietal releases in wheat, rice, maize, beans, and potatoes.

The functional form implied by the induced innovation model is (14).

Diminishing returns to search dictates the logarithmic specification. The G_I and G_F variables are not in logarithmic form because they are not part of the NARS search per se. That is (except indirectly) IARC germplasm affects NARS productivity, but NARS do not produce IARC germplasm.

Table 2 reports definitions and means for variables.

V_N is the number of varietal releases based on NARS crosses over the period, where n indexes countries.

B_N is the number of scientists engaged in CGI research on the crop at the beginning of the period. B_N was estimated in two stages. First the total number of senior agricultural scientists for the period and country was computed from the ISNAR data base (Pardey, Roseboom, and Anderson, 1991). Then a search of the FAO Agrostat data base for publications on plant breeding and related activities by crop, as well as on social science research, animal and pasture research and other fields of agricultural science. Publication shares for plant breeding on the crops in question were then formed for each country. These shares were then multiplied by the ISNAR scientist data to obtain our measure of B_N.

G_F is measured as the cumulated number of IARC crosses released as varieties in the country. This definition of germplasmic input attempts to correct for the fact that only a subset of IARC-crossed material is relevant in a given country. If the country actually released an IARC cross as a variety, this is taken to be an indication of relevance.

G_I is measured as the cumulative NARS crossed released at the beginning of the period.

Table 2. Variable Definitions: Means by Crop

Variable	Definitions	Wheat (66)	Rice (54)	Maize (32)	Beans (45)	Potatoes (51)
I. Endogenous Variables						
B_N	Number of scientist man years in NARS CVI program	298	206	126	25.6	61.1
V_N	Number of NARS crossed varietal releases	30.6	19.5	10.5	4.36	11.6
II. Exogenous Variables						
G_I	International Germplasm Stocks: Cumulated number of IARC crossed varieties released in the countries	19.0	6.31	1.88	4.09	9.98
G_N	National Germplasm Stocks: Cumulated NARS crossed varietal releases (V_N) in previous periods.	21.1	15.4	6.15	1.06	6.61
HA	Hectares (000) planted to the crop at the beginning of the period	2847	4613	244	377	1470
RPOPDEN	Population Density at the beginning of the period, Rural Population/area in crops and pasture (FAO)	256	411	523	268	230
GDP/c	GDP per capita in US dollars beginning of period, World Bank Atlas Method (World Bank Tables)	2784	2820	1954	2577	3410
Tech 2	Technology Capital Indicators from Evenson, 2000; Measures of Technological Capacity	.19	.11	.29	.27	.08
Tech 3		.48	.38	.54	.37	.51
Tech 4		.31	.28	.21	.35	.37
Climate2	Climate class indicators, from Evenson, 2000	.26	.39	.64	.62	.58
3		.40	.22	.27	.25	.24
4		.31	.16	.18	.19	.24
5		.31	.06	0	0	.06
6		.18	.11	.18	.13	.12
7		.09	.06	0	.06	.06

Specification (14) can be compared to a more general "Cobb-Douglas" log-linear form. In earlier work Mean Square Error tests showed (13) to be superior to the Cobb-Douglas functional form in all crops.

Table 3 reports estimates of (14) for five major crops in developing countries. Table 3 also reports estimates based on pooled crops. Two specifications are reported. The first specification treated the B_N variable as an exogenous variable. The second specification is a 2SLS specification where the B_N variable is predicted in a first stage (Evenson and Gollin, 2002, Chapter 21). Table 3 reports second stage estimates. For both pooled specifications the country-specific germplasm stock is the preferred specification, lending support to the proposition that the relevant germplasm stock for developing countries is not the world (or even the developing countries) frontier, but only a country-specific part of the world frontier.

Table 3 reports exclusion tests as well as tests of equation (13) versus a Cobb-Douglas specification. These estimates thus support the Adoption Invention/Innovation model. The international recharge term interaction is positive and highly significant in all specifications. The national germplasm term is also positive in all but the beans specification.

Table 3. Estimates -- NARS Varietal Production Specification Dependent Variable: NARS Varietal Releases

Independent Variables	2SLS (Second Stage)						3SLS Pooled
	Wheat	Rice	Maize	Beans	Potatoes	Pooled	
Ln (Bn)	4.813	11.926	6.742	1.287	2.490	4.918	7.702
	(1.54)	(2.32)	(2.79)	(.71)	(.69)	(2.94)	(3.26)
Ln (BN) x GI	.0966	.1443	.8919	.3496	.3314	.1985	.2395
	(1.85)	(1.53)	(4.21)	(4.55)	(6.24)	(6.61)	(6.29)
ln (BN) x GN	.0141	.0835	.0236	-.00015	.0427	.0600	.0146
	(.58)	(3.45)	(.72)	(.05)	(1.47)	(4.50)	.73
D Beans						-2.32	1.69
D Rice						-3.69	-9.48*
D Potatoes						-6.78	-8.42*
D Maize						-.35	2.09
# Obs	66	54	32	45	51	248	248
R^2	.711	.593	.849	.742	.741	.533	.596
P-Values							
Equation R^2 (2)	.0000	.0000	.0000	.0000	.0000	.0000	.0000
R^2 (3)	.0000	.0214	.0032	.369	.429	.0000	.0000*
Excluded Variable x^2	5.04	16.6	1.17	.83	16.4		
.05 Value	11.07	12.59	11.07	12.59	16.84		

C.3. Implications for NARS Productivity

The recharge role of IARC programs in the Green Revolution was very important to the production of MVs. Table 4 reports elasticities for independent variables on NARS MV production.

These elasticities show:

a) That NARS breeding resources (B_N) are subject to diminishing returns with elasticities well below one.
b) That International (IARC) germplasm (G_I) has an important productivity enhancing impact for pooled crop estimates.
c) That National (NARS) germplasm stocks (G_N) also have a productivity impact, but of smaller magnitude than the IARC germplasm.
d) That the sum of the production elasticities is approximately one or greater, indicating that the recharged NARS breeding programs were not subject to diminishing returns.

Table 4. MV Production Elasticities

2SLS (Second Stage)							3SLS Pooled
Independent Variables	Wheat	Rice	Maize	Beans	Potatoes	Pooled	
MV Production Elasticities							
B_N	.23	.72	.81	.62	.52	.45	.60
G_I	.23	.20	.50	.73	.92	.38	.46
G_N	.04	.28	.04	0	.08	.14	.04
Sum	.50	1.20	1.35	1.35	1.52	.97	1.10

D. IMPLICATIONS FOR NARS INVESTMENT

Table 2 also reports variables utilized in a NARS-CGI investment equation. IARC germplasm has two effects on NARS investment. One is the complementary effect reflected in Tables 3 and 4.

The second is a substitution effect associated with the fact that IARCs produce competing varieties.

The investment specification underlying Table 5 includes the following variables:

G_I:	International germplasm
G_N:	National germplasm
HA:	Hectares planted to the crop
Popden:	Rural population density
GDP/c:	GDP per capita

and interaction with G_I.

Table 5 reports estimates of the investment specification. Note that in the pooled estimates, the international germplasm variable (G_I) interacts positively with hectares planted (HA) and population density (Popden).

Table 6 reports elasticity estimates (and associated P values) evaluated at the mean and at the mean plus one standard deviation (in parenthesis). For the G_I elasticities, the second set of elasticities shares evaluations at the mean plus one standard deviation for both the hectare interaction and the Popden interaction terms.

The elasticities show:

1. That NARS program investments respond to hectares planted to the crop, but with elasticities below one. This is probably indicating that there are significant scale economics to plant breeding programs.
2. That NARS program investments respond positively to population density. For the pooled estimate the Popden elasticities are approximately 0.5, the

same as those for hectares. However, this population density effect is reflecting concern with land scarcity. This "Boserup" effect is quite strong. Countries with low population densities perceive that they can expand production by expanding area cropped.

3. Income (GDP/c) elasticities are low and not statistically significant when population density and hectares planted are considered.

4. International germplam (G_I) elasticities evaluated at the mean are very low. When evaluated at the mean plus one standard deviation for hectares planted and population density, they are positive and substantial (0.21 to 0.4).

Table 5. Estimates - NARS CGI Investment. Dependent Variable: ln(BN) by Period

Independent Variables	2SLS (Second Stage)						3SLS Pooled
	Wheat	Rice	Maize	Beans	Potatoes	Pooled	
Ln(GI)	-1.82 (1.35)	1.164 (.56)	.1884 (2.40)	-2.921 (1.13)	-1.074 (.37)	-2.061 (2.36)	-2.041 (2.56)
ln(GN)	-0.87 (.85)	.150 (1.33)	.251 (1.04)	-.018 (.09)	.013 (.09)	-.03 (.43)	-.055 (.97)
ln(HA)	.495 (3.45)	.745 (4.06)	.581 (1.83)	.533 (2.08)	.390 (2.19)	.347 (6.03)	.332 (6.24)
ln(Popden)	1.341 (5.88)	.708 (2.44)	.313 (.52)	.281 (.63)	-.022 (.05)	.367 (2.39)	.534 (2.39)
ln(GDP/C)	-.339 (.74)	.863 (2.01)	-2.76 (.61)	-.275 (.86)	1.065 (1.73)	117 (.76)	.125 (.89)
ln(GI) x ln(HA)	.108 (1.87)	.029 (.46)	.170 (1.02)	.066 (.67)	.069 (.84)	.103 (4.39)	.122 (5.63)
ln(GI) x ln(Popden)	-.095 (.75)	.237 (1.59)	.971 (1.57)	.122 (.63)	.149 (.69)	.112 (1.65)	.094 (1.52)
ln(GI) x ln(GDP/C)	.112 (.78)	-.015 (.10)	1.409 (2.16)	.150 (.17)	-.092 (.34)	.007 (.09)	-.022 (.32)
Number of Observations	66	54	32	45	51	248	248
R^2	.711	.593	.849	.742	.741	.533	.496
F	22.9	13.16	6.36	5.70	6.82	29.5	

This appears to be indicating that NARS programs with large acreages and high population densities are responding positively to the complementary impact of IARC germplasm.

The complementary effect outweighs the substitution effect. Conversely, for countries with small acreages and low population densities, the substitution effect outweighs the complementary effect.

When weighted by actual hectares and population densities, these estimates show that the weighted net elasticity is approximately 0.18.

Table 6. Elasticities -- NARS CGI Investment Estimates

Independent Variables	2SLS (Second Stage)						3SLS Pooled
	Wheat	Rice	Maize	Beans	Potatoes	Pooled	
NARS CGI Investments Elasticity Calculations							
HA***	.75 (.95) (.000)	.78 (.81) (.000)	.67 (.86) (.026)	.59 (.66) (.026)	.51 (.59) (.007)	.50 (.63) (.000)	.52 (.67) (.000)
Popden***	1.12 (.93) (.000)	.99 (1.26) (.044)	.84 (1.56) (.005)	.39 (.52) (.279)	.24 (.46) (.704)	.49 (.63) (.000)	.47 (.58) (.000)
GDP/C***	-.08 (.14) (5.26)	.84 (.83) (.641)	.49 (1.50) (.032)	-.14 (.02) (.653)	.80 (.79) (.022)	.13 (.14) (.319)	.09 (.07) (.330)
GI****	-.05 (.18) (.10) (.143)	2.80 (2.85) (3.08) (.612)	-.68 (-.39) (.41) (.028)	-.28 (-.02) (.10) (.255)	-.16 (-.02) (.09) (.704)	-.11 (.11) (.21) (.015)	-.14 (.12) (.40) (.009)
GN****	-.087 (.40)	.150 (.192)	.251 (.315)	-.018 (.930)	.013 (.920)	-.03 (.67)	-.066 (.334)

* Evaluated at mean GI and mean + 1 SD GI

** P values sum of coefficient.

*** Evaluated at mean Ha , mean + 1 SD Ha, mean + 1 SD Popden.

**** Evaluated at mean.

CONCLUSION

This paper provides a test of the Evenson-Kislev "Research as Search" model utilizing data from NARS and IARC plant breeding programs in developing countries. Data for five crops – wheat, rice, maize, beans and potatoes – were analyzed. These were the dominant Green Revolution crops.

Two tests of the model were developed. The first was a "functional form" test. The Research as Search model implies the functional form shown in (7). This form was compared to a Cobb-Douglas form. The second was a "recharge" test, where IARC-produced germplasm (G_I) was treated as a shifter of NARS breeding functions (see (14)). This recharge specification also implies a specific functional form.

The functional form tests showed that the data preferred the "Research as Search" functional form over the simple Cobb-Douglas form.

The recharge tests showed that IARC-produced germplasm did shift NARS breeding functions in a significant way. For the pooled estimates the NARS breeding resource elasticities showed strong diminishing returns (the elasticity was approximately 0.6). With IARC recharge (elasticities of 0.4), NARS breeding programs were not subject to diminishing returns. From 1970 to 1990, NARS breeding resources doubled. So did the production of NARS-crossed MVs.

Finally, this paper evaluated the net impact of IARC program investments on NARS program investments. This effect has two parts. The recharge effect is positive. The competition or substitution effect is negative. That is, IARC-crossed MVs compete with NARS-crossed MVs.

This analysis showed that there are implicit scale economies affecting NARS investments. The analysis also showed that population densities stimulate NARS investments. The IARC germplasm effect on NARS investments was related to both size of program (hectares planted) and population density. For small programs and for countries with low population densities, competition effects of IARC germplasm dominated. For larger countries and population dense countries, recharge effects dominated. For all developing countries (weighted by population density and hectares planted), the net impact of IARC germplasm was positive. The doubling of IARC investment from 1965 to 1985 stimulated 18 percent more NARS investment.

A final comment is in order here. Organizations providing research support to NARS breeding programs do not provide recharge. Recharge comes from programs dedicated to recharge support. The IARCs did accept a rehcarge support role vis-à-vis NARS programs. The estimates of the "research as search" model strongly supports the merit of the recharge support role.

REFERENCES

Ahamd, S. (1966). On the Theory of Induced Innovation. *The Economic Journal, Vol. 76* (302), 344-357.

Binswanger, H.P., and Vernon W.R., with Ben-Zion, U. (1978). *Induced Innovation: Technology, Institutions, and Development.* Baltimore: John Hopkins University Press.

Evenson, R.E. (2000). *Productivity and Agricultural Growth in the Second Half of the 20th Century: State of Food and Agriculture.* Rome: FAO.

Evenson, R.E., and Gollin, D. (Eds.) (2002). *Crop Variety Improvement and its Effect on Productivity: the Impact of International Agricultural Research.* Oxfordshire, UK: CABI publication.

Evenson, R.E., and Kislev, Y. (1976). A Stochastic Model of Applied Research. *Journal of Political Economy, Vol. 84* (2), 265-281.

Gollin, D., and Evenson, R.E. (1997). Genetic Resources, International Organizations, and Rice Varietal Improvement. *Economic Development and Cultural Change, Vol. 45* (3), 471-500.

Kennedy, C. (1964). Induced Bias in Innovation and the Theory of Distribution. *The Economic Journal, Vol. 75,* 541-547.

Kortum, S. (1997). Research, Patenting and Technological Change. *Econometrica, Vol. 65*, 1389-1419.

Nordhaus, W.D. (1973). Some Skeptical Thoughts on the Theory of Induced Innovation. *Quarterly Journal of Economics, Vol. 87*, 208-219.

Pardey, P.G., Roseboom, J., and Anderson, J.R. (Eds.) (1991). *Agricultural Research Policy: International Quantitative Perspective.* Cambridge, United Kingdom: Cambridge University Press.

Samuelson, P.A. (1966). Rejoinder: Agreements, Disagreements, Doubts and the Case of Induced Harrod-Neutral Technical Change. *Review of Economics and Statistics, Vol. 48*, 444-448.

Stigler, G.J. (1961). The Economics of Information. *Journal of Political Economy,Vol. 69*, 213-25.

In: The Economics of Natural and Human Resources...   ISBN 978-1-60741-029-4
Editor: Ayal Kimhi and Israel Finkelshtain   © 2009 Nova Science Publishers, Inc.

Chapter 11

ECONOMIC CONSEQUENCES OF KNOWLEDGE SPILLOVERS

Yacov Tsur[*,1] and Amos Zemel[2]*

ABSTRACT

Empirical evidence attests to non-negligible productivity effects of human-capital spillovers. We study implications of these externalities for welfare measurement, investment in education and patterns of knowledge-based economic growth. Estimating the productivity spillovers for an economy with Cobb-Douglas technology and iso-elastic preferences and using empirical parameter values, we find substantial effects in all three categories. A simple, self-financed education policy that implements the socially optimal outcome is offered.

A. INTRODUCTION

Human capital spillovers occur, inter alia, when workers' productivity increases with the education level of other workers in their geographic and economic vicinity. This phenomenon has long been identified as a potentially important determinant of economic growth, capable of explaining some of the large variations observed across national incomes (Romer 1986, Lucas 1988). Empirical assessment of these effects, however, has been elusive (Acemoglu and Angrist 2000, Jaffe et al. 1993, Thompson and Fox-Kean 2005). This issue has recently been addressed by Moretti (2004a) who investigated manufacturing plants in different U.S. cities and identified the productivity effect of human capital spillovers from inter-city

[1] Department of Agricultural Economics and Management, The Hebrew University of Jerusalem, POB 12 Rehovot 76100, Israel. Email: tsur@agri.huji.ac.il.
[2] The Jacob Blaustein Institutes for Desert Research and Department of Industrial Engineering and Management, Ben Gurion University of the Negev, Sede Boker Campus, 84990, Israel.

variations in the share of college graduates. Moretti's findings attest to the presence of non-negligible productivity spillovers associated with higher education.

In this work we study consequences of productivity spillovers for welfare measurement, investment in education and patterns of growth. Our underlying growth model allows to derive these spillover effects in terms of simple analytic expressions and to evaluate them for a reference economy with Cobb-Douglas technology and iso-elastic preferences, using received parameter estimates. We find substantial spillover effects in all three categories.

Welfare measurement in a growing economy has been studied by Aronsson and Löfgren (1996), Weitzman (1997), Weitzman and Löfgren (1997), and Asheim (1997, 2004) – the former for endogenous growth with knowledge spillovers and the others for exogenous growth. Following this line of research, we derive a "knowledge spillover premium" that modifies the NNP to obtain a valid welfare measure in the case of knowledge-based growth with knowledge spillover externalities, and estimate its magnitude at around 12 percent. This value is considerably smaller than the 40 percent estimate of Weitzman (1997) and Weitzman and Löfgren (1997), where technological progress is assumed to be entirely exogenous. The difference can be attributed (at least in part) to the intra-firm human capital effect that is endogenous in our framework, thus not included in the premium parameter (that corrects only for external effects).

The other spillover effects also turn out to be substantial. We find that accounting for knowledge spillovers increases investment in education by about 50 percent and the ensuing (balanced) growth rate by 30 percent. Such considerable gains call for policy intervention and we offer a simple, self-financed education policy that implements the socially optimal outcome, providing an education subsidy that is financed by either a flat income tax (during the transition phase) or a flat consumption tax (during the balanced growth phase). The mechanism's budget is balanced at each instant of time and requires no lump-sum transfers. This simple mechanism – with flat subsidy and taxes – is restricted to Cobb-Douglas economies. In a more general setting, time-varying subsidies and taxes based on stocks rather than flows (e.g., human capital subsidy rather than education subsidy) are needed to implement the socially optimal outcome, as discussed by Romer (1986) and Aronsson and Löfgren (1996) among others (see Gradstein et al. 2005 and references therein). While education in general generates myriad of extramarket benefits (e.g., reduced criminal activity, healthier life style, informed political decisions – see Wolfe and Haveman 2002, Moretti 2004b, and Gradstein et al. 2005), here we focus only on productivity spillovers. As estimates of these spillovers are primarily linked to higher education (Moretti 2004a), our considerations also focus on this form of education.

The literature on human-capital-based economic growth can be traced back to Arrow's (1962) learning-by-doing model and Shell's (1966, 1967, 1973) treatment of knowledge assets as an additional sector subject to policy decisions – both were early attempts to endogenize Solow's (1956, 1957) residuals. Recent literature follows Lucas (1988) who assumed that learning is a time-consuming activity and incorporated spillovers (see Barro and Sala-i-Martin 2004, Chapter 5, for an overview and extensions). Indeed, Aronsson and Löfgren (1996) based their growth framework on Lucas (1988). Here we follow Shell (1967) by treating learning as an income-consuming activity. While the cost of primary and secondary schooling in developed nations is borne, for the most part, by the public, the cost of higher education is largely private (Wolfe and Haveman 2002). Productivity spillovers are primarily linked to higher education (Moretti 2004a), and their analysis should include the income component of education investment.

In the following section we describe the economic setting. A complete dynamic characterization of both the transient and steady state phases of the private and social growth processes is described in Section 3. The optimal growth processes exhibit a turnpike property (Samuelson 1965, Cass 1966), reaching a certain path (the turnpike) *as rapidly as possible* (in a sense precisely defined in the text) and proceeding along it thereafter. Tsur and Zemel (2005, 2007a, 2007b) obtained the same growth pattern in a number of growth contexts. Other growth models that behave in this fashion are discussed in Barro and Sala-i-Martin (2004, Chapter 5). In Section 4 we discuss welfare measurement and specify the "knowledge spillover premium" associated with the NNP index. In Section 5 we estimate the knowledge spillover effects on welfare, investment in (higher) education and growth rates for a reference economy characterized by Cobb-Douglas technology and iso-elastic preferences using empirical parameter values. Section 6 describes the education policy that internalizes the spillover externalities and establishes its optimal properties for the reference economy. Section 7 concludes and the appendix contains technical derivations.

B. THE ECONOMY

To allow a sharp focus on the effects of knowledge spillovers, we consider a simplistic endogenous growth setting, in which competitive firms hire capital and labor to produce a composite good, and households choose their temporal evolution of consumption and education-saving investments. We briefly describe the economic setting below.

Firms: Firm i employs capital (K_i) and labor (L_i) to produce the output (Y_i) according to the technology $Y_i = B(H)F(K_i, A(h)L_i)$, where h represents individual (intrafirm) worker's level of human capital, $A(h)$ is a labor-augmenting productivity function, $B(H)$ is an inter-firm technology index that depends on aggregate knowledge $H = Lh$, and $L = \Sigma_i L_i$ is aggregate labor. The productivity index B represents the state of technology adopted by the economy up to the present time and incorporates the spillover effects of knowledge. These external effects may emanate from the knowledge flow (learning) or from human capital stocks (Chamley, 1993). Here we assume the latter. The external effects are specified as output augmenting but could enter as labor augmenting (as in Bils and Klenow 2000) without changing the nature of the results. The production function F is assumed to be linearly homogenous, thus can be expressed as $F(K_i, A(h)L_i) = L_i A(h) f(k_i/A(h))$, where $k_i = K_i/l_i$ is firm i's capital per worker and f is assumed increasing and strictly concave over $(0,\infty)$ with $f(0) = 0$, $f(\infty) = \infty$, $f'(0) = \infty$ and $f'(\infty) = 0$.

At each point of time, firms observe the aggregate stock of human capital, the wage rate w and the capital rental rate r and demand the capital per worker that maximizes profit per worker $A(h) f(k_i/A(h))B(H) - rk_i - w$. A necessary condition is

$$f'(k_i/A(h))B(H) = r. \qquad (2.1)$$

The labor market clearing wage rate w corresponds to a vanishing profit, yielding

$$[A(h)f(k_i/A(h)) - k_if'(k_i/A(h))]B(H) = w. \tag{2.2}$$

Multiplying (2.1) by K_i and (2.2) by L_i, adding the results and summing over all firms, we find

$$rK+wL = LA(h)f(k/A(h))B(H) = Y,$$

where $Y = \sum_i Y_i$ is aggregate output. Dividing through by L, we obtain

$$rk+w = A(h)f(k/A(h))B(H) \equiv y(k,h,H). \tag{2.3}$$

Equation (2.3) relates household income to the current levels of physical and human capital.

Households: The representative household decides on the evolution of asset holdings (k), human capital (h) and consumption (c). We follow Shell's (1966, 1967, 1973) approach, taking learning as an income-consuming activity and assume that knowledge accumulation ($\dot{h}$) is proportional to learning outlays,

$$\dot{h}_t = \alpha_t y(k_t, h_t, H_t) \tag{2.4}$$

where α_t is the fraction of income devoted to learning at time t (human capital depreciation could be added without affecting the nature of the results). The remaining income is allocated between consumption and saving, giving

$$\dot{k}_t = (1 - \alpha_t)y(k_t, h_t, H_t) - c_t \tag{2.5}$$

(k-capital depreciation is included in y). Here we assume that investment in physical capital is reversible, i.e., consumption can derive from the stock of capital at no extra cost.

The representative household derives utility from consumption according to an increasing and concave utility function $u(c)$ with a constant utility discount rate ρ. Given the capital-knowledge endowment (k_0, h_0), a feasible consumption-investment plan (c_t, α_t) satisfies (2.4), (2.5), $h_t \geq 0$, $k_t \geq 0$, $c_t \geq 0$ and $0 \leq \alpha_t \leq 1$ for all $t \geq 0$, and generates the value

$$\int_0^\infty u(c_t)e^{-\rho t}dt \tag{2.6}$$

The upper bound $\alpha_t = 1$ entails investing all income in education, so that consumption is funded exclusively from savings. Alternative exogenous bounds can be assumed with very little effect on the results. The optimal plan is the feasible plan that maximizes (2.6). We denote by $V(k,h)$ the value of (2.6) under the optimal plan given the endowment $k_0 = k$ and $h_0 = h$.

In solving the intertemporal allocation problem, households treat aggregate knowledge H as exogenously given, even though it is recognized that in equilibrium $H_t = Lh_t$. A social planner, on the other hand, accounts for these spillover effects of knowledge. The household's and social planner optimal plans are called *private* and *social*, respectively.

C. DYNAMIC CHARACTERIZATION

The simple structure of the allocation problem (2.4)-(2.6) allows the characterization of the optimal plans over the whole time horizon. Here we describe the main features of the private and social plans; a detailed account with formal derivations can be found in Tsur and Zemel (2004). The significance of the differences between these plans will be studied in the following sections. The optimal learning policy at each point of time takes one of three distinct regimes: no learning ($\alpha=0$), maximal learning ($\alpha=1$), or *singular* learning (with an intermediate learning fraction, as explained below). Consumption and saving are optimally adjusted to the chosen learning regime. With this classification we describe the optimal *h-k* processes in terms of two characteristic curves defined in the state space.

The first curve consists of the locus of (h,k) states at which the marginal product of human capital, $y_h \equiv \partial y(k,h,H)/\partial h$, equals that of physical capital, $y_k \equiv \partial y/\partial k$, implying that no additional gains can be made by reshuffling investment between k and h when they both increase. This curve differs between the private and social plans because the evaluation of the marginal product of h (y_h) depends on whether the productivity index $B(H)$ is taken as an exogenous parameter (private) or as a function of $H = Lh$ (social). Let $\eta_A(h) = A'(h)h/A(h)$ and $\eta_B(H) = B'(H)H/B(H)$ denote the elasticities of internal and external knowledge effects, respectively, $x = k/A(h)$ and $z(x) \equiv f(x)/f'(x) - x$. Noting (2.3), the marginal product of human capital is given by

$$(p) \ y_h = f'(x)z(x)A'(h)B(H), \ (so) \ y_h = [f'(x)z(x) + f(x)\eta_B(H)/\eta_A(h)]A'(h)B(H)$$

$$(3.1)$$

where p and so signify *private* and *socially optimal*, respectively. The marginal product of (physical) capital is $y_k = f'(x)B(H)$ for both plans. The no-arbitrage condition $y_k = y_h$, then, implies

$$(p) \ z(x) = \frac{1}{A'(h)}, \ (so) \ z(x) + \frac{\eta_B(Lh)}{\eta_A(h)}(z(x) + x) = \frac{1}{A'(h)} \qquad (3.2)$$

Notice, recalling $f'(x) > 0$ and $f''(x) < 0$, that $z(x)$ is increasing. Solving for $x = k/A(h)$, we see that (3.2p) defines a curve in the *h-k* plane, which we call the *private singular curve* and denote by $k_p^S(h)$. The analogous solution of (3.2so) defines the *social singular curve*, denoted $k_{so}^S(h)$. We use the notation $k^S(h)$ to represent either $k_p^S(h)$ or $k_{so}^S(h)$ when no confusion arises. It turns out that $k^S(h)$ is the unique locus of (h,k) points along which the singular learning policy is supported. Thus, when this policy is adopted, the consumption rate must be adjusted to the learning rate so as to keep the (h,k) process along the singular curve.

The second term of (3.2*so*), representing the contribution of the external effects, is positive. Since $z(x)$ is increasing, this term implies that $k_p^S(h) > k_{so}^S(h)$.

To understand the economic significance of the singular curve note that above the curve, when $k > k^S(h)$, the relation $y_k < y_h$ holds, so that physical capital is less productive than knowledge hence investment in human capital is more attractive than saving. The opposite situation holds below the singular curve. Along the singular curve the two forms of capital are equally productive at the margin and the decision maker (household for the private plan and the social planner for the social plan) should be indifferent between investing in one or the other. Indeed, we find that if the economy grows indefinitely, the optimal (h,k) process first approaches the singular curve at a most-rapid-learning rate: maximal learning ($\alpha=1$) above the curve and no learning ($\alpha=0$) below it. Once the singular curve has been reached, singular learning (with $0 < \alpha < 1$) is adopted, adjusting the optimal process to evolve along the singular curve. As this behavior is akin to turnpike models of growth (Samuelson 1965, Cass, 1966), we refer to the singular curve also as the *turnpike*. It is recognized that the extreme most-rapid learning at the transient phase (which arises due to our description of the diminishing returns to learning only via the knowledge stock h but not via the learning fraction α) is not too realistic. With a more general specification, the approach to the turnpike is more gradual, but the identification of the singular curve as the locus along which the economy grows in the long run retains its validity.

The second characteristic curve in the (h,k) plane is defined by equating the marginal product of capital y_k (or equivalently the capital rental rate r – see (2.1)) with the utility discount rate ρ. Using (2.3), this condition becomes

$$f'(k/A(h))B(H) = \rho. \tag{3.3}$$

Solving for k, we find

$$k(h) = A(h) f'^{-1}(\rho/B(Lh)). \tag{3.4}$$

The properties of A, f and B ensure that $k(h)$ is increasing. The function $k(h)$ represents the optimal steady state of k when no learning takes place. We thus refer to $k(h)$ as the *stagnation curve* and observe that the same curve applies to both the private and social plans. Indeed, if the private or social knowledge-capital processes ever stagnate at a finite steady state, this state must lie on the stagnation curve.

These observations are summarized in:

PROPERTY C.1: (i) The optimal knowledge and capital processes must either converge to a steady state on the stagnation curve or grow indefinitely along the singular curve. (ii) For a growing economy, the optimal (h,k) processes approach the singular curve at a *most-rapid-learning rate*, i.e., no learning ($\alpha = 0$) below the curve and maximal learning ($\alpha = 1$) above it, and evolve along it thereafter.

What are the conditions under which economies grow? As it turns out, these conditions depend on the relative location of the two characteristic curves at large knowledge levels. Two cases are considered, classifying economies into one of two possible types. The first type is characterized by the singular curve lying above the stagnation curve at large h, i.e.,

(i) $\lim_{h \to \infty} [k^S(h) - k(h)] > 0$,

while economies of the second type are characterized by

(ii) $\lim_{h \to \infty} [k^S(h) - k(h)] \leq 0$.

The geometric relations can be expressed in terms of the model functions. For example, condition (i) for the private plan reduces to $f'^{-1}(\rho/B(Lh)) < z^{-1}(1/A'(h))$ at large h. More transparent relations are derived in Section 5 for Cobb-Douglas economies. Economies that satisfy condition (i) are referred to as *stagnating* and those satisfying condition (ii) are called *potentially growing*. Economies of the first type eventually stagnate at a finite steady state, whereas those of the second type have the capacity to grow indefinitely, pending sufficient capital-knowledge endowment.

The type classification depends on the production functions and on the utility discount rate ρ but not on the instantaneous utility $u(c)$, which does not enter the definitions of $k^S(h)$ or $k(h)$. Notice that because the singular curve takes on different forms under the private and social plans, the same economy can be of a different type under each of these plans. With the social singular curve lying below its private counterpart, an economy that is potentially growing under the private plan maintains its type under the social plan, and its growth rate is, in fact, larger. However, a private stagnating economy can obtain either type under the social plan. Quantitative estimates of these effects are given in Section E.

In similarity with other growth models (e.g., Skiba 1978), the long run behavior of an economy depends also on the initial capital-knowledge stocks. For example, a potentially-growing economy may not be able to realize its growth potential if its endowment is too small. Similarly, the evolution trajectory and the eventual steady state of a stagnating economy may also depend on its endowment. The complete description of the large variety of growth patterns obtained with this model in terms of the geometry of the characteristic curves is provided in Tsur and Zemel (2004, 2007b) and will not be further pursued here.

D. KNOWLEDGE SPILLOVERS AND WELFARE MEASUREMENT

We turn now to study effects of knowledge spillover externalities on welfare measurement via national accounts, such as the NNP, and the appropriate welfare index for growing economies. For this purpose, we ignore the transient phase and consider a growing economy that has already reached the turnpike growth phase. We derive below a correction factor to the NNP under the private plan and estimate this factor in the following section. A similar correction to the NNP due to the presence of externalities associated with environmental catastrophes is derived in Tsur and Zemel (2006).

Following Weitzman (2000), we carry out the analysis with the instantaneous utility normalized such that the initial consumption flow can serve as the numeraire:

$$u(c_0) = c_0 \text{ and } u'(c_0) = 1. \tag{4.1}$$

This normalization does not affect the optimal plans. The current-value Hamiltonian corresponding to the intertemporal problem of seeking the consumption-learning plan (c_t, α_t), $t \geq 0$, that maximizes (2.6) subject to (2.4)-(2.5) is

$$\mathfrak{I}_t = u(c_t) + p_t^k[(1-\alpha_t)y_t - c_t] + p_t^h \alpha_t y_t \tag{4.2}$$

where p_t^k and p_t^h are the current-value prices of physical and human capital, respectively, expressed in terms of the initial consumption rate. Along the turnpike, these prices must be equal (otherwise, the Maximum Principle implies that corner values of α will be adopted), hence we denote $p_t^k = p_t^h = p_t$ and reduce (4.2) to

$$\mathfrak{I}_t = u(c_t) + p_t(y_t - c_t). \tag{4.3}$$

Observe that $y-c$ measures the total investment rate (in both human and physical capital), hence, in view of (4.1), $\mathfrak{I}_0$ represents the NNP at the initial time. The necessary condition $\partial \mathfrak{I}/\partial c = 0$ and the normalization (4.1) imply that $\mathfrak{I}_0 = y_0$, i.e., the initial NNP is given by y_0.

Let V_0 represent the value of the optimal plan at $t = 0$, i.e.,

$$V_0 = \int_0^\infty u(c_t^*)e^{-\rho t}dt, \tag{4.4}$$

with starred quantities indicating optimal turnpike processes, and define the present value of the flow of spillover externalities by

$$Z = \int_0^\infty (\partial y_t^* / \partial t)p_t^* e^{-\rho t}dt \tag{4.5}$$

Under the private plan, the explicit time dependence of y stems from the knowledge spillovers, $\partial y_t^* / \partial t = A(h_t^*)f(k_t^* / A(h_t^*))B'(H_t)\dot{H}_t > 0$ (H is treated as an exogenous process), implying that $Z > 0$. Under the social plan, however, H is related to the state variable h. Thus $y(k,h,H)$ does not have any exogenous time dependence and Z vanishes at all times.

To appreciate the economic significance of Z, recall Weitzman's (1976) result for *comprehensive* accounting, $y_0 = \rho V_0$, which serves as the justification for using the comprehensive (or "green") NNP as a welfare measure for the economy. With externalities such as those introduced by knowledge spillovers to the private plan, however, this simple rule fails and the NNP must be corrected to obtain an appropriate measure of welfare. Indeed, with the above notation we find (in similarity to equation (18) of Aronsson and Löfgren 1996):

PROPERTY D.1: The initial-time NNP for an economy that grows along the turnpike satisfies

$$y_0 = \rho V_0 - Z \tag{4.6}$$

To verify Property D.1, consider the present-value Hamiltonian $L_t = \Im_t e^{-\rho t}$. Recalling (4.3) and introducing the present-value price $\lambda_t = p_t e^{-\rho t}$, we write

$$L_t = u(c_t)e^{-\rho t} + \lambda_t(y_t - c_t) \tag{4.7}$$

Integrating the envelope property $dL_t/dt = \partial L_t/\partial t = -\rho u(c_t)e^{-\rho t} + \lambda_t(\partial y_t/\partial t)$ along the optimal path and recalling that $L_0 = \Im_0 = y_0$ and $\lim_{t \to \infty} L_t = 0$ (Michel 1982), establishes (4.6).

Thus, Z measures the bias introduced by the spillover externalities. Weitzman (1997) and Weitzman and Löfgren (1997) considered similar bias terms in the context of exogenous growth models and estimated the bias in terms of a "technological progress premium" parameter Θ, defined by the relation

$$y_0(1 + \Theta) = \rho V_0 \tag{4.8}$$

In view of (4.6), the analogous parameter in the present endogenous growth setting is

$$\Theta = Z / y_0 \tag{4.9}$$

In the following section we use the general forms of (4.5) and (4.9) to derive an explicit expression of the "knowledge spillover premium" term Θ for an economy with Cobb-Douglas technology and iso-elastic preferences and compare it with the results of Weitzman (1997) and Weitzman and Löfgren (1997). Numerical estimates for the welfare bias Θ and for the other growth effects of knowledge spillover externalities are obtained using empirical values for the relevant parameters.

E. ESTIMATES OF KNOWLEDGE SPILLOVER EFFECTS

The general derivations of the previous sections obtain more concrete and interpretable forms when recast in terms of a specific economy for which empirical estimates of the relevant parameters are available. We consider here a reference economy with a Cobb-Douglas production technology and iso-elastic preferences, using the parameter values from Weitzman (1997), Arrow et al. (2004) and Moretti (2004a). In this economy,

$$f(x) = \theta x^\beta, \quad 0 < \beta < 1, \tag{5.1a}$$

$$A(h) = h^a, \quad 0 < a < 1 \text{ (hence } \eta_A(h) = A'(h)h/A(h) = a), \tag{5.1b}$$

$$B(H) = (H/L)^b, \quad 0 < b < 1 \text{ (hence } \eta_B(H) = B'(H)H/B(H) = b), \tag{5.1c}$$

$$u(c) = c_0^{*\sigma} \frac{c^{1-\sigma}}{1-\sigma} - c_0^* \frac{\sigma}{1-\sigma}, \quad \sigma > 1 \tag{5.1d}$$

where c_0^* is the optimal initial consumption rate and the normalization constants of (5.1d) are chosen to satisfy (4.1). Since the optimal solution is invariant with respect to this normalization, the optimal policy, including c_0^*, can be determined with any arbitrary constants, independent of the initial consumption. We use the notation

$$\eta = \beta/(1-\beta) \quad \text{and} \quad \varphi = \theta \beta^\beta (1-\beta)^{1-\beta}. \tag{5.1e}$$

The singular and stagnation curves (defined by (3.2) and (3.4)) specialize to

$$(p) \ k_p^S(h) = \frac{\eta}{a} h, \quad (so) \ k_{so}^S(h) = \eta h \tag{5.2}$$

and

$$k(h) = (\beta \theta / \rho)^{1/(1-\beta)} h^{a+b/(1-\beta)} \tag{5.3}$$

respectively. Recalling the type classification of Section 3, we see that $a + b/(1-\beta) < 1$ implies stagnation under both the private and social plans and rules out sustained growth. We thus assume $a + b/(1-\beta) \geq 1$ and focus on the threshold case

$$a + b/(1-\beta) = 1. \tag{5.4}$$

Under (5.4), the stagnation curve (5.3) reduces to the straight line

$$k(h) = (\beta \theta / \rho)^{1/(1-\beta)} h \tag{5.5}$$

Since the turnpike and stagnation curve are straight lines emanating from the origin, they cannot intersect at positive h values. The analysis of Section C, then, implies that the economy is stagnating when the turnpike lies above the stagnation curve and is potentially growing when

$$(p) \ \rho < a^{1-\beta} \varphi, \quad (so) \ \rho < \varphi. \tag{5.6}$$

(cf. 5.1e). It is verified that under (5.1) the right-hand side of (5.6) equals the marginal product of capital ($\partial y/\partial k$) along the turnpike (5.2), which, according to (2.1), determines the interest rate:

$(p)\ r_p = a^{1-\beta}\varphi,\qquad (so)\ r_{so} = \varphi.$ \hfill (5.7)

We see from (5.6)-(5.7) that sustained growth requires the interest rate along the turnpike to exceed impatience. In this case, a potentially growing economy will realize its growth potential for any positive capital endowment. Moreover, under (5.1), (5.4) and (5.6) the optimal private and social (h,k) processes grow exponentially along their respective turnpikes. The turnpike values are derived in the appendix and summarized in Table 5.1, where the social parameters are obtained by setting $b = 0$ and $a = 1$ in their private counterparts.

The growth conditions (5.6) ensure that g_p and g_{so} are positive while $\sigma > 1$ implies that α_p lies between 0 and $a(1-\beta)$ and α_{so} lies between 0 and $1-\beta$. The endogenous exponential growth is directly linked to the constant returns to human capital h in the knowledge production function (2.4), implied in equilibrium by (5.4) along the singular curve, where k is proportional to h (Solow 2000 discusses equivalent assumptions in a variety of endogenous growth models). It is of interest to compare our "spillover premium" parameter Θ to its counterparts in Weitzman (1997, Equation 22) and Weitzman and Löfgren (1997, Equation 40).

While the denominators in all expressions measure the difference between the interest and eventual growth rates, the numerator of the value given in Table 5.1 is proportional to the spillover parameter b, hence only the fraction of the growth rate which can be attributed to the external spillover effects is included. In the above-cited references, in contrast, technological progress is entirely exogenous and the corresponding bias estimates are not diluted by factors analogous to b.

In this sense, our NNP is more "comprehensive", as it accounts for the internalized part of knowledge-induced growth, hence the associated bias term should be smaller. The estimates below confirm this expectation.

We evaluate now the knowledge spillover effects listed in Table 5.1 using the following parameter values: A capital share of $\beta = 1/3$ is commonly used and is adopted here. Following Arrow et al. (2004) the impatience parameter ρ is set at 0.5 percent. Moretti (2004a, p. 676 and Table 7 – see also discussion in p. 681) found the spillover parameter b to lie between 0.2 and 0.7, while the estimates of Acemoglu and Angrist (2000) are appreciably lower. We thus take the lower end of Moretti's range and set $b = 0.2$. Condition (5.4), then, implies that $a = 1-b(1-\beta) = 0.7$, so that the intra-firm labor augmenting share a is more than three times larger than its spillover counterpart b. We consider a private return on capital of $r_p = 4\%$ per year (cf. Weitzman and Löfgren 1997, p. 147) and a private growth rate of $g_p = 1.5\%$ per year, consistent with an intertemporal elasticity of $\sigma = 2.33$ – well inside the range considered by Arrow et al. (2004, p. 156).

With these values we obtain $\Theta = 0.12$, $g_{so}/g_p = 1.3$ and $\alpha_{so}/\alpha_p = 1.47$. Thus, the NNP along the private turnpike underestimates welfare by 12%, the growth rate under the social policy is 30% higher than its private counterpart and the faster growth is achieved by investment in education that is 47% larger.

The smaller estimate of Θ, as compared to the 40% estimate of Weitzman (1997) and Weitzman and Löfgren (1997), is due to the fact that our premium parameter Θ corrects only for the knowledge spillover externalities (the intra-firm, labor-augmenting productivity growth is endogenous in our framework), whereas the above-mentioned estimates consider technological progress that is entirely exogenous.

Table 1. Optimal turnpike variables

	Private	Social
Interest rate	$r_p = a^{1-\beta}\varphi$	$r_{so} = \varphi$
Growth rate	$g_p = \dfrac{r_p - \rho}{\sigma}$	$g_{so} = \dfrac{r_{so} - \rho}{\sigma}$
Learning (share of income)	$\alpha_p = a(1-\beta)\dfrac{g_p}{r_p}$	$\alpha_{so} = (1-\beta)\dfrac{g_{so}}{r_{so}}$
Saving (share of income)	$s_p = \beta\dfrac{g_p}{r_p}$	$s_{so} = \beta\dfrac{g_{so}}{r_{so}}$
Consumption (share of income)	$\dfrac{c_p}{y_p} = 1-(1-b)\dfrac{g_p}{r_p}$	$\dfrac{c_{so}}{y_{so}} = 1-\dfrac{g_{so}}{r_{so}}$
Spillover premium	$\Theta = \dfrac{bg_p}{r_p - g_p}$	$\Theta = 0$

The interest rate $r_p = 4\%$ is consistent with $\theta = 0.096$ (cf. (5.1e) and (5.7)), where θ is related to social infrastructure (Hall and Jones, 1999). When the social institutions are lacking or malfunctioning such that $\theta \le 0.012$, the growth condition (4.6p) is violated, transforming a growing private-learning economy into a stagnating type. Reducing θ further below 0.00945 leads to violation of condition (4.6so) as well, and transforms the social economy into a stagnating type. For intermediate values of θ (between 0.012 and 0.00945) the private learning policy entails stagnation while the social learning policy supports sustained growth.

F. EDUCATION POLICY

The failure of the competitive equilibrium to induce appropriate human capital investment calls for policy intervention. In actual practice such an intervention takes different forms, including state-financed schooling and training, and subsidized higher education (see Wolfe and Haveman 2002 for data on public spending on education in a number of countries). In this section we offer a mechanism that implements the socially optimal outcome for the economy specified in Section 5. The mechanism consists of a learning subsidy and linear taxes to cover the subsidy payments. The taxes vary between a flat income tax during the transitional phase (while the knowledge-capital processes approach the turnpike) and a flat consumption (or value added) tax along the singular curve. The tax proceeds match the subsidy outlays at each point of time, hence no lump sum transfers are needed. Aronsson and Löfgren (1996) offer a regulation scheme in a more general setting. By focusing on the Cobb-Douglas/iso-elastic economy we are able to specify a simple mechanism built on flat subsidy and taxes applied directly to the rates of learning, income and consumption (as in Bénabou, 2002).

Education subsidy: For every income unit spent on education, the household receives a coupon worth q income units that can be used to pay for additional education expense. This subsidy modifies the human capital accumulation process (2.4) to

$$\dot{h} = \alpha(1+q)y(k,h,H) \tag{6.1}$$

The value of q that provides the right learning incentives turns out to be $(1-a)/a$. To avoid overinvestment in human capital, that is to ensure that $\alpha(1+q)$ does not exceed unity, the subsidy is given only while $\alpha \le a$. The education subsidy can be succinctly defined in terms of

$$q = \begin{cases} (1-a)/a & if\ \alpha \le a \\ 0 & otherwise \end{cases} \tag{6.2}$$

It is verified in Tsur and Zemel (2004, appendix B) that this subsidy modifies the households' learning decisions (α_t) in such a way that their singular curve changes from $k_p^S(h)$ to $k_{so}^S(h)$.

Taxes: To finance the education subsidy, either a flat income tax at a rate m or a flat consumption tax at a rate v are used, depending on whether the economy is at the transitional phase above the turnpike or evolves along the turnpike, respectively. These taxes modify the household's saving process (2.5) to

$$\dot{k} = (1-\alpha-m)y - (1+v)c \tag{6.3}$$

The consumption tax v is applied along the turnpike $k_{so}^S(h)$ at the rate $bg_{so}/(r_{so}-g_{so})$

$$v = \begin{cases} bg_{so}/(r_{so}-g_{so}) & if\ k = k_{so}^S(h) \\ 0 & otherwise \end{cases} \tag{6.4}$$

Interestingly, the consumption tax rate of (6.4) agrees with the value given in Table 5.1 for the spillover premium parameter Θ when r and g take their social values.

Above $k_{so}^S(h)$ an income tax at the rate $1-a$ replaces the consumption tax, thus

$$m = \begin{cases} 1-a & if\ k > k_{so}^S(h) \\ 0 & otherwise \end{cases} \tag{6.5}$$

No subsidy or taxes are used below the singular curve.
Efficiency: The tax proceeds exactly match the subsidy payments when

$$q\alpha y = my + vc. \tag{6.6}$$

A q–v–m policy that satisfies (6.6) at all times is called balanced. The policy is efficient if it yields the socially optimal (h,k) process. Indeed, we establish (see Tsur and Zemel, 2004, appendix C, for a proof).

PROPERTY F.1: The education policy (6.1)-(6.5) is balanced and efficient.

The centerpiece of our mechanism is the education subsidy that modifies the household's singular curve from the private $k_p^S(h)$ to the socially optimal $k_{so}^S(h)$. The subsidy motivates households to increase the income share devoted to education from α_p to $a\alpha_{so}$, which is still below the socially optimal fraction α_{so} but with the subsidy (see equations (6.1) and (6.2)) ensures the correct (socially optimal) investment in education.

Along the turnpike, a consumption tax has no effect on household decisions (Rebelo, 1991, found this property to hold also for an extended Lucas model), thus can serve to finance the education subsidy. Applied at the rate $v=bg_{so}/(r_{so}-g_{so})$, this tax will raise the exact amount needed to cover the subsidy expense. This goal cannot be achieved with the income tax, since its distorting effects divert households away from the social turnpike $k_{so}^S(h)$. Above the turnpike, however, income tax is used temporarily to guide the process towards $k_{so}^S(h)$. At this stage, the income tax serves a dual role: first its distorting effects modify the saving-consumption balance and lead the (h,k) process towards the turnpike at the socially optimal pace. Second, its proceeds match exactly the subsidy payments, so that the consumption tax can be avoided until the turnpike is reached.

Below $k_{so}^S(h)$ (at (h,k) states satisfying $k < k_{so}^S(h)$), the socially optimal policy is to avoid learning and build up capital until the singular curve is reached. The regulator, then, has no reason to support learning and the subsidy is set to zero. As a result, taxes can also be avoided during this phase.

Applying the estimates of the previous section to equations (6.2) and (6.4), we obtain $q = 43\%$ and $v = 13\%$ along the turnpike. As knowledge spillovers are linked primarily to higher education (Moertti 2004a), the estimate of q suggests that about 43% of the cost of higher education should be publicly borne (according to Wolf and Haveman, 2002, the actual subsidy in the US during the 1990s was about 30%). The subsidy outlays are to be financed by a 13% consumption tax. The economy will then pull itself by the bootstraps to a (social) growth rate of 1.96 percent instead of the 1.5 percent (private) rate, as calculated in the previous section.

CONCLUSIONS

There is a wealth of evidence to suggest that external effects of human capital – social benefits not privately captured – are substantial. Recent theoretical investigations demonstrate the relevance of these externalities to welfare measures and national accounting as well as to national education policies. In this work we take advantage of the simple analytic structure of an endogenous growth model, which treats learning as an income-consuming activity, and of the recent estimates of the effects of human capital spillovers on productivity to consider these issues in a more quantitative manner.

For a reference economy with Cobb-Douglas technology and iso-elastic preferences, we estimate the effects of knowledge spillover externalities to be around 12% on the welfare index, 50% on investment in education, and 30% on the growth rate. We offer a simple mechanism, based on a flat education subsidy and a combination of income-consumption taxes, to implement the socially optimal policy. The mechanism is self-financed in that the linear income and consumption taxes, each levied during a different phase of the growth process, match the subsidy expenses at each point of time.

Growth failures in our model can happen for two reasons: either the economy fails to satisfy the growth condition (i.e., is of a stagnating type) or it passes the test (i.e., is of a potentially growing type) but lacks sufficient resources to realize its growth potential. The former situation is often due to poor social infrastructure, such as corruption, excessive bureaucracy, or insufficient enforcement of property rights. External infusion of capital can jumpstart economic growth for economies that satisfy the growth condition but not for those that fail in this respect (Burnside and Dollar 2000, Easterly 2003). For the latter economies, structural changes must take place in order to escape stagnation. A policy that provides the right education incentives may turn a stagnating economy into a growing one and in general accelerates growth.

APPENDIX: TURNPIKE GROWTH PROCESSES

In this appendix we derive the optimal growth processes along the private turnpike for the Cobb-Douglas economy specified in (5.1) and satisfying the growth condition (5.6). The corresponding social turnpike growth processes are obtained as a special case with $b=0$ and $a=1$.

The state equations are

(a) $\dot{h} = \alpha y$ and (b) $\dot{k} = (1-\alpha)y - c,$ (A.1)

where the specifications in (5.1) give

$$y = \theta h^{a(1-\beta)} k^{\beta} (H/L)^{b}.$$ (A.2)

Thus, for the private plan, where H is taken as an exogenous process,

(a) $y_k = \beta y / k$ and (b) $y_h = a(1-\beta)y/h.$ (A.3)

The condition for singular learning, $y_k = y_h$, then, yields a linear singular curve

$$k^{S}(h) = \chi h$$ (A.4)

with the slope

$$\chi = \eta / a .$$
(A.5)

Along the singular curve (A.4), the production function (A.2) reduces to

$$y^S = \theta \chi^\beta h^{1-b} (H/L)^b$$
(A.6)

We recall the notation $\eta = \beta/(1-\beta)$ and $\varphi = \theta \beta^\beta (1-\beta)^{1-\beta}$, and use (2.1) and (A.3a) to express the capital rental rate along the singular curve as

$$r = \beta y / k = a^{1-\beta} \varphi$$
(A.7)

Inserting (A.4-5) into (A.1) and using (5.4) gives the consumption fraction

$$c = [1 - \alpha G] y^S$$
(A.8)

where the constant G is given by

$$G = \frac{(1-b)}{a(1-\beta)} = 1 + \chi > 1.$$
(A.9)

In view of (A.8), the singular plan involves the single state variable h and is determined by

$$V^S(h_0) = Max_{\{\alpha\}} \left\{ \int_0^\infty u([1 - \alpha G] y^S) e^{-\rho t} dt \right\}$$
(A.10)

Subject to (A.1a), $h \geq 0$ and $0 \leq \alpha \leq 1/G$, where h_0 is reset to the knowledge state at which the singular plan begins. (Similarly, we reset the time at which the singular process starts to $t = 0$.) Here, the private marginal knowledge productivity is obtained by ignoring the contribution of the externality term $(H/L)^b$ of (A.6)

$$\partial y^S / \partial h \equiv y_h^S = \theta \chi^\beta (1-b) = rG$$
(A.11)

The current-value Hamiltonian for this problem is

$$L = u([1 - \alpha G] y^S) + \gamma \alpha y^S$$
(A.12)

The necessary conditions include

$$u'(c) = \gamma / G$$
(A.13)

and, using (A.11-A.13),

$$\dot{\gamma} = \rho\gamma - \partial L / \partial h = \gamma(\rho - r) \equiv -\gamma\Phi \qquad\qquad\qquad \text{(A.14)}$$

where

$$\Phi = r - \rho \qquad\qquad\qquad \text{(A.15)}$$

From (A.14), $\gamma = \gamma_0 \, exp(-\Phi t)$ and (A.13) implies $\dot{c}/c = \Phi u'(c)/[-u''(c)c]$ which for the isoelastic utility (5.1d) reduces to

$$\dot{c}/c \equiv g = \Phi / \sigma. \qquad\qquad\qquad \text{(A.16)}$$

Condition (5.6p) and $\sigma > 1$ ensure that consumption grows exponentially at the rate $0<g<r$. Because the optimal learning fraction α_t turns out to be constant along the singular curve, income, capital and knowledge are all proportional to consumption along the singular curve and thus grow at the same rate. To verify this, use (A.1a), (A.4), (A.7) and (A.9) to find $h = \alpha r G h/(1-b)$ and recall (A.8) to write the consumption rate as $c = (1-\alpha G)rGh/(1-b)$. Taking the time derivative, we find $g = \dot{c}/c = \dot{h}/h - \dot{\alpha}G/(1-\alpha G) = r\alpha G/(1-b) - \dot{\alpha}G/(1-\alpha G)$, yielding

$$G\dot{\alpha} = g(1 - G\alpha)(\Omega G\alpha - 1), \qquad\qquad\qquad \text{(A.17)}$$

where $\Omega = r/[g(1-b)] > 1$.

Integrating equation (A.17) gives $(\Omega G\alpha - 1)/(1 - G\alpha) = \psi \, exp[g(\Omega - 1)t]$ or $G\alpha = \dfrac{1 + \psi \, exp[g(\Omega - 1)t]}{\Omega + \psi \, exp[g(\Omega - 1)t]}$. To set the integration constant ψ, note that with $\Omega > 1$ any non vanishing value of ψ implies that $G\alpha$ converges to unity in the long run with $1 - G\alpha \approx exp[-g(\Omega - 1)t]$. (The notation $a(t) \approx b(t)$ signifies that the ratio $a(t)/b(t)$ approaches a constant as $t \to \infty$).

Thus, $h = c(1 - b)/[rG\alpha(1 - G\alpha)] \approx exp(g\Omega t) = exp[rt/(1 - b)]$ so that $h\gamma exp(-\rho t) \approx exp[(r/(1 - b) \quad \Phi - \rho)t] - exp[rbt/(1 - b)]$ (cf. (A.15)). The exponent on the right-hand side does not approach zero at large t, violating the transversality condition $\lim_{t\to\infty} L(t)exp(-\rho t) = 0$ (Michel 1982). It follows that the optimal integration constant ψ must vanish for all plans, reducing the learning fraction α to the constant

$$\alpha = 1/(\Omega G) = (1-\beta)ag/r, \qquad\qquad\qquad \text{(A.18)}$$

which ensures that $G\alpha = 1/\Omega < 1$. The consumption fraction, then, reduces to the constant

$$c/y^S = 1 - G\alpha = 1 - (1-b)g/r, \qquad\qquad\qquad \text{(A.19)}$$

and the remaining input is devoted to saving.

We turn now to derive the knowledge spillover premium Θ. To obtain the bias term Z, we use (5.1c) and write the explicit time dependence of y as

$$\frac{\partial y}{\partial t} = y\frac{\dot{B}}{B} = yb\frac{\dot{H}}{H} = ybg = y_0 bge^{gt} \tag{A.20}$$

where we have used the result that both y and H grow at the rate g. Similarly, we recall that the price $p(t)$ is proportional to y (with the normalization $p_0 = 1$ implied by 4.1) and write $p(t) = exp(-\Phi t) = exp[(\rho - r)t]$ (see A.15). Thus, (4.5) can be integrated to yield

$$Z = y_0 bg/(r-g). \tag{A.21}$$

Finally, we use (A.21) and (4.9) to obtain

$$\Theta = Z/y_0 = bg/(r-g). \tag{A.22}$$

REFERENCES

Acemoglu, D., and Angrist, J. (2000). How large are human capital externalities? Evidence from compulsory schooling laws. In Bernanke, B.S., and Rogoff K. (Eds.), NBER *macroeconomics annual*, *Vol. 15*, 9-59. Cambridge, MA: MIT Press.

Aronsson, T., and Löfgren, K-G. (1996). Social accounting and welfare measurement in a growth model with human capital, *Scandinavian Journal of Economics*, *Vol. 98*, 185-201.

Arrow, K. J. (1962). The economic implications of learning by doing. *Review of Economic Studies*, *Vol. 29*, 155-173.

Arrow, K., Dasgupta, P., Goulder, L., Daily, G., Ehrlich, P., Heal, G., Levin, S., Mäler, K.-G., Schneider, S., Starret, D., and Walker, B. (2004). Are we consuming too much? *Journal of Economic Perspectives*, *Vol. 18*, 147-172.

Asheim, G. B. (1997). Adjusting green NNP to measure sustainability. *Scandinavian Journal of Economics, Vol. 99*, 355-370.

Asheim, G. B. (2004). Green national accounting with a changing population. *Economic theory, Vol. 23*, 601-609.

Barro, R. J., and Sala-i-Martin, X. (2004). *Economic Growth* (second edition). Cambridge, MA: The MIT Press.

Bénabou, R. (2002). Tax and education policy in a heterogeneous-agent economy: What levels of redistribution maximize growth and efficiency? *Econometrica, Vol.70*, 481-517.

Bils, M., and Klenow, P.J. (2000). Does schooling cause growth? *American Economic Review, Vol. 90*, 1160-1183.

Burnside, C., and Dollar, D. (2000). Aid, policies and growth. *American Economic Review, Vol. 90*, 847-868.

Cass, D. (1966). Optimum growth in an aggregate model of capital accumulation: a turnpike theorem, *Econometrica,Vol.34*, 833-850.

Chamley, C. (1993). Externalities and dynamics in models of "learning or doing". *International Economic Review, Vol.34*, 583-609.

Easterly, W. (2003). Can foreign aid buy growth? *Journal of Economic Perspectives, Vol.17,* 23-48.

Gradstein, M., Justman, M., and Meier, V. (2005). *The Political Economy of Education: Implications for Growth and Inequality.* Cambridge, MA: MIT Press.

Hall, R. E., and Jones, C.I. (1999). Why some countries produce so much more output per worker than others? *Quarterly Journal of Economics, Vol. 114,*83-116.

Jaffe, A. B., Trajtenberg, M., and Henderson, R. (1993). Geographic localization of knowledge spillovers as evidenced by patent citations. *Quarterly Journal of Economics, Vol. 108,* 577-598.

Lucas, R.E. (1988). On the mechanics of economic development. *Journal of Monetary Economics, Vol. 22,* 3-42.

Michel, P. (1982). On the transversality condition in infinite horizon optimal problems, *Econometrica, Vol.50,* 975-985.

Moretti, E. (2004a). Workers' education, spillovers, and productivity: evidence from plant-level production functions. *American Economic Review, Vol. 94,* 656-690.

Moretti, E. (2004b). Estimating the social return to higher education: evidence from longitudinal and repeated corss-sectional data. *Journal of Econometrics, Vol. 121,* 175-212.

Rebelo, S. (1991). Long-run policy analysis and long-run growth. *Journal of Political Economy, Vol. 99,* 500-521.

Romer, P. M. (1986). Increasing returns and long-run growth. *Journal of Political Economy, Vol. 94,* 1002-1037.

Samuelson, P. A. (1965). A Catenary turnpike theorem involving consumption and the golden rule. *American Economic Review, Vol. 55,* 486-496.

Shell, K. (1966). Towards a theory of inventive activity and capital accumulation, *American Economic Review, Vol.56,* 62-68.

Shell, K. (1967). A model of inventive activity and capital accumulation. In Shell, K. (Ed.), *Essays on the theory of optimal economic growth* (67-85). Cambridge, MA: MIT Press.

Shell, K. (1973). Inventive activity, industrial organization and economic growth. In Mirrlees, J. A., and Stern, N. H. (Eds.), *Models of economic growth* (77-96). London, EN: Macmillan.

Skiba, A. K. (1978). Optimal ʹgrowth with a convex –concave production function. *Econometrica, Vol. 46,* 527-540.

Solow, R. M. (1956). A contribution to the theory of economic growth. *Quarterly Journal of Economics, Vol. 70,* 65-94.

Solow, R. M. (1957). Technical change and the aggregate production function. *Review of Economics and Statistics, Vol. 39,* 312-320.

Solow, R. M. (2000). *Growth theory: An exposition* (Second Edition). Oxford: Oxford University Press.

Thompson, P., and Fox-Kean, M. (2005). Patent citations and the geography of knowledge spillovers: A reassessment. *American Economic Review, Vol. 95,* 450-460.

Tsur, Y., and Zemel, A. (2004). Knowledge spillovers, learning incentives and economic growth, Discussion Paper 7.04. Center for Agricultural Economic Research, http://departments.agri.huji.ac.il/economics/tsur-spill.pdf.

Tsur, Y., and Zemel, A. (2005). Scarcity, growth and RandD. *Journal of Environmental Economics and Management, Vol. 49,* 484-499.

Tsur, Y., and Zemel, A. (2006). Welfare measurement under threats of environmental catastrophes. *Journal of Environmental Economics and Management, Vol. 52*, 421-429.

Tsur, Y., and Zemel, A. (2007a). Towards Endogenous Recombinant Growth. *Journal of Economic Dynamics and Control, Vol. 31*, 3459-3477.

Tsur, Y., and Zemel, A. (2007b). On the Dynamics of Knowledge-Based Economic Growth. *Journal of Optimization Theory and Applications, Vol. 135*, 101-115.

Weitzman, M. L. (1976). On the welfare significance of national product in a dynamic economy. *Quarterly Journal of Economics, Vol. 90*, 156-162.

Weitzman, M. L. (1997). Sustainability and technical progress. *Scandinavian Journal of Economics, Vol. 99*, 1-13.

Weitzman, M. L. (2000). The linearised Hamiltonian as comprehensive NDP. *Environment and Development Economics, Vol. 5*, 55-68.

Weitzman, M. L., and Löfgren, K-G. (1997). On the welfare significance of green accounting as taught by parable. *Journal of Environmental Economics and Management, Vol. 32*, 139-153.

Wolfe, B.L., and Haveman, R. H. (2002). Social and nonmarket benefits from education in an advanced economy, Conference Series [Proceedings] "Education in the 21st century: meeting the challenges of a changing world". Boston, MA: Federal Reserve Bank of Boston.

SECTION V: GOVERNANCE, RESOURCES AND AGRICULTURAL POLICIES

In: The Economics of Natural and Human Resources...   ISBN 978-1-60741-029-4
Editor: Ayal Kimhi and Israel Finkelshtain   © 2009 Nova Science Publishers, Inc.

Chapter 12

COMMODITY SUPPORT, INVESTMENT, AND PRODUCTIVITY

*Bruce Gardner**

ABSTRACT

This paper considers both short-run and long-run issues in the effects of commodity price support policies, with reference to the experience of U.S. farm programs. Because it is currently much in the news, and has not been well understood in popular accounts, the short-run discussion focuses on the recently enacted 2002 farm bill and the policies that preceded it. The longer-run discussion focuses on investment in agriculture and productivity growth as related to the economic environment created by commodity support policies.

A. THE U.S. 2002 FARM ACT

The Farm Security and Rural Investment Act of 2002 has replaced the programs of previous (1996) "Freedom to Farm" legislation that that was originally viewed, by economists at least, as a mechanism to phase out commodity support programs. The 1996 Act had made fixed payments averaging about $5 billion annually during 1996-2001 on crops (grains and cotton) with an aggregate market value of about $40 billion. In addition, the 1996 Act retained commodity support prices at roughly 20 percent below the average levels for these crops plus oilseeds during the 1980s and 1990s (see Figures 14.1-14.3 for corn, soybeans, and wheat).

The political reaction to a sharp drop in commodity prices during 1998-2001 spelled doom for the 1996 Act approach.

---

* Professor of Agricultural and Resource Economics, University of Maryland. The analysis of current farm programs is taken mostly from Gardner (2002b), and discussion of investment issues draws on Gardner (2002a).

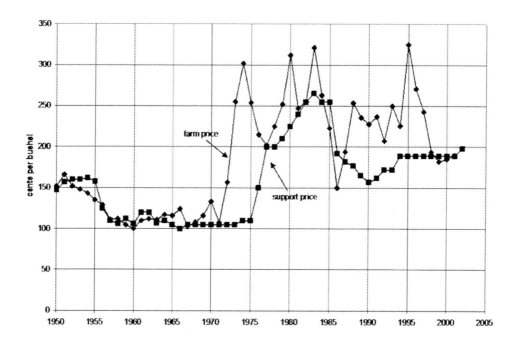

Figure 12.1. Corn Price and Support price.

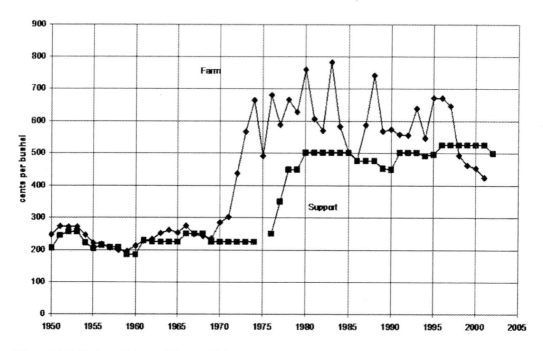

Figure 12.2. Soybean Price and Support Price.

Figure 12.3. Wheat Farm Price and Support Price.

Low prices caused support prices ("CCC loan rates") that were estimated to be costless in 1996 to generate loan deficiency payments and marketing loan losses of about $5 billion annually during 1998-2001.

Moreover, Congress appropriated $5.5 billion annually in additional "market loss assistance" payments for the 1999-2001 crops. So major-crop commodity support that had been estimated to cost $5 billion per year in 1996 ended up costing over $15 billion per year. The main thing the 2002 Farm Act has done is to lock in roughly this level of support, which had been legislated on an *ad hoc* annual basis in 1998-2001, for the crops planted in 2002-2007.

The 2002 Act was popular in Congress, having passed both houses of Congress easily, with no Bush Administration opposition. But outside the community of agricultural interests, the Act has been widely reviled. *Business Week* magazine: "It's a dreadful piece of legislation – bad for most farmers, bad for consumers, and horrendous for taxpayers" (May 7, 2002). *The New York Times* editorialized against the Act on several occasions, most recently on "The Hypocrisy of Farm Subsidies" on December 1, 2002. Most critical have been those speaking from the viewpoint of agricultural exporting nations, who see their producers of grains and cotton as unfairly having to compete with highly subsidized developed-country production.[1] Those concerns turn on two issues: the size of the subsidies and their effects in generating additional production.

---

[1] The issue has even seeped into discussion of philosophical morality. The *New York Times Book Review*'s reviewer criticized Peter Singer's new book on The Ethics of Globalization because "he fails to confront some of the issues that are most outrageous from a moral perspective, like the hypocritical agricultural subsidies in Europe and America and their dire consequences for poor nations" (December 1, 2002).

Budget Costs[2]: The Congressional Budget Office (CBO) estimated that the innovations of the 2002 Act will cost $80 billion over the ten Fiscal Years 2002-11.[3] Of this, $45 billion are for direct payments as an extension of current Production Flexibility Contract payments and new "countercyclical" payments (basically a re-institution of pre-1996 deficiency payments but without set-aside requirements). In addition there are estimated 10-year spending increases of $5.2 billion in marketing loans and loan deficiency payments, $4.9 billion for a new peanut program, $1.6 billion for a new dairy program, and $430 million for increasing support in the sugar program, partly offset by savings projected at $260 million from tightening payment limitation slightly, for a total of $56.7 billion in all commodity programs (Title I of the Act).

CBO's cost accounting scores legislation relative to a "baseline" of spending. The $80 billion is in addition to about $110 billion in spending that CBO estimated would have occurred with continuation of 1996 Act programs (but not Market Loss Assistance payments). Projected total spending on commodity, conservation, and related programs (but not including food stamp and some other nutrition and health programs) is thus about $190 billion for the next ten years.

To place prospective outlays under the 2002 Act in historical perspective, Figure 12.4 shows data since 1980. Over the next several years, when the uncertainties of baseline prices, though still substantial, are less egregious than in the 10-year projection, commodity program spending is projected at nearly $20 billion per year. This is a lot, but as the figure shows it is about $3 billion per year less than the federal government has been spending over the last three years. Nonetheless, the level is high compared to the $10 to $12 billion average annual cost of 1988-1997, or the $11 billion annual baseline spending for 2002-05 that was on the books before the 2002 bill was enacted.

Market-Distorting Effects: It is possible that market distortions that the 2002 Farm Act creates are quite small. It is arguable that the additional spending on direct and countercyclical payments, though large, is essentially a set of lump-sum payments that farmers cannot change through their decisions about what to produce, how much to produce, or the production practices followed. Therefore one may expect small if any output effects or price effects, and few if any deadweight losses due to market distortions.

What does this argument miss? One issue is the updating of acreage bases for payments, which blunts the point that the payments do not influence production decisions. Now farmers will have an incentive to maintain acreage in order to be in a favorable position for future updating.

Second, the addition of soybean base into the acreage for direct payments means reduced incentives for farmers to substitute vegetables or other nonprogram crops for grains and oilseeds. This is a subtle point since producers who received PFC payments under the FAIR Act were already restrained from expanding vegetable acreage through loss of all payments if they grow such crops on contract acreage (a disincentive enacted at the behest of vegetable growers). Midwestern vegetable processors have argued that under the 2002 Farm Bill, this provision will more seriously hinder the expansion of processing vegetable acreage.

[2] This section is largely taken from Gardner 2002b.
[3] Ten-year projected spending is estimated in accordance with Congressional budgetary procedures, even though the Act only authorizes programs for the next six years. The CBO's assumption is that the programs will be reauthorized to cover the ten-year period. – total spending is projected to average about $19 billion per year.

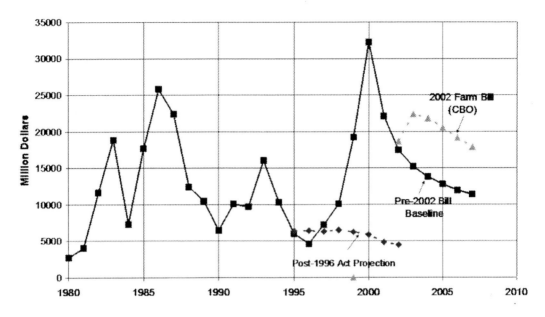

Figure 12.4. Commodity Program Outlay Projections.

Under the 1996 FAIR Act such expansion could occur because soybean acres were not part of the Production Flexibility Contract payment base, so vegetables could be grown on those acres, typically 40 to 50 percent of a farm's acres in some Corn Belt areas. But under the 2002 Act virtually 100 percent of a farm's acreage will often be in the payment base, and under the rules any expansion of vegetable acreage would cause the loss of all payments. Thus, the 2002 Act incentives to keep cropland in program crops are stronger than was the case under the FAIR Act.

A third issue is a set of individually small but collectively significant changes: the market-distorting sugar support price is effectively increased by one cent per pound (4.5%), the new Dairy Market Loss Program makes payments on a current production base, projected to be about 50 cents per hundred pounds (5%), part of the new peanut support system is a marketing loan program that makes payments on a current production base, and similar marketing loan programs are introduced for wool, mohair, honey, and pulses (chickpeas, lentils, and dry peas). These are significant new production-inducing subsidy programs.

Finally, the new Conservation Security Act and expansion of the Environmental Quality Improvement Program (EQIP) pay subsidies for investment in conservation practices on cropped acreage (or "working lands") and these investments are unlikely to cause yield reduction, while they may generate some increased acreage by making it profitable to grow crops on marginal acreage that might otherwise not be cropped. The Farmland Protection title, to the extent its purposes are achieved, will keep land in farming that would otherwise be converted to nonagricultural uses. However, the 2002 Act also has features that may work to reduce crop output. It creates new incentives under the Conservation Reserve Enhancement Program (CREP) for farmers in relatively high-rental-value areas where water quality is a problem (like the Chesapeake Bay watershed) to take land out of crops. It also raises the maximum land area in the overall CRP program by 2.8 million acres, Some of the new conservation programs could encourage farmers to try organic or other low-input production methods that would result in lower yields. The overall impact of the Conservation Title is not predictable in direction at our current state of knowledge.

An estimate of the production effects of the commodity titles of the 2002 Act has been made by the Food and Agricultural Policy Research Institute (FAPRI). They estimate that the area planted to the nine major crops (wheat, corn, soybeans, cotton, rice, sorghum, barley, oats, sunflowers) will be increased by 2 million acres (0.8 of 1 percent) in 2002 and 2003 as compared to the baseline. Wheat and corn plantings are estimated to be increased by about 1 million acres each, and soybean acres decreased by about 1.2 million (because the loan rate is decreased for soybeans and target prices determining countercyclical payments for corn are favorable relative to soybeans). Correspondingly the estimated price effects of the 2002 Act in 2003 are to reduce corn and wheat prices by about 5 cents per bushel (2.5 and 1.5 percent, respectively) and to increase the soybean price by 8 cents (1.7 percent) per bushel (FAPRI, 2002, p. 2).

B. PRE-2002 POLICIES

These effects outlined above are in addition to what the pre-2002 policies were already doing. If the standard of comparison is the absence of any U.S. commodity program support, we need also to estimate the effects of those programs. The effects to be considered, for the major crops of grains and oilseeds, arise from three main sources: the marketing loan program, direct payments, and crop insurance programs. The effects to be considered are those during the 1999-2001 marketing years (rather than the first years under the 1996 FAIR Act) because the market conditions of 1999-2001 are reasonably close to those of today.

Marketing Loan Programs. The most important element of USDA's these programs is "loan deficiency payments," a payment on the full amount of a producer's declared output that makes up the difference between the support "loan rate" price. The key analytical issue for purposes of estimating market distortion is determining what the expected producer price is, including the subsidy (the LDP). The simplest approach would be to just use the loan-rate levels ($1.89 for corn, $2.58 for wheat, $5.26 for soybeans, and 51.92 cents per pound for cotton during 1998-2000). But that approach would be mistaken. One reason is that the loan rate is a price floor, but if market prices rise above that level, the farmer gets the market price. So the appropriate price expectation is the probability of market price being at or below the loan level times the loan level plus the probability of price being above the loan level times the expected price given that outcome. This latter outcome did not occur in any of the years 1999-2001, but that does not mean the probability was zero *ex* ante (although it may reasonably be taken as small).

A second reason one cannot take the loan level as the relevant price expectation is that loan deficiency payments have provided revenues to producers that exceed the loan rate in each of the last three years, so farmers can be expected to count on this in making their planting decisions. Assuming the loan program was expected *ex ante* to generate the *ex post* benefits that actually occurred, the data indicate producer incentive prices average about 20 percent above the market prices for grains and oilseeds.

Westcott and Price (2001) estimated of the output effects of marketing loan supports by removing price wedges attributable to LDPs and other marketing loan provisions as of 1998, and simulating the effects for each commodity to 2005. They use a model embodying a complete set of commodity supply and demand elasticities and cross-elasticities, with baseline projections of yields and export demand. Taking an average of their results for 1999-2001, i.e., two to four years after the loan program is taken away, they estimate the percentage changes in prices and quantities attributable to the program (table 1).

"Freedom to Farm" Payments. The substantive issue with these payments is their effect on output and hence prices. A farm's payments cannot be increased by the farmer planting a larger acreage, or by increasing crop yields. But reasons have been given why the payments may nonetheless result in commodity production higher than would be the case in the absence of the program. Most notable among them are (1) wealth effects, (2) insurance effects, (3) anticipatory effects, and (4) ways around the decoupling.

(1) Guaranteed payments are an annual income flow analogous to what a farmer would receive from an increase in financial or other forms of wealth. If a farmer would respond to a wealth increase by investing some of the gain in the farm operation, then even decoupled payments would have an output effect. Standard theory would say this effect should be negligible, because investment should be governed by the expected rate of return, and decoupled payments do not increase the rate of return to investment. But suppose the farmer was credit-constrained, i.e., the expected rate of return on investment in the farm was higher than the interest rate in credit markets, yet a loan could not be obtained because the farmer had reached the credit limit as seen by the lender (or because of some other credit market imperfection). Then quite possibly the farmer would invest decoupled payments in the farm and thereby increase output.[4]

(2) If a farmer is risk averse, and increasing agricultural production increases the variability of income, and the farmer has nonetheless not fully hedged, then a payment program that reduces income variability will tend to increase output. Lump-sum payments add a constant to income and so do not reduce the variance. But, as emphasized by Hennessy (1998), increases in wealth reduce marginal risk aversion for some standard representations of production risk and farmer utility, so the payments might induce more output by reducing the obstacle that risky production would otherwise place in the farmer's way. Moreover, the payments may in practice not be a constant addition to income, but may be increased by Congressional action when commodity prices are unexpectedly low. In fact this occurred with the Market Loss Assistance payments that supplemented the PFC payments in 1998-2001. Payments that are expected to operate in this way will reduce farmers' anticipated risks in farming.

Table 1. Projected impacts of Marketing Loan Programs

Commodity	Market price	Acreage
Wheat	-2.2	1.5
Corn	-1.4	0.4
Soybeans	-3.7	1.4
Cotton[5]	-9.0	6.0

[4] A story goes that a farmer won the lottery and was asked what he would do with the winnings. He replied: I'll just keep farming until the money is gone.

[5] The cotton figures are Westcott-Price estimates only for quantity. I estimate producer price based on a demand elasticity of −2/3.

(3) Apart from wealth effects or risk aversion, a farmer might feel impelled to maintain acreage and production levels because at some future date the program is likely to be restructured and the base for payments updated (as is actually happening with the 2002 Farm Act). This creates an incentive to refrain from reducing output in the face of low prices and thus works in the direction of keeping production higher than is warranted by market conditions.

(4) The payments are not actually totally decoupled. A producer is not allowed to grow most fruits and vegetables on land covered by the program. So there is an incentive to keep growing program crops even if market conditions indicate higher returns from switching to those alternatives.

Whether any of these effects are quantitatively important is an empirical issue, and one that is impossible to estimate with precision from the data available. Westcott and Young (2001), following up on Young and Westcott (2000), use estimates of wealth effects on planted acreage, developed from pre-1990 data by Chavas and Holt (1990), to estimate that during the period of the FAIR Act PFC payments had "the possible increases in aggregate planted acreage range from 225,000 to 725,000," or about 0.3 percent of total cropland (p. 11). Adams et al. (2001) consider 1997-2000 acreage data directly for 11 major U.S. program-crop states. They find a positive effect of PFC plus market loss assistance (supplemental PFC) payments, but the effect has only marginal statistical significance. FAPRI's simulations imply that $10 billion in payments, about the average level in 1998-2001, would cause about 2.75 million acres of U.S. cropland to be devoted to program crops that would not have been in the absence of the FAIR Act, 1 percent of the acreage planted to those crops. The implied output effect of about 1 percent means the payments introduced in the FAIR Act had about half the downward world price effect of the marketing loan program. In view of the weak statistical significance of the underlying coefficient, the estimates are best taken as an upper limit of the program's effects.

Crop Insurance and Other Risk Management Programs. The Federal Crop Insurance Program has increased its subsidies and hence participation in the program since the 1994 Crop Insurance Reform Act. The subsidies are now sufficiently large to provide a significant incentive to produce crops in locations where production is sufficiently risky that producers would arguably choose to produce less risky crops or pasture the land instead of cropping it, if subsidized insurance were not available. Estimates of the effects are difficult to make with confidence, and attempts to provide such estimates have resulted in greatly varying findings both for shifts among crops and for aggregate crop acreage. Estimates in the literature imply that $3 billion in crop insurance subsidies would increase aggregate U.S. crop acreage by 0.5 to 10.0 percent, a remarkably wide range of uncertainty (see Glauber and Collins 2002, Young, Vandeveer, and Schneff 2001, Orden 2001, Keaton, Skees and Long 2001, Skees 2001). The most careful and detailed of these studies suggest the lower end of this range is most plausible. Young, Vandeveer, and Schneff project average acreages and yields during 2001-2010 in the absence of subsidized crop insurance. They estimate 960,000 acres would be withdrawn from grain, soybean, and cotton production (less than ½ of 1 percent), with more than half of this acreage from the Great Plains, a primarily wheat-growing area. Their implied estimate is that production of wheat would decline about 0.8 percent, cotton 1.7 percent, feed grains 0.2 percent, and soybeans 0.1 percent.

Overall Effects from the Literature. Although any estimate is conjectural, the set of most-reasonable estimates indicate that the marketing loan program increases the U.S. output of grains and soybeans by about 2 percent, the direct payment program, including the 2002 Act's changes, about 1 percent, and crop insurance subsidies by 1+ percent, for a total effect of 4 to 5 percent more of these commodities being produced in 1999-2002 than would have been the case in the absence of commodity support programs.

Given elasticities of demand for these products in aggregate that range from possibly −0.4 (short run) to −1.0 (intermediate run), an argument could be made for average world commodity price effects ranging from a decline of 4 percent to a decline of 12 percent. The latter figure, however, would only be at all plausible for a short-run (a year or less) scenario.[6] Considering adjustments in supply and demand in both the United States and in other countries, the most likely point estimate from the literature taken together, for impacts two to three years after a policy shock is about a 4 percent output effect with a demand elasticity of − 0.7, giving a world price decline of 6+ percent for the average of grains and soybeans, attributable to U.S. commodity support policies currently in place.

B.1. Long-Run Policy Effects

The long-run consequences of commodity support policies are a quite different matter. One has to consider government programs that have a longer-term focus (conservation, agricultural research), and the long-term effects of price supports through farmers' investment and technology adoption decisions.

Longer-run programs. The Conservation Reserve Program (CRP) idles 34 million acres (10 percent of all land used for crops) as of 2001. If that program were to end, what would the output effects be? Most land in the CRP is designated as highly erodible or having other characteristics that make cropping it more than usually threatening to water quality (such as land within 100 feet of a stream or lake). These lands are expected to have lower than average yields when cropped, but analysis by the Economic Research Service of USDA has estimated that yield capacities of CRP land are not far below corresponding cropped acreage on average; but 58 percent of CRP land is in the relatively low-yielding Great Plains states and only 18 percent is in the Corn Belt. So bringing this land back into production would have a disproportionately large effect on wheat production. Assuming two-thirds of CRP land would return to crop production with 85 percent of the yield of average U.S. cropland, assumptions consistent with USDA-ERS analyses, a reasonable estimate of the effect on aggregate grain and soybean output is that the CRP has decreased output by the equivalent of ($34 \cdot 0.67 \cdot 0.85=$) 19 million U.S. average-qulaity cropland acres, for about a 7 percent reduction due to the Conservation Reserve Program. Thus the CRP slightly more than offsets the production increasing effects of marketing loans, crop insurance, and direct payments as the operated in 1998-2001.

---

[6] Direct evidence in 2002 supports the idea that short-term effects of U.S. production on world prices are substantial. Between June and December, USDA's estimate of supply from the U.S. 2002 crops of corn and soybeans, and wheat declined by percentages of 9 ½ and 7, respectively. Over the same period, futures prices and USDA projections of year average farm-level commodity prices for corn and wheat each rose 20 percent. Given an unchanging supply-demand balance in the rest of the world (approximately correct according to USDA estimates for corn and soybeans, although not for wheat where Australia's production prospects also significantly weakened), and given no significant U.S. supply response to price after June, these percentages imply elasticities of demand for U.S. corn and soybeans of −0.48 and −0.35, respectively.

In its benefit-cost analysis of the CRP, USDA estimates imply that 34 million acres placed in the program increase the prices of wheat, corn, and soybeans by 11 percent, 13 percent, and 12 percent respectively (USDA, 1997, p. 7602). These estimated effects are probably too large as long-run impacts, but even if the long-run effects are only half as large, they still roughly offset the price-reducing effects of the USDA's current commodity support programs.

However, if one is going to include the production effects of the Conservation Reserve Program, one ought also to consider research and extension programs that generate new technology, which has increased total factor productivity (TFP) and reduced costs, and thus increased output. TFP in U.S. agriculture has increased about 1.8 percent annually over the last fifty years, but we have no reliable evidence on how much lower that rate of increase would have been in the absence of publicly supported research and extension. Even if only ten percent of TFP growth is attributable to U.S. policies, the cumulative effects by 2000 could easily be enough to offset the land idling of the CRP.

C. PRICE SUPPORT, FARMER INVESTMENT, AND PRODUCTIVITY GROWTH

The preceding section's family of arguments and short-run supply-demand analysis is the basis for the bulk of economists' assessments of commodity support. Longer-run effects that are more difficult to quantify are the consequences of commodity support programs for investment and productivity growth. Here there is dispute even as to the sign of the effect. On the one hand, subsidizing an industry or providing free insurance against financial loss reduces the incentives of managers to keep an eye on costs and avoid ruinous speculative production decisions. Thus, federal loan guarantees have been blamed for subsequent financial disasters. On the other hand, assurance against catastrophic risks may induce cautious producers to invest capital and adopt new productive but unproven technology that turns out well.

The latter line of argument has received more respectful attention in the agricultural than in the industrial context. This is especially true when considering the negative subsidies, i.e., taxes, that have been imposed upon agriculture in developing countries. T.W. Schultz argued that because of pervasive underpricing of agricultural products in developing countries, "farmers are not making the necessary investments, including the purchase of superior inputs" (1979, p. 7). Mundlak (1988) and Fulginiti and Perrin (1993) provided evidence that less taxation of agriculture would increase productivity in such countries. This finding is not inconsistent with the idea that subsidies reduce productivity, since either a tax or subsidy can move producers off the efficiency frontier. But the Schultzian point is friendlier to the idea that commodity support might increase productivity by inducing technology adoption.

Willard Cochrane and Mary Ryan state that 1930s commodity programs "provided the stable prices, hence price insurance, to induce the alert and aggressive farmers to invest in new and improved technologies and capital items, and the reasonably acceptable farm incomes and asset positions to induce lenders to assume the risk of making farm production loans" (Cochrane and Ryan, p. 373). Sally Clarke, concentrating mainly on farmers' investments in tractors in the Midwest in the 1930s, concluded that "farmers' willingness to invest turned in large part on the long-term changes initiated by the New Deal farm policy"(1994, p. 200). Gavin Wright (1986) claimed that mechanization of pre-harvest operations was available since the 1920s but was not adopted until the Cotton Program of the 1933 Agricultural Adjustment Act and its successor programs made sharecropper and tenant labor expensive through regulations that attempted to raise returns to farm labor at the same time the demand for labor was reduced by supply control. This induced growers to adopt labor saving technology and thus helped to force labor off of Southern farms, even before the mechanical cotton picker and World War II off-farm opportunities accelerated out-migration in the 1940s.

Wallace Huffman and Robert Evenson (1993) attempted to sort out the effects of research, farmers' schooling, and commodity supports using a multivariate econometric model, mainly with state-level data from 1950 to 1982. They found that while they could reject the hypothesis that price supports led to increased productivity, about 95 percent of the growth in productivity that they can explain is attributable to lagged effects of research and extension, with only about 5 percent attributable to commodity programs. Lachaal (1994) finds evidence that for subsidies of the U.S. dairy sector, the induced inefficiency effect prevails, so that commodity support reduces productivity growth. But in both Huffman-Evenson and Lachaal so much of the price-support action works over time nationally rather than cross-sectionally that it can be questioned whether price support effects can be empirically disentangled from other variables that change over time.

D. DATA EVIDENCE

D.1. Investment in Agriculture

The Census of Agriculture asks farmers for their inventories of certain items of equipment – the items asked about vary over time but since the 1930s has covered tractors and the main harvesting machinery. These data do not cover a great many capital items, notably new types of equipment. Moreover, Census inventory data do not provide enough information about the age, condition, and features of the equipment to construct a total capital stock estimate. Independently of the Census, the Economic Research Service of USDA collects a broader range of data from equipment manufacturers, dealers, and other sources. Using this information together with farm buildings and other fixed capital such as irrigation equipment, the Bureau of Economic Analysis of the Department of Commerce constructs a measure of "fixed reproducible tangible wealth" (to distinguish this form of wealth from natural resources, financial assets, and intangible capital such as brand-name goodwill and intellectual property).

USDA also publishes data on expenditures for capital goods by farmers each year, as well as an estimate of capital consumption (depreciation of the existing capital stock). The difference between capital goods purchased and depreciation is a measure of net investment in U.S. farms. The USDA measure, along with an implicit BEA measure obtained as the change in BEA's estimate of the capital stock (structure and equipment) on farms are both shown in Figure 12.5. The USDA investment measure differs from the BEA measure, primarily because BEA includes investment in agriculture by persons who are not farmers.

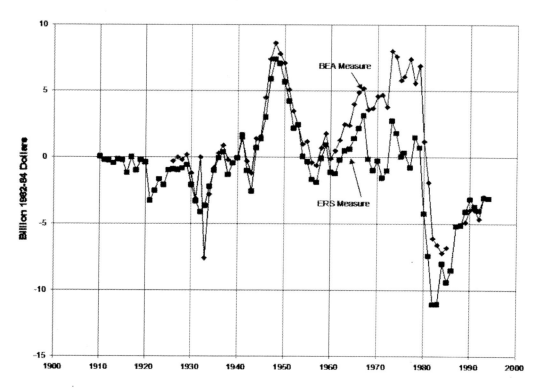

Figure 12.5. Real Net Investment on Farms.

The data according to either measure indicate the ill effects of the long period of unfavorable economic conditions in agriculture, with net investment by farmers being negative throughout the 1920s and 1930s. The economic meaning is that the farmers were to some extent living off their capital stock, by letting it depreciate. In this context, the increase in investment at the end of the 1930s and early 1940s is really quite modest. The take-off in net investment doesn't occur until 1946, after which the rise is spectacular. The timing is suggestive in two important ways. First, since overall productivity growth began to accelerate during 1935-1940, and had definitely begun its permanently faster growth before 1945, it is a mistake to tie the acceleration of productivity growth to farmers' investment in capital equipment. Second, while the New Deal programs undoubtedly gave farmers reasons for less pessimism, the investment data do not indicate a real switch to ebullient willingness to invest any time in the 1930s and early 1940s. Wartime restrictions helped keep a lid on some investment until 1945, but even so the facts of overall investment limited the extent to which the putative increase in underlying optimism could be converted into productivity-increasing new equipment.

To make a substantial difference, more than just a year or two of investment is required, especially after years of depreciation. Figure 12.6 shows the time series of BEA's stock of machinery and equipment on farms. Even in 1947 after two years of accelerated investment, the capital stock had only just recovered to its level of 1930. But by 1980 the capital stock had tripled. These considerations cast doubt on the Cochrane-Clarke hypothesis at least as it pertains to the New Deal programs fostering productivity growth by stimulating investment during the late 1930s.

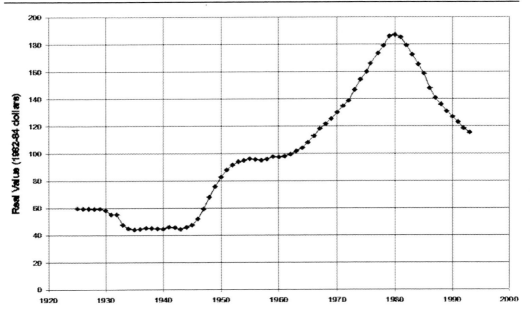

.Figure 12.6. Capital Stock on Farms.

D.2. Productivity Growth and Investment

Even if investment could be linked to commodity programs, it is a further step to claim investment as the vehicle for technology adoption and productivity growth. As mentioned above, the most striking structural shift in U.S. TFP growth was its marked and sustained acceleration after the mid-1930s. This acceleration is not associated with an uptick in investment; but it is associated with the introduction of the New Deal commodity support programs.

A second striking statistical episode is the continued growth of U.S. agricultural productivity even while investment in agriculture plummeted after 1980. Both output per worker and TFP kept increasing at an undiminished rate while U.S. manufacturing and overall productivity slowed down after the mid-1970s. That productivity slowdown has been attributed to a number of factors, of which the most widely agreed upon appears to be the rapid rise in the cost of energy following the OPEC oil marketing strategy change of 1972. Agriculture was cushioned from the immediate impact of energy price increases because farm output prices soared at the same time. But by 1978 grain prices had collapsed and farmers were marching on Washington in a show of political discontent unique in the last half of the century. Economic problems in agriculture only deepened with the wave of farm business failures that characterized the "farm crisis" of the mid-1980s. Commodity program spending and financial assistance responded with massive assistance to agriculture but by the mid-1990s the Federal government's role in agriculture was waning, and farmland prices had still not returned to the levels of 1981 in nominal much less real terms.

Notwithstanding those problems, agricultural productivity continued to grow at the 1940 to 1970 pace. Why? This subject has been much less investigated than the mid-1930s acceleration, but the data suggest the science-and-research hypothesis as perhaps the most plausible reason. Not only was commodity program support dwindling over the last decade of the century, but net investment ceased after 1980 and the farm capital stock declined, and the decline in farm numbers that may have fostered increased efficiency of labor use slowed down (the United States counted more farms in 2001 than in 1990). Increased environmental concerns as well as input costs led to lower use of chemical inputs after 1980, inputs which appear to have generated increased output value far in excess of their cost. In the face of these obstacles, improved technology and improvements in farmers' knowledge and ability to put that technology to work appear to be the most likely remaining explanatory factors for continued agricultural productivity growth.

One crucial aspect of the preceding data is suspect, namely the huge and sustained capital stock reduction. There are differences in measured capital input series available that are sufficiently large to make a difference in productivity measurement. Comparing the capital input series from Acquaye, Alston, and Pardey (2000) to the USDA-ERS index for durable equipment, both agree that capital in agriculture has been falling since about 1980 (peak at 1979 in AAP and 1981 in USDA). But the rate of decline is 3.9% annually in USDA and 0.9% annually in AAP. This 3% difference in the rate of decline, with capital accounting for about a sixth of agricultural inputs, means use of the AAP index would reduce the measured rate of multifactor productivity growth by about 0.5%, for example from 2.0% to 1.5% annually over the 1980-1992 period.

I suspect that both the USDA and AAP capital input indexes have been understating the true rate of growth of capital (or overstating the decline) for the period since 1970. My hypothesis is that the chief culprit is the treatment of depreciation. As discussed in Ball, et al (2000), USDA uses a concave function of decay of capital as contrasted with the more often used geometric decay. This means a given capital item decays slowly early in its life but then falls rapidly to zero as its lifetime ends. In contrast, with geometric decay an item loses most of its effectiveness early, but retains more as it gets older (as compared to the USDA approach). While Ball et al. cite good reasons for believing that capital holds its effectiveness better in its early life than geometric decay allows, I question the rapid fall-off to zero levels for "aged" capital.

The treatment of older capital is important because so much of the capital equipment in U.S. agriculture is quite old. The implication is that of the 4.5 million tractors reported on farms in The 1997 Census of Agriculture found 3.9 million tractors on U.S. farms. Of these 400,000 were reported as manufactured in 1993 or later. The 1992 Census reported 400,000 tractors manufactured between 1988 and 1992.[7] Thus at least 3.1 of the 3.9 million tractors on farms in 1997 are 10 years old or more.[8] This is important because ERS, following BEA practice, uses a tractor lifetime of 9 years, after which it is depreciated to zero. Probably many of the older tractors do not carry out much useful work, and thus are properly depreciated to low or zero values. But other old equipment is providing valuable services. Indeed Peterson (2002), surveying used equipment prices, finds even 20 to 30-year old tractors holding up well in value. The existence of so many productive older tractors indicates a substantial understatement of the capital stock. And, since recent-year sales relative to the Census inventory figures are lower in 1997 than in earlier Censuses, such bias as exists has been increasing over time since the 1970s.

---

[7] Separately, ERS data on sales of tractors indicate that about 1 million have been sold over the last 15 years (adding up reports of annual sales).

[8] "At least," because some of those bought in 1988-92 and counted in 1992 may have been junked and not included in the 1997 stock.

Similarly startling percentages of old equipment can be inferred Census data on other equipment, e.g., combines where of 460,000 on farms in 1997, at least 360,000 were manufactured before 1988. The ERS-BEA useful life of this machinery (all farm machinery except tractors) is assumed to be 14 years, indicating the understatement of the stock is less than for tractors, but still not small.

Another source of possible understatement of growth (or overstatement of decline) in the farm capital stock is that machinery less well covered statistically (and not counted in the Agriculture Census) includes corn planters and pesticide applicators, for example, machinery which has become more sophisticated and likely a larger fraction of the farm capital stock in recent years.

D.3. Short-Term Acreage Effects of Post-1996 Policies

In order to provide an informal reality check for the earlier estimates of commodity program effects (not counting long-term effects of conservation or research programs), consider the time series data on corn, soybean, and wheat acreage, as shown in Figure 12.7. The period between 1970 and 1981 is one in which a huge increase in plantings of these crops occurred, from 160 to 240 million acres, a 50 percent increase. This expansion was induced by price rises in which farm-level corn and soybean prices more than doubled and wheat prices tripled. During the commodity crash and consequent farm income crisis of the 1980s, this acreage fell back, partly in response to lower prices and partly because of federal acreage-idling programs of pre-1996 legislation. The acreage reductions of 1983, 1986, and 1987 are specific consequences of these programs.

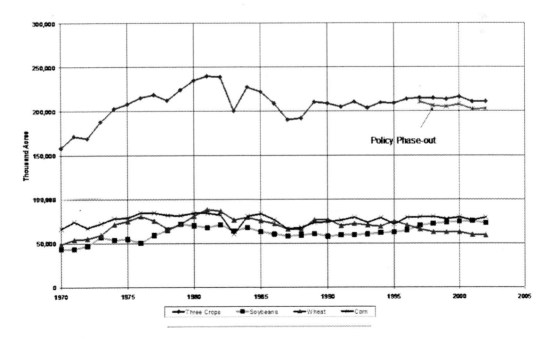

Figure 12.7. U.S. Acreage Planted, 1970-2001.

Table 2. Increase in Crop Planted Acreages, 1994/95 to 2001/02*

	Corn	Soybeans	Wheat	3 crops
change in million acres (percentage change below each entry)				
Midwest	150	6,550	-1,802	4,897
	0.3%	16.6%	-23.1%	5.2%
Plains	2,030	6,083	-5,462	2,651
	12.0%	69.2%	-13.2%	3.9%
South	-293	-1,380	-49	-1,721
	-5.6%	-11.8%	-1.1%	-8.1%
All other states	564	876	-1,255	185
	10.2%	41.8%	-7.8%	0.8%
US Total	2,452	12,128	-8,567	6,013
	3.3%	19.5%	-12.3%	2.9%

* Averages of two crop years.
Midwest: IA,IL,IN,MI,MI,MN,MO,OH,WI
Plains: KS,ND,NE,OK,SD,TX
South: AL,AR,FL,GA,KY,LA,MS,NC,SC,TN,VA

By 1990-1995 relative stability in acreage emerged for aggregate grain and soybean acreage, but with a moderate continuing trend away from wheat and into soybeans. In this context the FAIR Act of 1996 was intended to let farmers respond more fully to market prices rather than deficiency payments (a goal already partly achieved in the 1990 Farm Act and likely responsible for some of the move to soybeans in 1990-1995).

What are the apparent consequences of moving to "freedom to farm" in the 1996 Act? What was most clearly expected was a further shift to soybeans, and indeed this shift occurred. Beyond price incentives, one reason was the desire of some Corn Belt growers to introduce a two-year corn-soybean rotation for pest control purposes, but who had been trapped into continuous corn or nearly so by the loss of corn deficiency payments if they shifted to soybeans beyond the limits allowed under the limited flexibility provisions of the 1990 Act. However, regional data make it clear that the move to soybeans was not just a Corn Belt adjustment. Table 2 shows planted acreages for the main regions comparing the two years just before the FAIR Act (1994 and 1995 average) with the last two years (2000 and 2001 average). Soybean acreage increased by about the same amount (6 million acres) in both the Corn Belt and Great Plains, and by a much larger percentage in the latter.

Aggregate acreage for the three crops increased most in the Corn Belt. As Figure 12.8 shows, the main jump in acreage occurred in 1996. The predominant causes were the high commodity prices that persisted over a year from mid-1995, and the end of legislated acreage reduction programs.

Figure 12.8. U.S. Corn Acreage Planted.

The effect of the FAIR Act's marketing loan, PFC payment, and crop insurance programs was to maintain that higher acreage. This can be seen most clearly by plotting the data in price-quantity space. Figure 12.9 shows corn acreage planted and the average price received by farmers for the preceding crop.[9] It is noteworthy that the 1998-2002 levels of plantings are clustered in the lower right-hand corner of price-quantity space. This means that the acreage-response supply function lies below the supply function of earlier years. Why? One reason is that the real cost of producing corn has declined (note that prices are deflated to give real values), attributed to technological advances -- improved seed, machinery, etc. There is an overall tendency for successive observations to lie lower and to the right, as the division of the data into the 1980s (squares), early 1990s (triangles), and 1998-2002 (diamonds) indicates. In addition, corn programs, particularly set-asides, make a difference. This is most obvious in the case of the Payment-in-Kind acreage idling program of 1983, which brought planted corn acreage down to 60 million.

---

[9] This price is called the lagged price in the diagram, because it is received from marketing the crop preceding the crop whose planted acreage is shown. But the time during which the prices are observed actually coincides with the planting period. For example the price that corresponds to planted acreage in 2001 corn is the average price received for the 2000 crop. Most of the crop is sold in the months immediately following the harvest, in October 2000 to January 2001, just a few months before planting the 2001 crop; but some sales whose prices make up the season average price of 2000-crop corn occur throughout the marketing year, which goes through August 2001. Therefore, it is possible that observation of plantings could influence the "lagged" price to some extent, and we would not be able to identify the acreage-proxied supply function precisely.

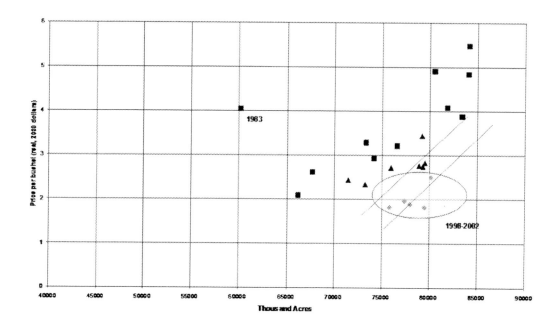

Figure 12.9. Corn Acreage Planted and Lagged Price, 1980-2002.

The 7.5 percent corn acreage reduction in the 1995 program in responsible for the left-most triangle in the 1990-1997 data and the only such year in which corn had an acreage reduction program.

The data suggest that the loan deficiency payments and perhaps the market-loss assistance payments of 1998-2001 also have played a role. Sketching in supply functions (adjusted for acreage reductions in years when they occurred) as shown in Figure 12.9 indicates that the curve shifted down by about 65 cents per bushel between 1991-97 and 1998-2002. If technical progress reduced costs by 2 percent per year during this period (USDA's estimate of the long-term average total factor productivity growth for US agriculture), this could have accounted for a shift of about 12 percent over the six years from the midpoint of the 1991-97 period to the midpoint of the 1998-2002 period, which at an average price of $2.50 would amount to 30 cents. This leaves a 35-cent apparent supply shift unaccounted for. That is, in 1998-2002 farmers are planting an acreage of corn that, based on farmers' historical behavior, would have required a price 35 cents per bushel higher than the actual price we observe in 1998-2002. (If there were no cost reductions, and the underlying real cost situation has remained the same since 1991, then the apparently missing price incentive is 65 cents per bushel).

Recall from the earlier discussion of marketing loans that the average marketing loan benefit for 1999-2000 was 26 cents per bushel. This explains a substantial part of the apparent supply shift – if producers expect a 26-cent marketing loan benefit, they will commit acreage to corn that they would commit if the market price (which doesn't include the marketing loan benefit) was 26 cents higher and there were not marketing loans (as there were not in the higher-priced years of 1991-1997). Since the total apparent supply shift (measured vertically) is 65 cents, this leaves a 9-cent (if corn production costs were reduced 12 percent) to 39-cent (if costs were not reduced at all) shift to be explained by other factors. The prime candidate is the Production Flexibility and Market Loss Assistance payments made under the FAIR Act.

To estimate the additional corn production created by the policies, we need to convert the vertical shift to a horizontal one. For this transformation only one parameter is necessary, the elasticity of supply. Assuming it is 0.3, the horizontal shift is 1.2 (12 percent cost reduction) to 4.5 percent (no cost reduction). Taking the midpoint, and assuming no yield effects, the implication is that policies in place under the FAIR Act generated about 3 percent more corn than would have been the case under pre-1996 policies.

The preceding calculations can be carried out statistically by means of a linear regression estimating the inverse (price dependent) supply function, explaining prices during 1980-2002 as a function of time period (1991-97 or 1998-2002, with 1980-1990 being the intercept), time trend (for technical change over time), and acreage. The resulting equation has a trend decline in real price of 5.0 cents (1.7%), a FAIR Act effect of 59 cents (compared to 1991-1997), and an elasticity of supply of 0.32. All the variables are statistically significant at the 5 percent level and the adjusted R^2 is 0.85. Carrying out the calculation of the preceding paragraph, we have an estimated acreage effect of the FAIR Act on production of 59/302·0.32=0.06, i.e., six percent more output than would have occurred under pre-FAIR Act policies. A problem is that with errors in variables, the inverse estimating equation overstates the elasticity. Estimating the same equation with acres as dependent variable and price on the right-hand side gives an elasticity of 0.20, which would imply a FAIR Act effect of four percent. This is a lower bound for the elasticity (because of the possible identification problem mentioned above as well as errors in variables).

Figure 12.10 provides a similar set of data for soybeans.

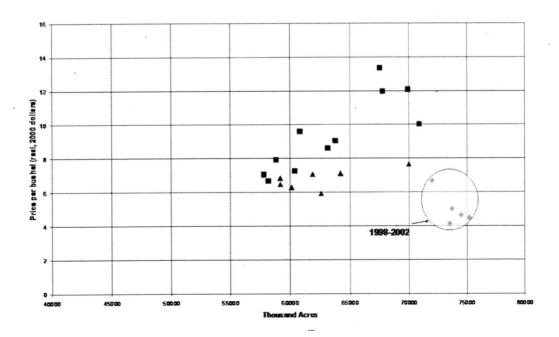

Figure 12.10. Soybean Acreage Planted and Lagged Price, 1980-2001.

These data indicate an even larger soybean acreage effect in 1998-2002. Despite record-low real prices, acreage keeps increasing. In part, following the discussion earlier, this is attributable to the FAIR Act's removal of previously existing disincentives to grow soybeans. This effect is not a matter of subsidies on soybeans. Since our means of identifying the FAIR Act's production effect was simply to use a dummy variable for the 1998-2002 period, we cannot sort out the two effects by the method used above for corn. Indeed, the soybean data call into question the estimate of the corn effect as estimated, because it too could be in part a result of corn acreage moving to soybeans as a result of FAIR Act soybean provisions rather than corn subsidies. Moreover, we cannot use the regression analysis to correct for the problem by using soybean prices in the corn equation, because what we are hypothesizing is not a market-response phenomenon, but rather the result of the removal of a prior policy disincentive to plant soybeans.

The most straightforward way to avoid the problems of corn-soybean entanglement is to look at the acreage of corn and soybeans together, as a corn-soy aggregate. Figure 12.11 shows these data. Applying the procedures used above, I obtain an elasticity of aggregate corn-soybeans supply of 0.2 and a production effect of the FAIR Act of 6 percent. Even a corn-soybean aggregate does not tell the whole story, because there has been a substitution of both of these crops, but especially soybeans, for wheat. For the three-crop aggregate, the data indicate an acreage effect of about 4 percent, which would imply a slightly smaller production effect because in substituting corn and soybeans for wheat we are getting more yield per acre. Earlier, based on other studies, I conjectured an output effect of the FAIR Act for these three crops ranging from 2 to 10 percent, but with a point estimate of 4 percent. The analysis of the raw data in Figures 14.9 to 14.11, without any specific analysis of the policy instruments used, gives a quite similar estimate of effects, providing more confidence that the true effect is not at the extreme high end of that range, and most probably in the 3 to 5 percent range.

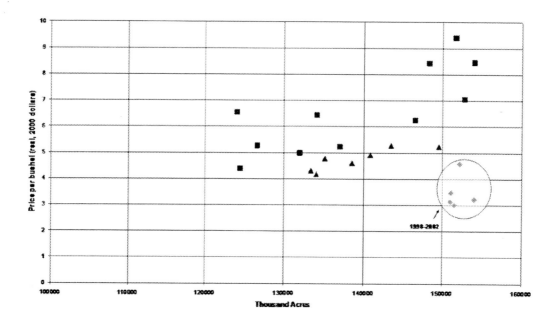

Figure 12.11. soybean and Corn (Aggregated) Acreage Planted and Lagged Price, 1980-2002.

Accordingly Figure 12.7 plots the path labeled "policy phase-out" as an estimated 4 percent less acreage during 1999-2001 as the difference between the U.S. area actually planted to corn, soybeans, and wheat and the area the would have been planted in the absence of the PFC payments, market-loss payments, marketing loan payments, and added crop insurance subsidies that were paid in those years.

REFERENCES

Acquaye, A., Alston, J., and Pardey, P. (2000). A Disaggregated Perspective on Post-War Productivity Growth in U.S. Agriculture. presented at USDA-ERS Conference on Productivity Measurement, March.

Adams, G., Westhoff, P., Willott, B., and Young II, R.E. (2001). Do 'Decoupled' Payments Affect U.S. Crop Area? Preliminary Evidence from 1997-2000. *American Journal of Agricultural Economics, Vol.83*, 1190-1195.

Chavas, J., and Holt, M.T. (1990). Acreage Decisions Under Risk: The Case of Corn and Soybeans. *American Journal of Agricultural Economics, Vol.72*, 529-538.

Clarke, S.H. (1995). *Regulation and the Revolution in U.S. Farm Productivity*. New York: Cambridge University Press.

Cochrane, W.W., and Ryan, M.E. (1976). *American Farm Policy, 1948-1973*. Minneapolis: University of Minnesota Press.

FAPRI (Food and Agricultural Policy Research Institute). (2002). Farm Security and Rural Investment Act of 2002: Preliminary FAPRI Analysis. Mimeo, May 6.

Gardner, B.L. (2002a). *American Agricultural in the 20th Century*. Cambridge: Harvard University Press.

Gardner, B.L. (2002b). U.S. Agricultural Policies Since 1995. Inter-American Development Bank Conference, October.

Fulginiti, L.E., and Perrin, R.K. (1993). Prices and Productivity in Agriculture. *Review of Economics and Statistics, Vol. 75*, 471-482.

Glauber, J.W., and Collins, K.J. (2002). Risk Management and the Role of the Federal Government. In Just, R., and Rope, R. (Eds.), *A Comprehensive Assessment of the Role of Risk in U.S. Agriculture* (469-488). Boston, MA: Kluwer Academic Publishers.

Hennessy, D.A. (1998). The Production Effects of Agricultural Income Support Policies under Uncertainty. *American Journal of Agricultural Economics, Vol. 80*, 46-57.

Huffman, W.E., and Evenson, R. (1993). *Science for Agriculture*. Ames, IA: Iowa State University Press.

Keaton, K., Skees, J., and Long, J. (1999). The Potential Influence of Risk Management Programs on Cropping Decisions. Presented at American Agricultural Economics Association meetings, 1999.

Lachaal, L. (1994). Subsidies, Endogenous Technical Efficiency and the Measurement of Productivity Growth. *Journal of Agricultural and Applied Economics, Vol. 26*, 299-310.

Martinez, A. (2002). Review of *One World: The Ethics of Globalization. New York Times Book Review*, December 1.

Mundlak, Y. (1988). Endogenous Technical Change and the Measurement of Productivity. In Capalbo, S., and Antle, J. (Eds.), *Agricultural Productivity Measurement and Explanation*. Washington, D.C.: Resources for the Future.

Orden, D. (2001). Should There Be a Federal Safety Net. USDA Agricultural Outlook Forum, February.

Peterson, G. (2002). Pricing Out Horsepower: Tractors Actually Increase in Value Beyond 15 Years of Age. *Successful Farming*, April.

Schnepf, R., and Heifner, R. (1999). Crop and Revenue Insurance. UDSA, *Agricultural Outlook, August*, 15-18.

Schultz, T.W. (1979). On Economic and Politics of Agriculture. In Schultz, T.W. (Ed.), *Distortions of Agricultural Incentives*. Bloomington: Indiana University Press.

Skees, J.R. (2001). The Bad Harvest. *Regulation*.

U.S. Department of Agriculture. (various years). *Agricultural Statistics*. Washington, D.C.: Government Printing Office.

U.S. General Accounting Office. (1976). Alleviating Agricultural Producers' Crop Losses. Washington D.C.

Westcott, P.C., and Price, M.J. (2001). Analysis of the U.S. Commodity Loan Program with Marketing Loan Provisions. Agricultural Economic Report No. 801, April.

Womach, J. (2000). Agricultural Marketing Assistance Loans and Loan Deficiency Payments.In *CRS Report for Congress* (98-744), Congressional Research Service, December.

Young, C.E., and Westcott, P.C. (2000). How Decoupled is U.S. Agricultural Support for Major Crops. *American Journal of Agricultural Economics, Vol. 82*, 762-767.

Young, C.E., Vandeveer, M.L., and Schneff, R.D. (2001). Production and Price Impacts of U.S. Crop Insurance Programs. *American Journal of Agricultural Economics,* Vol. 83, 1196-1203.

In: The Economics of Natural and Human Resources...   ISBN 978-1-60741-029-4
Editor: Ayal Kimhi and Israel Finkelshtain   © 2009 Nova Science Publishers, Inc.

Chapter 13

ARE "DECOUPLED" FARM PROGRAM PAYMENTS REALLY DECOUPLED? AN EMPIRICAL EVALUATION

*Barry K. Goodwin and Ashok K. Mishra**

ABSTRACT

This analysis utilizes farm-level data to evaluate the extent to which U.S. farm program benefits, particularly direct payments, bring about distortions in production. The issue is important in WTO negotiations and in the debate over the distortionary effects of decoupled ("green-box") payments. Our results suggest that the distortions brought about by AMTA payments, though statistically significant in some cases, are very modest. Larger effects are implied for market loss assistance payments. Probit models suggest that AMTA payments do not influence the likelihood that agents will acquire more land. Our results are reinforced using an aggregate county-level acreage model.

A. INTRODUCTION

U.S. agricultural policy underwent significant changes with the 1996 Federal Agriculture Improvement and Reform (FAIR) Act. In principle at least, the FAIR Act was meant to signal a transition toward a new policy environment characterized by diminished government involvement in agricultural markets. Market price supports and deficiency payment programs

* Barry K. Goodwin is William Neal Reynolds Professor in the Departments of Agricultural and Resource Economics and Economics at North Carolina State University. Ashok K. Mishra is Associate Professor, Department of Agricultural Economics and Agribusiness, Louisiana State University AgCenter, Baton Rouge. This chapter is reprinted with permission from the *American Journal of Agricultural Economics*, where it was originally published (Vol. 81, No. 1, February 2006, pp. 73-89). A portion of this work was done while Goodwin was at the Ohio State University. This research was supported by the North Carolina Agricultural Research Service, the OSU-OARDC, the Andersons' Endowment, and the OECD. We benefited significantly from the helpful comments of Jesús Antón, Harry DeGorter, Bruce Gardner, Matt Holt, Jeffrey Hopkins, Teresa Serra, Paul Westcott, Ed Young, Carl Zulauf, and an anonymous referee. We gratefully acknowledge the helpful comments of seminar participants at the University of Arizona, Hebrew University of Jerusalem, and Oregon State University. Views, opinions, and conclusions are the authors' alone and do not reflect those of the USDA or other organizations.

were replaced by a program with fixed payments (called "production flexibility contract" or "Agricultural Market Transition Act"[AMTA] payments) and a loan deficiency payment program intended to establish minimum support prices for program crops, including soybeans. AMTA payments were based upon historical production (base yields and acreages) of program crops (i.e., corn, wheat, cotton, grain sorghum, etc.) and thus were considered to be "decoupled" from production decisions. In principle, AMTA payments were intended to decline each year until the FAIR Act expired in 2002.

The extent to which the FAIR Act actually constituted a change in U.S. farm policy is a topic of substantial debate, especially in light of the substantial amount of ad hoc support that followed it and the 2002 Farm Bill that was signed into law on May 13, 2002. The 2002 Bill provided generous increases in support and extended the fixed, decoupled AMTA-type payments for another six years. Not only were the payments extended under the 2002 Act, producers were also given the opportunity to update their base acreages and yields which determine the payments and, perhaps more importantly, to include historical soybean acreage in their base. Provisions for updating this historical base, especially if such provisions were anticipated by growers, may call into question the extent to which the payments are actually decoupled.

Anticipation of future opportunities for updating base acreage reflects an embedded optionality that may influence current and future production decisions, thus breaking the "decoupled" nature of the programs. Such policy actions raise questions regarding the credibility and time consistency of agricultural policies. As Kydland and Prescott (1977) have noted, rational agents react to expected future policies, even when such expectations are counter to the policy rules currently in place. The generous ad hoc support that preceded the 2002 Farm Bill and the substantial benefits provided by the 2002 legislation may generate important credibility problems for agricultural policymakers.

The distortionary effects of domestic farm programs became an important issue in the Uruguay Round of the General Agreement on Tariffs and Trade/World Trade Organization (GATT/WTO) negotiations in the 1980s and 1990s. Along with the conventional focus on export subsidies and market access, domestic farm programs were targeted for reductions in support and other reforms. A philosophy underlying the Uruguay Round agreement on agriculture (URAA) involved a classification scheme whereby domestic policies were characterized by the extent to which they were considered to be "trade-distorting." Policies that were considered to be minimally trade distorting, such as conservation programs, domestic food aid, and research and extension expenditures were termed to be "green box" policies and not subject to limits on overall domestic support. Because they were presumed to be decoupled from production, AMTA payments were considered to be a "green-box" policy and thus are not subject to the negotiated reductions in support. A point of contention underlying this classification system involves the lack of a precise definition of "minimally trade distorting."

The extent to which fixed payments are truly decoupled from production decisions has recently come under debate. Various mechanisms by which decoupled payments may affect production decisions have been discussed. Hennessy (1998) pointed out that agents with declining absolute risk aversion (DARA) preferences will be willing to assume more risk as wealth increases (i.e., because of decoupled farm payments), since such an increase lowers their aversion to risk. Chau and de Gorter (2000) argued that AMTA payments may allow producers to cover fixed costs and thus may allow marginal farmers that would otherwise be forced to shut down to remain in production. In a similar vein, Roe, Somwaru, and Diao (2002) point out that decoupled payments may improve producers' access to credit by raising wealth directly and through increases in land values. They also note that expectations about future farm programs may tie program benefits to production, though they conclude that the distortionary effects of decoupled programs are likely to be modest. It should also be noted that psychological factors regarding farmers' preferences for remaining in production agriculture may be relevant to exit decisions. Foster and Rausser (1991) have provided conceptual and empirical support for such motivations that, at first glance, may appear to be economically irrational. A recent USDA study used an aggregate, computable general equilibrium (CGE) model to conclude that decoupled payments had no effect on production and further suggested that coupled market loan payments had a very modest effect on acreage (Burfisher and Hopkins, 2003). Of course, inferences from CGE models may be limited by their highly aggregate nature. The link between direct payments and investment is also important. In a dynamic sense, wealth transfers today may affect investment decisions and thus have important impacts on production in the future.[1]

The objective of this analysis is to evaluate empirically the effects of decoupled farm program payments on the production decisions of producers. To this end, we utilize a set of detailed farm-level data, collected under the USDA's agricultural resource management survey (ARMS) program. The focus is on farms in the Corn Belt, the major agricultural production region of the United States. We consider acreage devoted to the production of the three principal crops in this region—corn, soybeans, and wheat.[2] Individual farm data are used in conjunction with county aggregates to evaluate the extent to which AMTA payments may appear to have been linked to production decisions in the period that has followed the implementation of the 1996 FAIR Act.

B. EMPIRICAL FRAMEWORK AND ECONOMETRIC METHODS

Agents will act to maximize the expected utility of wealth, including changes brought about by discounted future expected profits. In each period, wealth is given by initial wealth, plus profits derived from production, direct government payments, and nonfarm activities. The agent's problem can thus be characterized as maximizing the expected value of :

$$V_t = \sum_{t=0}^{T} U\left\{ \delta^t \left(\sum_i P_{it} Q_{it}(A_{it}, X_{it}, A_{it-1}, \varepsilon_t) - w'X - C(A_{it-1}) + G_t + PS(P_{it}) + W_{t-1} \right) \right\} \quad (1)$$

where W_t is wealth, P_{it} is the price received for output i, $Q(\cdot)$ is output of product i, which is assumed to be a function of lagged acreage (A_{t-1}, representing rotational issues), acreage, and an exogenous shock, given by ε_t, X_t represents a vector of variable inputs, purchased at

---

[1] For a detailed discussion and analytical model of investment, and production decisions made by producers with heterogeneous lines of credit, see Rausser, Zilberman, and Just (1984).

[2] We note at the outset that corn and soybeans are the main crops and that wheat is primarily grown for crop rotation reasons in this region. Our evaluation is of an empirical nature only and thus we do not attempt to identify the exact mechanism (if any) by which decoupled program payments affect production. Instead, we focus on determining whether any such effect can be empirically identified.

price w_t, and $C(\cdot)$ represents fixed costs that also are influenced by lagged acreage. Government policies affect the producer's problem in several ways. First, prices received P_{it} may reflect support mechanisms such as loan deficiency payments. Second, payments based upon market conditions, such as market loss assistance payments (MLA also known as "double-AMTA" payments) may be received at harvest, and thus expectations regarding such payments will play a key role in production decisions. Such payments are represented by $PS(P_{it})$, which represents the fact that such payments may be conditioned on market prices. Finally, direct decoupled payments G_t will be important for their effects on wealth.

A number of restrictions are relevant to the producer's problem, including capacity constraints and those constraints describing the availability and cost of borrowed capital. If capital markets are perfect, wealth can be adjusted to accommodate situations where revenues are not sufficient to cover costs. However, borrowers are likely to face credit constraints, determined by their credit worthiness. In such cases, decoupled payments may indeed be relevant to production. Agents select acreage and other inputs to maximize the expected value of the utility function. This yields reduced form acreage equations of the form:

$$A_t = f(A_{t-1}, P_t, w_t, G_t, PS_t, W_{t-1}) \tag{2}$$

Output prices and payments based upon market conditions at harvest (PS_t) are unknown at the time planting decisions are made and thus actions will reflect agents expectation of the harvest-time values of these variables. Thus, an estimable, reduced-form acreage response equation will assume the form:

$$A_t = f(A_{t-1}, P_t^*, w_t, G_t, PS_t^*, W_{t-1}) \tag{3}$$

where asterisks correspond to expected harvest-time values, conditional on information available to agents at planting.

In cases where an agent's risk preferences are influenced by their level of wealth (such as constant relative risk aversion [CRRA] or decreasing absolute risk aversion [DARA]), their production decisions may be influenced by their level of wealth. In this way, decoupled payments G_t as well as initial levels of wealth will be important. Of course, as we discuss in greater detail below, for the typical commercial farm in the United States, the support provided by AMTA and other decoupled programs is likely to be small relative to a farm's overall wealth level.[3]

Our analysis is conducted using individual farm data collected under the ARMS project by the National Agricultural Statistics Service of the USDA. The ARMS data are collected annually by means of a survey of individual farmers. The ARMS data represent the USDA's primary source of information about U.S. agricultural production conditions, marketing practices, resource use, and economic well-being of farm households. We focus on data taken

---

[3] However, as a referee has pointed out, decoupled payments may have a second avenue by which wealth is affected—through increased asset values. One certainly expects that expected future benefits will be capitalized into asset values and AMTA payments may provide important signals about future policy benefits. In this light, our arguments regarding the significance of AMTA payments relative to a farm's overall level of wealth pertain only to the direct payment effects. We acknowledge that effects on asset values may also be pertinent. Our measure of wealth is an aggregate of self-assessed asset values less total liabilities.

from four years of the NASS survey—1998–2001. These years were chosen as representative of the FAIR act policy environment. In addition, the survey collected detailed policy information for these four years. County data from a variety of other sources were matched to the ARMS survey data. In particular, county data for crop acreages were taken from the USDA-NASS database and county-level program payments were summarized from unpublished USDA data.

Although the ARMS data provide a rich and valuable set of detailed farm household data, the database does have an important limitation—the lack of repeated sampling on individual farms. That is, the sample is taken randomly each year and it is thus impossible to observe the same farm in more than a single year.[4] This implies an important reliance on cross-sectional variability and prevents one from conditioning observed events on the preceding year's experience or on fixed farm effects. For example, though it is possible to observe an individual grower's corn acreage in a given year, it is not possible to examine how this acreage compares to the preceding year's acreage. The potential for confounding effects to complicate the identification of policy responses certainly exists. For example, those farms receiving large AMTA payments had a large base in program crops prior to the FAIR Act. To the extent that fixities make producers slow to adjust acreage, correlation between AMTA payments and current acreage may reflect correlation of both variables with historical acreage. However, it should be noted that we can intuitively assign a direction that such a bias might be expected to take. If both AMTA payments and current acreage are strongly correlated with historical production, we would expect to see a stronger effect of AMTA payments on current acreage than what might be expected in the absence of such correlation. The results that follow should be interpreted with this caveat in mind.

To address this issue, we consider an alternative evaluation of policy effects at the county level. This essentially involves treating each county as a farm. In this case, we are able to condition current production on lagged production. Our reliance on cross-sectional data also raises important concerns regarding simultaneity biases. Many production decisions are made jointly and thus the inability to measure predetermined (i.e., lagged) values of certain variables may make addressing this concern difficult. We attempt to adjust for this issue by relying on exogenous variables to the extent possible. For example, AMTA payment receipts are certainly exogenous to an individual in any given year. Likewise, we utilize county-level farm average MLA payments for the preceding year to represent expectations regarding MLA support. However, one could potentially question the extent to which some explanatory variables, such as insurance purchases and the ratio of debts to assets, may be endogenous to production decisions. Although we partially address this issue below, it remains an important caveat that merits additional research.

Unpublished data on season-average loan rates were obtained from the Farm Service Agency (FSA) of the USDA. Chicago Board of Trade (CBOT) futures market prices for corn, soybeans, and wheat were taken from the Bridge database. An expected price for each county was taken by calculating a state average basis for each state using season average prices collected from USDA-NASS and then adjusting the planting time price for the harvest time contract for the annual, state average basis charge. This yielded a state average expected

---

[4] This limitation will be addressed in future versions of the ARMS surveys in that surveys will revisit a subsample of farms

harvest-time market price.[5] The greater of the expected cash price or the county loan rate was taken to represent the expected commodity price. Unpublished county-level data describing farm program payment receipts in each farm program category were obtained from the USDA. These data were used to measure county-level aggregates of farm program receipts in the form of AMTA payments and MLA payments. These were placed on a per-farm and per-acre basis using county level data on the number of farms and number of farm acres in each county, taken from the 1997 *Agricultural Census*.

Our analysis is intended to focus on mainstream, commercial farms. Thus, we eliminated any farm from the ARMS survey that was defined (using the ERS farm typology index) as a limited resource, lifestyle, or retirement farm. In addition, any farm with less than 50 acres of total land was dropped from our sample. In light of the considerable heterogeneity of crop types, production practices, and policy types across different regions, it is important that a relatively homogeneous group of farms be evaluated. Thus, our analysis is focused on the Corn Belt region of the United States—which we define using the USDA-ERS farm resource region designation of the "Heartland." This region comprises a homogeneous grouping of counties in Illinois, Indiana, Iowa, Kentucky, Minnesota, Missouri, Nebraska, Ohio, and South Dakota. Our focus in on acreage of corn, soybeans, and wheat—overwhelmingly the primary crops in this region.

We have emphasized the important role of risk preferences as a factor determining planted acreage of crops and the potential effects of decoupled payments. The measurement of risk preferences in empirical models is difficult, since preferences are not directly observable and available survey data generally do not collect information about such preferences. We represent risk preferences in our empirical models by using a proxy variable, constructed as the ratio of total expenditures on insurance over total farm expenses. We hypothesize that more risk-averse farms will tend to devote more of their total production expenditures to insurance. We are able to directly measure a farm's wealth. Our measure of wealth is given by total assets less total debts. In order to prevent double counting of AMTA payments, we subtract AMTA payment receipts from total wealth. All financial values are converted to real terms by dividing by the producer price index.

A number of important econometric issues underlie our empirical analysis. An important characteristic of the ARMS data relates to the stratified nature of the sampling used to collect the data. Two estimation approaches have been suggested for problems such as this involving stratification. The simplest involves a jacknife procedure, where the estimation data are split into a fixed number of subsamples and the estimation is repeated with each subsample omitted.[6] An alternative approach involves repeated sampling from the estimation data in a bootstrapping scheme. Ideally, rather than random sampling from the entire estimation sample, an appropriate approach to obtaining unbiased and efficient estimation results

---

[5] We utilized the average daily close prices in February for December corn and November soybean futures and the average daily price in September for the July wheat futures on the CBOT. It should be noted that our specification does not explicitly account for basis risk differences across farms in the Corn Belt. To consider the potential effects of this assumption, we considered an alternative model that included state fixed effects. Taken together with the annual dummy variables, such a specification accounts for any state-level basis effects. Very similar estimates were obtained. These results are available on request.

[6] Under the jacknife approach, the sample is divided into *m* subsamples. Estimation programs created by ERS use 15 subsamples. This approach is subject to a number of limitations. First, it is not clear that the stratification scheme does not alter likelihood functions beyond simple weights, though this remains an important topic for

involves random sampling from individual strata (see, for example, Deaton, 1997). In the ARMS data, however, this is not possible since the strata are not identified. The database does, however, contain a population weighting factor, representing the number of farms in the population (i.e., all U.S. farms) represented by each individual observation. This can be used in a probability-weighted sampling scheme whereby the likelihood of being selected in any given replication is proportional to the number of observations in the population represented by each individual ARMS observation. We utilize a probability-weighted bootstrapping procedure.

The specific estimation approach involves selecting N observations (where N is the size of the survey sample) from the sample data. The data are sampled with replacement according to the probability rule described above.[7] The models are estimated using the pseudo-sample of data. This process is repeated a large number of times and estimates of the parameters and their variances are given by the mean and variance of the replicated estimates.[8]

An important econometric problem also involves the fact that a censoring issue underlies our empirical acreage models. Not every farm produces every crop in each year. In particular, 90.32% of farms in our sample produced corn, 89.41% produced soybeans, and 37.44% produced wheat. This may reflect specialization issues for individual farmers or crop rotation patterns. To address this censoring issue, we utilize the recently introduced modeling procedures of Shonkwiler and Yen.[9]

C. EMPIRICAL RESULTS

Our empirical analysis is conducted in three segments. In the first, a large sample of data drawn from individual farms is used to consider three acreage equations—for corn, soybeans, and wheat. In a second segment of the analysis, we consider an evaluation of several alternative measures of farmland usage. In particular, we consider factors, including farm program payments, affecting the ratio of nonharvested to harvested farm acres. The 1999 ARMS survey contained two additional measures of farmland usage pertinent to our analysis. The first considered the extent to which owned farmland was placed in uses other than crop production and orchards (e.g., pasture, conservation reserve, fallow, etc.). The second involved a query of producers regarding whether they had acquired ownership of new land over the year. Production distortions from decoupled programs may manifest themselves

---

future research. Similarly, the appropriateness of the pre-defined jacknife weights in a subsample of the overall data such as our case is unclear.

[7] To be precise, if observation i represents n_i farms out of the total of M farms in the population, the likelihood that observation i is drawn on any given draw is n_i/M. It should be acknowledged that our approach may result in less efficient estimates than would be the case were sampling from individual strata possible. This could occur in cases where inferences are being made about variables used in designing the stratification scheme in that such information is being ignored by not drawing from individual strata. To the extent that this is relevant to our analysis, the t-ratios reported below represent conservative estimates.

[8] We utilize 2,000 replications in the applications that follow.

[9] Shonkwiler and Yen propose a two-step estimation procedure, whereby a discrete variable indicating a noncensored observation is evaluated using a probit model and then used to construct correction terms that account for censoring. We apply White's heteroskedasticity-consistent covariance matrix in our estimation. It should be noted that a specific form of heteroskedasticity is implied by the two-step procedures. However, our reliance on cross-sectional variability in a heterogeneous sample leads us to suspect that other unknown forms of heteroskedasticity may also be relevant. Thus, we use a more general correction.

through the acquisition of new productive resources—i.e., land. Thus, we consider the extent to which new land acquisitions were associated with farm program payments by using a probit model to evaluate the probability that an agent acquired land in 1999.[10] Finally, a third segment of our investigation expands our empirical analysis to a consideration of acreage allocations at the county level. In our analysis of county-level data, the sampling undertaken in the ARMS survey is not dense enough to permit the construction of reliable county aggregates and thus a slightly different specification is adopted.[11]

C.1. Farm-Level Acreage Analysis

Variable definitions and summary statistics for our sample of the "Heartland" region farms are presented in Table 1. Our sample consists of 4,121 farm-level observations. The average farm planted 373 acres of corn, 386 acres of soybeans, and 41 acres of wheat. Of course, these averages reflect the substantial proportion of farms that did not grow wheat in a given year, such that the average acreage for farms growing wheat was much higher (115 acres). Aggregate price risk and other factors that are likely to be constant across all farms in a given year are likely to be important factors affecting acreage decisions. We include annual dummy variables to capture such fixed annual effects. These factors represent price risk (assumed to be constant across all farms in the region in a given year), systemic yield risk and weather, and other unobservable factors that may be relevant to production.[12]

The first segment of our empirical analysis considers acreage response equations for individual farms in the "Heartland" region.

Equations for corn, soybeans, and wheat, the dominant crops in the region, were estimated. Parameter estimates and summary statistics are presented in Table 2.[13] Parameters representing price effects are of the correct sign, though the price coefficient for corn is not statistically significant.

The estimates correspond to acreage elasticities of 0 and 1.39 for corn and soybeans, respectively. A large elasticity (1.25) is implied for wheat, though when the elasticity is evaluated using acreage for only those farms growing wheat, a more reasonable estimate of 0.46 is implied.

The role of AMTA payments is central to our analysis of the production effects of direct farm payments. Conceptual considerations suggest three different avenues through which decoupled payments might operate to influence production.

In the first avenue, risk-averse agents may find that the additional wealth provided by AMTA payments lowers their aversion to risk and thus encourages greater production of risky commodities.

---

[10] Data on land acquisition and disposal were only available in 1999.

[11] In particular, the ARMS survey consists of approximately 10,000 farm observations per year. With 3,142 counties in the United States, this implies an average of about 3 farms per county. Of course, stratified sampling and the geographic concentration of agriculture affects this count. Thus, the sample is not dense enough to permit county-level analysis.

[12] We also considered models that omitted these fixed effects. Results were similar and the overall implications of the analysis were robust to the inclusion of fixed annual effects.

[13] First-stage probit models (not presented here) included lagged county-level yields, acreage, operator age, farm machinery assets, and assets associated with irrigation equipment.

We represent individuals' risk aversion by including the proportion of total expenses accounted for by insurance purchases (which includes all forms of insurance purchased by the farm).[14]

Table 1. Variable Definitions and Summary Statistics

Variables	Definition	Mean	Std. Dev.
Corn acres	Corn acreage	372.966	478.737
Soybean acres	Soybean acreage	385.896	493.274
Wheat acres	Wheat acreage	41.220	133.329
Corn price	Max(basis adjusted futures price, county loan rate)	2.467	0.243
Soybean price	Max(basis adjusted futures price, county loan rate)	5.619	0.716
Wheat price	Max(basis adjusted futures price, county loan rate)	3.276	0.499
Farm size	Total farm size	1,007.680	1,131.780
Disaster	Disaster payments received per acre ($/acre)	5.278	8.855
MLA	County average market loss payments (t− 1)	7.567	7.359
AMTA	AMTA payments received ($/acre)	13.744	12.907
Debts/assets	Debt-to-asset ratio	0.191	0.221
Insurance	Ratio of insurance expenses to total expenses	0.042	0.036
Wage	State average farm wage rate ($/hour)	8.023	0.574
Fertilizer price	State average nitrogen price ($/lb.)	0.202	0.044
Gas price	State average gasoline price ($/gallon)	0.903	0.156
Not Harvested	Proportion of farm acres not harvested	0.167	0.189
Mean Yield	Average normalized yield (farm yield/county yield)	0.995	0.176
Not Cropped	Proportion of owned acres not in crops or orchards	0.232	0.254
Acquire land	1 if farm acquired owned land in 1999, 0 otherwise	0:049	0.217
Livestock	Ratio of livestock sales to total sales	0.303	0.364

Note: Numbers of observations are 2,615 for all variables except for Not Harvested, which had 2,263 observations and Not Cropped and Acquire Land, which each had 806 observations.

We allow the response to AMTA payments to vary according to this effect by including an interaction term. Following Pope and Just (1991), we also include the farm's level of wealth (total assets, less total debts, and AMTA payment receipts). We adjust for AMTA payments to prevent double counting, although for the typical farm such payments represent small changes to overall wealth. We also have hypothesized that agents that are capital constrained may respond to AMTA payments by increasing production (acreage). We represent the likely degree of financial leverage for an individual farm by considering the ratio of total debts to total assets. Again, we include an interaction term with the AMTA

---

[14] As a referee has pointed out, this specification is only indirectly related to the conceptual framework outlined above. We acknowledge the potential limitations associated with this measure of risk aversion, including possible distortions brought about by actuarially unfair crop insurance. This measure is used in lieu of any direct or indirect representation of risk preferences.

payments variable to permit farms to have variable responses to the payments according to their degree of financial leverage. Finally, we have hypothesized that any anticipation of the opportunity afforded producers to update program parameters under the 2002 Farm Bill may have affected acreage decisions. Such an effect is impossible to gauge directly using our data, though AMTA payments should convey an important signal regarding the expected benefits of future farm policy for an individual farm. Thus, the overall effect of AMTA payments depends on parameters involving a direct effect plus the interaction effects with insurance and leverage.

The direct effect of AMTA payments on acreage decisions is statistically significant in the corn and soybean equations, though the estimated coefficients are quite small in every case. In the case of corn, the coefficient implies that an additional $1.00 per acre in AMTA payments would increase corn acreage by 0.92 acres. In the case of soybeans, the direct effect of such an increase is 0.61 acres. Finally, for wheat, an additional $1.00 of AMTA payments raises wheat acreage by 0.36 acres, though the effect is not statistically different from zero. In elasticity terms, the corresponding elasticities (not including the interaction terms) are 0.0317 for corn, 0.0204 for soybeans, and 0.0428 for wheat. The corner solutions implied by the large number of farms that grow no wheat are accounted for by the δ_i correction term, which is significant only in the case of the wheat acreage equation.[15]

Of course, in a strict interpretation, these direct effects yield an elasticity value applying to farms with no insurance and no debt. The debt to asset interaction terms are not statistically significant in any of the equations. This may suggest that the capital constraints discussed above and identified in other work (e.g., De Gorter, 2000) do not have an important effect on acreage decisions, at least for this sample of farms. A similar result is implied in the case of the insurance-AMTA interaction terms, which are negative though statistically insignificant in every case. It is important to note that, even if such a crude measure captures the relative degree of risk aversion for producers, it is impossible to determine exactly how this degree of risk aversion changes with AMTA payments. The overall elasticities, including both the insurance and debt-to-asset ratio interaction effects, are 0.0344, 0.0246, and 0.0333 for corn, soybeans, and wheat, respectively. Note that the parameter estimates for the wheat effect may be somewhat misleading in light of the relatively small number of farms that produce wheat. The elasticity estimates account for the censoring and thus results that are similar to the other crops are obtained for wheat after adjusting for censoring.

The overall implications are that the AMTA payments implied very small though in some cases statistically significant acreage responses. The exact mechanism by which AMTA payments are affecting acreage response—wealth effects, changes in risk preferences, capital constraints, or changes related to the anticipation of future benefits—is not identified by our analysis. It is, however, clear that allegations regarding the substantial production effects (which were termed "flashing amber box" effects by DeGorter, 2000) are not supported, at least for these data. This is not to say that there is not at least a limited potential for distortions to arise as a result of the provision of AMTA payments. We have examined only one dimension of production distortions—acreage allocation effects. It is possible that, although acreage is not significantly changed, agents change their production and marketing techniques in a manner that produces distortions. For example, the risk effects discussed above could assert themselves through changes that involved the adoption of riskier production practices

---

[15] This is not surprising in light of the prevalence of corner solutions for wheat as compared to corn and soybeans.

Table 2. Parameter Estimates and Summary Statistics: Farm-Level Acreage Equations

Variables	Corn	Soybeans	Wheat
Intercept	−20.7016	−551.9640	98.2126
	(128.1941)	(120.4402)*	(226.4504)
Corn price	24.4231	−93.9133	−2.5116
	(40.6762)	(38.4238)*	(63.1047)
Soybean price	−3.9111	101.6672	−32.1289
	(35.6250)	(31.4855)*	(49.9225)
Wheat price	6.2037	−1.4071	44.8814
	(5.7010)	(5.6236)	(12.6058)*
Farm size	0.3558	0.3996	0.0712
	(0.0169)*	(0.0132)*	(0.0269)*
MLA/acret−1	5.8076	0.8315	−0.6167
	(0.7530)*	(0.6124)	(0.7917)
AMTA/acre	0.9152	0.6103	0.3569
	(0.2708)*	(0.2508)*	(0.3669)
AMTA×debts/assets	0.8715	0.7729	−0.2148
	(0.7893)	(0.6360)	(1.4696)
AMTA×Insurance	−2.1575	−0.5598	−0.9231
	(2.8920)	(2.8453)	(3.3561)
Wage	8.3341	13.0637	9.3424
	(5.5331)	(4.7221)*	(7.9739)
Fertilizer price	−577.2572	594.5935	−45.2468
	(185.2804)*	(165.2445)*	(283.5646)
Gas price	−20.6282	0.8496	−40.4422
	(49.5540)	(42.1453)	(96.2913)
Wealth	1.6122	−1.1645	−1.2250
	(1.1822)	(1.3840)	(1.9362)
Livestock	−59.7864	−98.8104	−17.7424
	(5.9478)*	(6.2063)*	(6.3333)*
Debts/assets	9.0658	2.4683	5.4313
	(16.7142)	(14.7324)	(27.1922)
Insurance	−128.5892	−99.2492	−109.5046
	(44.9584)*	(36.1050)*	(39.4763)*
D 99	−42.2477	73.7970	−15.3287
	(23.4889)*	(21.3507)*	(34.9640)
D 00	32.0945	−51.6104	−0.1945
	(59.5269)	(48.9233)	(82.5079)
D 01	−21.7965	38.4174	0.9480
	(33.5510)	(30.2467)	(35.6587)
δi	−23.0843	3.7451	−43.3174
	(24.1447)	(18.1616)	(7.5143)*
R2	0.7835	0.8060	0.3488

Note: Numbers in parentheses are standard errors. An asterisk indicates statistical significance at the α= 0.10 or smaller level. Note that δi is the censoring correction term.

(e.g., decreased application of fertilizer and chemicals) rather than a simple expansion or reallocation of crop acreage. It is also important to recognize that, for reasons discussed above, a positive bias in the effects of such payments may be inherent in these results.

A second important dimension of farm program support in the post-FAIR environment involves the provision of ad hoc disaster assistance, including MLA payments. In the case of the ARMS survey data, information regarding MLA payments is grouped together with overall disaster relief. It is important to note that these payments are generally based upon market conditions at harvest and thus cannot be anticipated with certainty when acreage decisions are made. In this light, we are interested in obtaining a proxy measure of producers' expectations regarding the MLA payments. Again, the fact that we are unable to observe an individual farm over time limits our analysis. Ideally, we would prefer to have information about the payment receipts of producers in the year preceding the period in which planting decisions are made. As an alternative, we utilize the county average of MLA payments per farm acre in the preceding year MLA_{t-1}. It is important to note that MLA payments were based upon base acreages, and thus would be expected to be more highly associated with events in traditional program crop markets (i.e., corn and wheat). This is not to say that MLA payments are not expected to affect soybean production, since many payment recipients produced soybeans in their crop mix and prices of corn and wheat are correlated with soybean prices.

A somewhat stronger effect seems to be implied for expected MLA payments than was the case for AMTA payments, at least for corn. The coefficient on the preceding year's MLA payments is highly significant for corn, though it does not appear that MLA payments had a significant effect on wheat or soybean acreage. In addition, the effect for corn is quite strong, implying that an additional dollar of MLA payments per acre in the preceding year tends to raise corn acreage, other things constant, by 5.7 acres. The corn MLA elasticity is 0.10. In that large acreage responses are not implied for wheat or soybeans, one would assume that such an increase would involve a reallocation of land away from other crops or the introduction of uncultivated land (e.g., pasture or fallow land) into corn production. Of course, these are changes at the margin and thus large shifts in program payments could conceivably have different effects. Implications that MLA payments had larger effects on corn than on wheat and soybeans are not really surprising since ad hoc support to oilseed producers was much smaller than that directed to those producers with corn and wheat base acreage. Recall that MLA payments were paid on those crops that had base acreage under the old farm programs, though an "oilseed program" also made payments on soybeans. Payments made under the oilseed program are included in the MLA statistics. The fact that wheat acreage is not strongly affected is also not a surprise. Wheat is not a major crop in the Corn Belt states evaluated in this study and is generally grown for crop rotation purposes.

Provision of the MLA payments may have served as a signal to producers that income shortfalls for such crops that are based upon low market prices may be offset to a degree by ad hoc MLA payments. However, the conceptual link is somewhat tenuous since the MLA payments, though indirectly based upon market conditions for an individual crop, are not based upon a producer's specific level of production of that crop (or on production of any crop for that matter). In particular, an individual producer may have received MLA payments for a crop regardless of whether that particular crop was grown in the relevant year. The determining factor involved base acreage, which is reflected in AMTA payments. The link with market conditions may also be subject to challenge, since the statutory authority underlying the MLA payments does not tie their provision to prices or conditions in a particular market. However, by definition, the payments are intended to assist producers because of poor market conditions. Thus, in spite of such ambiguity, the link between market conditions and MLA payments seems to exist, though the exact connection is certainly subject to debate. In light of their link to market conditions, MLA payments would appear to assume the role of informally supporting prices.

Using aggregate data, Pope and Just (1991) found that wealth tended to be positively correlated with the acreage of potatoes in Idaho. They interpreted this finding to represent differences in risk preferences that result from constant relative risk aversion preferences. We included total farm wealth in each of the acreage models. In every case, total wealth does not appear to be significantly correlated with acreage of the three crops. It should be acknowledged, however, that we control for the scale of a farm by including total acreage. One would certainly expect that total acreage of a farm operation would be highly correlated with wealth, such that the effects of wealth on acreage may be captured in the effect of total acreage when both are included as regressors in the acreage models. In every case, as would be expected, total farm acreage is positively correlated with acreage of each crop. This raises a concern as to whether AMTA payments may provide an incentive for producers to acquire additional farmland, thus making total farm size heavily correlated with the fixed payments. We address this possibility below in a consideration of factors influencing the acquisition of new land in 1999.[16] Certainly, this possibility raises concerns regarding the potential endogeneity of total farm acres to individual crop acreages or other variables in the model. While acknowledging this possibility and the fact that we have assumed total acreage to be fixed for a farm, we would argue that crop acreages are more likely to respond to the total scale of a farm than would be the opposite case.[17] As expected, the scale of a farm, represented by total size, is highly correlated with the total number of acres grown for any of the crops. The coefficients correspond to crop mixes that are similar to what is realized for the region. For example, the average allocation of farm acreage to each of the three crops in the region was 32% for corn, 33% for soybeans, and 5% for wheat.

We included the proportion of total farm sales accounted for by livestock farms. It is not surprising that farms with livestock production have fewer acres of corn, soybeans, and wheat. An interesting result lies in the response to fertilizer price changes. Regions with higher fertilizer costs tend to grow more soybeans and less corn. This is expected since corn is much more demanding in terms of fertilizer requirements.

In all, our analysis of farm-level data suggests that AMTA payments had a relatively modest, though statistically significant effect on the acreage of corn, soybeans, and wheat in the "Heartland" region of the United States. The acreage responses are, however, very small, with elasticities for corn and soybeans (the major crops) being about 0.03–0.04. However, it does appear that the provision of MLA payments, which were disbursed alongside AMTA payments, may have resulted in a more substantial increase in corn acreage. Our results are

---

[16] It is important, however, that acreage of individual crops be conditioned on farm scale since larger farms will, by definition, have more acreage in individual crops. Our inclusion of both AMTA payments and farm size allows us to evaluate the extent to which AMTA payments affect acreage, conditional on holding farm size constant.

[17] Consideration of various instruments for evaluating the extent of any such endogeneity concerns remains a topic of current research. The lack of repeated sampling in the ARMS survey is an impediment to the identification of appropriate instruments.

similar to those obtained from an aggregate model by Burfisher and Hopkins (2003). Our results suggest that acreage is not affected by wealth, thus perhaps implying that any risk preference shifts caused by different levels of wealth do not appear to affect crop acreage. This is in contrast to the findings of other work (e.g., Chavas and Pope, 1985; Pope and Just, 1991; Hennessy, 1998) that has suggested important wealth effects on risk preferences and production. In interpreting these results, it is important to keep in mind the caveats raised above. In particular, our inability to observe individual farms over time may suggest a potential for an upward bias in the implied effects of AMTA and MLA payments on acreage. Thus, these elasticities should be interpreted within this context as upper bound estimates. We address this limitation in the aggregate analysis that follows below.

C.2. Analysis of Idled Acreage

An alternative and more general evaluation of the effects of fixed payments on production practices involves measures of the extent to which farmland is placed in alternative practices other than crop production. Such alternatives might include conservation reserves, pasture, forest, set-asides, fallow, and other idling practices. Two alternative measures of land idling/waste were constructed. In the first, we considered the ratio of total harvested acres to total farm acres to represent crop land usage. Thus, one minus this ratio yields a measure of the proportion of farm acres idled (*Not Harvested*). The 1999 ARMS survey collected detailed data relating to land ownership and land acquisition. Detailed information about the usage of owned land was elicited.

For this single year, we constructed an alternative measure (*Not Cropped*) reflecting the idling and waste of owned farmland resources. This measure is slightly different in that it pertains only to owned resources and thus omits production on leased acreage. It thus may provide a less accurate view of overall production/acreage effects of program payments. For our data, the alternative waste/idling measures ranged from 16.7% for Not Harvested to 23.2% for Not Cropped. Table 3 contains parameter estimates for each of the alternative measures of land usage.

In both cases, the results suggest that higher AMTA payments do tend to be associated with more intensive use of land.

This is not unexpected, since farms with more productive land are more likely to have less waste and are also more likely to have a crop base. In elasticity terms, the elasticity of the proportion of total farm acres idled with respect to AMTA payments is −0.33 for the first model and −0.16 for the second model. The AMTA interaction terms are significant in the first model but are not statistically significant in the second model. When the elasticities are evaluated at the mean values of the insurance and relative debt variables, AMTA elasticities are −0.31 and −0.22, respectively.

These results indicate that AMTA payments are correlated with lower amounts of land being put in fallow or set aside, though the extent to which this reflects the fact that farms with more crop land naturally are those that have higher historical base and thus higher AMTA payments is unclear. The preceding results would tend to suggest that this does not occur through substantial increases in corn, soybean, or wheat acreage.

Other factors affecting land usage have the expected signs. The average of the normalized yield across all crops grown on a farm has the expected negative effect, implying that farms with higher relative yields tend to have less land idled.[18] Higher soybean and wheat prices are associated with less land being idled.

Though a positive effect on idling is indicated for corn prices, the corn price effect is statistically significant only in the first model. This result is not consistent with expectations, though it may reflect basis pattern correlations with soil productivity or other local factors related to land use. Higher MLA payments (for the county in the previous year) imply less waste or idling of land in the first model, but do not have a statistically significant effect in the second model.

The elasticity for market loss payments is again quite large at −0.39, though this effect is statistically significant only in the first model. Thus, expectations regarding the provision of MLA payments appear to have a significant effect in reducing the idling and waste of farm acreage. In general, higher input prices, fertilizer and labor in particular, lead to more idling of land resources. Finally, wealth does not appear to be significantly related to land idling in the overall farm acreage measure, though wealth does reduce idling when only owned acreage is considered.

In general, the two models of land idling suggest that the provision of direct government payments, even in cases where the payments are not tied to production of a particular crop, may lead to less idling of land and thus may result in more land being in production. The larger sample that includes a consideration of the entire land operated by a farm suggests that the greatest effect is likely to be realized from MLA payments. This is as would be expected, since such payments are seemingly more tied to the market place, as they are triggered (at least in theory) by market events, which motivate legislators to other support.

In the case of our analysis of owned land usage in 1999, the results suggest that AMTA payments may be associated with less idling of land. This may reflect either the wealth or risk effects noted above. Alternatively, these results may provide evidence consistent with these policies easing capital constraints on agents and thus permitting greater use of land resources. However, the result is smaller than what is implied for all land operated by the farm. In all, although AMTA and MLA payments appear to exert a statistically significant effect in reducing idling of farm acreage, the elasticities are quite inelastic, ranging from −0.16 to −0.39 for AMTA and MLA payments. We must acknowledge, however, that this result may reflect the fact that land with base is likely to be more productive and thus less subject to idling than would be the case for land without program base.

C.3. Analysis of Land Acquisition

Finally, the 1999 ARMS survey data allowed us to consider the acquisition of new owned land resources by farms in that year. A relatively small proportion of the farms (4.94%) actually acquired land in 1999. We were interested in evaluating whether the provision of fixed payments might have been associated with the acquisition of new land—yet another indication of potential production distortions. Of course, for every agent buying land, another

---

[18] The normalized yield is calculated by taking the farm's yield and dividing by the NASS county-average yield for the year in question. This removes the effects of county-wide yield shocks and thus places yields in relative terms.

Table 3. Parameter Estimates and Summary Statistics:
Crop Land Idle/Waste Equations

Variable	Not Harvested	Not Cropped
Intercept	1.4630	1.1918
	(0.1965)*	(0.5658)*
Mean yield	−0.2109	−0.1218
	(0.0183)*	(0.0363)*
Corn price	0.1634	0.2394
	(0.0538)*	(0.1656)
Soybean price	−0.0646	−0.0178
	(0.0471)	(0.1209)
Wheat price	−0.0249	0.0336
	(0.0099)*	(0.0588)
Farm size	0.0000	0.0000
	(0.0000)*	(0.0000)
AMTA	−0.0040	−0.0029
	(0.0004)*	(0.0012)*
County corn acres$t-1$	0.0000	0.0000
	(0.0000)*	(0.0000)*
MLA	−0.0091	−0.0041
	(0.0010)*	(0.0044)
AMTA×debts/assets	−0.0025	−0.0027
	(0.0006)*	(0.0040)
Wage	−0.0388	−0.0580
	(0.0071)*	(0.0373)
Fertilizer price	−3.1040	−1.7329
	(0.3051)*	(1.2815)
Gas price	0.0680	−0.5104
	(0.0775)	(0.3079)*
AMTA×insurance	0.0148	−0.0106
	(0.0040)*	(0.0176)
Wealth	−0.0002	−0.0062
	(0.0006)	(0.0032)*
Livestock	0.1818	0.0944
	(0.0101)*	(0.0274)*
D 99	−0.0396	
	(0.0468)	
D 00	−0.0460	
	(0.0766)	
D 01	0.3340	
	(0.0903)*	
Number of observations	4,121	884
R2	0.2871	0.1496

Note: Numbers in parentheses are standard errors. An asterisk indicates statistical significance at the α= 0.10 or smaller level.

is selling and thus it is not clear that such transactions actually lead to more production.[19] Land transactions could lead to more land being used in production or, if new owners idle their newly acquired land, even less production. Parameter estimates and summary statistics for a probit model of the land acquisition decision are presented in Table 4. An interesting result is that the direct effect of AMTA payments on the decision to purchase land is not statistically significant.

The effect does not appear to vary with the ratio of debts to assets though it does vary significantly with insurance purchases. The results suggest that farms that are strong insurers are less likely to be acquiring new land. The overall marginal effect of AMTA payments, which is largely driven by the insurance interaction term, is given by $f(X\beta)\beta_i$, where $f(\cdot)$ represents the normal probability density function (pdf). The overall marginal effect, incorporating the insurance and leverage ratio interaction effects, is -0.0007, implying that raising AMTA payments $1 per acre would lower the probability of acquiring new land by 0.07%.

If we consider the direct effect, for farms with no insurance and no debts, the marginal effect implies that increasing AMTA payments by $1 per acre raises the likelihood of acquiring new land by 0.01%.

Thus, the estimates suggest that the provision of AMTA payments may lead to more land ownership transactions, though the effect is not significant for the average farm in our sample and is very small even for farms that have no insurance or debts. This may reflect a general lack of capital constraints that could inhibit the acquisition of land.

Even if a larger effect were indicated, one could not necessarily conclude that this will involve the introduction of new land into production, since this may merely involve the exchange of ownership of land that was already in production.[20]

C.4. County-Level Acreage Analysis

Although the preceding empirical analysis provides rich inference by using farm-level data, our analysis is clearly limited by its reliance on cross-sectional variation—individual farms are not observed over time. This limits our ability to condition on historical values of key variables and thus may complicate the identification of causal effects of policy variables. For example, AMTA payments are based upon historical base acreage for program crops. It is likely that farms that planted a large number of acres to corn in the post-FAIR policy environment also had considerable acreage in corn during the pre-FAIR regimes, and thus are also receiving large AMTA payments.

---

[19] A full understanding of the effects of policy on the acquisition and disposal of land and other productive assets requires a conceptual model of the land market of the sort developed by Rausser, Zilberman, and Just (1984) and observations on land bid and offer schedules. Such an analysis is beyond the scope of this article, especially in light of our limited data on land acquisitions. The topic remains an important issue for future research.

[20] We were concerned that, to the extent that land purchased may be debt financed, the debt-to-asset ratio may be endogenous to land purchases. To address this concern, we estimated an alternative two-stage probit model in which the debt to asset ratio was allowed to be endogenous. The resulting estimates (not presented here) were very similar.

**Table 4. Probit Parameter Estimates and Summary Statistics:
Discrete Land Acquisition Equations**

Variables	Parameter
Intercept	−1.4983
	(8.2596)
Mean yield	0.4934
	(0.4602)
Corn price	−0.2064
	(3.0764)
Soybean price	−1.0394
	(1.5241)
Wheat price	−0.0989
	(1.1711)
Farm size	0.0003
	(0.0001)*
AMTA	0.0142
	(0.0125)
County corn acrest−1	0.0000
	(0.0000)*
MLA	−0.0197
	(0.0509)
AMTA×debts/assets	0.0196
	(0.0251)
Wage	0.1125
	(0.7324)
Fertilizer price	18.3291
	(18.0226)
Gas price	0.7396
	(5.3605)
AMTA×insurance	−0.5745
	(0.2141)*
Wealth	0.0057
	(0.0159)
Livestock	−0.3641
	(0.3367)
McFadden's R2	0.1400

Note: Numbers in parentheses are standard errors. An asterisk indicates statistical significance at the α= 0.10 or smaller level.

Thus, a large acreage of corn may be correlated with large AMTA payment receipts, although it is not necessarily the case that AMTA payments are "causing" producers to plant corn. As we have noted, to the extent that such an effect is present, one would expect the overall effect would be to infer a larger influence of AMTA payments on acreage than actually exists.[21]

Ideally, in cases where adjustment is costly or occurs with a lag, one will condition on the outcomes of prior planting decisions (i.e., in the preceding year or perhaps under the previous policy regime).

As we have previously noted, the ARMS data are too sparsely sampled to permit one to derive meaningful county-level aggregates or averages.[22] Thus, our county-level analysis does not include the basic measures of risk aversion (i.e., insurance purchases), financial leverage (the ratio of debts to assets), and wealth. However, we are able to observe other basic factors typically associated with planting decisions, including measures of AMTA payment receipts (per farm acre in the county) and average MLA payments (per farm) in each county.

Table 5 presents parameter estimates and summary statistics for county-level acreage equations for corn, soybeans, and wheat, estimated over the same 1998–2001 period. The aggregate results suggest positive supply elasticities for soybeans and wheat. The corn acreage response to price is again not significantly different from zero. Lagged acreage of each respective crop exerts a strong influence on acreage, representing the conventional partial adjustment process that is universally found to be relevant to planted acreage.

Probably of greatest interest is the finding that AMTA payments again appear to have a positive relationship with crop acreages at the county level, though once again the effect is very small.

The AMTA effects on acreage are statistically significant for soybeans. In the case of soybeans, the results imply that an additional dollar per acre of AMTA payments will add 168 acres of soybeans.

No statistically significant effect is revealed for corn or wheat. Such a small marginal effect implies very modest elasticities. In particular, the AMTA acreage elasticities for corn and wheat are essentially zero for corn. In the case of soybeans, the AMTA elasticity is 0.018. In every case, the county-level estimates imply a smaller elasticity than do the farm-level estimates.

In both cases, however, the estimated elasticities are very modest and suggest that the fixed payments have only a very small effect on acreage. These results are largely in agreement with those presented at the disaggregated level.

In the case of MLA payments, a significant relationship with acreage is implied only for corn and soybeans, where an additional dollar per acre of MLA payments appears to raise county acreages by 225 and 138 acres, respectively. Again, this corresponds to a very small elasticity estimate of less than 0.01 in each case, which although statistically significant, is very close to zero. Thus, at the county level, the results do not imply large effects from AMTA payments or the MLA payments. It should be acknowledged that our county-level models rely on aggregated data for which much of the variation in explanatory factors has been removed. Indeed, the fixed-effects parameters may account for much of the variation, especially in policy, that affected production in the post-FAIR years.

---

[21] That is, we know the direction that any such bias in our inferences would assume. Any such correlation that is not captured by our model would tend to exaggerate the effects of AMTA payments on acreage. Thus, our estimates provide a conservative upper bound on the effects of decoupled payments on acreage decisions.

[22] The stratification scheme used in collecting the ARMS data also complicates aggregation.

**Table 5. Parameter Estimates and Summary Statistics:
County-Level Acreage Equations**

Variable	Corn	Soybeans	Wheat
Intercept	4,736.5240	−8,364.1000	−13,602.5000
	(2,972.2720)	(2,773.0480)*	(1,721.0730)*
Corn price	−888.7030	−7,965.4400	6,056.8820
	(2,063.8230)	(1,937.5000)*	(1,215.3980)*
Soybean price	2295.6350	3577.1780	−996.3100
	(933.6118)*	(874.6612)*	(548.0211)*
Wheat price	−3,201.1500	1,970.7100	1,021.4200
	(461.1421)*	(434.7740)*	(273.1260)*
County farm acres	0.0103	0.0158	0.0020
	(0.0024)*	(0.0023)*	(0.0009)*
Acrest−1	0.9522	0.9432	0.9215
	(0.0056)*	(0.0057)*	(0.0058)*
AMTA/farm	−46.7855	167.7565	−0.1713
	(47.1465)	(40.5604)*	(24.4509)
MLA/farmt−1	225.5854	138.1505	13.9352
	(45.9700)*	(43.0587)*	(26.0915)
Fertilizer price	−35,752.9000	−644.1460	−2,477.2500
	(4,167.9660)*	(3,898.4240)	(2,448.8470)
Income CV	−0.3431	11.8935	−1.9650
	(20.8113)	(19.4296)	(12.2548)
D 98	−532.7320	−596.3490	275.3825
	(430.7310)	(404.3131)	(254.4218)
D 99	−288.9660	−70.6130	13.5886
	(453.3811)	(425.1351)	(267.3603)
D 00	−6.1379	178.6800	436.9469
	(441.3311)	(414.2154)	(260.4836)*
System-weighted R2		0.9875	

Note: Numbers in parentheses are standard errors. An asterisk.

Results for the other factors hypothesized to be relevant to acreage shifts are very similar to what was obtained for the disaggregated, producer-level data. A large effect is implied for input prices. Again, higher fertilizer prices appear to have large effects on acreage, with shifts being implied from corn and wheat to soybeans. Finally, we wanted to determine the extent to which farm financial risk might have had important acreage effects. Recall that it is difficult to obtain such a measure for individual farms in the ARMS sample since we do not observe the farms over time. However, such a measure can be constructed at the county level. We considered a measure of risk at the county level—the ten-year coefficient of variation on net farm income for the county, calculated from the U.S. Department of Commerce's Regional Economic Information System database. This measure was not statistically significant in any of the equations. Whether this reflects weaknesses in our measure of risk or rather implies that acreage decisions are not especially sensitive to income risk is unclear.

We repeated the county-level acreage response analysis using the level of acreage produced in each county in 1995 (immediately before the FAIR act was implemented) rather than lagged acreage. Our goal was to condition on acreage prior to the implementation of the FAIR act and the beginning of AMTA payments. The results were very similar to those included in Table 5 and thus are not presented here.[23]

CONCLUSION

The objective of our analysis was to utilize farm-level data to consider the extent to which U.S. farm program benefits, particularly the AMTA and MLA payments, may bring about distortions in production. Previous research has pointed out that wealth effects operating through risk preferences or the effects of payments on capital-constrained borrowers may result in distortions, in spite of the fact that the benefits of these programs are not directly tied to the production of a particular crop. Decoupled payments may delay or prevent farmers from being forced to exit production. The issue is important in light of the recent U.S. Farm Bill, which expanded these decoupled payments, as well as the upcoming WTO negotiations and the debate over the distortionary effects of such decoupled ("green-box") payments on markets. To address this question, we consider farm level and aggregate empirical models of acreage allocations to evaluate the extent to which decoupled payments have affected production decisions.

We utilize farm level data to consider acreage allocation decisions. This analysis is reinforced by an aggregate analysis of county-level acreage allocations. The overarching question underlying our analysis pertains to whether decoupled payments evoked a discernable acreage effect. Our focus is empirical and thus we do not develop a detailed conceptual framework for considering policy. Several important findings emerge from our analysis. First, there is modest evidence that AMTA payments may lead to increased production of corn, soybeans, and wheat. However, the acreage effects are very small. For an analysis of individual, farm-level data, acreage elasticities for the major crops, corn and soybeans, are about 0.025 to 0.035. Though statistically significant, a 95% confidence interval ranges from about 0.01 to 0.04. These results suggest that even a very large increase in these decoupled payments would not be expected to significantly increase acreage.[24] A somewhat different implication is implied for MLA payments that, at least for corn, appear to have a more significant effect on acreage. In particular, the elasticity of corn acreage with respect to MLA payments was 0.10, suggesting that such payments may indeed lead to more corn production. In order to examine the extent to which unobserved correlation with historical production patterns may have affected our farm-level estimates, we considered a county-level analysis that allowed us to condition on previous acreage levels. In this case, even smaller effects were suggested, with acreage AMTA and MLA elasticities of 0.01 or less. Our analysis does not imply important wealth effects, at least for our sample of Corn Belt farms.

---

[23] These results are available from the authors on request.

[24] Note that the standard caveats regarding the use of local marginal effects to interpret large policy changes are applicable here. Care must be used in interpreting these estimates when considering the elimination of decoupled payments or the counterfactual question of never having had decoupled payments in the first place.

We also considered how decoupled payments may affect the acreage idling decisions of producers. AMTA payments appear to evoke modest though generally significant effects, leading to less idling of land. A larger effect is implied by MLA payments, at least in the case of the models of the entire farm. Increasing MLA payments tends to make producers less likely to idle or waste land.

Finally, we considered probit models of the acquisition of new owned land for 1999. In this case, our results suggest that AMTA payment benefits did not appear to lead to strong incentives for agents to acquire new farmland assets. Likewise, MLA payments do not appear to be correlated with incentives to acquire ownership of new farmland.

Overall, our results imply that decoupled farm program payments have only modest effects on acreage. In particular, although these payments do have a statistically significant effect on acreage of the major crops in the U.S. Corn Belt, the effects are very small, with elasticities in the order of 0.01–0.03. This result is not surprising given the fact that such payments, though often large, are decoupled and represent relatively minor changes in the overall wealth of the typical Corn Belt farm. In particular, AMTA payments over these years averaged 1.8% of the typical farm's overall net worth. The conclusions are not as favorable for the neutral position of the ad hoc MLA payments. Our results implied an acreage elasticity of 0.10 for corn in response to MLA payments. These payments were linked to market events and thus bring about distortionary effects, although the payments were disbursed along with decoupled payments. Of course, producers' expectations regarding such payments, which are received after production decisions are made, are unobservable and thus our results are conditional on our proxy measurement of such expectations.

A number of research questions remain unanswered by our analysis. Our cross-sectional analysis is limited by our inability to observe an individual farm over time. As we discuss above, this limits our ability to condition our analysis on certain factors and thus may make it difficult to identify those effects we are evaluating. Having noted this possibility, it should also be pointed out that one would expect that this would lead to biases that would tend to overstate the importance of AMTA payment benefits on acreage decisions. Thus, even in light of the potential for such effects, our results do not imply large acreage effects as a result of AMTA payments. These limitations suggest that our estimates should be viewed as an "upper-bound" estimate on the effects of decoupled payments on the acreage of corn, soybeans, and wheat in the Corn Belt region. It is also important to acknowledge that our empirical model is broad in its focus and that a deeper understanding of the exact mechanisms underlying the effects of decoupled payments on production conditions requires a more complex conceptual framework that recognizes the dynamic nature of production and investment decisions. Development of such a framework is an important next step in this avenue of research.

Anecdotal evidence suggests another important effect necessarily neglected by our analysis. Farmers may have anticipated the opportunity to update program parameters such as yields and base. Thus, farmers may not have wanted to move to nontraditional crops or to idling land because they would not want to lose the opportunity to secure an updated base. The 2002 Farm Bill certainly supports such a suspicion. The 2002 Act provided a number of generous provisions for farmers to update their program base and yields that determine the fixed payments. In light of this fact, farmers may have been slow to adjust to market conditions or other factors outside of policy arena because they were anticipating the provisions to allow base yields and acreages to be updated. This may complicate an analysis of the production effects of farm program payments since AMTA payments were based upon historic base acreages and farmers may have anticipated having the opportunity to update base in the near future.

This raises an interesting question. Were farmers surprised by the generous provisions of the 2002 Farm Bill and did this legislation affect their expectations for future farm policy benefits? Allowing producers to update their base acreage and yields which form the basis for fixed payments certainly must be interpreted as tying the program benefits more closely to production decisions. To the extent that farmers expect that current production will be an important determinant of future program benefits, their production decisions may be altered by policy, even when such policy is administered through fixed payments. This is, of course, a research question that must await future policy developments. It will be important to evaluate acreage decisions under the new farm legislation to determine whether the 2002 provision to allow updating of program yields and base had an important effect on the relationship between fixed payments and acreage decisions.

Our analysis has been based upon the ARMS survey data. In the future, repeated sampling of individual farms may allow much richer inferences to be drawn from these data. In addition, potentially important endogeneity concerns that we have largely ignored are certainly an important area for future research. This research must be updated as new data on production patterns and policy benefits under the new Farm Bill become available.

REFERENCES

Burfisher, M.E., and Hopkins, J. (2003). Decoupled Payments: Household Income Transfers in Contemporary U.S. Agriculture. Agricultural Economics Report No. 822, Economic Research Service, USDA , Washington DC.

Chau, N.H., and De Gorter, H. (2000). Disentangling the Production and Export Consequences of Direct Farm Income Payments. Paper presented at the AAEA Meetings, Tampa , Florida , August.

Chavas, J.P., and Pope, R.D. (1985). Price Uncertainty and Competitive Firm Behavior: Testable Hypotheses from Expected Utility. *Journal of Economics and Business, Vol. 37,* 223–35

Deaton, A.S. (1997). *The Analysis of Household Surveys: A Microeconometric Approach to Development Policy.* Baltimore : Johns Hopkins University Press and the World Bank.

De Gorter, H. (2000). A Comparison of U.S. and E.U. Government Policies for the Cereals Sector: Implications for the WTO Trade Negotiations. Paper prepared for Unigrains, October 25.

Foster, W., and Rausser G.C. (1991). Farmer Behavior under Risk of Failure. *American Journal of Agricultural Economics, Vol. 73,* 276–88.

Hennessy, D.A. (1998). The Production Effects of Agricultural Income Support Policies under Uncertainty. *American Journal of Agricultural Economics, Vol. 80,* 46–57.

Kydland, F., and Prescott, E. (1977). Rules Rather Than Discretion: The Inconsistency of Optimal Plans. *Journal of Political Economy , Vol. 87,* 473–92.

Pope, R.D., and Just, R.E. (1991). On Testing the Structure of Risk Preferences in Agricultural Supply Analysis. *American Journal of Agricultural Economics, Vol. 73*, 743–48.

Rausser, G.C., Zilberman, D., and Just, R.E. (1984). The Distributional Effects of Land Controls in Agriculture. *Western Journal of Agricultural Economics, Vol. 9*, 215–32.

Roe, T., Somwaru, A., and Diao, X. (2002). Do Direct Payments Have Intertemporal Effects on U.S. Agriculture? Unpublished, University of Minnesota.

Shonkwiler, J.S., and Yen, S.T. (1999). Two-Step Estimation of a Censored System of Equations. *American Journal of Agricultural Economics, Vol. 81*, 972–82.

In: The Economics of Natural and Human Resources...   ISBN 978-1-60741-029-4
Editor: Ayal Kimhi and Israel Finkelshtain   © 2009 Nova Science Publishers, Inc.

Chapter 14

THE ORGANIZATION OF AGRICULTURAL EXPORTS: LESSONS FROM REFORMS IN ISRAEL

Israel Finkelshtain and Yael Kachel[*]

ABSTRACT

We study the impact of far-reaching reforms of the agricultural export sector in Israel. The reforms included the abolition of statutory export monopolies, and the privatization of export operations. A comparative study of three main export products (avocado, grapefruit and pepper) reveals differences in the development of export performance after liberalization. These differences seem to be related to demand conditions in export markets and barriers to entry to production and export. Econometric results indicate that the potential to exploit market power in export markets is very small; hence the abolition of centralized exports presumably did not cause a decline in export revenues. Results are inconclusive with regard to the question if the reforms increased the efficiency of export operations. Research results indicate that the impact of reforms on export performance and growers revenues may have been dampened by noncompetitive market structures for export services which developed after reforms.

A. INTRODUCTION

The organization of the agricultural export sector in Israel has changed very much in the last decade. Motivated by government policy to decrease public intervention in the economy and to privatize state monopolies, the agricultural export sector was reformed. The two main aspects of these reforms were (a) the abolition of statutory export monopolies, and (b) the privatization of export operations. Exports were opened up to competition by granting export licenses to private firms while parastatal monopoly exporters ceased export operations or started to compete with private firms.

---

[*] Israel Finkelshtain is Associate Professor, and Yael Kachel is post-doctoral fellow, at the Department of Agricultural Economics and Management of the Hebrew University.

The liberalization of the agricultural export sector caused a drastic change in industry structure with probably far-reaching consequences for conduct and performance. Economic theory does not provide an unequivocal answer to the question of how to best organize exports from the welfare point of view of a single country. Both centralized and competitive systems have their advantages and disadvantages. From a theoretical point of view, centralized marketing by a statutory organization may maximize the welfare of the export country if the centralized organization is able to exercise market power on export markets and to exploit economies of scale. On the other hand, there are certain potential losses associated with control and incentive problems in organizations that are not exposed to competition. If the losses from centralization are greater than the gains that can be realized, the 'free market' alternative is optimal. The far-reaching reforms in the Israeli agricultural export sector offer the opportunity to analyze the performance of alternative forms of organization of agricultural exports.

The reforms in the organization of agricultural exports were introduced gradually and encompassed after a few years most agricultural exports. Before the reforms two State Trading Enterprises were responsible for all horticultural exports from Israel: the Citrus Marketing Board of Israel (CMBI) exported all citrus fruit while Agrexco (a company owned by growers and by the government) exported all other fruits and vegetables. Reforms commenced in 1991 with a comprehensive reform in the citrus sector including the abolition of single-desk exports and the privatization of export operations. Agrexco and a few commercial companies took over citrus exports. The Citrus Marketing Board continued to exist but no longer marketed the fruit. It fulfilled some regulatory functions like granting export licenses and managing the "Jaffa" brand name. Starting from 1992/93, exporters could apply for export licenses for specific fruits and vegetables in addition to Agrexco, but just if they were able to demonstrate that they will export at least 30% of total exports of the specific product. Later on, this condition was abolished, but Agrexco continued to export a large share of Israeli fruit and vegetable exports. For flowers, the export monopoly was already abolished more than 20 years ago but the Flower Board kept the exclusive concession for exports to the main market, the flower auctions in Holland, while Agrexco provided the logistic services for flowers sold through the auctions. At the end of the nineties also the flower sector was reformed and exports to the auctions were opened to additional exporters.

There are other countries which abolished agricultural export monopolies. The South African ministry of agriculture commissioned a report to investigate the marketing of agricultural products under various marketing boards. The Kassier Report (1992) - named after the chairman of the committee of inquiry - concludes that the activities done under the authority of the Marketing Act did not achieve the goals and objectives of the act, e.g. efficient production was not promoted and producer prices were stabilized in certain industries but income was not. Vink and Kirsten (2000) argue that the deregulation of South African agriculture has resulted in a net welfare gain to the commercial agricultural sector and present empirical evidence in support of this argument. Mather (2002) investigates attempts of South African citrus growers to cooperate and establish voluntary regulations after liberalization of exports in 1997. According to this report, the impact of liberalization for growers has been mixed. Although growers can select an exporter as result of the liberalization, returns have declined and appear to have become more volatile. Monopoly exports of citrus and tomatoes from Morocco were abolished at the end of the 80's but some cooperation in exports continued afterwards. Moroccan exporters cooperated in export logistics and even exported together to markets further away (Kachel 1996). Aloui argues in a comparative analysis of Moroccan strawberry and tomato exports that one of the main reasons for the success of tomato exports is the high integration of export operations after the abolition of monopoly exports.

The experience of other countries with export liberalization is mixed. Also in Israel, different sectors developed differently after the reforms. Previous research shows that in the citrus sector main performance indicators continued to decline after the reform (Kachel, 2005). On the other hand, vegetable exports increased substantially in recent years following the liberalization of exports. Differences in the reform process and in the resulting market structure might be a reason for these observed differences in performance. In all sectors exports are now carried out by private exporters and by Agrexco. But sectors differ in (1) arrangements customary before the reforms, (2) market structure in export markets, and (3) horizontal and vertical (for example the ownership of packing stations) market structure in the market for "export services" in Israel.

In this chapter we report a study of the success of reforms in the agricultural export sector in Israel. The detailed analysis of the changes of the export regime and its consequences focuses on a few main export products: grapefruit (the main citrus fruit exported), avocado (the main fruit exported beside citrus) and pepper (the main vegetable exported). We commence with a short description of the development of agricultural production and exports. In the next section, we compare economic indicators describing the structure and performance of the selected agricultural export sectors preceding and following the reforms. The evaluation of each product is followed by a comparative analysis to identify factors which may be responsible for differences observed in the performance of the sectors.

B. THE DEVELOPMENT OF AGRICULTURAL PRODUCTION AND EXPORTS[1]

The value of agricultural production declined in the 80's as a result of a large decline in output prices parallel to a substantial increase in production. During the 90's the value of agricultural production was more or less steady – around 15 billion NIS (in 2004 prices). Recent years witnessed an increase in the output value to about 19 billion NIS in 2005 (Figure 14.1). Main outlets for agricultural production are the local market and the processing industry. Exports account for 25% of agricultural output (2005). Increasing agricultural exports are responsible for nearly half of the output value increase observed since 2000.

Favorable exchange rates in main export markets (a strong Euro) account for part of the increase in the value of export. Probably also the liberalization of exports contributed to the increase.

---

[1] Data source for all data presented in this section: Central Bureau of Statistics (CBS). All nominal values were deflated by the CPI and are reported in 2004 prices. The Figures present the agricultural output value according to uses (domestic market, export, industry, other). "Other" stands for "intermediate produce" which is agricultural produce that re-enters the agricultural production process (e.g., locally grown barley used for livestock feed). Data on intermediate produce also include data on destruction of agricultural produce, and as of 1986 - sales to Judea, Samaria and the Gaza Area.

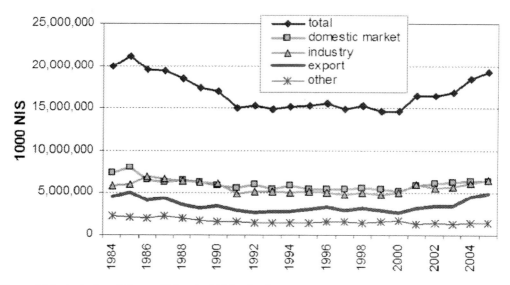

Figure 14.1. Agricultural Output Value (in 2004 prices).

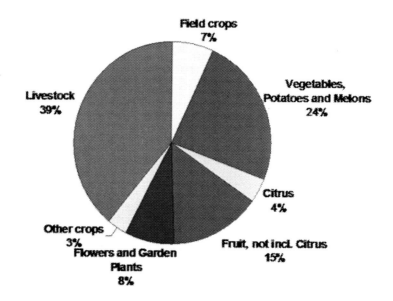

Figure 14.2. Total Agricultural Output in 2004 – 18 Mrd. NIS.

Crops comprise about 60% of total agricultural output, while horticultural crops (fruit, vegetables and flowers) are the main products. Fruit (including citrus) and vegetables account for 43% of the agricultural output (Figure 14.2).

The various horticultural sectors are characterized by different structures and development. The vegetable sector produces mainly for the domestic market which generates 63% of the output value (2005). Exports account for 31% while just a small share of vegetable production is supplied to the processing industry. In recent years, the vegetable sector developed very rapidly, driven by an increase of sales to the domestic market and to export markets (Figure 14.3).

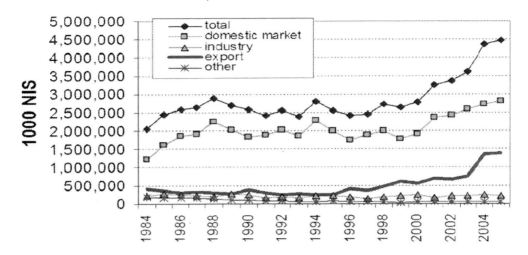

Figure 14.3. Vegetable Output Value (including Potatoes and Melons) (in 2004 prices).

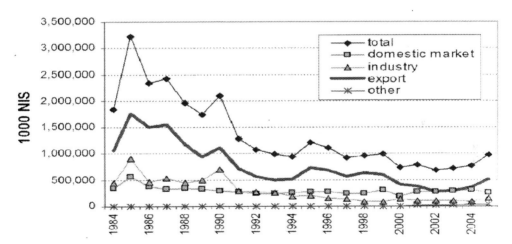

Remark: For citrus, each year relates to the season beginning the year before, e.g. 1984 = season 1983/84.

Figure 14.4. Citrus Output Value (in 2004 prices).

In the past, *citrus* was one of the main agricultural sectors and one of Israel's main export products. In 2004, citrus accounted for just 4% of the agricultural output and for 9% of agricultural exports. The output value of citrus fruit declined very much in the 80's, reflecting a decline in production and exports and a crisis of the sector which led to the extensive reforms. After the abolition of centralized export operations by the Citrus Marketing Board in 1991 citrus exports (and the output value) increased somewhat but since the mid-nineties the trend of decline in output and exports resumed. In recent years citrus exports recovered somewhat, influenced by favorable exchange rates and especially by an increase in demand for Israeli grapefruit following extensive damages by hurricanes to grapefruit production in Florida (Figure 14.4).

In the past, the citrus sector was very much export-oriented. In the second half of the 80's, less than 10% of citrus production was sold in the domestic market. Citrus fruit not satisfying the standards of the fresh fruit market were processed. In recent years, the value of citrus sold in the domestic market is approaching the value of citrus fruit exported as fresh fruit.

Contrary to citrus, *other fruits* are produced mainly for domestic consumption while the processing industry accounts for a very small share of total production. Output values for other fruits stagnated in the 90's and increased in recent years. Also fruit exports started to increase after a long period of stagnation (Figure 14.5).

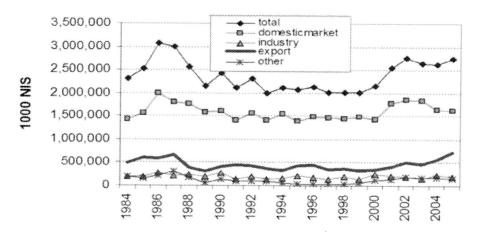

Figure 14.5. Fruit Output Value, not including Citrus (in 2004 prices).

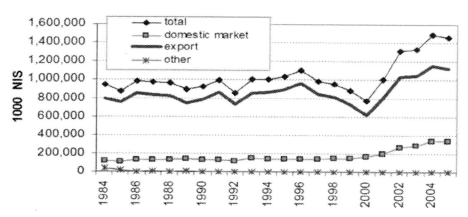

Remark: For flowers, each year relates to the season beginning the year before, e.g. 1984 = season 1983/84.

Figure 14.6. Flower Output Value (in 2004 prices).

Flowers are an export product. Until recently, exports accounted for about 85% of the output value. Since 2000, the local market for flowers developed substantially, and the share of exports in the total output value of flowers decreased to 77% (2005). The value of flower exports declined at the end of the 90's after a period of stagnation but recovered in recent years (Figure 14.6).

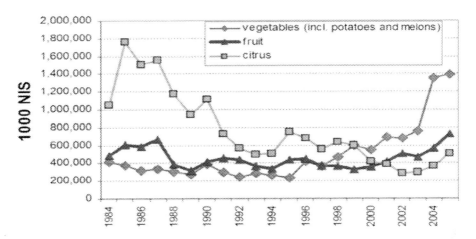

Figure 14.7. Export Value According Sectors (in 2004 prices).

Israeli exports of unprocessed agricultural products are comprised almost exclusively of horticultural products. We focus in our analysis on citrus, fruit and vegetable exports and analyze in detail the most important export product in each product category. Exports in each of these sectors developed very differently.

Citrus exports declined very much, exports of other fruits are more or less stable with an increase in recent years, while vegetable exports increased substantially (Figure 14.7).

Avocado accounts in recent years (avg. 2003-2005) for about 35% of total fruit exports (not including citrus), a decline from 65% at the end of the eighties. The most important vegetable exported is pepper, accounting for 31% of the export value of vegetable exports and even more in the last two years. The export of vegetables in recent years increased mainly as a result of increases in pepper and potato exports. Grapefruit exports account for about 48% of total citrus exports.

C. COMPARATIVE ANALYSIS OVER TIME[2]

In this section, the development of the avocado, the pepper and the citrus sector is studied. We compare economic indicators in the decade before the reforms to the decade afterwards. Our objective is to evaluate the success of the reforms in the different sectors.

The analysis is based on output data (Source: CBS) and import data of the European Union (Source: EUROSTAT). Output quantities and values are reported according to the use of the output (domestic market, export, industry, intermediate produce = other). We calculate unit values (value per mt of production) and use these unit values as indication for prices received by growers. These data are based chiefly on monthly reports from wholesalers, production boards, and from industrial enterprises, on produce received from the farms for the

---

[2] The comparison is based on data from the CBS (development of the various sectors) and data of the European Union (EUROSTAT data for imports to the European Union = sum of imports to 15 EU countries).

domestic market, for export and for manufacturing. The agricultural output value usually excludes board fees and marketing commissions (CBS). The CBS collects these data on a monthly and on a yearly basis. But while the yearly data are verified and updated, the monthly data are not, and there are years where are substantial differences between yearly data and aggregated monthly data.

EUROSTAT collects trade data from EU member states based on customs data supplied by the member state and data collected from trading firms for the trade between EU countries. We use import data to the EU15 - that is total imports to the 15 member states of the European Union before the recent enlargement to 25 member states. We calculate unit values from data on import quantities and values. These unit values are an indication of import prices. These data may not be reliable because of the nature of the fruit and vegetable trade. Sales are often on a consignment basis and therefore the final price is not known at the time of customs declaration. In addition, unit values calculated for suppliers from the EU depend on the reliability of data reported by traders.

In this section, we compare output data and EU import data for Israel before and after the reforms in the selected sectors. In addition, we compare Israeli import quantities and prices to those of main competitors. To evaluate if export liberalization led to cost savings we compare the difference between import prices (unit values on CIF basis) and export prices (unit values on FOB prices) before and after reforms. This difference just accounts for part of the marketing costs (mainly transportation and insurance).

All nominal output values were deflated by the CPI and are reported in 2004 prices. EU trade data are presented in Euro and in real NIS. We use Euro for the comparison of import prices for Israeli products with those of competitors in order to evaluate the effect of the liberalization on relative prices in export markets.

C.1. The Avocado Sector

The Development of the Avocado Sector

The avocado sector is characterized by important changes in the last decade. Agrexco was the only avocado exporter till 1998[3]. From export season 1998 99, additional companies started to export avocado. Exports are still very concentrated, with Agrexco accounting for about 70%, and two additional exporters for the balance.

The avocado sector was in a crisis in the second half of the eighties. After a record harvest in season 1986/87 (135,000 mt), production declined, parallel to a decrease of avocado prices in export markets. As a result of the large decline of production also the output value declined (Figure 14.8).

---

[3] Till the mid-eighties there was an additional avocado exporter (Hilron) competing with Agrexco.

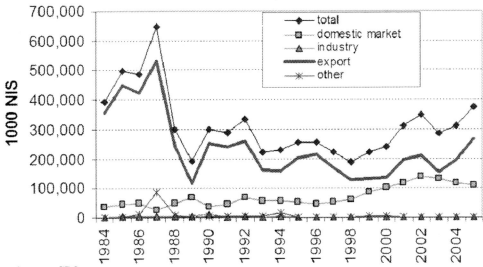

Data Source: CBS.

Figure 14.8. Avocado Output Value (in 2004 prices).

A comparison of output quantities and prices in the decade before the opening of exports to the seven years that passed since the reforms reveals the following changes (see Table 1):

- Average export quantities are slightly lower (-3%), contrasting with an increase in domestic consumption of 112%. The increase in domestic consumption is caused by a large increase in per capita consumption (from 3.5 kg to 6.2 kg per year) in addition to the population increase.
- Avocado production increased (+34%) parallel to the increase in domestic consumption.
- Average output values per mt for avocados exported are nearly identical in both periods. Also average output values for avocado sold on the domestic market did not change. The value of one mt exported is substantially higher than the value of one mt sold on the domestic market.
- Overall, average grower prices (as indicated by the unit output value) are somewhat lower in the period after liberalization (-11%). This decline may be overstated because data indicate that there was no collection of price information for avocado sold to the processing industry and to intermediate uses in most of the period before liberalization, and instead the much higher price of the domestic market was used to derive the value of avocado supplied to these uses.
- The total value of avocado production increased by 20%.

Table 1. Development of the Avocado Sector (Averages per Season)

	Production	Domestic Market	Industry	Export	Intermediate
Quantity in mt					
Avg. 88/9-97/8	57,756	19,011	715	36,991	1,039
Avg. 98/9-04/5	77,663	40,339	1,081	35,763	481
Change in %	34%	112%	51%	-3%	-54%
Real Value in 1000 NIS					
Avg. 88/9-97/8	248,400	53,770	2,290	189,194	3,147
Avg. 98/9-04/5	297,917	113,556	403	182,813	1,146
Change in %	20%	111%	-82%	-3%	-64%
Real Unit Value in NIS/mt					
Avg. 88/9-97/8	4,301	2,828	3,202	5,115	3,027
Avg. 98/9-04/5	3,836	2,815	373	5,112	2,384
Change in %	-11%	-0%	-88%	-0%	-21%

Remarks: The data in the Table are based on aggregated data per season. Till 1994, no separate price was collected for avocado supplied to the processing industry and to intermediate uses. Prices reported were identical to prices in the domestic market. This explains the large decline in the price for avocado for processing.

Data Source: CBS.

Avocado Imports to the European Union

The European Union (EU15) is the main market for Israeli avocados. Israel is one of four main avocado suppliers to the European Union; the others are Spain, South Africa and Mexico. There are a few additional smaller suppliers increasing their market share in recent years – Kenia, Chile and Peru. The Israeli export season is from October to April. The main competitors in this period are Spain and Mexico. Israel's market share in this period is 40% (average 98/99-2004/05), higher than market shares of Spain (33%), and Mexico (13%) in the same period[4].

A comparison of avocado import data to the EU from Israel and its main competitors in the decade before reorganization of exports and in the years afterwards enables preliminary conclusions about the influence of this reform on export performance (Table 2). We compare the period after the opening of exports (October 1998 to April 2005) to the decade before. The data are monthly averages for the Israeli export season (October – April) in both periods.

Avocado supplies to the EU originate mainly in countries outside the EU. The only EU country producing substantial quantities of avocados for export is Spain. The increase in average monthly EU avocado imports by 23% suggests an increase in avocado demand (Table 3). The imports from Spain increased by 47%, compared to an increase of only 12% of avocado imports from Israel. In contrast, avocado imports from Mexico declined. Imports from Mexico are completing the avocado supply during periods with low supply from Spain and Israel. In recent years, imports from additional suppliers (Chile, Peru) in the counter season increased and may have caused the decline in imports from Mexico.

---

[4] Total avocado imports to the EU are calculated as sum of imports from Extra – EU countries and imports from Spain. Spain is, according to FAO data, the only commercial avocado producer in the EU, therefore we assume that imports from other EU countries are re-exports.

Table 2. Avocado Imports to the EU in October - April (Monthly Average)

	Spain	Israel	Mexico	EU-Extra	EU-Extra + Spain
Quantity in mt					
10/88-4/98	2,811	4,419	1,739	7,363	10,174
10/98-4/2005	4,133	4,948	1,624	8,374	12,508
Change in %	47%	12%	-7%	14%	23%
Value in 1000 Euro					
10/88-4/98	3,140	5,111	2,030	8,640	11,780
10/98-4/2005	5,460	6,477	2,545	11,630	17,090
Change in %	74%	27%	25%	35%	45%
Euro/mt					
10/88-4/98	1,117	1,157	1,167	1,173	1,158
10/98-4/2005	1,321	1,309	1,567	1,389	1,366
Change in %	18%	13%	34%	18%	18%
Real Value in 1000 NIS					
10/88-4/98	18,220	30,291	11,836	51,125	69,344
10/98-4/2005	26,428	30,983	12,516	56,368	82,796
Change in %	45%	2%	6%	10%	19%
Real Unit Value in NIS/mt					
10/88-4/98	6,483	6,855	6,807	6,943	6,816
10/98-4/2005	6,394	6,261	7,707	6,731	6,620
Change in %	-1%	-9%	13%	-3%	-3%

Remarks: Unit values are weighted monthly averages. EU-Extra = Imports from countries not belonging to EU15.
Data Source: EUROSTAT (The data are for EU15 countries).

Table 3. Comparison of Monthly Unit Import Values for Avocado in Euro/mt
(Simple Average, October – April)

	Spain	Israel	Mexico	Diff. to Spain	Diff. to Mexico	Number of Observations.
10/88 – 4/1998	1,168	1,236	1,181	68	55	70
10/98 – 4/2005	1,353	1,378	1,504	25	**-126**	49

Remark: For the price comparison with competitors we use simple monthly averages in order to compare price levels in during the Israeli export season without taking into account differences in the monthly distribution of supplies (e.g. higher supplies of Mexican avocado at the beginning of the Israeli season when prices are generally high). Just the price difference to Mexico is statistically significant (printed **bold**).
Data Source: EUROSTAT (The data are for EU15 countries).

Unit values (the CIF value of imports divided by the quantity) provide an indication of import prices. The average unit value in Euro for EU avocado imports increased by 18%.

Mexico managed to increase import prices for its avocados by a third while prices for Israeli and Spanish avocados increased much less (13%. and 18%, respectively). A translation of import values to real NIS reveals a decline in real import prices for Israeli avocados (-9%).

A comparison of Israeli import prices to those of its main competitors in the period before and after the opening of exports to competition does not indicate a relative change in prices that may be attributed to competition among Israeli exporters and a resulting decline in bargaining power. Unit values for Spanish and Israeli avocados are similar in both periods, with slightly higher average prices for Israel (the differences are not statistically significant at the 5% level[5]). Unit values for Israeli and Mexican avocados were similar in the first period while Mexican prices are significantly higher in the second period. We cannot explain the reason for this change without further research (a possible reason is an increase in Mexican avocado quality). It is not reasonable to attribute this change to increased competition among Israeli exporters – in this case we should expect a similar change in relative prices compared to Spain.

Table 4. Comparison of Unit Values (CIF and FOB) for Israeli Avocados
(Weighted Average, October to April)

	Real CIF Prices in NIS/mt	Real FOB Prices in NIS/mt	FOB/CIF	CIF - FOB
10/88 – 4/1998	6,855	5,332	0.78	1,522
10/98 - 4/2005	6,261	5,079	0.81	1,182
change in %	-9%	-5%	4%	-22%

Remark: We performed the comparison of CIF and FOB unit values also based on yearly CBS data which are updated and probably more accurate than monthly data. In this case the data indicate an even larger decline in the CIF – FOB margin after liberalization.
Data Sources: EUROSTAT, CBS.

We examine the development of the margin between export FOB prices and CIF import prices for a first indication of possible cost savings in export operations resulting from liberalization. For Israeli avocados, the price difference declined 22% in the second period (Table 4). This may indicate a success of the reform in increasing efficiency of export operations and a corresponding decline of marketing margins.

C.2. The Citrus Sector

The Development of the Citrus Sector

After the establishment of Israel, citrus production expanded rapidly to a record production of 1.7 million mt in the mid-seventies. Production was export-oriented. The domestic market consumed just a small percentage of production while fruit not suitable for fresh consumption was diverted to the processing industry. During the 80's, citrus exports declined by more than half (see Figure 14.4 above). The steep fall in exports and shrinking profitability of citrus growing led to increasing criticism of the operations of the Citrus

---

[5] All statistical tests reported are performed at the 5% significance level.

Marketing Board. As a result it was decided to cancel the export and domestic marketing monopoly of the board. In the season 1991/92, several commercial companies began exporting Israeli citrus for the first time. The domestic market was opened to competition in April 1991. The Citrus Marketing Board continued to exist and perform some regulatory functions, common promotion and RandD but it ceased selling operations. In 2004, the CMBI was united with three other boards to form the Plants Production and Marketing Board.

The development of grapefruit production mirrors that of total citrus production; merely the decline in exports and production is smaller (Figure 14.9). Florida grapefruit production was hit hard in 2004/05 by hurricanes which caused long term damage to the sector and increased in turn the prospects for Israeli grapefruit exports.

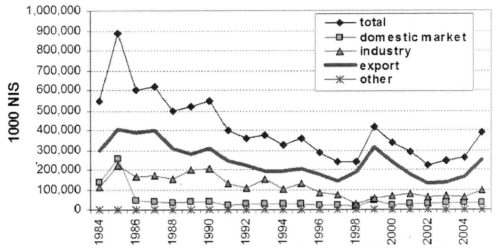

Data Source: CBS (Each year relates to the season beginning the year before, e.g. 1984 = season 1983/84.)

Figure 14.9. Grapefruit Output Value (in 2004 prices).

We compare the last five seasons before the reform of the citrus sector to the average of the fourteen seasons which passed since then (Table 5). Because of the rapid decline of production and exports in decadé before the liberalization we choose a short period of five seasons only immediately before liberalization.

The following are the main changes observed in the citrus sector after liberalization:

- The decline in production continued – citrus production after liberalization is lower by almost 40% compared to the five seasons immediately before liberalization.
- Production declined as a result of the decline in exports (parallel to the decline in exports also the supply to the processing industry declined which is a by-product to fresh fruit production).
- Production supplied to the domestic market increased by 35%. Per capita citrus consumption hardly increased (from 24.6 kg to 25.2 kg), despite a substantial decline in citrus prices on the domestic market (as indicated by the unit values in Table 5).
- Unit output values declined substantially for all main uses (export, domestic market, industry). The percentage decline is lowest for export unit values (-21%).

- The percentage of production supplied to the processing industry declined (from 56% to 48%), the percentage supplied to the domestic market increased (from 9% to 20%), while the percentage exported declined slightly (from 35% to 32%).
- The changes in the grapefruit sector mirror those observed for all citrus. The main difference: the decline in production and exports for grapefruit is smaller.

Table 5. Development of the Citrus Sector (Average per Season)

	Production	Domestic Market	Industry	Export	Intermediate
Total Citrus					
Quantity in mt					
Avg. 01/90-7/86	1,221,050	111,050	686,590	422,730	680
Avg. 05/04-2/91	759,397	150,442	360,738	244,011	4,206
Change in %	-38%	35%	-47%	-42%	519%
Real Value in 1000 NIS					
Avg. 01/90-7/86	1,904,969	313,757	491,461	1,099,343	408
Avg. 05/04-2/91	918,871	262,020	147,681	499,552	9,618
Change in %	-52%	-16%	-70%	-55%	2256%
Real Unit Value in NIS/mt					
Avg. 01/90-7/86	1,560	2,825	716	2,601	600
Avg. 05/04-2/91	1,210	1,742	409	2,047	2,287
Change in %	-22%	-38%	-43%	-21%	281%
Grapefruit					
Quantity in mt					
Avg. 01/90-7/86	369,010	14,420	241,980	112,610	0
Avg. 05/04-2/91	319,090	19,372	203,139	96,573	7
Change in %	-14%	34%	-16%	-14%	
Real Value in 1000 NIS					
Avg. 01/90-7/86	517,343	35,813	172,959	308,571	0
Avg. 05/04-2/91	310,251	29,725	84,401	196,115	10
Change in %	-40%	-17%	-51%	-36%	
Real Unit Value in NIS/mt					
Avg. 01/90-7/86	1,402	2,484	715	2,740	
Avg. 05/04-2/91	972	1,534	415	2,031	1,361
Change in %	-31%	-38%	-42%	-26%	

Data source: CBS.

Overall, the performance of the Israeli citrus industry did not improve after liberalization. Production, exports and grower prices continued to decline. To investigate the reasons for this development and the role of export liberalization we chose grapefruit exports for a more detailed analysis. Grapefruits accounted for 27% of export quantities before liberalization, nowadays it is the main export product in the citrus sector with a share of 40% in the period after liberalization. In addition, Israeli grapefruit account for significant market shares in export markets.

Grapefruit Imports to the European Union

We compare average import quantities and values to the European Union during the supply season of Israeli grapefruit (September – June). Monthly EU import data are available from 1988 only, therefore the period before liberalization comprises only four seasons (without the beginning of the first season).

EU countries receive their grapefruit supplies mainly from countries outside the EU, with the exception of Spain which grows grapefruit for export. Additional EU imports from other EU countries are probably mainly re-exports. Total EU grapefruit consumption (EU-Extra + Spain) is slightly lower in the second period (Table 6). Imports from the two main suppliers, the U.S. and Israel, declined – with a much larger decline in imports from Israel. The average market share of Israeli grapefruit decreased from 25% to 18%. On the other hand, imports from Turkey and Spain increased. The import unit value for Israeli citrus increased in Euro but decreased in real NIS.

Table 6. Grapefruit Import to the EU in September - June (Monthly Average)

	Turkey	USA	Israel	Spain	EU-Extra	EU-Extra + Spain
Quantity in mt						
1/88-6/91	1,507	12,571	9,459	749	36,394	37,142
9/91-6/2005	3,126	11,663	6,490	1,557	34,106	35,663
Change in %	107%	-7%	-31%	108%	-6%	-4%
Value in 1000 Euro						
1/88-6/91	714	7,529	4,323	382	18,729	19,111
9/91-6/2005	1,711	6,536	3,420	886	18,187	19,073
Change in %	140%	-13%	-21%	132%	-3%	0%
Euro/mt						
1/88-6/91	474	599	457	510	515	515
9/91-6/2005	547	560	527	569	533	535
Change in %	15%	-6%	15%	12%	4%	4%
Real Value in 1000 NIS						
1/88-6/91	4,860	51,699	29,555	2,589	127,657	130,246
9/91-6/2005	8,523	33,690	17,649	4,532	93,847	98,379
Change in %	75%	-35%	-40%	75%	-26%	-24%
Real Unit Value in NIS/mt						
1/88-6/91	3,225	4,113	3,125	3,459	3,508	3,507
9/91-6/2005	2,727	2,889	2,720	2,910	2,752	2,759
Change in %	-15%	-30%	-13%	-17%	-22%	-21%

Remarks: Unit values are weighted monthly averages. EU-Extra = Imports from countries not belonging to EU15.

Data Source: EUROSTAT (The data are for EU15 countries).

Table 7. Comparison of Unit Import Values for Grapefruit in Euro/mt
(Simple Average, September – June)

	Turkey	USA	Israel	Spain	Diff .to Turkey	Diff. to USA	Diff. to Spain	Number of Obs.
1/88-6/1991	497	636	464	495	-33	**-172**	-31	30
9/91-6/2005	534	585	540	570	16	**-45**	**-30**	122

Remark: The price difference to Turkey is not statistically significant in both periods, the difference to
   the U.S. is significant in both periods, while the difference to Spain is significant in the second
   period only (significant differences are printed **bold**).
Source: EUROSTAT.

Unit values indicate that import prices for Israeli citrus are mostly lower than those of its main competitors, although the difference to Spain and Turkey is small (Table 7). In contrast, US grapefruit obtained significantly higher grapefruit prices in the period before liberalization.

In the second period, the price premium for US grapefruit compared to Israeli grapefruit declined considerably but is still significant. The price for Israeli grapefruit also improved compared to Turkish grapefruit and Israeli import prices are higher in the second period. The price comparison indicates that there was an improvement of Israeli grapefruit prices relative to those of competitors in the period after liberalization of exports.

A comparison of CIF import prices and the FOB export prices for Israeli grapefruit in both periods point to an increase in the margin (Table 8). This result contradicts results reported by Kachel (2005) which indicate a decline in the margin after liberalization of exports. Probably different observation periods and different data sources (CMBI instead of CBS) are responsible for the divergence.

Table 8. Comparison of Unit Values (CIF and FOB) for Israeli Grapefruit

	Real CIF Prices in NIS/mt	Real FOB Prices in NIS/mt	FOB/CIF	CIF - FOB
Avg. 86/7-90/1	3,234	2,740	0.84	514
Avg. 91/2-04/5	2,685	2,031	0.76	654
Change in %	-17%	-26%	-10%	27%

Remark: The calculation of unit values is based on seasonal data for FOB prices because monthly FOB
   data looked not very reliable. CIF prices are based on yearly data because monthly data for EU
   imports are just available from 1988.
Data Sources: EUROSTAT, CBS.

C.3. The Pepper Sector

The Development of the Pepper Sector

The pepper sector expanded impressively in the last decade, resulting from an increase in domestic consumption and especially in exports (Figure 14.10). For pepper, exports were opened to competition gradually: already in 1991 a grower group in the South of the country (The Arava Growers) received an export license and started to compete with Agrexco. Exports were completely opened in season 1999/2000, inducing substantial entry into the pepper export business. Today tens of export companies are exporting pepper in addition to Agrexco and the export share of Agrexco declined to about 50%. In the following analysis, we compare these three distinctive periods.

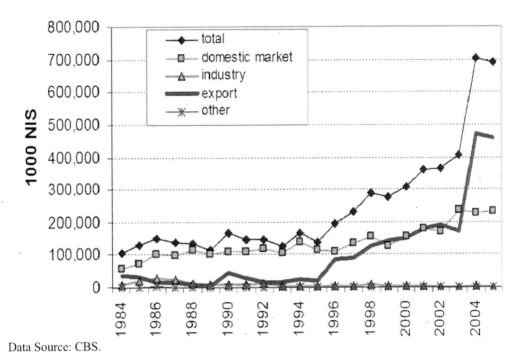

Data Source: CBS.

Figure 14.10. Pepper Output Value (in 2004 prices).

The main changes in the pepper sector are summarized below (see Table 9):

- Production increased substantially (from 48,000 mt in 88-91 to 114,000 mt in 2000-05).
- Total domestic consumption of pepper increased as well as per capita consumption. In contrast, quantities supplied to the processing industry declined.
- Exports increased impressively from just about 3,000 mt in 88-91 to 40,000 mt in 2000-05. The increase in exports continues, and exports in 2005 reached 62,000 mt.
- The unit output value for exports is substantially higher than those obtained for other uses.
- The real unit export value declined from period to period. The decrease from the first period (one exporter) to the second period (two exporters) is small (-3%). In the last period (many exporters) average real export prices declined an additional 6%.
- Despite this decline, average unit values for pepper production increased substantially as a result of the large increase in exports.

Table 9. Development of the Pepper Sector (Average per Season)

	Production	Domestic Market	Industry	Export	Intermediate
Quantity in mt					
Avg. 88-91	47,760	36,369	7,877	2,854	660
Avg. 92-99	72,282	55,865	5,642	9,085	1,690
Avg. 2000-2005	114,111	70,723	2,483	40,347	558
Change 92-99 / 88-91	51%	54%	-28%	218%	156%
Change 00-05 / 92-99	58%	27%	-56%	344%	-67%
Real Value in 1000 NIS					
Avg. 88-91	140,024	109,530	8,881	21,010	602
Avg. 92-99	196,019	124,803	5,642	65,003	571
Avg. 2000-2005	472,543	199,554	2,641	270,245	102
Change 92-99 / 88-91	40%	14%	-36%	209%	-5%
Change 00-05 / 92-99	141%	60%	-53%	316%	-82%
Real Unit Value in NIS/mt					
Avg. 88-91	2,932	3,012	1,127	7,363	912
Avg. 92-99	2,712	2,234	1,000	7,155	338
Avg. 2000-2005	4,141	2,822	1,064	6,698	183
Change 92-99 / 88-91	-8%	-26%	-11%	-3%	-63%
Change 00-05 / 92-99	53%	26%	6%	-6%	-46%

Data Source: CBS.

Pepper Imports to the European Union

A comparison of import quantities and prices of Israeli pepper in main export markets to those of main competitors provides additional information on the performance of this sector. The European Union is the main export market for Israeli pepper while the main competitors in this market are Spain and the Netherlands. We compare average import quantities and prices in the months November to May which is the export season of Israeli pepper (Table 10). EU pepper imports from Israel increased substantially. Nevertheless, Israel is still a small pepper supplier to the EU market, with a share6 in total EU pepper imports in November to May of about 8%. EU import quantities from Spain and the Netherlands increased even more than those from Israel, despite the large growth rates in Israeli exports.

Prices obtained for Israeli pepper (as indicated by unit import values) are lower than the prices for Dutch pepper but higher than prices for Spanish pepper (Table 11). Over the years, the price difference to Dutch pepper declined, while the price difference to Spanish pepper increased.

---

[6] Probably Israel's actual share in imports is somewhat higher because total imports include re-exports. On the other hand, part of the EU pepper consumption is produced locally and not imported; therefore import shares are higher than actual market shares.

Table 10. Pepper Imports to the EU in November - May (Monthly Average)

	Netherlands	Israel	Spain	Total Imports
QUANTITY in mt				
(1) 1/88 - 5/91	5,035	213	19,897	28,890
(2) 11/91 - 5/99	8,570	1,069	30,531	44,056
(3) 11/99 - 5/2005	12,892	4,395	37,984	65,110
Change (2) / (1)	70%	402%	53%	52%
Change (3) / (2)	50%	311%	24%	48%
VALUE in 1000 Euro				
(1) 1/88 - 5/91	9,412	285	20,671	34,595
(2) 11/91 - 5/99	17,191	1,634	33,619	57,186
(3) 11/99 - 5/2005	27,173	7,773	50,789	99,156
Change (2) / (1)	83%	473%	63%	65%
Change (3) / (2)	58%	376%	51%	73%
Euro/mt				
(1) 1/88 - 5/91	1,869	1,338	1,039	1,197
(2) 11/91 - 5/99	2,006	1,528	1,101	1,298
(3) 11/99 - 5/2005	2,108	1,768	1,337	1,541
Change (2) / (1)	7%	14%	6%	8%
Change (3) / (2)	5%	16%	21%	19%
Real Value in 1000 NIS				
(1) 1/88 - 5/91	63,447	1,949	141,803	236,337
(2) 11/91 - 5/99	91,578	8,205	180,041	304,974
(3) 11/99 - 5/2005	131,031	38,758	245,669	481,857
Change (2) / (1)	44%	321%	27%	29%
Change (3) / (2)	43%	372%	36%	58%
Unit Value in NIS/mt				
(1) 1/88 - 5/91	12,602	9,136	7,127	8,181
(2) 11/91 - 5/99	10,686	7,673	5,897	6,922
(3) 11/99 - 5/2005	10,163	8,818	6,468	7,401
Change (2) / (1)	-15%	-16%	-17%	-15%
Change (3) / (2)	-5%	15%	10%	7%

Remarks: Unit values are weighted monthly averages.
Data Source: EUROSTAT (The data are for EU15 countries).

All price differences are statistically significant. The price comparison indicates that prices of Israeli pepper relative to those of main competitors improved. There is no indication for a price decline caused by increased competition among Israeli exporters.

The evidence from a comparison of FOB export prices and CIF import prices for Israeli pepper is inconclusive (Table 12). The margin is the highest in the first period with Agrexco as only exporter, declines more than half in the second period, but increases again very much in the third period. However, these large differences in margins are not statistically significant. Monthly margins for pepper display a high variability, casting doubt on data reliability.

Table 11. Comparison of Unit Import Values for Pepper in Euro/mt
(Simple Average, November – May)

	Netherlands	Israel	Spain	Diff. to NL	Diff. to Spain	Number of Obs.
1/88 - 5/91	1,649	1,181	1,141	-468	40	20
11/91- 5/99	1,853	1,398	1,107	-455	291	55
11/99-5/2005	2,056	1,728	1,332	-317	407	42

Data Source: EUROSTAT.

Table 12. Comparison of Unit Values (CIF and FOB) for Israeli Pepper
(Weighted Average, November-May)

	Real CIF Prices in NIS/mt	Real FOB Prices in NIS/mt	FOB/CIF	CIF - FOB
(1) 1/88 - 5/91	9,136	7,602	0.83	1,534
(2) 11/91- 5/99	7,673	7,010	0.91	663
(3) 11/99 - 3/2005	8,810	7,517	0.85	1,293
Change (2) / (1)	-16%	-8%	10%	-57%
Change (3) / (2)	15%	7%	-7%	95%

Remark: Margins were also calculated based on yearly data. The main difference in results compared to those in presented in the table is a larger margin in the last period because of a lower FOB unit value in this period.

Data Sources: EUROSTAT; CBS.

D. MARKET POWER IN EXPORT MARKETS – ECONOMETRIC ANALYSIS

In the discussions preceding reforms it was argued that the abolition of centralized exports will lead to a "wild" competition among Israeli exporters, a decrease in prices for Israeli products, and shrinking grower profits. In this section we estimate residual import demand functions for main Israeli fruit and vegetables. Our objective is to examine these claims.

D.1. The Citrus Sector

In previous research (Kachel 2005, Kachel and Finkelshtain 1999) we analyzed the possibility to exercise market power in Israeli citrus exports. The objective was to examine whether centralized exports by the CMBI succeeded to increase export revenues. The research focused on orange and grapefruit exports to the UK and Germany. It is based on monthly import data for the years 1978 to 1992 for the German market and 1978 to 2002 for the British market.

The methodological approach belongs to the school of "New Empirical Industrial Organization" (NEIO), that is, firms' actual behavior is inferred from market data. Time series of prices and quantities are analyzed in order to evaluate both the potential for market power and its actual exercising (Bresnahan 1989, Carlton and Perloff 1990). The estimation procedure proceeds as follows. The first step is the estimation of the inverse residual import demand functions for different markets and different products. These provide the information regarding the possibility to exercise market power in the various export markets. If demands are not perfectly elastic there is scope for the exporting firm to use market power and the analysis should proceed to the next step. In the second step an equation representing the exporter's behavior is estimated.

We estimated a system of simultaneous equations, employing the method proposed by Fair (1970, 1984) to account for simultaneity and serial correlation of residuals. Estimation results (Table 13) show that the CMBI as a centralized export institution had little scope to exploit its organizational structure to increase revenues in exports markets. Import demands for Israeli oranges and grapefruits in both the U.K. and Germany are very elastic and provide a very limited potential for exploiting monopolistic market power. For Israeli oranges, we estimated an import demand elasticity of -4.4 in the U.K. market and an elasticity of -30 in the German market[7]. For Israeli grapefruit imports, the U.K. demand is more elastic ($\eta = -14.6$) compared to the demand of the German market ($\eta = -5.9$). These differences are consistent with differences in market share and with previously published studies of consumer preferences in the two markets. The results imply that the CMBI could employ third degree price discrimination between the German and British markets. Nevertheless, the estimation of behavioral equations shows that the CMBI did not exploit this potential[8]. To summarize, we find that despite conditions supporting the presence of market power like substantial market shares and high brand awareness the hypothesis that the market conduct of the CMBI was competitive is not rejected.

These results question the claim of supporters of centralized exporting as a means to increase growers' revenues.

D.2. The Avocado Sector

We employed a similar methodology to analyze Israeli avocado exports. We estimated the following inverse demand function for Israeli avocado imports to the European Union (15 countries), based on monthly import data for 1988 to 2005[9]:

$$p_t^I = \beta_0 + \beta_1 q_t^I + \beta_2 q_t^S + \beta_3 q_t^M + \beta_4 D^{lib} + \beta_5 D^{lib} q_t^I + \beta_6 p_{t-1}^I + \beta_7 D^{89/90} + \varepsilon_t$$

where t is the date, p_t^I is the import price (unit value) for Israeli avocados, q_t^I, quantities of Israeli avocados imported in t, q_t^S and q_t^M, quantities of avocados from main competitors

---

[7] The coefficient for Israeli orange quantities in the German market is not significant.
[8] Estimation results are not presented here, for details see Kachel (2005).
[9] The estimations are based on data for the months October till April, the main supply season of Israeli avocados.

(Spain and Mexico, respectively), D^{lib}, a dummy variable for the period of liberalized exports, and $D^{89/90}$, a dummy accounting for an exceptional season characterized by extremely low yields in Israel as a result of weather damages.

Table 13. Demand for Israeli Citrus in the U.K. and in Germany

Explanatory Variables:	Oranges – U.K. (Linear Specification)		Oranges – Germany (Linear Specification)	
	Coefficient	t-Statistic	Coefficient	t-Statistic
Constant	373.2	16.58	960.0	7.93
Quantity Israel	-0.0080	-7.83	-0.0034	-1.37
Quantity Other Suppliers	-0.0075	-9.23	-0.0038	-2.64
Quantity Easy Peelers	-0.0075	-10.23	-0.0016	-0.63
Quantity Grapefruit	-0.0074	-3.71	-0.0068	-1.03
Quantity Israeli Grapefruit	-0.0004	-0.09	0.0020	0.23
Expenditure Citrus	$1.96*10^{-5}$	10.45	$2.59*10^{-6}$	1.54
Explanatory Variables:	Grapefruit – U.K. (Logarithm. Specification)		Grapefruit – Germany (Logarithm. Specification)	
	Coefficient	t-Statistic	Coefficient	t-Statistic
Constant	5.15	7.84	4.38	6.73
Quantity Israel	-0.0685	-3.44	-0.1706	-4.81
Quantity Other Suppliers	-0.0603	-2.38	-0.1173	-3.13
Quantity Easy Peelers	-0.0385	-2.76	-0.0347	-3.60
Quantity Grapefruit	-0.1352	-3.32	-0.2061	-3.40
Quantity Israeli Grapefruit	0.0006	0.07	0.0368	2.55
Expenditure Citrus	0.2126	3.96	0.3929	4.61

Remarks: Dependent variables: Import prices for the respective market and fruit. Coefficients significant at the 5% level are printed bold. Regressions included additional explanatory variables (Dummy and Trend variables) not presented in the table. The R-square for the presented results ranged from 0.76 to 0.90. For more details see Kachel (2005).

The regression was estimated with the 2SLS estimation procedure to account for simultaneity. Regression results (Table 14) show that Israeli avocado quantities have a significant negative influence on the price obtained. Also the coefficients for quantities of competitors are negative and significant like expected. The own price elasticity at the sample average is about -5. This suggests a quite elastic demand for Israeli avocados and consequently a limited potential to increase export revenues by exercising market power.

To account for possible changes of residual import demand as a result of export liberalization we included a dummy for liberalization as fixed effect and as a slope shifter. For example, the demand for Israeli avocados might decrease after liberalization as result of granting export licenses to additional exporters because of increasing transaction costs or decreasing expenditure for promotion. Regression results indicate that there was no significant change in the level or slope of the residual demand function after liberalization.

Table 14. EU15 Demand for Israeli Avocados

Explanatory Variables	Coefficient	t-value
Israeli Quantity in mt	-0.061	-4.64
Dummy for Liberalization (Constant)	-30.24	-0.20
Dummy for Liberalization (Slope)	0.024	0.90
Quantity of Spain	-0.04	-2.65
Quantity of Mexico	-0.03	-2.33
Lagged Israeli CIF Price (t-1)	0.58	8.36
Dummy for Season89/1988	89.77	0.81
Constant	975.3	6.65
R^2	0.83	
Number of Obs.	105	

Remarks: Dependent variable: Import prices for Israeli Avocados. The equation was estimated using instrumental variable regression (2SLS) with robust STD. We tested for autocorrelation of residuals with the Breusch-Godfrey Serial Correlation LM Test; test results indicate that residuals are not correlated.

Coefficients significant at the 5% level are printed bold.

Overall, conclusions are similar to those obtained for citrus exports. Despite large market shares the price elasticity for Israeli avocados is high, limiting the scope to exploit market power. Also for avocados, the estimation of a behavioral equation indicates that the existing market power was not exploited by the single-desk exporter[10].

D.3. The Pepper Sector

Regression results for Israeli pepper exports to the European Union did not show any evidence that Israeli supply quantities influence prices obtained. This is not surprising given that the market share of Israeli pepper in the EU market is small. This result provides evidence that no gains are to expect from one-hand exports with regard to the possibility of price discrimination and the increase of export revenues. On the other hand, it indicates, that Israeli pepper exports can still be increased without a negative influence on the price level in the EU export market. There are indications that EU import data for Israeli pepper may not be completely reliable, hence the results for pepper have to be interpreted with caution.

E. THE MARKET FOR EXPORT SERVICES – ECONOMETRIC ANALYSIS

One of the dangers of privatization in general and especially in the market for export services for agricultural products is the possibility that the state monopoly will be exchanged by a private monopoly or oligopoly which can exploit its power to decrease grower revenues. In this case, the efficiency gains from privatization may be smaller than the damage caused by

---

[10] Estimation results are not presented here because of space constraints but can be obtained from the authors upon request.

the noncompetitive market structure of the privatized sector. We use econometric methods to analyze the functioning of the market for export services after the reforms.

In the econometric analysis for avocado and pepper, FOB prices (collected by the CBS) are explained by CIF prices (EUROSTAT unit values) and additional variables. Under perfect competition, we expect that changes in CIF prices are transmitted fully to growers; hence the coefficient of the CIF price is expected to be close to one[11]. In this case, the constant is expected to be negative and indicate transportation and insurance costs. If the coefficient of the CIF price is significantly smaller than one, this is an indication that changes in CIF prices are not fully translated to changes in FOB prices. For the period before liberalization, this may be an indication for cross-subsidization practiced by the monopoly exporter. For the period after liberalization, this may be an indication that the market for export services is not competitive.

E.1. The Avocado Sector

Avocado CIF and FOB prices were analyzed with the help of three regressions, one for all observations (1988-2005), one with data for the period before export liberalization (1988-4/1998), and one for the period since liberalization (10/1998-2005). High values for the R^2 (0.6 to 0.7) indicate that a large part of the variance of FOB prices is explained by the variables included in the regressions (Table 15). The estimated coefficients for the CIF price for all three regressions are smaller than 0.7 and statistically significant different from 1. This result indicates that changes in CIF prices are not translated completely to FOB prices. Regression results suggest that the reform did not influence much the way CIF prices are related to FOB prices. Constant and slope dummies for the regression including all observations are not significant. In addition, the coefficients of the CIF price are identical in the second and third regression.

E.2. The Pepper Sector

In contrast to results for the avocado sector, the R^2 for the estimated pepper price equations is much lower (less than 0.2). One reason for the large unexplained variation in FOB prices may be changes in the transportation technology (a move to sea transport from air transport), or changes in transport costs, but probably the reason are problems with the quality of price data in the pepper sector.

In the case of pepper, the coefficients for the CIF price are lower than 0.5, an even larger departure from the expected value close to 1. It is important to note that the price coefficient increased in the last period which is characterized with significant entry into pepper export operations. This result may indicate an increase in competition in the market for pepper export services.

---

[11] Most export costs (e.g. packing and transportation) are fixed on a per unit basis and do not depend on the selling price of the product. There are some costs (e.g. commissions) which are calculated as a percentage of the selling price but these costs account only for a small share of the selling price (about 15%).

Table 15. Price Equation for Avocado from Israel (Dependent Variable: FOB Price)

Explanatory Variables	OLS		AR(1) Correction	
	Coefficient	t-value	Coefficient	t-value
All Observations (10/88 - 3/05)				
CIF Price	0.64	11.64	0.67	7.45
Dummy for Liberalization (Constant)	156.7	0.20	790.1	0.74
Dummy for Liberalization (Slope)	-0.003	-0.03	-0.08	-0.56
Constant	876.6	2.06	602	0.90
R^2	0.61		0.68	
DW	1.23		1.45	
Before Liberalization (10/88 - 4/98)				
CIF Price	0.63	10.2	0.66	6.01
Constant	876.6	1.81	709	2.12
R^2	0.61		0.70	
DW	1.07		1.12	
After Liberalization (10/98 - 3/2005)				
CIF Price	0.63	8.68		
Constant	1,033	2.08		
R^2	0.62			
DW	1.69			

Table 16. Price Equation for Pepper from Israel (Dependent Variable: FOB Price)

Explanatory Variables	All Observations (05/3-88/1)		First and Second Period (1/88-5/99)		Third Period (11/99-3/05)	
	Coeff.	t-value	Coeff.	t-value	Coeff.	t-value
CIF Price	0.337	4.75	0.304	3.60	0.416	3.09
Dummy for "Arava" exporter	435	1.05				
Dummy for additional exporters	-264	-0.82				
Constant	4,439	6.69	5,027	7.57	3,970	3.44
R^2	0.18		0.16		0.20	
DW	1.7		1.75		1.62	

E.3. The Citrus Sector

The Israeli citrus industry after liberalization is characterized by a highly concentrated export sector. In the first years after liberalization, 3 to 4 main exporters exported about 90% of all Israeli citrus. In recent years, there is a duopoly of two main exporters responsible for about 90% of exports, and in addition a number of small exporters. The high concentration of the sector for citrus export services raises concerns that exporters may exploit market power in their transactions with citrus growers.

Contracts offered by exporters differ in the degree of information provided to growers about the final price for their fruit. For example, exporters may agree to pay a certain price, or they may pay growers just after selling the fruit abroad without any ·guarantee on price (consignment contract) and with very limited possibilities for growers to evaluate the performance of exporters. In contrast to the text book contract theory which predicts contracts with profit sharing, during most of the 90's the common contract in the Israeli citrus industry was consignment based. In recent years it is common to offer a minimum price.

In previous research we developed a model characterizing contract choice in the Israeli citrus industry (Kachel et al. 2003, Kachel 2005). The citrus market for export services is modeled as a two-stage game. In the first stage, each of the exporters chooses, non-cooperatively, the type of contract offered to growers. In the second stage, given the contract type chosen in the first stage, exporters engage in price competition. The model shows that exporters may decrease price competition among themselves by means of limiting the amount of price information provided to growers in contracts offered.

Empirically, we find that there is a very weak relationship between the price export firms pay growers and the share of each exporter in citrus fruit supplied by growers. Low price elasticities are characteristic for a market with very little price information where growers choose exporters randomly or based on factors other than price. In addition, the analysis of price margins in grapefruit and orange exports indicates a substantial oligopoly markup of exporters, decreasing grower prices and contributing to a decline in citrus production in the longer term.

CONCLUSION

We study the influence of far-reaching reforms in main agricultural export sectors in Israel on the performance of these sectors. The reforms included the abolition of statutory export monopolies, and the privatization of export operations. A comparison of the three sectors studied shows differences in the development of exports. Citrus exports continued to decrease after the reform, and the overall performance of the sector did not improve. Avocado exports decreased slightly after reforms, while other fruit exports started to increase in recent years. In contrast, pepper exports increased very much and induced the expansion of pepper production and the entry of numerous new exporters. It seems that the differences in performance are mainly related to demand conditions in export markets.

In addition, entry barriers are influencing the speed of adaptation to changing market conditions. The vegetable sector is characterized by low entry barriers to growing (annual growing cycle) and exporting (packing operations are mainly owned by growers). In contrast, fruit production is characterized by a multi-annual production cycle and higher investments, which is slowing the speed of the adaptation process. In addition, packing stations in the citrus sector were initially mainly owned by export companies – creating an additional entry barrier into citrus exports. In the avocado sector, growers (kibbutzim) own the main packing stations. A large part of avocado growers are organized in a common organization and may be able to obtain higher revenues through joint bargaining A relatively higher price transmission in avocado exports compared to citrus and pepper exports may be an indication.

Results are clear-cut with regard to the question if the opening of export operations to competition caused a loss of market power in export markets. First, there is no indication that prices for Israeli products declined after reforms relative to those of its competitors. On the contrary, relative import prices for pepper and grapefruit improved which probably indicates an improvement in quality. In addition, we estimated residual import demand functions for Israeli products to investigate formally the possibility to exploit market power on export markets. Estimation results show that avocado and citrus supplies from Israel have a significant but small influence on prices obtained. Import demand is very elastic and therefore the potential to exploit market power is quite limited. Econometric results for behavioral equations indicate that centralized exports did not manage to take advantage of this limited potential. To summarize, we find that despite conditions supporting the presence of market power like substantial market shares and high brand awareness the hypothesis that the market conduct of the CMBI was competitive is not rejected. These results question the claim of supporters of centralized exporting as a means to increase growers' revenues.

Results are inconclusive with regard to the question if the reforms increased the efficiency of export operations and led to a saving of marketing costs. We compared import to export prices and found that the margin decreased substantially after reforms in the case of avocado exports. For grapefruit, results obtained here contradict those in an earlier study (Kachel 2005), probably as result of different time periods and data sources. For pepper, the differences observed in margins in three distinctive periods are not significant. A large variability in margins over time especially for pepper exports cast some doubt on data reliability. In addition, the price margin we calculated from the unit value data available contains just part of the marketing costs (mainly overseas transportation and insurance).

The high concentration of exports in the hand of just a few exporters, especially in the citrus and in the avocado sector, raises the concern that the market for export services for agricultural products is not competitive and exporters can exploit their power to decrease grower revenues. Previous theoretical research by the authors shows that exporters can use information as strategic tool to reduce price competition among them. Our model predicts that exporters will use consignment contracts to conceal price information, reduce price competition and pay lower grower prices. Empirical research confirms that the market structure for export services in the citrus sector is noncompetitive. The analysis for avocado and pepper provides a first indication that also in these sectors export services may be noncompetitive but further research is necessary.

To summarize, research results indicate that the impact of reforms on export performance and growers revenues may have been dampened by noncompetitive market structures for export services which developed after reforms. In addition, performance depends on further factors which may dominate the effects of reform. In the pepper sector, which shows an impressive export performance in the years after reform, exports are relatively less concentrated than exports in the less successful citrus and fruit sectors. But it seems that the main reason for success in this sector was the introduction of production methods for high-quality pepper which can be supplied to European markets in periods of lower domestic supply.

There is a need for further reforms to increase competitiveness in the market for export services. These reforms should include an abolition of the partial exemption for wholesalers (including exporters) from the enforcement of antitrust laws, if these wholesalers are not owned by growers. In addition, regulations are necessary to increase transparency and fairness in the relationship of exporters with growers.

REFERENCES

Aloui, O., (Without Year). Performance in the Agro-Exports' Sector: Tomatoes and Strawberries in Morocco, Consultancy Report Prepared for UNCTAD.

Bresnahan, T. F., (1989). Empirical Studies of Industries with Market Power. In Schmalensee, R., and Willig, R.D. (Eds.), *Handbook of Industrial Organizations* (1011-57). North-Holland, New-York and Oxford: Elsevier Science Publishers B.V.

Carlton, D. W., and Perloff, J. M. (2001). Modern Industrial Organization, *American Journal of Agricultural Economics, Vol. 83* (No.1), 254-255.

Fair, R.C. (1970). The Estimation of Simultaneous Equation Models with Lagged Endogenous Variables and First Order Serially Correlated Errors. *Econometrica, Vol. 38,* 507-516.

Fair, R.C. (1984). *Specification, Estimation, and Analysis of Macroeconometric Models.* Cambridge: Harvard University Press.

Kachel, Y. (2005). The Influence of Industry Structure on Performance: The Case of the Israeli Citrus Industry. Unpublished PhD Thesis, Hebrew University of Jerusalem.

Kachel, Y. (1996). Growing and Marketing of Citrus Fruit in Morocco. Department of Market Research, Ministry of Agriculture. (in Hebrew).

Kachel, Y., Finkelshtain, I.,and Kislev, Y. (2003). Equilibrium Contracts in the Israeli Citrus Industry. Presented at the 81st Seminar of the European Association of Agricultural Economics, Economics of Contracts in Agriculture, KVL Copenhagen, June.

Kachel, Y., Finkelshtain, I. (1999). Marketing Boards and Monopolistic Conduct: the Case of the Israeli Citrus Export to Europe. In IAMO (Institute of Agricultural Development in Central and Eastern Europe) (Eds.), *Studies on the Agricultural and Food Sector in Central and Eastern Europe.* Kiel, Germany: IAMO.

Kassier, W. E. et al. (1992). Report of the Committee of Inquiry into the Marketing Act. commissioned by the Ministry of Agriculture, South Africa.

Mather, C. (2002). Regulating South Africa's Citrus Export Commodity Chain(s) after Liberalization. School of Geography, Archaeology and Environmental Studies, University of the Witwatersrand, 2002.

Vink, N., and Kirsten, J.(2000). Deregulation of Agricultural Marketing in South Africa: Lessons Learned. *Free Market Foundation Monograph No. 25.*

SECTION VI: LABOR AND MANAGEMENT ON FARM HOUSEHOLDS

In: The Economics of Natural and Human Resources…   ISBN 978-1-60741-029-4
Editor: Ayal Kimhi and Israel Finkelshtain   © 2009 Nova Science Publishers, Inc.

Chapter 15

THE EFFECT OF FAMILY COMPOSITION ON THE OFF-FARM PARTICIPATION DECISIONS IN ISRAELI FARM HOUSEHOLDS

*Ayal Kimhi and Eddie Seiler**

The Hebrew University, Israel and Eddie Seiler, Fannie Mae, U.S.A.

ABSTRACT

This paper studies the dependence of the off-farm participation behavior of farm operators and their spouses on the demographic composition of the household. Specifically, we examine the effect of the existence and work decisions of adult children of the farm couple. We found little evidence for a genuine effect of adult children on the participation decision of the father. The mother, on the other hand, tends to reduce her tendency to participate in off-farm work in the presence of adult children, even after controlling for observed characteristics.

A. INTRODUCTION

The time allocation decision of farmers has long attracted researchers because many farmers divide their labor supply between farm work and off-farm work, a phenomenon which is rarely observed in other sectors of the economy (Shishko and Rostker 1976). Other than the scientific attractiveness of multiple job-holding among self-employed farmers, understanding this phenomenon is important for the design of rural policy in general and

* Ayal Kimhi is with the Agricultural Economics Department, The Hebrew University, Rehovot, Israel. Eddie Seiler is a former Post-Doctoral Fellow at the Hebrew University and currently at Fannie Mae. This research was supported by Research Grant Award No. IS-2762-96 from BARD - the United States – Israel Binational Agricultural Research and Development Fund. The authors acknowledge the helpful comments and suggestions of participants in the annual meetings of the American Economic Association and the European Society for Population Economics, the Second Mediterranean Social and Political Research Meeting, and the Workshop on the Economics of Water and Agriculture. Special thanks to Elana Dror and Haim Regev from the Central Bureau of Statistics in Israel for providing the data.

agricultural policy in particular. Many policy instruments are initiated in order to improve farm income or reduce income variability of farmers. Policy makers do not fully appreciate the importance of earnings from off-farm sources, which serve as a buffer against farm income fluctuations. Moreover, any farm-related policy should take into account the ability of farmers to act on the extensive margin between farming and off-farm activities in addition to their actions on the intensive margin between different farm activities. Understanding how farmers allocate their time between farming and off-farm occupations is therefore crucial for designing successful farm policies.

The empirical applications of the time allocation model have thus far been limited to husband and wife only because of two main reasons. One is the lack of sufficient data on the time allocation of other family members. The other is the limitation imposed by the availability of suitable econometric techniques. As family farming is still dominant all over the world, data on farm households are readily available in many countries. This research will use data from a detailed family farm survey conducted in Israel, which include the time allocation patterns of all farm-family members older than 14 years. Econometric tools such as quasi-maximum likelihood estimation (Kimhi 1994), and minimum distance estimation (Kimhi and Lee 1996), enable the joint estimation of a large number of participation and labor supply equations. Hence the purpose of this research is to extend the time allocation analysis to other members of the farming family.

Previous research (Kimhi 1996) has found that household composition affects the tendency of different household members to provide off-farm labor. This is explained by the differential income effects resulting from the household's joint budget constraint and the time and money costs imposed by different household members. In particular, farm couples are more likely to work off the farm when the number of other adults in the household increases. Kimhi (2004) extended the previous work in several directions: (a) using a more recent data set; (b) focusing on other adults in the household who are immediate descendents of the farm couple (and the descendents' spouses); (c) estimating the off-farm participation equation of the descendents jointly with the off-farm participation equations of the farm couple. The results showed that the parents (farm operator and spouse) reduce their tendency to work off the farm as the number of adult children in the household rises. The sample was composed of farms from three types of localities: Moshavim (cooperative villages), private Jewish localities and private Arab localities. It was found that the type of locality has a significant, and in some cases quite large, effect on the off-farm labor participation decision. The question is whether it is safe to assume that the difference between the types of localities affects the participation decision only through the intercept of the regression equation. In this paper we want to examine whether the previous results hold if we concentrate on farms in Moshavim only. Moshavim is the largest group of households, hence it makes sense to examine them first. In addition, this will enable a better comparison with the previous results of Kimhi (1996) that were obtained with 1981 data, which included only farms in Moshavim.

B. BACKGROUND AND PREVIOUS RESULTS

The literature is rich in applications of the agricultural household model to time allocation problems. The traditional approach has been to estimate off-farm participation equations and labor supply equations of farm operators (e.g., Sumner 1982). In the last decade, researchers have moved to estimate two-equation models in which the off-farm labor supply equations of husbands and wives are jointly determined (e.g., Huffman and Lange 1989; Tokle and Huffman 1991; Lass and Gempesaw 1992). The results of these studies indicated that off-farm labor supply of husbands and wives are positively correlated. Recently, this approach has been extended to include farm work participation equations (Kimhi 1994) and labor supply equations as well (Kimhi and Lee 1996). Buttel and Gillespie (1984) have also found that men's and women's farm and off-farm labor supply decisions are correlated.

However, farm families are not made of a husband and a wife only. On the contrary, farm families are often larger than non-farm families, including several generations who function as an extended family. The importance of within-family succession serves as an incentive for adult children to work together with their parents on the family farm (Kimhi 1995). Blanc and Perrier-Cornet (1993) found that European successors often work as laborers for their parents for ten years or more before receiving ownership. Hence, the existence of other family members allows the farm operator and spouse to have more flexibility in their time allocation decisions.

This claim is supported by the empirical results of Kimhi (1996), who studied the effect of family composition on the labor participation decisions of Israeli farm couples. Children under 3 years of age decreased the tendency of spouses to participate in either farm work or off-farm work, decreased operators' farm participation but increased their off-farm participation. Older children (up to 18 years of age) increased farm participation and decreased off-farm participation of both adult family members. The number of other adults (19 to 51 years old) increased (decreased) off-farm (farm) participation of both spouses. It seems that other adults are net substitutes in farm work. Further, a measure of other adults' farm work was included as an explanatory variable, and the results did not change much, though the coefficients tended to be larger in absolute value. This variable had a strong positive (negative) effect on farm (off-farm) participation probability. Finally, the joint participation model was estimated separately for households with and without other adults. The results implied that the time allocation of farm operators and their spouses depends strongly on the existence of other adult household members. Overall, the previous results indicate that there are substitutability and complementarity relations between the labor supplies of different household members to the two sectors. Hence, a joint estimation is recommended if consistent estimators are desired.

C. THEORY AND EMPIRICAL METHODS

In most empirical applications, the time-allocation decisions in family farms were modeled as if they are derived from a joint household utility model, that is, each and every family member acts so as to maximize a utility function defined over consumption and leisure of all family members. This is the framework used by Huffman (1991) in his comprehensive theoretical survey of the farm-household models. In particular, utility is maximized subject to a household budget constraint, a set of individual time constraints, and a set of non-negativity constraints on off-farm labor. Kimhi (1994) suggested that in a household setting, nonnegativity constraints on farm work should also be included. The optimal solution to the maximization problem can be characterized by Kuhn-Tucker conditions,. The farm work and off-farm work participation conditions are a subset of the Kuhn-Tucker conditions. In this paper we focus on the off-farm labor participation equations of all adult family members.

Off-farm participation models with up to two participation equations were modeled by maximum likelihood models in most of the studies of joint husband-wife work decisions. The quasi maximum likelihood method (Kimhi 1994) can be used for more than two equations. The method is illustrated here for the case of three equations. Let the participation equations be $\alpha_i \cdot X_i + v_i \leq 0$ (i=1,2,3), where strict equality indicates participation. Assuming normality, one can obtain probit estimators α^*_i (i=1,2,3) as first-stage estimators that are consistent but inefficient, since they ignore the correlation among the participation equations. The second stage involves maximizing a bivariate probit log-likelihood function of the form:

$$\pounds_{ij} = \Sigma \ln B(d_i\alpha^*_i X_i, d_j\alpha^*_j X_j, d_{ij}\rho_{ij}),$$ (1)

with respect to ρ_{ij}, for each possible $(i,j) \in \{(1,2), (1,3), (2,3)\}$. Summation is over individuals; B is the bivariate normal probability function; ρ_{ij} is the correlation between v_i and v_j; I_k equals one if participation occurs, zero otherwise; and $d_i=2I_i-1$ and $d_{ij}=d_id_j$. Since maximizing $\pounds_{ij}$ for each possible (i,j) is equivalent to maximizing $\pounds = \pounds_{12} + \pounds_{13} + \pounds_{23}$, $\pounds$ can be maximized over all the parameters in one stage. This is the most efficient QML estimator subject to the condition that the level of integration is not higher than two. The method is appropriate for any number of equations. The true covariance matrix of the estimators should be calculated as $H^{-1}WH^{-1}$ where H is the matrix of second derivatives of quasi-likelihood function $\pounds$ and W is its gradient outer-product matrix.

D. DATA

The data come from a farm survey that was conducted in Israel in 1995 (State of Israel, Central Bureau of Statistics 1998). The survey encompassed a representative 10% sample of farms, and included approximately 3000 farms of various kinds. In this paper we only use data on family farms in Moshavim (cooperative villages). Despite the cooperative structure of Moshavim, these farms can be treated as private family farms for all practical purposes.[1] Sampling in Moshavim was conducted in two stages: 130 Moshavim were sampled in the first stage out of around 350 Moshavim in the country. These Moshavim included approximately 9000 family farms. Among these, 2100 family farms (as well as 150 partnership and business farms) were sampled in the second stage.[2] The sample was stratified according to farm size, branch, and region, and an appropriate weight was attached to each observation.

The survey questionnaire included very detailed questions about farm production activities, as well as personal and family characteristics (age, education, tenure, ethnic origin).

---

[1] Kimhi (1998) provides a detailed description of the historical institutional structure of Moshavim. However, by 1995 most Moshavim had very little cooperation left.

[2] The sample in Moshavim included inactive farms, accounting for over 25% of family farms.

Regarding time allocation, each family member was asked if he/she engaged in agricultural activities on the farm up to 1/4 of a full-time job, up to 1/2, 3/4, full time, or not at all. A similar question was asked about non-agricultural farm activities, and about off-farm work.

We use only a small subset of the variables in this data set.

Among the time allocation variables, we only use a dummy for working/not working in each sector, and ignore the level of work. This is because the vast majority of those who work off the farm do it on a full-time basis. Also, we add together those who work off the farm and those who participate in non-agricultural activities on the farm, because the latter are a very small group. Other personal characteristics that we use are age, a dummy for being born in Israel, a dummy for being born in Asia or Africa (this relates to the respondent or his/her father), and three educational dummies: one for finishing high school, one for having more than high school education, and one for having some kind of agricultural education. The latter dummy variable is independent of the former two dummies, in the sense that finishing agricultural high school qualifies for both the first and the third dummies. Family-related variables include two location dummies (north and south), the number of children up to age 14, the number of adolescents up to age 21, and dummies for the number of adults in the household: group=1 is for husband and wife only, group=2 is for husband, wife, and on adult child, group=3 is for husband, wife, and two adult children (or an adult child and his/her spouse), and group=4 is for husband, wife, and more than two adult children or spouses. An adult child is a child older than 21 years.[3] Other types of households, including single-parent households, households with elderly parents, and other forms of extended families, were excluded from the current analysis. There were 1494 families left in the data set comprising of groups 1 to 4. Variables related to the farm operator include tenure, which is the time since the current owner operates the farm, and two dummies for method of receiving the farm, one for succession and one for purchase (the excluded group includes those who received the farm through the settlement agencies). Variables related to farm production include level of specialization, land, capital, and types of products. Level of specialization includes two dummy variables: one for specialized farms, in which one branch accounts for at least 90% of total value added,[4] and another for diversified farms, which include all other farms with positive production. The excluded group includes inactive farms. Land size includes all the land that is permanently held by the farm.[5] Capital stock is the value of buildings, machinery, equipment, and livestock.[6] We also include dummy variables indicating production in each of the following branches: flowers and nurseries, poultry, field crops and vegetables, and cattle.[7]

---

[3] It is important to note that the number of adult children includes only those who are currently residing on the farm, either as part of the parents' household or as a separate "succeeding" household, hence it has nothing to do with the number of children the parents ever had.

[4] Value added is "normative", meaning that it was calculated using weights attached to physical measures of production, such as size of crop areas and number of animals.

[5] This could be larger or smaller to the size of land that is actually operated. This variable could easily be thought of as exogenous or at least predetermined (Kimhi 1998).

[6] The use of capital stock as an explanatory variable could be problematic, due to possible endogeneity (Ahituv and Kimhi 2002).

[7] Although a farm could have production in more than one branch, we exclude the dummy for fruits in order to avoid collinearity with the specialization dummies through the inactive farms.

E. DESCRIPTIVE STATISTICS

Table 1 includes descriptive statistics of the personal characteristics of the different household members.[8] We can see that overall, some 60% of the operators and spouses work off the farm, while 70% of oldest children do so. However, the fraction of operators and spouses who work off the farm declines with the number of adult children in the household, while that of the oldest children rises.

This could very well be an age effect. As can be seen from the table, the ages of operators, spouses, and oldest children rise with the number of adult children, reflecting life-cycle effects. While the parents are already in the age range in which the tendency to work off the farm declines, the children are still in the age range in which the tendency rises with age. Opposite to the results of Kimhi (1996), we do not find that adult children substitute for their parents' farm labor. This could be due to several reasons. First, Kimhi (1996) treated all adult household members equally, while here we only deal with immediate descendents. Second, only 25% of oldest children work on the farm, reflecting the highly diminished role of agriculture in Moshavim in 1995 relative to 1981. Finally, these are only raw results; perhaps they will change after we control for observed differences among the groups of households.

The fractions of operators and spouses who were born in Israel declines sharply as the number of adult children increases, and so does the fraction of those of Asian or African origin. This is most likely to reflect the age pattern, as well. Among adult children, these variables do not vary systematically across the groups of households. Education does not vary systematically across the groups either. It is interesting to note that 70% of adult children are males. This could be due to two reasons. First, children's spouses are also included when present, are male spouses of female children are likely to be older. Second, there could be a higher tendency for male children to live on the family farm alongside their parents.

Table 2 includes descriptive statistics of the operator, family, and farm variables. We can first observe that the majority of groups 1 and 2 are found in the north and south of the country, while the majority of groups 3 and 4 are found in central locations. This can be explained by the residential value of living on the farm, which is much higher in central regions due to higher housing prices. The number of adolescents goes up from group 1 to group 2, while the number of younger children goes down. This reflects the fact that households with a single adult child are in a more advanced stage in the life cycle than households without an adult child, as we have learned from the age statistics.[9] The opposite is observed when moving from group 2 to group 3. Here the increase in the number of young children is perhaps due to the third generation. The same trend continues to group 4.

Average tenure increases monotonically from group 1 to group 4, again reflecting the stage in the life cycle. The fraction of operators who have succeeded their parents on the farm is highest in group 1, while the fraction of operators who have purchased their farms from previous owners declines monotonically from group 1 to group 4. This reflects the fact that most Moshavim have been established between the late 1940s and the early 1950s, so older operators are more likely to have obtained their farms directly from the settlement institutions.

---

[8] We do not show the statistics for adult children other than the oldest, since they will not be included in the estimated model, as will be explained below.

[9] On the other hand, group 1 can include elderly households in which children have grown up and left.

Table 1. Descriptive Statistics of Personal Variables

Variable	All	Group 1	Group 2	Group 3	Group 4
Male Operator or Spouse					
WORKS ON FARM	0.61	0.58	0.62	0.69	0.71
WORKS OFF FARM	0.60	0.66	0.60	0.48	0.45
AGE	53.05	49.04	57.37	58.97	60.06
BORN IN ISRAEL	0.43	0.56	0.28	0.29	0.15
ASIA/AFRICA ORIGIN	0.29	0.36	0.22	0.20	0.08
HIGH SCHOOL	0.60	0.59	0.62	0.66	0.54
HIGHER EDUCATION	0.14	0.12	0.15	0.11	0.20
AGRICULTURAL EDUCATION	0.07	0.07	0.08	0.06	0.07
Female Operator or Spouse					
WORKS ON FARM	0.29	0.26	0.37	0.33	0.29
WORKS OFF FARM	0.59	0.66	0.51	0.57	0.36
AGE	49.37	45.59	52.97	54.84	56.90
BORN IN ISRAEL	0.48	0.61	0.38	0.32	0.20
ASIA/AFRICA ORIGIN	0.34	0.38	0.32	0.30	0.18
HIGH SCHOOL	0.59	0.59	0.58	0.57	0.59
HIGHER EDUCATION	0.14	0.14	0.13	0.11	0.17
AGRICULTURAL EDUCATION	0.06	0.06	0.05	0.07	0.09
Oldest Adult Child or Spouse					
WORKS ON FARM	0.24		0.25	0.21	0.25
WORKS OFF FARM	0.74		0.69	0.75	0.81
MALE	0.70		0.63	0.72	0.80
AGE	29.31		26.48	30.00	33.01
BORN IN ISRAEL	0.93		0.94	0.91	0.92
ASIA/AFRICA ORIGIN	0.49		0.51	0.42	0.58
HIGH SCHOOL	0.55		0.49	0.58	0.62
HIGHER EDUCATION	0.11		0.13	0.12	0.06
AGRICULTURAL EDUCATION	0.06		0.05	0.06	0.08
OBSERVATIONS	1494	798	277	258	161

Note: off-farm work includes on-farm non-agricultural activities.

Highly specialized farms comprise 52% of group 4, compared to 34%-38% in the other groups. The fraction of diversified farms is lower in groups 1 and 4 than in groups 2 and 3. The fraction of inactive farms (the excluded category) decreases monotonically from group 1 to group 4. It could be that inactive farms are less attractive to adult children for succession purposes, and it could also be that farms without successors become inactive. The causality is not clear here. Among active farms, the statistics imply that groups 1 and 4 are the most specialized. We do not have a good explanation for this.

Table 2. Descriptive Statistics of Family, Operator, and Farm Variables

Variable	All	Group 1	Group 2	Group 3	Group 4
NORTH	0.24	0.25	0.30	0.18	0.15
SOUTH	0.26	0.28	0.28	0.18	0.25
ADOLESCENTS	0.76	0.77	0.89	0.71	0.57
CHILDREN	1.39	1.71	0.61	1.05	1.40
TENURE	24.83	20.41	29.00	31.01	34.06
SUCCEEDED	0.18	0.20	0.12	0.16	0.13
PURCHASED	0.31	0.35	0.30	0.24	0.20
SPECIALIZED	0.38	0.37	0.34	0.38	0.52
DIVERSIFIED	0.25	0.22	0.32	0.33	0.23
LAND	30.59	30.50	32.68	28.99	30.08
CAPITAL	102.10	89.61	102.66	128.18	133.48
FLOWERS	0.11	0.11	0.10	0.15	0.06
POULTRY	0.21	0.17	0.25	0.28	0.25
FIELD CROPS	0.21	0.20	0.21	0.21	0.31
CATTLE	0.03	0.03	0.04	0.03	0.07
OBSERVATIONS	1494	798	277	258	161

Landholdings are only slightly different across the groups, and not in a systematic way. This is due to the fact that landholdings were determined at time of establishment, which was long before household structure was determined. It also implies that land in itself is not valuable enough to affect household structure. On the other hand, capital stock increases monotonically from group 1 to group 4. As opposed to landholdings, capital stock was gradually accumulated over the years since establishment. The positive association between capital stock and number of adult children residing on the farm can be explained similarly to the explanation of the level of inactivity above, again without the ability to determine causality. Regarding the branch dummies, we observe that group 4 is different than the other groups. Field crops and cattle are more frequently found on farms in group 4. This could be associated, at least in part, with the higher agricultural activity on these farms, and in the case of cattle, also with the higher capital stock. Flowers are less frequently found among farms in group 4, while poultry is less frequently found among farms in group 1. We do not have a good explanation for this.

F. RESULTS

We first apply the quasi-maximum likelihood estimation of the off-farm participation equation for the whole sample, allowing for different intercepts for the different groups of households. The model includes 3 different equations: for the male operator or spouse, for the female operator or spouse, and for the oldest adult child. We tried to add an equation for a second adult child, but the model did not converge, probably because the number of observations with more than one adult child is not large enough. The estimation was performed using Gauss.[10] The procedure accounts for the different probability weights attached to different households, and for missing values. Most cases of missing values were in the work participation variables: many respondents did not answer these questions. While we believe that a large fraction of those thought the questions were not relevant for them because they did not work at all, there is no way to confirm this, and hence we exclude these individuals from the model by attaching zero weights. A few additional observations were excluded because of missing schooling data.[11]

The results are in table 3. We first observe that the three off-farm participation equations are positively correlated. This could be due to two reasons. First, it could be that unobserved household-specific components are important determinants of off-farm labor participation, even after controlling for all the observed attributes. Second, it could be easier for other household members to work off the farm when one member already does so, for various reasons.[12] The group dummies do not have significant coefficients in the males' equation, but they all have significantly negative coefficients in the females' equation, implying that the tendency of farm women to work off the farm is smaller when adult children are present. This is similar to the raw statistics in table 1. The tendency of adult children to work off the farm increases with the number of adult children, again showing similar pattern as in the raw statistics.

Age has a typical inverted U effect on participation probability. Females are more likely to work off the farm if they were born in Israel. This variable is considered as a proxy for country-specific human capital that affects potential earnings positively. Ethnic origin does not have a significant effect in any of the equations. Education has a positive effect on males' participation, as expected, but a negative effect on females' participation, contrary to intuition. Participation is lower in northern and southern regions, as in the raw statistics. Both north and south dummies are significant in the females' equation, while only the south dummy is significant in the males' equation. None of the regional dummies was significant in the children's equation. The numbers of children and adolescents did not have significant effects in any of the equations.

Tenure has a negative effect on males' off-farm labor participation and a positive effect on children's. Participation is higher in farms purchased from a previous owner. This hints to the existence of a phenomenon of purchasing farms for residential purposes. The level of farm specialization does not seem to have an effect on the off-farm participation decision, but the male operators of active farms are much less likely to work off the farm than the male

---

[10] The code is available from the corresponding author upon request.

[11] It should be emphasized that when data were missing for an individual we excluded that individual only, not the whole household.

[12] To test these two explanations, a panel data set with at least three periods is necessary (Ahituv and Kimhi 2002).

operators of inactive farms. This is a natural result stemming from the lower value of reservation wage on inactive farms. Landholdings have a significantly positive effect on the probability of working off the farm for both males and females, but not for adult children. This is a surprising result. If land was important as a factor of production, we would have expected the opposite. It is clear, then, that landholdings are not an important for farm production, and its significant effect is probably due to its correlation with unobserved factors.

Table 3. Quasi-Maximum Likelihood Estimation Results

Variable	Estimate	t-statistic	
CORRELATION MALE/FEMALE	0.3475	6.1370	**
CORRELATION MALE/CHILD	0.2744	4.6060	**
CORRELATION FEMALE/CHILD	0.4661	6.5540	**
Male Operator or Spouse			
CONSTANT	-0.2643	-0.1850	
GROUP 2	0.0526	0.3800	
GROUP 3	-0.2126	-1.3830	
GROUP 4	-0.1261	-0.6760	
AGE	0.1172	2.1250	*
AGE SQUARED	-0.0015	-2.8890	**
BORN IN ISRAEL	-0.0054	-0.0460	
ASIA/AFRICA ORIGIN	0.0183	0.1610	
HIGH SCHOOL	0.1710	1.4290	
HIGHER EDUCATION	0.3073	1.9830	*
AGRICULTURAL EDUCATION	-0.1657	-0.8220	
NORTH	-0.1404	-0.9640	
SOUTH	-0.4483	-3.0760	**
ADOLESCENTS	0.0816	1.3850	
CHILDREN	-0.0340	-0.9160	
TENURE	-0.0093	-2.1920	*
SUCCEEDED	-0.0657	-0.4110	
PURCHASED	0.2618	2.0110	*
SPECIALIZED	-0.8115	-5.0100	**
DIVERSIFIED	-0.8003	-4.1790	**
LAND	0.0047	1.6670	*
CAPITAL	-0.0019	-5.1240	**
FLOWERS	-0.4813	-3.3520	**
POULTRY	-0.2354	-1.6790	*
FIELD CROPS	-0.6146	-4.6010	**
CATTLE	-0.2793	-1.2220	
% correct predictions			
Participants	89.47		
Non- participants	60.83		

Table 3. (Continued)

Variable	Estimate	t-statistic	
Female Operator or Spouse			
CONSTANT	-4.9879	-4.0090	**
GROUP 2	-0.5163	-3.4080	**
GROUP 3	-0.3504	-2.2640	*
GROUP 4	-0.6403	-3.1760	**
AGE	0.2934	5.3230	**
AGE SQUARED	-0.0034	-5.7810	**
BORN IN ISRAEL	0.1925	1.7980	*
ASIA/AFRICA ORIGIN	-0.0026	-0.0240	
HIGH SCHOOL	-0.2010	-1.6970	*
HIGHER EDUCATION	-0.2376	-1.4890	
AGRICULTURAL EDUCATION	0.1318	0.6860	
NORTH	-0.3222	-2.2860	*
SOUTH	-0.4316	-3.0360	**
ADOLESCENTS	-0.0796	-1.2900	
CHILDREN	-0.0405	-1.0350	
TENURE	-0.0021	-0.4650	
SUCCEEDED	-0.0503	-0.3370	
PURCHASED	0.1187	0.9010	
SPECIALIZED	-0.1747	-1.1760	
DIVERSIFIED	0.0123	0.0680	
LAND	0.0149	5.3030	**
CAPITAL	-0.0011	-3.5960	**
FLOWERS	-0.3238	-2.5510	**
POULTRY	-0.3123	-2.1260	*
FIELD CROPS	-0.3302	-2.5760	**
CATTLE	-0.3000	-1.2490	
% correct predictions			
Participants	90.24		
Non- participants	51.68		
Oldest Adult Child or Spouse			
CONSTANT	-2.5971	-1 4570	
GROUP 3	0.2055	1.1570	
GROUP 4	0.4542	2.0930	*
MALE	-0.2111	-1.2310	
AGE	0.1800	1.6790	*
AGE SQUARED	-0.0027	-1.6920	*
BORN IN ISRAEL	0.1902	0.7140	
ASIA/AFRICA ORIGIN	0.1600	0.9710	
HIGH SCHOOL	-0.1470	-0.8930	
HIGHER EDUCATION	-0.2152	-0.9510	
AGRICULTURAL EDUCATION	-0.1248	-0.4850	
NORTH	-0.2946	-1.5010	

Table 3. (Continued)

Variable	Estimate	t-statistic	
SOUTH	-0.1844	-0.8960	
ADOLESCENTS	0.1175	1.2160	
CHILDREN	-0.0067	-0.1110	
TENURE	0.0141	1.7570	*
SUCCEEDED	0.2027	0.8120	
PURCHASED	0.5348	2.7640	**
SPECIALIZED	-0.4296	-1.7370	*
DIVERSIFIED	-0.3685	-1.2860	
LAND	-0.0011	-0.2680	
CAPITAL	-0.0023	-5.7930	**
FLOWERS	-0.0323	-0.1750	
POULTRY	-0.0605	-0.3140	
FIELD CROPS	-0.0390	-0.2190	
CATTLE	0.2397	0.7320	
% correct predictions			
Participants	95.45		
Non- participants	19.58		

* coefficient significant at 5%.
** coefficient significant at 1%.

Capital stock, on the other hand, has a significantly negative effect on the off-farm participation probabilities of all household members, as expected. Males' participation was lowest in the presence of field crops or vegetables, the second lowest in flower farms, and the third – in poultry farms. For females, all three branches have similar negative effects on participation. None of the branch dummies was significant in the children's equation, and the cattle dummy was not significant in any of the equations.

Next, we want to examine the importance of the constraint imposed on the previous model, that the participation equations in the different groups of households are only different in their intercepts. For this, we estimate the model separately in each of the four groups. In table 4 we report the results for the first three groups. The model of group 1 includes only two equations, so is in fact a bivariate probit model.

The model of group 4 did not converge, probably due to the relatively small number of observations. A quick look at the table reveals that the coefficient estimates vary considerably across the groups of households. Interestingly, the correlation coefficients between the child's equation on one hand and the parents' equations on the other hand are not statistically significant.

We conclude that the fact that the correlation coefficients turned out significant in table 3 is a result of the assumption of equal probit coefficients across the groups. Hence, if we adopt the results of table 4, we can conclude that the off-farm participation decisions of the oldest adult children are independent of the participation decisions of the parents. In this case, we can use the child's participation decision as a valid explanatory variable in the parents' participation equations.

The results of this attempt are reported in table 5. All models are now of the bivariate probit type. Except for the females' equation in group 3, none of the coefficients of children's off-farm work participation is statistically significant.[13]

Table 4. Off-Farm Participation Results by Groups of Households

Variable	Group 1 Estimate	t-stat.		Group 2 Estimate	t-stat.		Group 3 Estimate	t-stat.	
CORR. MAL/FEM	0.3787	4.8610	**	0.4116	3.2980	**	0.2715	1.8760	*
CORR. MAL/CHI				0.1217	0.8980		0.0808	0.5150	
CORR. FEM/CHI				0.1257	0.9770		0.3040	1.5920	
Male Operator or Spouse									
CONSTANT	0.2637	0.1730		1.2643	0.2300		-10.967	-2.0340	*
AGE	0.0890	1.4760		0.0399	0.2110		0.5928	3.1980	**
AGE SQUARED	-0.0012	-2.0490	*	-0.0008	-0.5420		-0.0060	-3.6880	**
BORN IN ISRAEL	0.0131	0.0860		-0.0890	-0.3370		-0.6654	-2.1240	*
ASIA/AFRICA ORIGIN	0.0242	0.1740		-0.0977	-0.3360		0.5840	1.5860	
HIGH SCHOOL	0.0526	0.3450		0.2667	0.9340		0.3820	1.2360	
HIGHER EDUCATION	0.3477	1.5770		0.0735	0.2040		0.0073	0.0170	
AGRIC. EDUCATION	-0.0228	-0.0770		0.2922	0.7100		-0.7894	-1.6490	*
NORTH	-0.2046	-1.0050		-0.3073	-1.0070		-0.0516	-0.1370	
SOUTH	-0.3793	-1.8790	*	-1.0576	-3.3950	**	-0.2699	-0.7120	
ADOLESCENTS	0.1061	1.3270		0.3537	2.8510	**	-0.2176	-1.3220	
CHILDREN	-0.0283	-0.5420		-0.0367	-0.3200		0.0735	0.7120	
TENURE	-0.0096	-1.8780	*	0.0054	0.5720		-0.0463	-2.3610	**
SUCCEEDED	-0.2016	-0.9360		-0.0550	-0.1330		0.1505	0.3550	
PURCHASED	0.2088	1.2080		0.3184	1.1320		-0.1702	-0.4680	
SPECIALIZED	-0.7193	-3.3790	**	-1.0366	-2.7420	**	-1.4563	-3.1170	**
DIVERSIFIED	-0.8913	-3.6580	**	-0.8004	-1.7770	*	-0.8066	-1.5380	
LAND	0.0049	1.2190		0.0251	3.2060	**	-0.0071	-0.8650	
CAPITAL	-0.0022	-5.0040	**	-0.0022	-3.2610	**	-0.0010	1.0900	
FLOWERS	-0.4879	-2.6990	**	-0.9572	-2.9740	**	-0.1605	-0.4680	
POULTRY	-0.0913	-0.4630		-0.4815	-1.5200		-0.4959	-1.4670	
FIELD CROPS	-0.6114	-3.4420	**	-1.4397	-4.6870	**	-0.7593	-2.1250	*
CATTLE	-0.0030	-0.0090		0.2338	0.4850		-0.7982	-1.2770	

---

[13] In groups 3 and 4, the participation of either the oldest or the second-oldest child was taken into account.

Table 4. (Continued)

Variable	Group 1 Estimate	t-stat.		Group 2 Estimate	t-stat.		Group 3 Estimate	t-stat.	
Female Operator or Spouse									
CONSTANT	-4.2573	-2.9670	**	-19.506	-2.8810	**	-23.847	-2.9860	**
AGE	0.2411	3.6600	**	0.8343	3.2520	**	1.0919	3.6240	**
AGE SQUARED	-0.0028	-3.8670	**	-0.0085	-3.5150	**	-0.0112	-3.9190	**
BORN IN ISRAEL	0.2421	1.6780	*	-0.0073	-0.0250		0.2294	0.7520	
ASIA/AFRICA ORIGIN	-0.0806	-0.5790		-0.1378	-0.5210		0.4927	1.6350	
HIGH SCHOOL	-0.1350	-0.8310		-0.1838	-0.6560		-0.6777	-2.1580	*
HIGHER EDUCATION	-0.3318	-1.5360		0.3145	0.7980		-1.1216	-2.5570	**
AGRIC. EDUCATION	0.5740	2.2200	*	0.1039	0.1940		-0.9081	-1.5240	
NORTH	-0.2360	-1.2230		-0.1383	-0.4120		-1.2292	-3.2110	**
SOUTH	-0.2165	-1.1440		-0.9487	-2.7140	**	-1.3322	-3.7720	**
ADOLESCENTS	0.0369	0.4480		-0.0346	-0.2180		-0.6071	-2.7940	**
CHILDREN	-0.0611	-1.1290		0.1885	1.4620		0.2730	2.2020	*
TENURE	-0.0061	-1.0170		0.0066	0.6430		-0.0493	-2.4070	**
SUCCEEDED	0.1037	0.5170		-0.7847	-2.0540	*	-0.6436	-1.6400	
PURCHASED	0.2142	1.2490		-0.3239	-1.0280		-0.3084	-0.9490	
SPECIALIZED	-0.2824	-1.4650		-0.2685	-0.7010		0.5682	1.2890	
DIVERSIFIED	0.1094	0.4450		-0.2036	-0.4170		0.2668	0.5560	
LAND	0.0153	3.6940	**	0.0148	2.3600	**	0.0362	3.8620	**
CAPITAL	-0.0011	-2.7920	**	-0.0007	-0.9310		-0.0020	-2.3380	**
FLOWERS	-0.2283	-1.3300		-0.7388	-2.4020	**	-0.8845	-2.5760	**
POULTRY	-0.1583	-0.7910		-0.9608	-2.5260	**	-0.1543	-0.3740	
FIELD CROPS	-0.2823	-1.6470	*	-0.8547	-2.5950	**	-0.7619	-1.8670	*
CATTLE	-0.4464	-1.2430		1.3127	2.3880	**	-1.3164	-1.3330	
Oldest Adult Child or Spouse									
CONSTANT				-6.3710	-2.1740	*	-2.3479	-0.7600	
MALE				-0.4488	-1.6100		-0.1485	-0.5360	
AGE				0.3987	2.1710	*	0.1771	0.9700	
AGE SQUARED				-0.0059	-2.0730	*	-0.0028	-1.0760	
BORN IN ISRAEL				0.7140	1.2950		-0.1806	-0.4490	
ASIA/AFRICA ORIGIN				0.3453	1.0710		0.1134	0.4360	
HIGH SCHOOL				0.2024	0.7620		-0.5173	-1.8140	*
HIGHER EDUCATION				-0.2520	-0.6650		-0.8590	-2.2340	*
AGRIC. EDUCATION				-0.8648	-1.6940	*	-0.2684	-0.6230	

Table 4. (Continued)

Variable	Group 1		Group 2			Group 3		
	Estimate	t-stat.	Estimate	t-stat.		Estimate	t-stat.	
NORTH			-0.1769	-0.5380		-0.5750	-1.6290	
SOUTH			-0.1016	-0.2670		-0.5887	-1.6810	*
ADOLESCENTS			0.1568	1.0040		0.1976	1.1550	
CHILDREN			-0.1011	-0.8370		-0.0801	-0.7030	
TENURE			0.0028	0.2430		0.0199	1.5640	
SUCCEEDED			-0.1745	-0.3990		0.3359	0.8830	
PURCHASED			0.0031	0.0090		1.0596	3.0050	**
SPECIALIZED			-0.7691	-1.9730	*	0.1403	0.3480	
DIVERSIFIED			-0.4867	-1.0150		0.0644	0.1410	
LAND			-0.0018	-0.2370		0.0162	2.0770	*
CAPITAL			-0.0018	-2.8610	**	-0.0030	-4.0740	**
FLOWERS			-0.2859	-0.9140		0.0563	0.1790	
POULTRY			-0.3893	-1.0390		0.2501	0.7760	
FIELD CROPS			0.2510	0.7740		-0.4835	-1.6150	
CATTLE			0.2783	0.4500		-0.1114	-0.2010	
SPECIALIZED			-0.2685	-0.7010		0.5682	1.2890	

* coefficient significant at 5%.
** coefficient significant at 1%.

We therefore conclude that the demographic composition of the household has an effect on the off-farm labor participation decisions of its members, but once household composition is controlled for, the participation decisions of adult children do not affect the participation decisions of their parents.

Table 6 compares the performance of the different models by looking at the predictions of the fraction of participants in the off-farm labor market. The table includes actual frequencies and predicted frequencies. The predicted frequencies include the three different models.

"Joint estimation" is the model with equal coefficients for the different groups of households except for the intercepts.

"Separate estimation" is the model with all the coefficients different. The last model (w/kids' work) is the one with children's participation status considered exogenous.

For each of the first two models, we also calculate the frequencies at the sample means of the explanatory variables, where the means are taken over all the groups of households. This last calculation allows us to examine the effect of the group alone, without the effects of the different variable means across groups.

For both males and females, the predicted frequencies are higher than the actual frequencies for all groups of households, but they follow a similar pattern, namely a general decline with the number of adult children (except for a rise from group 2 to group 3 among females, which is reproduced by the predicted frequencies in the joint estimation but not in the separate estimation). This is true for the joint estimation as well as the separate estimation, although the decline is somewhat more moderate in the latter. When controlling for children's off-farm work status, the only qualitative change is that the males' predicted frequency rises slightly from group 3 to group 4.

Table 5. Bivariate Probit Participation Results with Child's Participation Given

Variable	Group 1 Estimate	t-stat.		Group 2 Estimate	t-stat.		Group 3 Estimate	t-stat.	
CORR. MAL/FEM	0.4579	3.2610	**	0.3188	1.7790	*	0.1639	0.8030	
Male Operator or Spouse									
CONSTANT	0.7783	0.1430		-10.873	-2.0750	*	6.2525	0.8730	
AGE	0.0549	0.2930		0.5925	3.3490	**	-0.0344	-0.1550	
AGE SQUARED	-0.0009	-0.6090		-0.0060	-3.8860	**	-0.0010	-0.5540	
BORN IN ISRAEL	-0.1163	-0.4370		-0.6899	-2.2190	*	2.3234	4.1640	**
ASIA/AFRICA ORIGIN	-0.1853	-0.6530		0.6390	1.7010	*	0.2107	0.3480	
HIGH SCHOOL	0.2044	0.7430		0.4270	1.3650		0.3234	0.6630	
HIGHER EDUCATION	0.0843	0.2500		0.1092	0.2650		1.0831	1.5480	
AGRIC. EDUCATION	0.2196	0.5520		-0.7246	-1.5990		-1.0221	-1.1350	
NORTH	-0.2753	-0.9110		-0.1046	-0.2640		0.0292	0.0550	
SOUTH	-1.0995	-3.4870	**	-0.2954	-0.7760		-0.0033	-0.0070	
ADOLESCENTS	0.3550	2.8010	**	-0.2485	-1.5320		-0.0040	-0.0160	
CHILDREN	-0.0345	-0.3040		0.0740	0.7250		0.1177	1.1570	
TENURE	0.0039	0.4150		-0.0466	-2.3990	**	0.0043	0.2640	
SUCCEEDED	-0.0024	-0.0060		0.1335	0.3260		-0.6914	-1.1030	
PURCHASED	0.3242	1.1340		-0.1861	-0.5170		0.8684	1.8650	*
SPECIALIZED	-1.0416	-2.8490	**	-1.5051	-3.2360	**	-0.3672	-0.7390	
DIVERSIFIED	-0.7688	-1.7560	*	-0.8695	-1.6750	*	-0.1917	-0.3000	
LAND	0.0250	3.1460	**	-0.0082	-0.9740		-0.0269	-2.1410	*
CAPITAL	-0.0022	-3.1270	**	-0.0009	-1.0210		-0.0003	-0.3040	
FLOWERS	-0.9339	-2.9690	**	-0.1557	-0.4540		-1.7019	-3.0200	**
POULTRY	-0.4970	-1.6420		-0.4812	-1.4460		-0.8492	-1.4360	
FIELD CROPS	-1.4044	-4.4750	**	-0.7308	-2.0450	*	-1.6654	-3.4880	**
CATTLE	0.1824	0.3820		-0.8958	-1.4070		-1.6159	-2.2930	*
CHILD WORKS OFF	0.1230	0.5290		-0.0456	-0.1660		0.4271	1.0170	
% correct predictions									
Participants	90.19			88.95			89.51		
Non- participants	56.32			69.81			83.72		

Table 5. (Continued)

Variable	Group 1 Estimate	t-stat.		Group 2 Estimate	t-stat.		Group 3 Estimate	t-stat.	
Female Operator or Spouse									
CONSTANT	-19.573	-3.1300	**	-23.702	-3.0070	**	-51.082	-5.1520	**
AGE	0.8284	3.5040	**	1.0882	3.6490	**	1.9894	5.7630	**
AGE SQUARED	-0.0083	-3.7640	**	-0.0112	-3.9560	**	-0.0190	-6.1530	**
BORN IN ISRAEL	-0.0048	-0.0170		0.1840	0.5940		0.9558	2.1360	*
ASIA/AFRICA ORIGIN	-0.1399	-0.5330		0.4635	1.5380		0.4033	0.8520	
HIGH SCHOOL	-0.2498	-0.9000		-0.6908	-2.1360	*	-0.4149	-0.7720	
HIGHER EDUCATION	0.3502	0.9370		-1.1760	-2.6770	**	-0.9681	-1.3690	
AGRIC. EDUCATION	0.0691	0.1330		-0.9971	-1.6250		-0.5735	-0.9590	
NORTH	-0.0891	-0.2690		-1.1997	-3.0490	**	-0.5981	-0.8610	
SOUTH	-0.8875	-2.5650	**	-1.2942	-3.5910	**	-0.5206	-1.0840	
ADOLESCENTS	-0.0157	-0.1000		-0.6830	-2.9910	**	-0.0659	-0.3030	
CHILDREN	0.2014	1.5990		0.2942	2.3190	*	-0.1791	-1.1370	
TENURE	0.0062	0.6210		-0.0554	-2.5580	**	0.0015	0.0850	
SUCCEEDED	-0.7516	-1.9370	*	-0.7002	-1.7510	*	0.1694	0.2470	
PURCHASED	-0.2603	-0.8270		-0.3626	-1.0930		0.0076	0.0110	
SPECIALIZED	-0.2994	-0.7750		0.4914	1.0850		-0.4537	-0.7680	
DIVERSIFIED	-0.2534	-0.5290		0.1784	0.3590		-0.2861	-0.3820	
LAND	0.0143	2.2960	*	0.0353	3.7010	**	0.0251	2.2440	*
CAPITAL	-0.0008	-1.1430		-0.0017	-2.0080	*	-0.0030	-2.0510	*
FLOWERS	-0.6720	-2.2070	*	-0.9360	-2.7260	**	-0.4428	-0.7720	
POULTRY	-0.8706	-2.3300	**	-0.1013	-0.2410		-0.5183	-0.8490	
FIELD CROPS	-0.7643	-2.3740	**	-0.7257	-1.7200	*	-0.2627	-0.4720	
CATTLE	1.3165	2.4360	**	-1.4738	-1.5050		-1.5273	-1.6310	
CHILD WORKS OFF	-0.0371	-0.1520		0.4753	1.7410	*	-0.0523	-0.0900	
% correct predictions									
Participants	94.05			82.62			86.86		
Non- participants	40.68			65.35			78.48		

* coefficient significant at 5%.
** coefficient significant at 1%.

Table 6. Comparing Off-Farm Participation Frequencies

Model	Group of Households				
	1	2	3	4	All
Males					
Actual frequency	0.623	0.553	0.442	0.409	0.562
Joint estimation					
Predicted	0.759	0.657	0.512	0.467	0.674
At the means	0.521	0.542	0.436	0.471	0.504
Separate estimation					
Predicted	0.727	0.625	0.599	0.475	
At the means	0.482	0.466	0.496	0.854	
Predicted w/kids' work		0.627	0.487	0.519	
Females					
Actual frequency	0.555	0.412	0.460	0.277	0.489
Joint estimation					
Predicted	0.820	0.542	0.598	0.303	0.688
At the means	0.621	0.418	0.483	0.370	0.533
Separate estimation					
Predicted	0.786	0.555	0.518	0.371	
At the means	0.553	0.241	0.274	0.008	
Predicted w/kids' work		0.544	0.516	0.360	
Children					
Actual frequency		0.546	0.621	0.742	0.621
Joint estimation					
Predicted		0.850	0.918	0.959	0.901
At the means		0.620	0.700	0.776	0.687
Separate estimation					
Predicted		0.800	0.757		
At the means		0.624	0.645		

Note: the actual frequencies are somewhat different from those reported in table 1 because of the different treatment of missing values.

When using the sample means of the explanatory variables to generate predicted frequencies, the results change remarkably for males, but not for females. Specifically, the males' predicted participation frequency at the means does not change much from group 1 to group 2, and rises from group 3 to group 4.[14] This means that much of the decline of males' off-farm work participation with the number of adult children is due to the changes in explanatory variables rather than to the genuine effect of the adult children. This conclusion goes in line with the lack of statistically significant correlation between the males' and children's participation equations in the separate estimation.

The children's predicted participation frequencies rise from group 2 to group 4 in the joint estimation, similar to the actual frequencies, but decline from group 2 to group 3 in the separate estimation. When calculated at the sample means, the predicted frequencies in the joint estimation have a similar pattern, but they show a moderate rise from group 2 to group 3 in the separate estimation.

CONCLUSION

This paper takes a deeper look at the phenomenon observed in previous research, that the off-farm labor participation behavior of farm operators and their spouses depends on the demographic composition of the household. Using data from a 1995 family farm survey, we estimate jointly the off-farm participation equations of the farm operator, his or her spouse, and their eldest adult child. We find that the number of adult children has a statistically significant negative effect on the off-farm participation of females, but most of the difference seems to be between females with no adult children and females with one or more adult children. Males' participation decisions did not seem to be affected by the number of adult children. When allowing all the coefficients of the participation equations to vary with the number of adult children, we found that the participation equations of the children were not significantly correlated with the participation equations of their parents. The children's work status did not come out with a statistically significant coefficient when included among the explanatory variables.

An analysis of the predicted frequencies of off-farm labor participation revealed that for males, most of the variation among the groups of households defined by the number of adult children is due to observed differences across the groups, and not to genuine effects of the number of adult children or their work status. For females, the negative dependence of off-farm participation on the number of adult children holds even after controlling for variations in the explanatory variables. These conclusions contradict the results of previous research, but this is subject to several qualifications. First, previous research looked at the effects of the number of all adults in the household, not only children, and included different forms of households, other than the nuclear households considered here. Second, the previous research looked at the joint farm and off-farm labor participation decisions, while here we only examined off-farm participation. Finally, it could be that the effects of household composition changed directions and importance from 1981 to 1995. While all these qualifications could and will be studied in future research, the last one is perhaps the most interesting and deserves more attention.

---

[14] Note that the predicted frequencies from the separate estimation in group 4 at the means are way off the mark for both males and females, hence we will disregard group 4 in the separate estimation. Recall that the quasi-maximum likelihood separate estimation did not converge when including the children's equation, probably

REFERENCES

Ahituv, A., and Kimhi, A. (2002). Off-Farm Work and Capital Accumulation Decisions of Farmers Over the Life-Cycle: The Role of Heterogeneity and State Dependence. *Journal of Development Economics, Vol. 68*, 329-53.

Blanc, M., and Perrier-Cornet, P. (1993). Farm Transfer and Farm Entry in the EC. *Sociologia Ruralis, Vol. 33*, 319-35.

Buttel, F.H., and Gillespie, G.W. (1984). The Sexual Division of Farm Household Labor: An Exploratory Study of the Structure of On-Farm and Off-Farm Labor Allocation among Farm Men and Women. *Rural Sociology, Vol.49*, 183-209.

Huffman, W.E. (1991). Agricultural Household Models: Survey and Critique. In Hallberg, M.C., Findeis, J.L., and Lass, D.A. (Eds.), *Multiple Job-holding among Farm Families* (pp. 79-111). Ames, Iowa: Iowa State University Press.

Huffman, W.E., and Lange, M.D. (1989). Off-Farm Work Decisions of Husbands and Wives: Joint Decision Making. *Review of Economics and Statistics* LXXXI, 471-80.

Kimhi, A. (1994). Quasi Maximum Likelihood Estimation of Multivariate Probit Models: Farm Couples' Labor Participation. *American Journal of Agricultural Economics, Vol.76*, 828-835.

Kimhi, A. (1995). Differential Human Capital Investments and the Choice of Successor in Family Farms. *American Journal of Agricultural Economics, Vol. 77*, 719-724.

Kimhi, A. (1996). Demographic Composition of Farm Households and its Effect on Time Allocation. *Journal of Population Economics, Vol. 9*, 429-439.

Kimhi, A. (1998). Institutional Environment, Ideological Commitment, and Farmers' Time Allocation: the Case of Israeli Moshavim. *Economic Development and Cultural Change , Vol. 47*, 27-44.

Kimhi, A. (2004). Family Composition and Off-Farm Participation Decisions in Israeli Farm Households. *American Journal of Agricultural Economics, Vol. 86*, 502-512.

Kimhi, A., Jae Lee, M. (1996). Joint Farm and Off-Farm Work Decisions of Farm Couples: Estimating Structural Simultaneous Equations with Ordered Categorical Dependent Variables. *American Journal of Agricultural Economics, Vol.78*, 687-698.

Lass, D.A., and Gempesaw, C.M. (1992). The Supply of Off-Farm Labor: A Random Coefficients Approach. *American Journal of Agricultural Economics, Vol.74*, 400-11.

Shishko, R., and Rostker, B. (1976). The Economics of Multiple Job Holding. *American Economic Review, Vol. 66 *, 298-308.

State of Israel, Central Bureau of Statistics. (1998). *Agricultural Survey 1995*, Publication No. 1081, Jerusalem.

Sumner, D.A. (1982). The Off-Farm Labor Supply of Farmers. *American Journal of Agricultural Economics, Vol.64*, 499-509.

---

due to the relatively small number of observations. It is likely, then, that the maximum likelihood estimates of the bivariate probit estimation of males and females that did converge are not of very high quality.

Tokle, J.G., and Huffman, W.E. (1991). Local Economic Conditions and Wage Labor Decisions of Farm and Rural Nonfarm Couples. *American Journal of Agricultural Economics, Vol. 73*, 652-70.

In: The Economics of Natural and Human Resources...   ISBN 978-1-60741-029-4
Editor: Ayal Kimhi and Israel Finkelshtain   © 2009 Nova Science Publishers, Inc.

Chapter 16

FARM HOUSEHOLD INCOME AND ON- AND OFF-FARM DIVERSIFICATION

Christoph Weiss and Kevin T. McNamara[*]

ABSTRACT

The paper analyzes the relationship between off-farm labor allocation and on-farm enterprise diversification as farm household income stabilization strategies with census data from the federal state of Upper Austria. The results suggest that both on-farm diversification and off-farm labor allocation are related to farm and household characteristics. Larger farms tend to be more diversified. Younger farmers are more likely to work off-farm. Larger farm households tend to allocate more labor to off-farm income activities.

A. INTRODUCTION

Farming is a risky business. Farm operators face a number of uncertain factors, including both weather and market conditions, that affect household income risk. The effect of recent policy changes (in particular the liberalization and globalization of agricultural markets) on the further risk associated with farming is open to question. Historically, government market intervention has sheltered domestic markets from international prices (Hazell, Jaramillo, and Williamson). If policy changes so that domestic prices actually track international price signals, farmers, as well as those involved in agriculture policy formulation, will be forced to consider the implications of larger fluctuations in commodity prices on income risk.[1]

---

[*] Kevin T. McNamara is professor, Department of Agricultural Economics, Purdue University, West Lafayette, IN. Christoph Weiss is professor, Department of Economics, Vienna University of Economics and B.A., Vienna, Austria. This chapter is reprinted with permission from the *Journal of Agricultural and Applied Economics*, where it was originally published (Vol. 37, No. 1, April 2005, pp. 37-48).

[1] Recent studies on the effects of agricultural market liberalisation on the domestic market prices instability include Thompson, Herrmann, and Gohout; and Chavas and Kim. Fraser examined the implications for producer compensation in the Agenda 2000 Cereal Reforms.

On-farm enterprise diversification can be an efficient risk management mechanism by stabilizing expected returns in an uncertain environment. Although the importance of this strategy has long been recognized (Heady), few studies have examined the relationship between farm enterprise diversification and farm household income variability using micro-data (White and Irwin; Pope and Prescott; Sun, Jinkins, and El-Osta; Purdy, Langemeier, and Featherstone; Mishra and El-Osta).

Changes in risk associated with specific activities causes fundamental structural changes in an economy. If producers are risk averse and perceive the variance of income to be greater in one enterprise than another, they will allocate less time to the higher risk enterprise. The reallocation of labor from agricultural to non-agricultural income activities has been an important farm household income management strategy of the post war prosperity in most industrialized countries. Following Huffman's seminal work, the last two centuries have seen considerable empirical research on farm household labor allocation. However, as Mishra and Goodwin stressed, limited attention has been devoted to assessing how farm enterprise risk influences farm's household labor allocation across farm enterprises and to off-farm earnings. Referring to a U.S. farmer attitudes survey, Mishra and Goodwin point out that farmers reported the primary reason they worked off-farm was to stabilize household income given the variability of their farm income. Analysis of Kansas farmers' off-farm labor supply decisions found a positive relationship between the coefficient of variation for farm income and off-farm work (Mishra and Goodwin). That is, the greater the variability of farm income, the higher farmers' off-farm labor participation.

This paper combines two strands of literature by analyzing the interrelationship between on-farm enterprise diversification and off-farm labor allocation as farm household income stabilization strategies, both theoretically and empirically.[2] A model was developed to examine the relationship between on-farm enterprise diversification and off-farm labor allocation and farm household income stabilization strategies. Then the data and econometric results are presented and discussed. The paper concludes with a discussion of the conclusions and implications.

B. THEORY

Theoretical models offer different arguments about farm household on-farm and off-farm diversification. These arguments can be divided into two groups: efficiency gains and risk reduction.[3] The standard theoretical framework for modelling efficiency issues related to off-farm diversification decisions, the farm household model, emphasizes the role of technologies and costs by focusing on the marginal productivity of labor both on and off the farm. The marginal income of farm labor declines with the amount of time spent working on the farm. If farm income falls below the farm households' reservation wage, household members will

---

[2] Different definitions of farm "diversification" are used in the literature. For an extensive discussion see Evans and Ilbery.

[3] In addition to these arguments, the industrial organization literature also mentions market power arguments, as well as the principal-agent relationship between corporate managers and shareholders (Montgomery). Given that these arguments have limited relevance for the agricultural sector, they were not discussed.

allocate time to off-farm labor if they can.[4] With respect to on-farm diversification, economies of scale and scope of the agricultural enterprise mix are important. If it is less costly to produce goods jointly instead of separately, the cost function exhibits "economies of scope." Although there is general acceptance of the synergy concept,[5] the sources of economies of scope are not easy to identify. Fernandez-Cornejo et al. explored causes of scope economies for German farms in detail.

Income risk arguments for non-farm enterprise diversification stress the importance of risk associated with agricultural production as the key motivation. Farm households (farm firms) benefit from diversification strategies that generate a more stable income stream. This argument, however, is not convincing for manufacturers. Jovanovic argued that, without bankruptcy risk and liquidity constraints, firms need not diversify to avoid risk – shareholders should.[6] And, there is ample evidence that shareholders typically diversify their portfolios. In the agricultural sector, however, the argument for enterprise diversification has more appeal. The role of the owner and the manager coincide in family farms (the "manager" receives all the rewards of his efforts). Farm operators, therefore, might have less incentive to diversify their investment portfolio off the farm. While research suggests the off-farm investment of U.S. farmers has increased in recent years (Mishra et al.), farm operators have a strong incentive to spread personal risks associated with farm investment through diversification of farm production enterprises.

The effects of price risk on farm operators' diversification decisions on- and off-farm can best be studied in an expected value-variance (EV) approach.[7] Suppose a farm family allocates total available labor, L, across n different farm enterprises (l_i, with $i = 1, ..., n$) and off-farm work l_0: $L = \sum_{i=1}^{n} l_i + l_0$. Farm output is produced according to the following production function $q_i = l_i^\alpha$, which, for simplicity is assumed to be identical for all farm products.[8] The only form of risk considered here are price fluctuations in the agricultural product market. For simplicity, assume the expected prices of all farm products p_i and the variances and covariances of p_i to be identical ($p_i = p$, and $\sigma_{ii} = \sigma_k^2$, $\forall\, i = 1,...,n$ and $\sigma_{ij} = \rho\sigma_k^2$, $\forall\, i \neq j = 1,...,n$; with $-1 \leq \rho \leq 1$). Expected income can be written as:

$$E(y) = \sum_{i=1}^{n} p_i l_i^\alpha + wl_0 - cn = np\left(\frac{L - l_0}{n}\right)^\alpha + wl_0 - cn , \qquad (1)$$

---

[4] A survey of this literature is available in Lass, Findeis, and Hallberg.

[5] Baumol formalized this concept in an extensive treatise.

[6] Jovanovic reviewed arguments as well as the available empirical evidence.

[7] The following model draws heavily on Robison and Barry. The EV approach has had widespread use in economic analysis. It can be derived from expected utility maximization (a) if an individual's utility function is assumed quadratic, reflecting preferences for expected values and variances only, or (b) if the distribution of returns are fully characterised by expected values and variances. For a detailed discussion see Robison and Barry.

[8] This (restrictive) assumption allows us to represent the degree of diversification with a single variable, the number of different farm enterprises (n). Robison and Barry point to the problems of deriving clear predictions when relaxing this assumption by allowing different production technologies.

where w is the wage rate in the off-farm labor market. In Equation (1), the acquisition of each farming enterprise involves a fixed fee, c, that represents the cost of learning to manage or supervise the enterprise.[9] The certainty equivalent income is:[10]

$$y_{CE} = E(y) - \frac{\lambda}{2}\sigma^2(y) = np\left(\frac{L-l_0}{n}\right)^\alpha + wl_0 - cn - \frac{\lambda}{2}(L-l_0)^2\left[\frac{1+(n-1)\rho}{n}\right]\sigma_k^2, \quad (2)$$

where $\lambda > 0$ represents the degree of risk aversion.

What are the optimal level of farm diversification (the number of farm enterprises, n) and the optimal time spent on off-farm work (l_0)? Maximizing y_{CE} with respect to l_0 and n gives:

$$\frac{\partial y_{CE}}{\partial l_0} = -\alpha\left(\frac{L-l_0}{n}\right)^{\alpha-1}p + w + \frac{\lambda(L-l_0)[1+(n-1)\rho]\sigma_k^2}{n} = 0, \quad (3)$$

$$\frac{\partial y_{CE}}{\partial n} = (1-\alpha)\left(\frac{L-l_0}{n}\right)^\alpha p - c + \frac{\lambda(L-l_0)^2(1-\rho)\sigma_k^2}{2n^2} = 0, \quad (4)$$

The optimal n and l_0 is easy to compute for the simple case of a linear farm production function $(\alpha = 1)$. Here we find $l_0^* = \frac{n(w-\alpha p)}{\lambda[1+\rho(n-1)]\sigma_k^2} + L$ and $n^* = \left[\frac{\lambda}{2c}(1-\rho)\right]^{1/2}(L-l_0)\sigma_k$. For the more general case of $\alpha \neq 1$, the comparative static results of this model are reported in the Appendix.

Similar to farm household models, we find the amount of off-farm labor increases with off-farm wages ($\partial l_0^*/\partial w > 0$). The model also suggests that off-farm work is more attractive for risk averse individuals ($\partial l_0^*/\partial \lambda > 0$) and in situations where risk associated with farming increases ($\partial l_0^*/\partial \sigma_k^2 > 0$), as long as ρ is not "too small" ($\rho > -1/(n-1)$). If ρ is very small (close to -1); however, perfect risk reduction is possible on-farm and no off-farm work will be chosen. Finally, off-farm labor increases with the total amount of family labor L ($\partial l_0^*/\partial L > 0$) and declines with farm size $\partial l_0^*/\partial p < 0$.[11]

With respect to the optimal degree of diversification, three terms determine the optimal n in Equation (4). The third term ($\frac{\lambda(L-l_0)^2(1-\rho)\sigma_k^2}{2n^2}$), which is always positive for $\rho < 1$, represents the gains in y_{CE} due to risk reduction. This gain has to be set against the losses due

---

[9] We do not consider product complementarity between the different activities here. For an analysis of the product diversification problem which features both producer risk aversion and product complementarity see Fraser (1990).

[10] Robison and Barry show that $\sigma^2 = (L-l_0)^2\{[(1+(n-1)\rho]/n\}\sigma_k^2$.

[11] Most of the comparative static results on off-farm labor supply correspond to those derived from "standard" farm-household models. For attempts to introduce risk and uncertainty into farm-household models see Finkelshtain and Chalfant; and Roe and Graham-Tomasi.

to the cost of learning to manage or supervise the additional enterprise ($-c$). The smaller the costs of including an additional product into the farm production mix, the larger diversification will be. Finally, the first term ($(1-\alpha)\left(\dfrac{L-l_0}{n}\right)^{\alpha}p$) represents the consequences of increasing n for farm productivity. Increasing (decreasing) returns $\alpha > 1$ ($\alpha < 1$) imply additional gains from specialization (diversification) of farm production, ceteris paribus. As expected, we find that diversification is more attractive for risk averse individuals ($\partial n^*/\partial\lambda > 0$), and in situations where risk associated with farming is substantial ($\partial n^*/\partial\sigma_k > 0$). Diversification increases as the correlation between the different returns from farming declines ($\partial n^*/\partial\rho < 0$). With respect to the relationship between the total amount of farm household labor available (represented by L), as well as farm size (represented by p) and diversification, we find $\partial n^*/\partial L > 0$ and $\partial n^*/\partial p > 0$ for $\alpha < 1$ and $\partial n^*/\partial p < 0$ for $\alpha > 1$. The impact of farm size on farm diversification thus provides information on the form of the underlying production technology.[12]

Finally, this model suggests on-farm and off-farm diversification are interrelated. In the optimum, we expect part-time farmers to have a lower level of on-farm diversification ($\partial n^*/\partial l_0^* < 0$). Given that off-farm employment is not associated with the risk of agricultural production, part-time farmers, ceteris paribus, will have more stable total income, reducing their incentive for on–farm diversification. Similarly, farmers with more on-farm enterprise diversification have lower probabilities of participating in off-farm employment activity, ceteris paribus ($\partial l_0^*/\partial n^* < 0$). Empirical tests of these hypotheses are presented and discussed in the following section.

C. DATA

The estimated model used panel data from 39,621 farm households in Upper Austria. The data were collected by the Census Bureau in Upper Austria in 1985 and 1990 as part of the farm census. The farm census collects information on farm operations and farm household characteristics (such as, age, sex, and schooling of various family members, the off-farm employment status).

Given the importance of dairy farming in Upper Austria, the size and on-farm diversification measures were based on the number and type of livestock (measured in "median large animal units"). The aggregate measure of farm size is broken down into nine sub-categories (calves, fattened cattle, cattle, piglets, sheep and goats, chicken, cows, fattened pigs, and brood sow). Indices based on these nine farm production enterprises were used to measure the degree of on-farm enterprise diversification.

Three indices are commonly used to measure diversification:

---

[12] Recent work by Gomes and Livdan focuses explicitly on the role of technologies and costs for diversification of production without, however, considering individual preferences with respect to risk.

1) a modified concentration ratio $D_C = \dfrac{Q - q^{max}}{Q}$,

2) the Berry-index (Berry) $D_B = [1 - \sum_{j=1}^{n} s_j^2]$, and

3) the entropy measure (Jacquemin and Berry) $D_E = \sum_{j=1}^{n} s_j \log(\dfrac{1}{s_j})$,

where $s_j = \dfrac{q_j}{Q}$. Here, q_j denotes the quantity of product j with $Q = \sum_{j=1}^{n} q_j$, q^{max} is the quantity of the most important product in the group of all 9 products ($q^{max} = \max(q_1, q_2, \ldots, q_n)$) and n is the number of products ($n = 9$). Note that complete specialization implies $D_C = D_B = D_E = 0$, whereas the maximum level of diversification is given by $D_C = D_B = 1$ and $D_E = \log(n)$. The properties of these diversification measures are discussed in Gollop and Monahan. In the following empirical model, we use $TD_E = D_E / D_E^{max}$ (with $0 \leq TD_E \leq 1$, where D_E^{max} is the maximum level of diversification over all farms) as the dependent variable, the results when using alternative diversification measures are very similar and are reported in the Appendix.

The census data report farm households' off-farm work participation as one of three groups: (a) 90% more on-farm, (b) less than 90% but 50% or more on-farm, or (c) 50% less on-farm. Farm households were classified as "full-time farmers" if more than 50% of household time was allocated to farm activities ($PT = 0$). Farm households with 50% or less time allocated to on-farm activities were classified as "part-time farmers" ($PT = 1$).

To guarantee a homogenous data base, the analysis used only farms included in both years and having all relevant data. A total of 39,621 farm households satisfied this criteria. Descriptions and summary statistics for each variable used in the empirical model are reported in Table 1.

D. RESULTS

The results of the econometric analysis are shown in Table 2. Columns (1) and (2) report parameter estimates of probit models on diversification (TD_E) and the probability of part-time farming (PT), respectively. All variables refer to observations from the 1990 farm census, we used lagged observations (from the 1985 farm census) as instruments (for TD_E in column (2)).

The estimation models are statistically significant at the 1% level, as measured by the likelihood ratio test. Model (2) correctly classifies 77.7% of all observations. Whereas 75.1% of all cases with the farm operator working off the farm ($PT = 1$) are correctly predicted. The percentage of families reporting no off-farm work correctly classified is somewhat higher with 80.6%.[13] The results reported in column (2) are consistent with detailed empirical analysis on off-farm employment using these data (Weiss). Discussion of the results focused

---

[13] Since the TD_E variable is not binary, this statistic cannot be calculated here.

on the determinants of diversification and the interaction between on and off-farm diversification.

Table 1. Definition and Descriptive Statistics of All Variables Used

Variable	Symbol	Part – time Farms Mean (Std. Dev.)	Full – time Farms Mean (Std. Dev.)	All Farms Mean (Std. Dev.)
Number of Observations	N	21,146	18,670	39,621
Modified Concentration -- Index of Diversification	D_C	0.277 (0.199)	0.413 (0.174)	0.341 (0.199)
Berry Index of Diversification	D_B	0.373 (0.231)	0.526 (0.187)	0.445 (0.225)
Entropy Measure of Diversification	TD_E	0.375 (0.234)	0.544 (0.208)	0.455 (0.237)
Part-time farming: married couple spends more than 50% of total working time on off- farm employment.	PT	1.000 (0.000)	0.000 (0.000)	0.529 (0.499)
Farm size is the Log of Livestock (measured in Median Large Animal Units)	$\ln(S)$	3.952 (1.267)	5.223 (0.884)	4.552 (1.271)
Number of family members in the farm household younger than 6 years	$\#FAM<6$	0.302 (0.633)	0.403 (0.733)	0.349 (0.683)
Number of family members in the farm household between 6 and 15 years	$\#FAM6<15$	0.545 (0.898)	0.753 (1.040)	0.643 (0.973)
Number of family members in the farm household between 15 and 65 years	$\#FAM15<65$	3.596 (1.428)	3.745 (1.475)	3.668 (1.452)
Dummy for farm operator married state in 1990. It is set equal to 1 if he (she) is married, and is zero otherwise.	$MARR$	0.846 (0.361)	0.769 (0.421)	0.809 (0.392)
The farm operators age in 1990	AGE	48.061 (12.735)	43.339 (10.401)	45.832 (11.928)
Dummy for agricultural specific schooling. Is set equal to 1 if the farm operator has a 'farm master' degree, and is zero otherwise.	$SCHOOL$	0.593 (0.491)	0.607 (0.488)	0.599 (0.489)

Empirical literature offers conflicting results as to the impact of farm size on farm enterprise diversification. White and Irwin, using aggregate U.S. Census Data, compared diversification across farm size classes and concluded that larger farms were more specialized. The opposite finding was reported in Pope and Prescott. Our results support the Pope and Prescott findings. The transformed Entropy measure (TD_E) increased with farm size ($\ln(S)$) and larger farms tended to be more diversified.[14] This is consistent with the prediction of Robison's and Barry's model outlined above, and to more recent theoretical work on diversification, that emphasizes the role of technologies and costs (Gomes, and Livdan). According to the authors, decreasing returns to scale implies that the returns to capital

---

[14] The size distribution of farms is skewed to the right with a skewness coefficient equal to 1.3 (Greene, p. 879). Given this skewed distribution, the natural logarithm of farm size is used in the empirical analysis.

accumulation decline as the farm enterprises expand until there is no further incentive for expansion of the current activity. This generates a powerful motivation for larger farms to diversify into new activities to obtain higher returns to capital accumulation. An increase in farm size also reduces the probability of entering into the off-farm labor market (column (2)), which corresponds to the existing empirical literature.

The results suggest personal characteristics of the farm operator, as well as the farm family influence on- and off-farm diversification decisions (Table 2, column (2)). The probability of off-farm work significantly decreases with the farm operators' farm-specific schooling (*SCHOOL*). No such relationship can be observed with respect to the degree of diversification on the farm. The parameter estimates for non-farm specific schooling were found to be insignificant in both models and are thus not reported here. The impact of the farm operator's age (*AGE*), is significantly different from zero in both models. Different arguments for a relationship between age and diversification have been offered. Pope and Prescott speculated that younger farmers are less risk averse, which would reduce the level of on-farm diversification (positive relationship between age and diversification). On the other hand, the farm operator's age might be positively correlated with wealth (which is not observed in the present data set). Given a decreasing absolute risk aversion as wealth increases, there would be an inverse relationship between age and diversification. Similarly, sociological studies based on direct interviews frequently indicate the farmers' intention to reduce working load and make life easier as they grow older. This could be achieved through specialization or reducing the number of farm enterprises. Column (1) in Table 2 reports a non-linear age-diversification relationship. On-farm diversification first declines with the farm operator's age, reaches its minimum at 48 years of age. and then increases. A similar non-linear pattern is reported in column (2) which is consistent with other research (Lass, Findeis, Hallberg).

Farm family size also appears to be an important determining out of both on- and off-farm diversification. An increase in the number of family members living on the farm in the age category between 16 and 65 years ($\#FAM_{15<65}$) is associated with a higher farm enterprise diversification. This result is consistent with the predictions derived from the theoretical model, given that a larger number of family members implies an increase in the total amount of family labor available on the farm. No significant effect is observed with respect to the number of younger family members ($\#FAM_{<6}$, and $\#FAM_{6<15}$). Similarly, we find that additional family members below 16 years of age impede the acceptance of additional off-farm work for the married couple, but later on provide the necessary labor resources on the farm, and thereby facilitate entering the off-farm labor market. If the farm operator is married (*MARR* = 1), diversification on the farm is lower and the probability of off-farm employment is higher, the impact of this variable in column (1) only being significantly different at the 10% level, however.

Dummy variables for regional differences (R_1 to R_6 as well as HZ_1 to HZ_4) were included where they contributed significantly to the explanatory power of the models. Farms located in less productive areas ($HZ_i = 1$ with $i = 1, 2, 3, 4$) report a significantly higher probability of participating on the off-farm labor market. A significant positive impact on farm diversification can only be observed for farms located in the most unfavourable production conditions ($HZ_4 = 1$). To evaluate the relationship between the two forms of diversification, (TD_E and *PT*), we carried out a number of estimation experiments along the lines suggested in

Table 2. Results of Instrumental-Variable Probit Models on Farm Production Diversification (TD_E) and Off-Farm Diversification (part-time farming)

Independent Variables Estimation Method:		Dependent Variable TD_E Parameter (t-value) (1)	Dependent Variable PT Parameter (t-value) (2)
Constant		-1.869*** (-18.94)	6.149*** (51.89)
Farm Size	ln(S)	0.378*** (58.45)	-0.642*** (-73.22)
Agricultural Schooling	SCHOOL	-0.014 (-1.04)	-0.034**(-2.33)
Age of Farm Operator/40	AGE	-0.342** (2.12)	-6.769***(-31.68)
(Age of Farm Operator/40)^2	AGE2	0.143** (2.06)	3.171*** (33.18)
(# of Fam. Memb. <6)	#FAM<6	0.005 (0.51)	-0.101*** (-8.62)
(# of Fam. Memb. 6<15)	#FAM6<15	0.002 (0.25)	-0.033*** (-3.98)
(# of Fam. Memb. 15<65)	#FAM15<65	0.019*** (4.08)	0.011** (2.11)
Married State	MAR	-0.034* (-1.69)	0.698*** (31.18)
Hardship Zone 1	HZ1		0.138*** (7.21)
Hardship Zone 2	HZ2		0.156*** (6.73)
Hardship Zone 3	HZ3		0.079*** (3.24)
Hardship Zone 4	HZ4	0.209* (1.66)	0.353** (2.25)
Region 1	R1		-0.879***(-18.42)
Region 2	R2	0.159*** (3.56)	-0.283*** (-12.56)
Region 3	R3	0.110**(2.37)	0.080*** (3.17)
Region 4	R4	0.087** (1.99)	-0.100*** (-4.99)
Region 5	R5	0.192*** (4.44)	
Region 6	R6	0.217*** (5.01)	
Diversification (Entropy)	TD_E		-0.514*** (-12.55)
LL(0)		-27,302.99	-27,391.84
LL(β)		-25,013.69	-19,755.37
LRT (DF)		4,578.61 (14)	15,272.94 (17)
R^2 McFadden (Veall/Zim.)		0.084	0.278 (0.479)

Notes: LL(β) and LL(0) is the log-likelihood function and the restricted log-likelihood function respectively, and LRT refers to the likelihood ratio test statistic. *** (** and *) indicate that the parameter estimate is significantly different from zero at the 99%-level (the 95% and 90%-level, respectively).

Maddala and Greene.[15] Unfortunately, in none of the numerous specifications tested did the bivariate probit model converge, the results of independently estimated probit models are thus discussed in Table 2. We used the lagged diversification and part-time variable for instrumentation. The results reported suggest on-farm and off-farm diversification decisions are closely related. The probability of off-farm diversification is found to decline significantly as the farm enterprise mix becomes more diversified. This corresponds to our predictions derived from a simple mean-variance model. Different estimation experiments indicate that *PT* does not contribute significantly to on-farm diversification.

CONCLUSION

The purpose of this paper was to examine the impact of various farm and household characteristics on farm household income diversification. Two forms of diversification (as well as their interaction) were considered: on production farm and off-farm diversification (off-farm employment). In contrast to the existing literature, we did not examine off-farm employment in a farm-household model, but derived testable predictions from an optimal portfolio selection framework.

Using linked census data for Upper-Austria from 1985 and 1990, we found that the degree of on-farm diversification, as well as the probability of off-farm diversification, was significantly related to farm and family characteristics. In particular, we provided evidence that larger farms are more diversified on the farm, whereas off-farm diversification is found to be less likely. A significant impact on the degree of on- and off-farm diversification is also reported for the farm operator's age and the number of family members living on the farm.

These results have important policy implications. Historically, government market intervention has sheltered domestic prices from international market price fluctuation. In the new economy of the European Union, domestic prices will be more closely tied to international price signals. A similar tendency to shift a larger portion of risk bearing function from the public sector back to the private sector can also be observed in non-EU countries. Our results imply that these changes will result in more off-farm diversification and/or more on-farm diversification. Which of the two strategies actually chosen by the farm operators will not only have important consequences for the performance of their individual farm, but will also influence the structure of the farm sector in the future.

---

[15] Maddala discusses alternative simultaneous-equations models with discrete endogenous variables. A general specification for a two-equation model would be: $y_1 = \gamma_1 y_2 + \beta_1' X_1 + \varepsilon_1$ and $y_2^* = \gamma_2 y_1 + \beta_2' X_2 + \varepsilon_2$, with $E[\varepsilon_1] = E[\varepsilon_2] = 0$, $Var[\varepsilon_1] = Var[\varepsilon_2] = 1$ and $Cov[\varepsilon_1, \varepsilon_2] = \rho$. The unobservable variable y_2^* are related to the observable variables y_2 as follows: $y_2 = 1$ if $y_2^* > 0$ and is zero otherwise. Maddala shows that this model is logically consistent if and only if γ_1 or γ_2 is equal to zero (p. 117f). To find the appropriate specification for a model with two endogenous variables TD_E ($\equiv y_1$) and PT ($\equiv y_2$), we first estimate three different models.

In model (1) we assume $\gamma_1 = \gamma_2 = 0$ and thus no direct relationship to exist. Model (2) assumes $\gamma_1 = 0$, whereas model (3) has $\gamma_2 = 0$. A likelihood ratio test does not reject model (1) against model (2). However, model (1) is rejected against model (3). We thus consider model (3) the most appropriate specification, the results of this specification are reported in columns (1) and (2) in Table 2.

APPENDIX

Table A.1. Results of Instrumental-Variable Probit Models on Farm Production Diversification (D_B) and Off-Farm Diversification (part-time farming)

Independent Variables Estimation Method:		Dependent Variable D_B Parameter (t-value) (1)	Dependent Variable PT Parameter (t-value) (2)
Constant		-1.694***(-17.35)	6.152***(52.03)
Farm Size	ln(S)	0.343***(54.50)	-0.646***(-74.31)
Agricultural Schooling	SCHOOL	-0.011 (-0.84)	-0.035**(-2.40)
Age of Farm Operator/40	AGE	-0.304*(1.90)	-6.742***(-31.65)
(Age of Farm Operator/40)^2	AGE2	0.125*(1.82)	3.159***(33.17)
(# of Fam. Memb. <6)	#FAM<6	0.001 (0.08)	-0.102***(-8.65)
(# of Fam. Memb. 6<15)	#FAM6<15	0.004 (0.48)	-0.033***(-4.00)
(# of Fam. Memb. 15<65)	#FAM15<65	0.012**(2.55)	0.010*(1.89)
Married State	MAR	-0.028* (-1.41)	0.701***(31.36)
Hardship Zone 1	HZ1		0.139***(7.29)
Hardship Zone 2	HZ2		0.159***(6.89)
Hardship Zone 3	HZ3		0.082***(3.36)
Hardship Zone 4	HZ4	0.189 (1.51)	0.355**(2.25)
Region 1	R1		-0.871***(-18.31)
Region 2	R2	0.129***(2.92)	-0.278***(-12.38)
Region 3	R3	0.085*(1.86)	0.084***(3.35)
Region 4	R4	0.058 (1.36)	-0.096***(-4.79)
Region 5	R5	0.137***(3.20)	
Region 6	R6	0.178***(4.18)	
Diversification (Berry)	D_B		-0.523***(-11.97)
LL(0)		-27,354.95	-27,521.31
LL(β)		-25,421.23	-19,837.46
LRT (DF)		3,867.44 (14)	15,367.70 (17)
R^2 McFadden (Veall/Zim.)		0.071	0.279 (0.479)

Notes: See Table 2.

Table A.2. Results of Instrumental-Variable Probit Models on Farm Production Diversification (D_C) and Off-Farm Diversification (part-time farming)

Independent Variables Estimation Method:		Dependent Variable D_C Parameter (t-value) (1)	Dependent Variable PT Parameter (t-value) (2)
Constant		-1.898***(-18.78)	6.105***(51.73)
Farm Size	ln(S)	0.330***(49.23)	-0.639***(-73.99)
Agricultural Schooling	SCHOOL	-0.101 (-0.74)	-0.036**(-2.41)
Age of Farm Operator/40	AGE	-0.284*(1.72)	-6.733***(-31.61)
(Age of Farm Operator/40)^2	AGE2	0.117*(1.64)	3.155***(33.13)
(# of Fam. Memb. <6)	#FAM<6	0.001 (0.10)	-0.101***(-8.62)
(# of Fam. Memb. 6<15)	#FAM6<15	0.002 (0.31)	-0.033***(-4.01)
(# of Fam. Memb. 15<65)	#FAM15<65	0.008*(1.75)	0.010*(1.89)
Married State	MAR	-0.027 (-1.35)	0.699***(31.32)
Hardship Zone 1	HZ1		0.135***(7.08)
Hardship Zone 2	HZ2		0.156***(6.74)
Hardship Zone 3	HZ3		0.079***(3.23)
Hardship Zone 4	HZ4	0.185 (1.41)	0.356**(2.27)
Region 1	R1		-0.866***(-18.22)
Region 2	R2	0.115***(2.49)	-0.275***(-12.22)
Region 3	R3	0.061 (1.27)	0.082***(3.24)
Region 4	R4	0.042 (0.93)	-0.097***(-4.86)
Region 5	R5	0.113**(2.54)	
Region 6	R6	0.150***(3.38)	
Diversification (Concentration)	D_C		-0.643***(-13.69)
LL(0)		-25,547.69	-27,521.31
LL(β)		-23,960.23	-19,815.64
LRT (DF)		3,174.91 (14)	15,411.34 (17)
R^2 McFadden (Veall/Zim.)		0.062	0.279 (0.481)

Notes: See Table 2.

Comparative static results of the model for $\alpha \neq 1$

From the first-order condition for the optimal l_0 reported in Equation (3) in the text, we

define: $\quad F \equiv -\alpha \left(\dfrac{L - l_0}{n} \right)^{\alpha - 1} p + w + \dfrac{\lambda (L - l_0)[1 + (n-1)\rho]\sigma_k^2}{n} = 0$. Applying the

implicit function theorem and using the second-order condition:

$$\frac{\partial^2 y_{CE}}{\partial l_0^2} \equiv A = \alpha(\alpha - 1)\left(\frac{L - l_0}{n}\right)^{\alpha - 1}\frac{p}{L - l_0} - \frac{\lambda[1 + (n-1)\rho]\sigma_k^2}{n} < 0 \text{, we find:}$$

$$\frac{\partial l_0}{\partial w} = -\frac{\partial F/\partial w}{\partial F/\partial l_0} = \frac{-1}{A} > 0 \text{;} \quad \frac{\partial l_0}{\partial L} = -\frac{\partial F/\partial L}{\partial F/\partial l_0} = 1 > 0 \text{;}$$

$$\frac{\partial l_0}{\partial p} = -\frac{\partial F/\partial p}{\partial F/\partial l_0} = \frac{\alpha(L - l_0)^{\alpha - 1}}{n^{\alpha - 1}A} < 0 \text{;} \quad \frac{\partial l_0}{\partial \rho} = -\frac{\partial F/\partial \rho}{\partial F/\partial l_0} = \frac{-\lambda(L - l_0)(n-1)\sigma_k^2}{nA} > 0 \text{;}$$

$$\frac{\partial l_0}{\partial c} = 0 \text{;} \quad \frac{\partial l_0}{\partial \lambda} = -\frac{\partial F/\partial \lambda}{\partial F/\partial l_0} = \frac{-\lambda(L - l_0)[1 + (n-1)\rho]\sigma_k^2}{nA} > 0 \text{ for } \rho > -1/(n-1) \text{;}$$

$$\frac{\partial l_0}{\partial \sigma_k^2} = -\frac{\partial F/\partial \sigma_k^2}{\partial F/\partial l_0} = \frac{-\lambda(L - l_0)[1 + (n-1)\rho]}{nA} > 0 \text{ for } \rho > -1/(n-1) \text{;}$$

Similarly, from Equation (4) we define:

$$F \equiv (1 - \alpha)\left(\frac{L - l_0}{n}\right)^{\alpha}p - c + \frac{\lambda(L - l_0)^2(1 - \rho)\sigma_k^2}{2n^2} = 0 \text{. The second-order condition for}$$

the optimal number of products n is:

$$\frac{\partial^2 y_{CE}}{\partial n^2} \equiv B = -\alpha(1 - \alpha)\left(\frac{L - l_0}{n}\right)^{\alpha}\frac{p}{n} - \frac{\lambda(L - l_0)^2(1 - \rho)\sigma_k^2}{2n^4} < 0 \text{. Using this, we find:}$$

$$\frac{\partial n}{\partial c} = -\frac{\partial F/\partial c}{\partial F/\partial n} = \frac{1}{B} < 0 \text{;} \quad \frac{\partial n}{\partial \rho} = -\frac{\partial F/\partial \rho}{\partial F/\partial n} = \frac{\lambda(L - l_0)^2\sigma_k^2}{2n^2 B} < 0 \text{;}$$

$$\frac{\partial n}{\partial p} = -\frac{\partial F/\partial p}{\partial F/\partial n} = \frac{-(1 - \alpha)(L - l_0)^{\alpha}}{n^{\alpha}B} \geq 0 \text{ if } \alpha \leq 1 \text{;} \quad \frac{\partial n}{\partial \lambda} = -\frac{\partial F/\partial \lambda}{\partial F/\partial n} = \frac{-(L - l_0)^2(1 - \rho)\sigma_k^2}{2n^2 B} > 0 \text{;}$$

$$\frac{\partial n}{\partial \sigma_k^2} = -\frac{\partial F/\partial \sigma_k^2}{\partial F/\partial n} = \frac{-\lambda(L - l_0)^2(1 - \rho)}{2n^2 B} > 0 \text{;} \quad \frac{\partial n}{\partial w} = 0 \text{;}$$

$$\frac{\partial n}{\partial L} = -\frac{\partial F/\partial L}{\partial F/\partial n} = \frac{-[\alpha(1 - \alpha)p(L - l_0)^{\alpha - 1}n^{-\alpha + 2} + \lambda(L - l_0)(1 - \rho)\sigma_k^2}{n^2 B} \geq 0 \text{ if } \alpha \leq 1$$

REFERENCES

Chavas, J-P., and Kim, K. (2001). An Econometric Analysis of the Effects of Market Liberalization on Price Dynamics and Price Volatility, Paper presented at the annual meetings of the American Agricultural Economics Association in Chicago, IL, August 2001.

Baumol, W.J. (1982). *Contestable Markets and the Theory of Industry Structure.* New York: Harcourt Brace Jovanovich.

Berry, C.H. (1971). Corporate Growth and Diversification. *Journal of Law and Economics, Vol. 14,* 371-83.

Evans, N.J., and Ilbery, B.W. (1993). The Pluriactivity, Part-time Farming, and Farm Diversification Debate. *Environment and Planning A, Vol.25,* 945-59.

Fernandez-Cornejo, J., Gempesaw, C.M., Eltrich, J.G., and Stefanou, S.E. (1992). Dynamic Measures of Scope and Scale Economies: An Application to German Agriculture. *American Journal of Agricultural Economics, Vol.74,* 329-42.

Finkelshtain, I., and Chalfant, J.A. (1991). Marketed Surplus Under Risk: Do Peasants Agree with Sandmo? *American Journal of Agricultural Economics, Vol. 73 ,* 557-67.

Fraser, R.W. (1990). Producer Risk, Product Complementarity and Product Diversification. *Journal of Agricultural Economics, Vol. 41,* 103-07.

_____. (2000). Risk and Producer Compensation in the Agenda 2000 Cereal Reforms: A Note. *Journal of Agricultural Economics, Vol. 51,* 468-72.

Gollop, F.M., and Monahan, J.L. (1991). A Generalized Index of Diversification: Trends in US Manufacturing. *The Review of Economics and Statistics, Vol. 73,* 318-30.

Gomes, J., and Livdan, D. (2002). Optimal Diversification. CEPR Discussion Paper No. 3461, London, UK.

Greene, W.E. (2003). *Econometric Analysis* (5th Edition). Englewood Cliffs: Prentice Hall.

Hazell, P.B.R., Jaramillo, M., and Williamson, A. (1990). The Relationship between World Price Instability and The Price Farmers Receive in Developing Countries. *Journal of Agricultural Economics, Vol. 41,* 227-41.

Heady, E. (1952). Diversification in Resource Allocation and Minimization of Income Variability. *Journal of Farm Economics, Vol. 34,* 482-96.

Huffman, W.E. (1980). Farm and Off-Farm Work Decisions: The Role of Human Capital. *The Review of Economics and Statistics, Vol. 62,* 14-23.

Jacquemin, A., and Berry, C.H. (1979). Entropy Measure of Diversification and Corporate Growth. *Journal of Industrial Economics, Vol. 27,* 359-69.

Jovanovic, B. (1993). The Diversification of Production. *Brookings Papers on Economic Activity: Microeconomics,* 197-247.

Lass, D.A., Findeis, J.L., and Hallberg, M.C.(1991). Factors Affecting the Supply of Off-Farm Labour: A Review of Empirical Evidence. In, Hallberg, M.C., Findeis, J.L., and Lass, D.A. (Eds.), *Multiple Job-holding among Farm Families* (pp. 239-62). Ames, Iowa: Iowa State University Press.

Maddala, G.S. (1983). *Limited Dependent and Qualitative Variables in Econometrics.* (Econometric Society Monographs No. 3). Cambridge: Cambridge University Press.

Mishra, A.K., and Goodwin, B. (2002). Farm Income Variability and the Supply of Off-Farm Labor. *American Journal of Agricultural Economics, Vol. 79,* 880-87.

Mishra, A.K., and El-Osta, H. (2002). Risk Management Through Enterprise Diversification: A Farm-Level Analysis. Paper presented at the American Agricultural Economics Association meeting in Long Beach, CA.

Mishra, A.K., El-Osta, H.S., Morehart, M.J., Johnson, J.D., and Hopkins, J.W. (2002). Income, Wealth, and the Economic Well-Being of Farm Households. ERS Agricultural Economic Report No. AER812, Washington, DC, July . p. 77.

Montgomery, C.A. (1994).Corporate Diversification. *Journal of Economic Perspectives, Vol. 8*, 163-78.

Pope R.D., and Prescott, R. (1980). Diversification in Relation to Farm Size and Other Socioeconomic Characteristics. *American Journal of Agricultural Economics, Vol. 62*, 554-59.

Purdy, B.M., Langemeier, M.R., and Featherstone, A.M. (1997). Financial Performance, Risk, and Specialization. *Journal of Agricultural and Applied Economics, Vol. 29*, 149-61.

Robison, L.J., and Barry, P.J. (1987). *The Competitive Firm's Response to Risk*. London: MacMillan Publishing Company.

Roe, T., and Graham-Tomasi, T. (1986). Yield Risk in a Dynamic Model of the Agricultural Household. In, Inderjit, J., Singh, L.S., and Strauss, J. (Eds.), *Agricultural Household Models: Extensions, Applications, and Policy*. Baltimore, MD: John Hopkins University Press.

Sun, T.Y., Jinkins, J.E., and El-Osta, H.S. (1995). Multinomial Logit Analysis of Farm Diversification for Midwestern Farms. Paper presented at the annual meeting of the American Agricultural Economics Association in Indianapolis.

Thompson, S.R., Herrmann, R., and Gohout, W. (2000). Agricultural Market Liberalization and Instability of Domestic Agricultural Markets: The Case of the CAP. *American Journal of Agricultural Economics, Vol. 82,* 718-26.

Weiss, C. R. (1997). Do They Ever Come Back Again? The Symmetry and Reversibility of Off-Farm Employment. *European Review of Agricultural Economics, Vol. 24* (1), 65-84.

White, T., and Irwin, G. (1972). Farm Size and Specialization. In, Ball, G., and Heady, E. (Eds.), *Size, Structure and Future of Farms*. Ames, Iowa: Iowa State University Press.

In: The Economics of Natural and Human Resources...   ISBN 978-1-60741-029-4
Editor: Ayal Kimhi and Israel Finkelshtain   © 2009 Nova Science Publishers, Inc.

Chapter 17

ON-FARM NON-AGRICULTURAL LABOR: ON THE DEVELOPMENT OF RURAL TOURISM IN WESTERN COUNTRIES

*Anat Tchetchik, Aliza Fleischer and Israel Finkelshtain**

ABSTRACT

In the last decades, western economies have experienced major structural changes in their rural areas as a result of globalization, and political, social and technological changes. Among these changes, the development of rural tourism has undoubtedly played an important role. Rural tourism is a rapidly growing industry in Europe and North America, experiencing an annual growth rate of 6%. In many rural areas it has become an important source of livelihood for the rural population. The aims of this chapter are twofold: first, to provide a comprehensive review of the academic literature that has accumulated in the last 20 years or so, focusing on the following issues: (1) explaining the rapid development of rural tourism by examining both demand and supply factors, (2) public policy in rural tourism in North America and Europe, and finally (3) studying the unique relationships between rural tourism and agriculture. The second aim is to give a detailed description of the rural accommodations market in Israel and present the results of several related studies (Fleischer and Tchetchik, 2005; Tchetchik, 2006; Tchetchik, Fleischer and Finkelshtain, 2008).

A. INTRODUCTION

In the last decades, western economies have experienced major structural changes in their rural areas as a result of globalization, and political, social and technological changes. Among these changes, the development of rural tourism has undoubtedly played an important role. Although people have recreated in the countryside for centuries, it was only after the Second

* Department of Agricultural Economics and Management, The Hebrew University of Jerusalem. Corresponding author: Aliza Fleisher, e-mail: fleische@agri.huji.ac.il. Financial support from the Center for Agricultural Economic Research and the Agricultural Chief-Scientist fund are appreciated

World War that the relationship between rural settings and leisure activities engaged therein changed significantly (Cloke, 1993). Recreation and tourism in many rural areas have undergone a transformation from minor economic activities to dominant sector of the rural economy. Today, with an average annual growth rate of 6% in Europe and North America, rural tourism is contributing more and more to rural economies. In England, for instance, the annual earnings from rural tourism amount to $14 billion and it provides 380,000 jobs (Arnold, 2004).

In Canada, it accounts for 3% of the rural labor force (Bollman, 2005) and in the US, during the years 2002-4, a reported 90 million adults took trips to rural destinations (Brown, 2005). In the northern region of Israel, 10% of the rural households are engaged in rural tourism (Tchetchik, 2006). Figures for other countries reveal similar participation rates (Lane, 1994).

To demonstrate the transformation that rural regions have undergone, one can look at the results of the Foot and Mouth epidemic in the UK in 2001. It was found that the losses to rural economies were mostly caused by losses in rural tourism, and moreover, farming emerged as the source of the problem (The Observer, March 11, 2001).

The development of rural tourism is well reflected in the academic literature through many disciplines, including: geography, sociology, economics, and environmental studies. Most of these studies deal with the different benefits derived from rural tourism, as well as with the potential for negative externalities that may occur.

In general, the beneficiaries from rural tourism are: (1) The rural/agricultural sector, as rural tourism is an alternative/complementary source of income and jobs. In fact, the entire local economy benefits from rural tourism, as the visitors dine at local restaurants, buy food, fill their cars with gas, shop, etc. (2) The visitors/consumers who enjoy the diversity of rural tourism facilities and activities. (3) Society as a whole, which benefits from the preservation of environmental quality, fresh air, green landscapes, and open spaces, as well as from the creation of more opportunities for communication between different sectors in society.

The need for government intervention becomes apparent when one takes into account these benefits as well as the potential for negative externalities associated with rural tourism (such as heavy traffic, waste, overcrowding and conflicts between the host community and visitors).

Indeed, the development of rural tourism has been accompanied by different policy and support measures. For example, currently, the EU is proposing to budget over US $17 billion from 2007 to 2013 in support of tourism-related projects in rural areas.

The aims of this chapter are twofold: first, to provide a comprehensive review of the academic literature that has accumulated in the last 20 years or so, focusing on the following issues: (1) explaining the rapid development of rural tourism by examining both demand and supply factors, (2) public policy in rural tourism in North America and Europe, and finally (3) studying the unique relationships between rural tourism and agriculture. The second aim is to give a detailed description of the rural accommodations market in Israel and present the results of several related studies (Fleischer and Tchetchik, 2005; Tchetchik, 2006; Tchetchik, Fleischer and Finkelshtain, 2008).

B. COMPREHENSIVE REVIEW OF THE LITERATURE

B.1 Definition and Description

There is no commonly accepted definition of rural tourism, mainly since rurality can represent the geographic, as well as social and cultural aspects of an area; more than that, different countries have different criteria for defining an area as rural.

Consequently, rural tourism has a plethora of definitions, from the very minimalist one: "any tourism activity that takes place in rural areas" (Commission of the European Communities, 1986), to more elaborate ones such as the definition by Lane (1994). Lane suggested that rural tourism is tourism located in rural areas, i.e. regions that are rural in scale, character and function, reflecting the unique patterns of the rural environment, economy, history and location. According to Lane, any activity that is not an integral part of the rural fabric and does not employ local resources cannot be considered rural tourism.

The rural tourism industry can be categorized by its products, such as Farm Tourism, Agritourism, Green Tourism and Ecotourism, each relating to a different aspect of the rural setting. Another categorization of rural tourism is based on the rural resources utilized in the course of the activity. An example is activities related to environmental quality;; in Europe and North America, groups go to the countryside to take part in tree planting, nature-reserve fencing, etc. Some authors include outdoor recreation in national parks and wilderness areas in the definition of rural tourism (Ladki, 1993 and Owens, 1984), others exclude them (Dernoi, 1991). Nevertheless, Lane's 'typology' of rural tourism is referred to in all subsequent key English-language publications and is widely accepted at an international level.

Although rural tourism includes a wide range of products and activities, the main emphasis is on rural accommodations. The spectrum of the latter ranges from campgrounds, self-catering and bed and breakfasts (B&B), to full-catering establishments including hotels and motels in rural communities. Rural accommodations businesses differ from traditional commercial tourism businesses in many aspects. The latter, composed of many rooms/units, are extensive in capital, and they usually rely on hired labor. Rural accommodations are usually small, based on family labor, include very few rooms/units, and do not require large capital investment. In the US, for example, according to the Small Business Administration, almost 99% of all tourism-related establishments in rural areas qualify as small businesses (Galston and Baehler, 1995).

B.2. The Development of Rural Tourism

Demand Factors

Although people were recreating in the countryside even before the second half of the 19th century, this activity was only available to a minority of landlords for hunting, horse-riding, etc. The development of demand for rural tourism has been the result of three major factors: technological progress, increases in income and increases in leisure time. Such technological progress took place during the 19th century with the laying of railroad tracks in Europe which enabled the growth of the entire tourism industry. A further development included elevators and cable cars, which turned many regions into popular rural tourism destinations, for example, Bernese Oberland in Switzerland, which attracts more than half a million visitors each summer (Flint, 1992).

In the US, while the early settlers avoided the wilderness of the west, during the 19th century those areas began to be perceived as recreation sources (Shaw and Williams, 1994).

However, it was only during the 20th century that rural tourism became widespread. Massive road paving in Europe, accompanied by increased private car ownership, especially after 1945, dramatically decreased traveling costs. These factors, together with increased available income and leisure, accelerated the demand for rural tourism.

In the last two decades, despite the emergence of new tourism products that compete directly with rural tourism, such as inland all-weather resorts that have become very popular in northern Europe, the demand for rural tourism has generally been sustained. Contributing to this are: (1) the move toward short-break holidays, these breaks are taken mostly in the countryside; (2) the evolution of the 'heritage industry' which perceives rural areas as the genuine representatives of national heritage (Hewison, 1987); (3) the notion that rural areas are beneficial to health, offering fresher air, cleaner water and the opportunity for outdoor recreation; (4) improvement in facilities aimed at recreation in nature such as four-wheel-drive vehicles and mountain bikes; (5) easier accessibility to rural areas due to improved transport and communication, and the removal of political and economic barriers.

Supply Factors

Huge technological advances in farming, which took place in the 20th century in developed economies, led to production surpluses of basic food (Bowler, 1985; Healey and Ilbery, 1985; Windhorst, 1989). A vicious circle was created, in which a cost-price squeeze in agricultural output pushed farmers to seek scale economies, through farm enlargement, specialization and intensification. The result was more production surpluses and further price decreases. Between 1987 and 1997, employment in agriculture was falling across the EU; one out of every three farming jobs was lost in Italy, Spain, Portugal and France (Bowler, 1985). The declining terms of trade in agriculture and the increase in the ratio of urban to farming incomes resulted in rapid urbanization. Thus, from a place where most of the population lived and derived its livelihood from farming, the countryside became, in a relatively short time, a place of low population density[1] and overproduction of agricultural output.

The EU reacted to these changes by a complete change in the development strategies and policies. It shifted its policy focus from encouraging agricultural production to restraining it and encouraging rural development instead. Economic diversification became the most dominant policy strategy and in this context, rural tourism, and specifically farm tourism, became an important element[2] (Ilbery et al., 1998).

Farm Tourism

Farm tourism is not a new phenomenon: farms in Austria and other countries have been hosting tourists for over a hundred years (Frater, 1982). In recent years, however, farm tourism in Europe has experienced enormous growth accompanied by structural change. Today, England, France, Germany and Austria dominate the global farm tourism market with

---

[1] Today rural areas in Europe comprise more than 80% of EU territory and 40% of its population.

[2] A detailed discussion of public policy in rural tourism is presented below.

20,000 to 30,000 enterprises per country (Weaver and Fennel, 1997). Over 23% of the farms in the UK are involved in tourism (Denman 1994a,b). The Ministry of Agriculture, Fisheries and Food has estimated that farm accommodations in England and Wales generate 70 million pounds per annum (MAFF, 1995).

Farm households engage in rural tourism by offering small-scale, high-quality accommodations and/or by developing tourist attractions, such as farm tours, farm festivals and more.

Farm tourism employs mostly idle labor already existing on the farm. Hjalager (1996), who investigated farm tourism in Denmark, found it to be widely accepted practice that wives and the older children are the most active participants in the operation of farm-tourism businesses.

A comparison of farmers who were not willing to diversify to those who had diversified revealed that the latter run a larger farm business, earn a higher net income, are younger, continue full-time education after school and receive formal agricultural training (Ilbery et al., 1998).

In recent years, from its position as a complementary activity, farm tourism has developed into a sector in its own right. It is a growing industry and many authors forecast a further growth in demand.

B.3. The Impacts of Rural Tourism

The main theme of rural tourism research from the 1960s to the early 1990s was the economic benefit from rural tourism to the farms, as well as the entire agricultural sector (Dernoi), 1983; Evens and Ilbery, 1992 and many others).

Many studies indicate that rural tourism makes an important contribution to the local economy at the level of both the individual farmer and the region as a whole. Vacationers not only lodge and dine in the rural accommodations, they also engage in recreational activities and shop in local stores. Taking into consideration the multiplier effect, the contribution to the local economy extends far beyond the farm household. A study conducted in four rural regions in England showed that on average, 44% of visitors' expenditures remain in the local economy (English Tourist Board, 1991). Other estimates suggest that each 10,000 pounds of tourists' expenditures create 3.5 to 4 direct positions and 0.5 indirect positions (Archer, 1974; Dower, 1980; Smith and Wylde, 1977).

While some authors view rural tourism as a panacea for rural areas, others are more skeptical. Oppermann (1996), who studied rural tourism in Germany, claims that it is hardly a serious second foothold for farm operators. It is, therefore, only a temporary alternative for farmers facing declining profits from agriculture. Oppermann claimed that the time involved in running a rural accommodations business was often underestimated or not considered by operators. Two factors limit the expansion of rural tourism: the first is government regulation that limits construction of residential housing outside residential zones, and the second relates to infrastructure. Specifically, many farms are not connected to the public sewage plant owing to their isolated location. The expansion to more than two accommodation units would require such a connection or the construction of a private sewage plant; both are very expensive. Other rural operators in this research are mostly restrained by the size of their house or land. Oppermann suggests that state and federal governments will either erase legal barriers to allow the expansion of farm tourism or else quit promoting it as an economic alternative.

Other potential negative effects that may accrue include: cost increase of public services such as waste disposal, resulting from increased demand, the creation of partial/temporary jobs, increases in land prices and even a situation in which local residents are unable to acquire more dwellings in the area, and over dependency of the community on one industry, the success of which is not under the local community's control.

B.4. Public Intervention

The rural tourism industry is vulnerable to market-failure results to a great extent. The massive development of tourist attractions and the large number of visitors can damage or even ruin the same amenities that define the attractiveness of the rural environment. Rural tourism development must therefore maintain a balance between the conflicting aims of conservation and development (Lane, 1994).

Public intervention in rural areas affects the tourism industry either directly or indirectly. Even in the absence of a specific rural tourism policy, government decision-making in such fields as zoning, transportation, communication and other infrastructures, land and water resource management, among others, has implications for rural tourism (Beeton, 1999).

Over the past decades, tourism development has received increasing recognition as a regional and national economic development tool. This has led to various reactions in government policy. Today, government intervention in rural tourism and recreation is widespread. The intervention can regulate, support, or maintain (at times simultaneously because government policies across sectors are not always coordinated or complementary) rural tourism and recreation activities. The actual extent of government intervention in rural tourism varies from country to country according to various political-economic-constitutional systems, and circumstances peculiar to each country and region. Public intervention is employed at all levels of government in: developed nations, the former socialist countries of Eastern Europe, less developed countries (e.g. Kenya, Cuba and Sri Lanka) and the Pacific region. However, while the goals of rural tourism development, e.g. economic growth and adaptation, employment generation, population retention, and conservation are fairly standard policy goals, the actual policy process by which they are achieved is not.

Europe

In the mid 1980s, the EU changed its Common Policy in Agriculture (CAP) from encouraging production to restraining it. This was the result of overproduction of agricultural commodities, a decline in farm income and environmental problems resulting from intensive agriculture.

In its original form, the CAP was aimed at increasing agricultural production, sustaining a proper standard of living for farmers, stabilizing the markets and ensuring a continuous supply of agricultural output at reasonable prices. These goals were achieved mainly through price mechanisms that ensured the prices paid to farmers for many products. As a result, supply surpluses of several agricultural products were created. By the beginning of the 1990s, supply surpluses of cereals, dairy and poultry products and vegetables were exterminated. Hence, while agriculture's contribution to the EU's GDP and employment had diminished, farmers' income was sustained. In order to halt this vicious cycle, the EU put restrictions on the production of cereal and milk. Subsidies were given to farmers to stop working their land, and to move from intensive to extensive production techniques (Ervin, 1988; Gasson and Potter, 1988; Ilbery, 1990). Since 1992, a large part of the EU's rural land has become available for other uses (Baldock and Beaufoy, 1993).

Populated rural areas are considered a national goal in many countries; therefore, policy measures in most developed countries have expanded their focus from support of agriculture to support of rural development to halt the process of urbanization.

Recognizing the important role played by rural regions in supporting the entire population's welfare, in 1993, the EU had allocated billions of ECU (European Currency Units) mainly to support rural regions. Among the four regional objectives was 5b: facilitating the development and structural adjustment of rural areas. In practice, the main beneficiaries of objective 5b funding, were tourism projects.

In recent years, the EU has identified tourism as a potential source of new income for rural regions, especially regions that have suffered a decline in agricultural activities. Today, rural tourism is being encouraged and is receiving support through various EU programs (Bates and Wacker, 1996; Slee, Farr and Snowdon, 1997).

The LEADER program (Links Between Actions for the Development of the Rural Economy) for instance, is one of the most interesting rural development plans in Europe (Nitsch and Straaten, 1995). The program was established in 1990 (as LEADER I and later continued as LEADER II), in order to promote an integrated approach to rural development, with a strong emphasis on local involvement. The two LEADER programs funded local action groups: a combination of public and private partners who jointly created a strategy and a set of means for the development of rural areas on a community scale (Jenkins, Hall and Troughton, 1998). Global grants were used to: (1) finance infrastructure to meet tourists' needs, (2) finance the development of buildings and rural sites, (3) promote activities, market studies and measures to extend the tourism season (Wanhill, 1997). The novelty of the LEADER programs was their emphasis on community participation. A project was not eligible for support unless it had a local partner. This was a bottom-up approach for rural development with a strong emphasis on tourism. Out of 217 LEADER regions, tourism was the dominant business plan in 71 of them (Calatrava and Aviles, 1993).

EU Regulation Number 2078/92 officially acknowledged the role of farmers as conservators of the landscape and protectors of natural resources. Accordingly, member countries have assigned acreage-bound subsidies to farmers supplying these services in their land cultivation methods. For example, in Austria, farmers who participate in the Market-Relief and Landscape-Compensation Program (MLCP) choose from a list of landscape-enhancing activities and receive subsidies according to given scores and scales. The upper bound in 1992 was 225 ECU per hectare.

Similar methods were applied to the UK in 1988 when the Ministry of Agriculture, Fisheries and Food (MAFF) came up with two policy instruments: the Farm Diversification Grant Scheme (FDGS) and the Farm Woodland Scheme (FWS). The FDGS referred specifically to farm-based diversification. It included three kinds of grants: (1) capital grants of up to £35,000 for non-agricultural structural diversification, (2) feasibility study grants of up to £3,000 for individuals and £10,000 for groups, (3) marketing grants (by the same amount as the feasibility study grants). Eligible enterprises for financial support from the

FDGS included: farm-based accommodations, educational ventures and various recreational activities.

Among FWS goals were: the diversion of land from agricultural production to help reduce agricultural surplus; enhancement of the landscape, the creation of new wildlife habitats, the encouragement of recreational use and the expansion ·of tourist interest; contributions to supporting farm income and rural employment (Ilbery, 1992).

The US and Canada

In the US, as far back as 1980, the federal government (US Department of Agriculture) encouraged farmers to consider farm tourism as a means of supplementing their income and assisted them with the establishment of vacation farm cooperatives. Eleven years later, in a 1991 survey of state-sponsored rural tourism programs, Luloff et al. (1994) found that 30 states had tourism programs specifically targeted to rural areas. The farm bill, passed in 1996, and the reorganization of the Ministry of Agriculture, with an emphasis on rural development, definitely implied an attitude change toward the countryside. With the USDA's reorganization, budgets and authorities of the Agency for Rural Development (USDA/RD) were enhanced. The agency's main duty is improving the quality of life of rural residents, through tight cooperation between private and public sectors. It coordinates grants, loans, and technical help that the Federal government provides. The agency maintains three main programs: rural dwelling services, rural infrastructure services, and rural business services. The latter provides loan guarantees and loan grants for small businesses.

As far as rural tourism is directly concerned, there has been no Federal policy aimed directly at it. The only significant US Federal legislation to address tourism directly was the National Tourism Act of 1973 that established the National Tourism Administration. Rural tourism policy was not mentioned in this act. Even when a national study identified a need for rural tourism policy (Edgell, 1999), neither Congress nor the president offered one. When Congress created the National Rural Tourism Foundation in 1992, it failed to authorize funding for the organization, which has struggled since its inception to meet its mandate. Yet, in the US, it is domestic tourism that makes rural tourism work. In the absence of any Federal guidance policy, assistance was provided by the states. Today, as many as 30 states employ specific tourism programs for rural areas, 14 other states includes rural tourism in their general tourism strategies, and the other six states have no rural tourism strategy (Luloff et al., 1994). Significant state policy efforts have involved the creation of tourism agencies, divisions, or departments within state agencies. Nevertheless, most of the programs are more promotional and marketing-oriented than leaning towards product development, and do not inherently espouse the broader socio-economic goals.

In Canada, despite the dominance of agricultural policy, there were times when the government developed specific rural emphasis schemes (Freshwater, 1991). These schemes were region-specific and tried to adopt an integrative approach that related labor with finance for infrastructure and aid to businesses. Yet, given the nature of the Canadian federal government, the schemes tended to involve the federal and provincial governments in the partnership. These programs faced big obstacles, most of them stopping shortly after initiation, others being absorbed into bigger plans. According to Freshwater (1991), more farm policy than rural policy is found in Canada and the US because farmers have a strong political lobby, originating from a time when farmers were the majority and from Jefferson's approach, which saw in agriculture the ideal basis for democracy. Farmers have strengthened their power over the years and they claim full custody of rural sector representation. But their strong position also derives from the organizational structure of the US and Canadian governments. In both countries, economic policy tends to be sector-oriented. As a result, interest groups are organized by sectors. In rural areas, besides agriculture and fishing, there is no industry with defined leadership.

Other assistance in the transformation of rural North America to one more heavily dependent on tourism has come from the higher-education establishments in the US and Canada. Through the Cooperative Extension Service, arising from the Morrill Act of 1862 which established the land grant system for state universities in the US, have come manuals, workbooks and other resources to help communities understand and manage tourism for their benefit. Rural tourism development has been a common theme of these publications. Canadian universities have also produced some excellent materials dealing with rural tourism issues.

In summary, rural tourism development in North America is a story of domestic tourism. International visitors, although welcome, will have very little impact on how rural tourism in the US, and to a lesser extent in Canada, develop.

B.5. The Relations between Agriculture and Rural Tourism

Cox and Fox (1992) described the relations between rural tourism and agriculture as symbiotic. Upon its introduction, rural tourism makes use of the resources and infrastructures already available in agricultural areas. As it develops, it further extends the infrastructures and creates more resources. The latter become available to the agricultural industry as well.

Yet, within this discussion, a distinction should be made between developed and developing countries. While less important for developed countries, attracting foreign tourists is of great importance for developing countries, which are in dire need of foreign currency. In this case, the flow of local agricultural products to the tourism industry is necessary to prevent a leakage from the economy as result of importing food products that match the visitors' demand. Cox and Fox (1992) recognized three potential sources of such flow: (1) to the tourism businesses, such as hotels, restaurants, etc., (2) directly to the visitors, (3) to the outside environment. The latter happens when tourists' tastes begin to favor local products. This change may lead tourists to demand those products once they return home.

The more the local farmers adjust to the demand of the tourist industry, the less leakage there will be from the economy. Latimer (1985) and Bowen (1998) found that in the Himalayas, farmers have adapted to visitors' demands by producing higher value products, such as pineapple, macadamia nuts, papaya and guava.

Forsyth (1995) researched the adoption of tourism by agricultural communities in northern Thailand. He found that tourism was only adopted by those with available cash and labor, and did not present a viable alternative to agriculture. Most of the poorest households did not have the resources to adopt rural tourism; instead, they intensified land cultivation. His findings are somewhat similar to Evens and Ilbery (1989) in their research of tourism adoption practices in England.

Barke and Newton (1994), in a study in the Alpujarras area near Granada in southern Spain, pointed out some problems caused to the agricultural industry by rural tourism, such as lack of labor and high land prices. Following the application of the LEADER program, the service sector's contribution to employment rose from 25% in 1982 to 66% in 1992, while agriculture's contribution to employment declined from 70% to 38%, respectively. This might be evidence that rather than helping farmers survive, rural tourism actually accelerated the downturn of agricultural businesses in the area.

Within the framework of rural tourism, farm tourism enterprises are more closely related to agriculture than other rural tourism operations. Clarke (1996) claims that there is a difference between tourism on farms and farm tourism. When accommodations are divorced from the farm environment then it is 'farm tourism', while in 'tourism on the farm', the farm environment and its essence are incorporated into the product (e.g., participation in the farm work and picking your own produce).

Busby and Rendle (2000) describe the transition from 'tourism on the farm' to 'farm tourism'. This transition occurs as farmers who become engaged in tourism on their farms slowly divorce themselves from agricultural activities. With this transition, the farm activities are no longer a necessary component. Clough (1997) extends this argument further by claiming that most of the visitors would be happy not seeing the working farm. These observations lead to the conclusion that there is a range of links between agriculture and tourism and that these links are getting weaker, especially from the visitor's point of view.

In summary, the relations between the two industries have been analyzed in the literature; most studies have explored the effects of rural tourism on the agricultural industry. There is, however, a lack of rigorous economic analysis studying the mutual effects within the same multi-product firm, i.e. a firm that manufactures agricultural products as well as providing tourism services.

C. RURAL TOURISM IN ISRAEL

C.1. Background

Growth

Rural tourism is the most continuously rapidly growing economic activity in rural areas of Israel. Since its inception towards the end of the 1980s (Fleischer and Pizam, 1997) the industry has been exhibiting an average annual growth rate of 15%. Prior to its introduction, residents of rural communities were engaged mainly in agricultural and off-farm activities. With the worsening of the terms of trade in agriculture and the resultant decline in real income, many farmers, similar to their counterparts in Europe and North America, adopted rural tourism as an alternative or complementary source of income.

By the year 2004, the rural accommodations industry accounted for 18% of the total domestic tourism market in terms of room nights. It consisted of 8,000 accommodations units, situated in about 210 villages: semi-cooperatives (Moshavim) and collectives (Kibbutzim), and non-agricultural rural towns. These spread out from the Lebanese border in the north to the Red Sea in the south. The increase in the number of accommodations units in the last two decades is depicted in Figure 17.1.

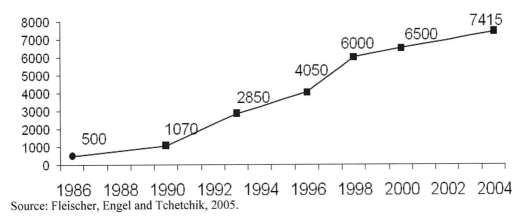

Source: Fleischer, Engel and Tchetchik, 2005.

Figure 17.1. Number of Rural Accommodations Units in Israel over 18 Years.

Following the increase in accommodations units was the establishment of attractions in the rural space such as restaurants and galleries, agro-tourism and other leisure activities. Data gathered by the Ministry of Agriculture indicates that by the end of 1999, there were more than 2,350 tourist attractions in the rural periphery.

The rural accommodations product has gone through some drastic changes during its existence. In the first stages, existing buildings in Kibbutzim and Moshavim were converted to serve as accommodations units. These units were very basic facilities, just adequate for accommodation. The season was short with an average annual occupancy of 80 to 90 nights (reflecting the fact that demand consisted mainly of families with children, confined to holiday/vacation periods). With the years, new types of units began appearing. These were mostly log cabins, highly luxurious and accessorized with facilities such as air-conditioning, TV, VCR, Jacuzzi, fireplace, etc. Extras such as wines, natural juices, chocolates and pastries started being served as part of the hospitality. As a result, prices have increased, the high season has expanded and new segments have entered the market. The Internet has been supplying an ideal, low-cost marketing channel for the firms' owners. It should be noted that the rural accommodations industry in Israel relies mainly on domestic tourists; it has not penetrated the incoming tourism market. Dependency on the domestic market implies a limited potential market. In this case, firms must rely heavily on repeat visits. This, in part, has driven new entrants to the market to position their units to the up-market, which has resulted in vast product differentiation.

Government Support

In the early stage of development, the Jewish Agency was the only organization giving support to the rural tourism industry. With the expansion of the industry and the recognition of its importance, the Ministry of Tourism started supporting it in 1993. Today the industry is regulated and supported by the ministries of Tourism and Agriculture as well as other non-governmental organizations. Three main support programs are being employed: a tourism village program, a small-business loan and guarantee fund, and a capital support fund for farmers. The Ministry of Tourism also operates "Tourism Incubators" jointly with the Jewish Agency in peripheral areas. Within these Incubators, business advisory services and business accompaniment are offered to rural tourism operators, as well as professional skills training. The Incubators cover 75% of the training costs and the operators pay the rest. Figure 17.2

presents the development of total funds, budgeted by the Ministry of Tourism to support rural tourism. The support budget is divided into direct support (a small-business loan and guarantee fund) and indirect support (a tourism village program).

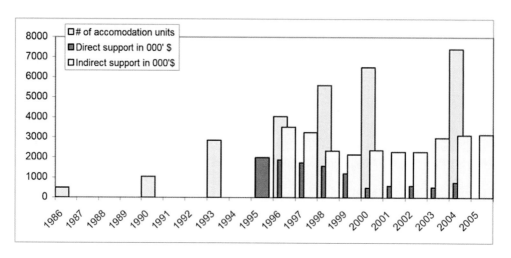

Figure 17.2. Ministry of Tourism's Support to Rural Accommodations.

C.2. Detailed Description of the Industry

The following section describes the rural accommodations industry in Israel, based on a dataset collected via a cross-sectional survey. The survey was conducted in the year 2000 and provided the database for a Ph.D. dissertation (Tchetchik, 2006). Updates and completions were taken from the Israeli rural tourism survey of 2004 (Fleischer et al., 2005).

The following figures provide descriptive statistics of the rural accommodations industry. Averages are given followed by the standard deviations in brackets. Differences among regions' averages are stated only where significant. Differences in averages were tested by T-test with a confidence level of 5%.

Firms

The typical firm consists of 3.6 (2.8) accommodations units. Regional differences exist: the Sea of Galilee's average is the highest while the Western Galilee's average is the lowest (Figure 17.3).

Businesses have been in existence for 6.3 (5.4) years on average: firms in the Upper Galilee, being the pioneers in rural accommodations, average 7.7 years while in the Western Galilee, rural accommodations is a relatively new phenomenon and hence the average firm has been around for 2.5 years.

As already mentioned, the industry is moving toward highly accessorized luxury units. The establishment of new log cabins reflects this trend: 22% (39%) of the sample's units are log cabins. Regional differences are found, as can be seen in Figure 17.4: specifically, in the Western Galilee, the ratio of log cabins is the highest, 55%, while in the Upper Galilee region, only 9% are log cabins.

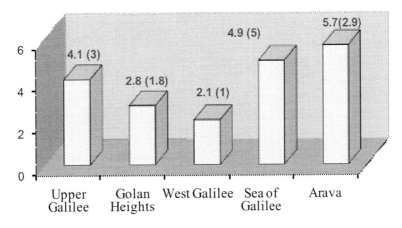

Figure 17.3. Average Number of Units per Firm by Region (S.D. in brackets).

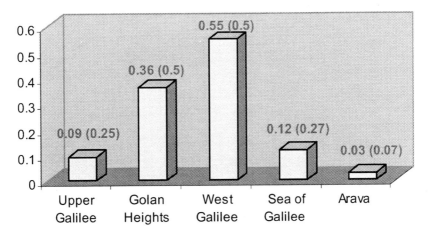

Figure 17.4. Average Share of Log Cabins per Firm by Region (S.D. in brackets).

These regional differences reflect the fact that while in the former region, rural accommodations are relatively new and positioned for the up-market, in the latter region, rural accommodations were established earlier on and are thus characterized by more standard units. This is also reflected in the investment in luxury elements in the unit (e.g. Jacuzzi, sauna, VCR, etc.). The average firm invested NIS 5,540 (4,520) per unit. As can be seen in Figure 17.5, rural accommodations in the Western Galilee are the most luxurious, with an average of NIS 7,300, while units in the Sea of Galilee are the least luxurious, with an average investment of NIS 3,100.

Another characterization of the rural accommodations relates to the service provided by the operators. The variable "Amenities" refers to the number of "extras" the guests are provided with as part of the hospitality. These include natural juices, homemade jams and pastries, wines, chocolates, bath oils, flowers, etc. The average firm's offer is 2.7 (2.3) amenities per unit.

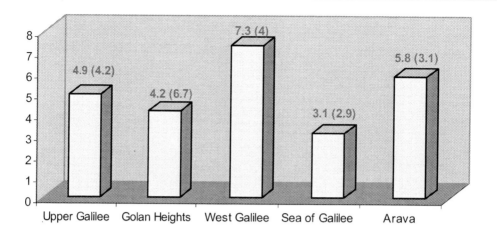

Figure 17.5. Average Investment in Luxury Elements by Region (S.D. in brackets).

In many rural accommodations, the firm's operator offers leisure activities, such as guided tours of the surrounding area, jeep trips, bicycle rides, body massages, etc. (These activities are not included in the accommodations price and are charged separately.) While the sample's maximum is five activities, the average firm offers one (0.9) leisure activities. Another kind of leisure activity offered is agro-tourism, such as guided tours of the agricultural area, picking your own fruit, taking part in livestock activities, etc. Operators, who are also farmers, can offer agro-activities and thus relate the accommodations more closely to agriculture. The average among farmers is 0.5 (0.7) agro-activities.

A fourth element of service is the "Personal Touch." It reflects the extent to which firms' operators demonstrate warm hospitality toward their visitors. For example, do they initiate welcoming conversation with their guests upon arriving, do they show concern for their guests' satisfaction during the hospitality and at the end of their stay. etc. The personal touch variable sums these elements. While the maximum possible value is 9, the average firm's score is 7.33 (0.95). This implies warm hospitality among Israeli rural accommodations operators. No significant differences were found among regions.

Since the external environment of the accommodations is important in determining the demand for rural accommodations, it is described with a focus on the surrounding scenery, and on the attractions in the village and in the area. The landscape viewed from the accommodations unit is described using two dummy variables. The first, "Open View," specifies whether there is an open view from the unit. The other dummy. "Spectacular View," is defined as a completely unobstructed open view of nature, such as the sea, mountains, forests, or agricultural fields, without any interference from man-made constructions: 85% of the firms have open views of landscapes from the units, while regionally, the Upper Galilee's average is the highest at 92%, and the Arava's average is the lowest. only 33%. As many as 46% of the firms enjoy the positive externality of a spectacular view.

Tourist attractions in the village include restaurants, river-rafting, horseback-riding, galleries, museums, etc. The average number of attractions in a village is 5.8 (5.1), while the most tourism-oriented village enjoys the presence of 16 attractions. As can be seen in Figure

17.6, villages in the Upper Galilee area are richer in attractions, while villages in the vicinity of the Sea of Galilee have only one attraction on average.

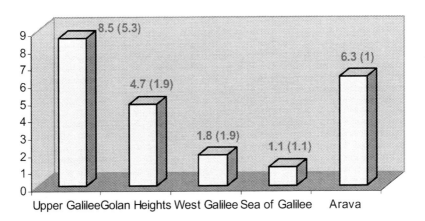

Figure 17.6. Average Number of Attractions in Settlement by Region (S.D. in brackets).

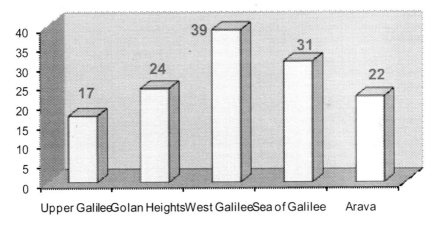

Figure 17.7. Number of Special Attractions by Region.

The tourist attractions in the surrounding area reflect an important regional influence on the demand for rural accommodations. Unlike full-resort accommodations, people stay at rural accommodations as a base for trips in the vicinity. Regional attractions include national parks, natural reserves, museums, archeological sites, etc. Focusing on attractions of great interest (as classified by the Israeli Karta Tourism Guide), it is found that on average there are 24.2 (9) attractions per region. Figure 17.7 demonstrates the regional distribution of special attractions. It reveals that the Western Galilee is the most affluent with special attractions whilst the Arava region is the least affluent with them.

Owners

Having described the internal and external environments of the accommodations, we now characterize their operators. As mentioned earlier, the rural accommodations business is typically a small-scale family business run by husbands and wives: 42% of the operators are also active farmers, 12.12% of the operators used to practice farming and left it once they got involved in rural accommodations; 40% of the males engaged in the industry also work off-farm/house at a 2/3 to full-time job, and 45% of the females work 2/3-time jobs off the farm/house.

Turning to the operators' education and managerial skills, it is found that on average, the educational level per household is of post-high school. Of the sample's operators (either husband or wife), 17% have managerial skills, that is, they have occupational experience as managers. Comparing regionally, Arava's operators were found to have no managerial experience at all.

C.3 Economic Indicators

Tchetchik et al. (2008) estimated various economic indicators of the rural accommodations industry. This section presents these results starting with per-firm economic indicators, then with a comparison to hotel accommodations and the regional importance of rural tourism, and ending with an industry-level account.

Per-Unit Performance

In this section, all figures are in 1999 NIS. Regional differences are stated for significant differences only.[3]

Occupancy

Average annual occupancy is 107 (48) nights per unit, i.e. a 30% occupancy rate. Regional differences were found: in the Western Galilee, occupancy is highest, whereas the Sea of Galilee's average is the lowest.

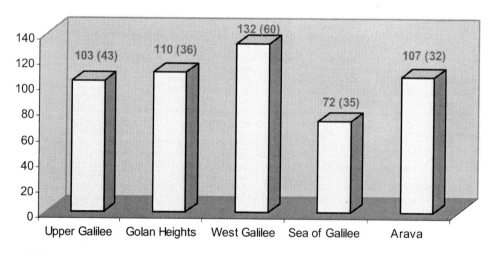

Figure 17.8. Average Annual Occupancy per Unit by Region (S.D. in brackets).

---

[3] Average differences were tested by T-test, at a confidence level of 5%.

Prices

Prices of rural accommodations are high during the high season, lower on off-season weekends and lowest on off-season mid-week days. Average weighted price is NIS 300 (69) per night. In Figure 17.9, the differences among prices in the different seasons as well as among regions are illustrated. The weighted average price in the Western Galilee is the highest, whereas the Sea of Galilee's weighted average price is the lowest.

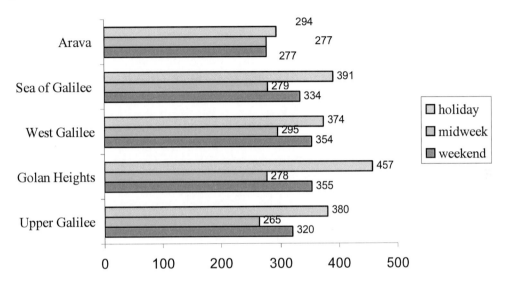

Figure 17.9. Average Price per Unit by Region (S.D. in brackets).

Revenue

The average annual revenue per unit is NIS 47,465 (26,222). This includes revenue from accommodations and from charges for extra breakfasts. Thus, the average annual revenue for a firm operating 3.6 units is NIS 171,400.

Not surprisingly, with the highest occupancy and prices, the annual average revenue in the Western Galilee is the highest, and in the Sea of Galilee, with the lowest occupancy and prices, the lowest (Figure 17.10).

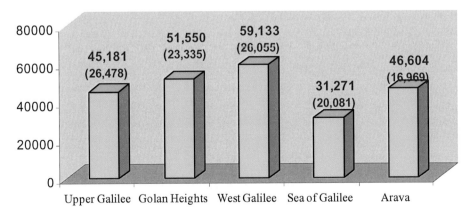

Figure 17.10. Average Annual Revenue per Unit by Region (1999 NIS, S.D. in brackets).

Capital

Seventy-three percent of the units were originally built for use as rural accommodations; the average cost for these units is NIS 96,500, including construction, facilities and furnishing. The other 27% were built for other purposes (such as farm storage) and were converted for use as accommodations. The average cost of conversion is NIS 48,000. Weighting the cost of new and converted units gives an investment of NIS 81,875 on average. Of the operators, 35.4% took active part in the construction and conversion work. Accounting for the value of owners' work[4] brings the average investment in an accommodations unit to NIS 84,605.

Additional money was invested in facilities outside the unit such as dining room, children's facilities, lobby, swimming pool, etc.; 25.3% of the operators reported investing in such facilities, at an average investment of NIS 73,140 per business. Taking all of the above costs into account yields an average investment of NIS 92,400 (43,000) per unit. This is equivalent to NIS 2,740 per square meter. No regional differences were found.

Operating Costs

Being a small family business based on environmental amenities, owner labor and low levels of service, operating costs in rural accommodations are relatively low. Most of the costs data was received from the survey, and completions for expenses such as telephone, water, and electricity were obtained from the "Galilee Development Authority" which gathered accurate annual costs for several accommodations units in the Upper Galilee. The average total annual expenditure is NIS 13,800 per unit (not including own-labor worth). This includes variable costs and fixed costs, i.e. finance and depreciation.

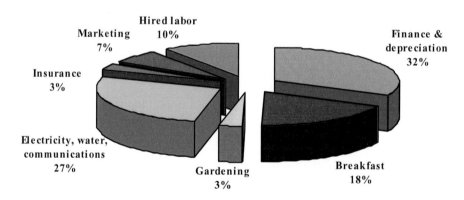

Figure 17.11. Distribution of Total Costs per Unit.

Labor

As illustrated in Figure 17.11, hired labor accounts for a small share of the total costs. The average is 86 hired labor hours, and 507 own labor hours, i.e. 1,825 own labor hours annually for the average firm. Assuming that a full-time job accounts for 2,260 hours annually, own labor in rural accommodations constitutes an 80% position on average, where hired labor per firm constitutes a 14% position. Whereas owner labor is uniquely devoted to

---

[4] The average value of owners' work was estimated at NIS 20,690 per firm.

managing, taking reservations and marketing, hired labor is devoted to tasks such as cleaning, gardening and maintenance.

Profits and Added Value

Calculating the profits in the rural accommodations industry in Israel reveals high profit margins and a high rate of return on investment. Table 1 presents the per-unit calculation for the year 1999.

Profits (after depreciation and finance expenses) account for 71% of revenue and constitute a 36% return on investments. If accounting for own labor costs, profit rate falls to 20% of revenue and constitutes a 10.3% return on investment.

Table 1. Per Unit Calculation for 1999

	NIS (1999 values)
Average annual revenue	47,465
Average annual added value	39,443
Average annual operative profit	38,083
Average annual profit before tax [1]	33,652
Annual average profit before tax [2]	9,652
Average capital investment	92,400
Average annual cost	13,800
from which hired labor cost	1,360

(1) After depreciation and finance expenses.
(2) After depreciation, finance expenses and estimated own labor costs.

Industry Level Performance

Table 2 provides aggregative figures for the industry's performance. It indicates that while the number of accommodations units has increased by 32%, aggregate revenue has increased by 52%. This is explained by the increase in average occupancy rate (by 27%), and the increase in real prices.

The fact that the rural accommodations market is exclusively domestic is reflected in the relatively small contribution of rural accommodations to the entire tourism product.

To gain additional insight into the industry's technology, it is instructive to compare the economic performance of a typical rural accommodations unit to the average hotel unit. Table 3 presents such a comparison.

While occupancy rate and revenues in the hotel industry are twice as large, the value added in the hotel industry is only 30% larger than in the rural accommodations. Moreover, when turning to profits (return to equity), the ranking is reversed. The return to equity in rural accommodations is 1.53 times that in the hotel industry. These differences are explained by the differences in hospitality technology.

Hotel hospitality requires many services beyond the room itself. Examples are facilities, such as a lobby, swimming pool, and dining room. These amenities are replaced in rural hospitality by the rural environment, the farmer's garden, the farm landscape, etc., the latter being byproducts of farming and the household residence.

Table 2. Industry Level Account (thousands of $ US 2005)

	1999	2004[1]
Number of accommodations units	6,156	8,105
Average occupancy rate	30%	38%
Aggregate annual revenue	75,955	115,419
Aggregate added value	63,118	95,912
Aggregate wages	2,176	3,306
Return to equity and owners' labor	60,942	92,605
% added value in agriculture added value	2.2	6.7
% added value in tourism added value	11.6	10

(1) Source: Fleischer et al., 2005.

Table 3. Comparison with the Hotel Industry in 1999 NIS

	Rural accommodations (per unit)	Hotel industry [1] (per room)
Occupancy rate	30%	61.8% [2]
Annual revenue	47,465	95,400
Added value	39,443	52,800
Employees (annual labor per unit)	0.14	0.69
Wages	1,360	38,500
Return to equity and owners' labor	33,652	10,800

(1) Source: Statistical Abstract of Israel 2000, no. 51.
(2) Of which half is the result of incoming tourism.

Considering that an average investment in a rural accommodations unit is $24,000, significantly less than the capital requirements for an average hotel room (between $80,000 and $100,000), the implication is that the rate of return to equity and owner's labor in the rural accommodations industry (approximately 37%) is much larger than the return rate in the hotel industry (approximately 13%). This provides an explanation for the rapid growth of the rural accommodations industry.

Importance to Regional Economy

As shown by the above indicators, the revenues from rural accommodations make up only a small share of the total agricultural and tourism aggregate products. However, in the northern regions of Israel, rural accommodations has become an important source of livelihood.

As can be seen in Figure 17.12, the average participation rate ranges between 6 and 10% of the total household population. For those families who operate rural accommodations businesses, the profits from tourism present an important source of income.

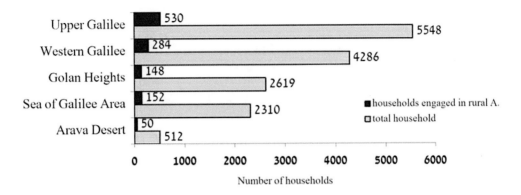

Figure 17.12. Participation in Rural Accommodations of Rural Population.

Table 4. Income Estimates for Operators of Rural Accommodations in 1999 NIS

Income source	Farmers		Non-Farmers	
	Annual income	% of income	Annual income	% of income
Rural tourism	131,627	50.7%	117,380	60.7%
Agriculture [1]	64,455	24.8%		
Off-farm occupation [2]	63,376	24.4%	75,945	39.3%
Total family income	259,459	100.0%	193,325	100.0%

(1) Norms of profit per unit of farming activity—Ministry of Agriculture and Rural Development.
(2) Wages by occupation—Central Bureau of Statistics, Statistical abstract of Israel 2000.

As can be seen in Table 4, tourism income makes up 50 and 60% of agricultural and non-agricultural households' incomes, respectively, while farm profits and wages from off-farm jobs are only secondary sources of the household's livelihood.

SOME EMPIRICAL RESULTS

Recognizing a dearth of rigorous economic analyses and accounting for the industry's special features, hedonic prices and discrete-choice models were employed to analyze the rural accommodations industry by Fleischer and Tchetchik (2005) and Tchetchik et al. (2008). Fleischer and Tchetchik (2005) estimated a linear hedonic price function. They divided the attributes of rural accommodations into four groups: (1) attributes of the unit itself, (2) attributes of the owner, (3) the level of tourism activity, (4) agricultural activities. The units are characterized by their luxury level, amenities, size, and the serving of breakfast. The owners' service orientation is an important characteristic of rural accommodations due to the personal touch that characterizes this type of hospitality. The level of tourism orientation is reflected in the number of tourism activities being offered on the premises, the existence of a tourism village infrastructure and the number of tourist attractions in the surrounding area. Agriculture is reflected as an attribute of the unit if the visitors are exposed to a working farm and/or open green rural landscape. The estimation results revealed that of the four variables that reflect the attribute of the unit, three are positive and significant. For each increase in NIS

1,000 in the luxury component, the hedonic price increases by NIS 4.84. Visitors are willing to pay NIS 28 more for log cabins and NIS 0.84 for every additional square meter. Tourism orientation of the accommodations has the highest impact on the hedonic price. This is true at the unit level, at the village level and at the regional level. The incremental contribution of activities and attractions to the price fades with increases in distance. For each increase in activity or number of attractions at the unit location, the price increases by NIS 9.7, at the settlement level by NIS 5.4 and in the surrounding area by NIS 2.2. The public investment in the planning and infrastructure of a tourism village pays off and visitors will pay NIS 20 more for this attribute. The rest of the accommodations attributes were not found significant.

Vanslembrouck et al. (2005) conducted a similar study in the Belgian rural tourism industry. The results indicate that the higher the number of people that can stay in the same room, the lower the price per person and per night. Quality and provision of catering have positive effects on the price of the accommodations. Most of the geographic characteristics do not have a significant influence on the price. Among the environmental attributes, five are clearly significant. Accommodations price appears to be negatively influenced by fodder crop production, which can be related to intensive livestock farming and the proportion of forests in the area. On the other hand, the price is positively correlated with permanent grassland. The later result was found in similar studies in France (e.g. Le Goffe and Delache, 1997).

Tchetchik et al. (2008) adopted a structural approach to estimate equilibrium in the rural accommodations industry. This approach allowed a distinction between the influence of agriculture on production cost and its effect on consumer preferences. Accounting for the vast product differentiation and the heterogeneity in consumer tastes and technologies, they applied a discrete-choice framework with product differentiation to model the rural

accommodations industry in Israel and to jointly estimate the effect of lodging and farm characteristics on consumer preferences and firms' costs. In particular, they applied the nested-logit model which was suggested by McFadden (1978) and Cardell (1997), and was successfully employed for the analysis of related issues, such as demand for recreation and fishing sites (e.g. Hauber and Parsons, 2000). However, while the literature on recreation demand focuses mainly on consumer preferences, the application of Tchetchik et al. (2008) , which follows Berry (1994) and Fershtman et al. (1999), allows a joint estimation of both the demand and cost parameters, using only aggregated firms' level data. The results of the model's estimation revealed an oligopolistic markup that averages 62% of the price. Decomposing the markup reveals that the most important source for the price-cost margin is vertical differentiation, contributing 50% of the markup. Second in importance are horizontal differentiation and lack of information. The rest is attributed to government regulations that restrict supply.

Evidence of technological synergy in the joint production of farming and rural hospitality was also found. For instance, the estimated regression shows that the cost per night for a business located on a flower farm may be as much as 42% lower than a tourism business without a farm. The sources for this synergy are several intrinsic characteristics of an active farm, such as the flexibility of farmers with their time and the ability to adjust their work schedule to meet the needs of the accommodations business. Another characteristic is the ability to employ idle hired labor for tasks such as cleaning, gardening and maintenance.

In the presence of synergy, exits of farmers can adversely affect the rural hospitality industry. Thus, agricultural-support policies that are intended to preserve small family farms may indirectly benefit the rural tourism industry.

The estimated parameters were employed to simulate the industry equilibrium under a variety of governmental policies and market structures. Presently, the industry is heavily regulated and government restrictions create a barrier to entry and development. The simulation results showed that the industry has growth potential and that the government may catalyze growth by lifting regulations and providing information. The government may also beneficially intervene in the market by investment subsidization and provision of local public goods, such as parks, promenades and improved transportation facilities.

Under these circumstances, the rural accommodations industry has a real potential for growth and for becoming an important source of livelihood in the rural economy.

CONCLUDING REMARKS

This section wraps up the literature review of rural tourism in different countries and the in-depth analysis of rural tourism in Israel by delineating what other countries can learn from the Israeli experience. Based on the thorough description of rural tourism operations worldwide it can be concluded that the rural tourism product is less country specific and more sectoral specific. Thus, the Israeli analysis, being unique in its comprehensiveness, can provide insights into operation and policy formulation of rural tourism in other countries.

Throughout the chapter it is shown that rural accommodations businesses share many similarities regardless of which country they operate in. Tourism has been developing in rural areas as a response to the declining terms of trade and employment in agriculture. In many rural regions as well as in Israel, tourism was found to be the fastest growing rural economic activity. It is typically based on the regional ambience and rural amenities which provide an important source of product differentiation. Rural accommodations consists of small family-based firms and usually it provides only an auxiliary income to the household. However, it was found in different regions that it has an important contribution to the whole rural economy through high multipliers. Moreover, accounting for the special interrelationship between agriculture and tourism, rural tourism enables farmers to remain on the farm and continue farming.

In many countries, Israel included, the national and local governments recognized the importance of tourism in halting the process of urbanization. They also acknowledged the role of farmers as conservators of landscape and protectors of rural amenities and the need for career retraining of farmers. All these factors provide the rationale for the medley of policy measures that support and regulate the development of rural tourism in different regions.

The interrelationship between agriculture and tourism was noted by other studies, however, the analysis of the Israeli case provides an insight into the dynamics of these two activities. A farmer engaged in both activities, tourism and agriculture, is a more efficient producer of tourism services. This is the case in Israel but due to the aforementioned similarities it is probably the same in other countries and policy makers should realize that supporting agricultural provides indirect support to tourism.

Another important insight is the realization that rural tourism is a highly differentiated market with welfare implications. The fact that rural tourism is regional-based and consists of small family businesses gives the rural tourism operators the ability to differentiate their business and thus receive above normal profits. This market structure is typical to most of the regions and thus governments should formulate their policy accordingly. For example, provide more information about the units to the public can enhance welfare.

It is important to note that the forces in the rural economies leading to the development of tourism activities are still undergoing structural changes. The lessons from the Israeli case study provide insights for policy makers in other countries in formulating their support and regulation measures of this process.

REFERENCES

Archer, B.H. (1974). The impact of recreation on local economies. *Planning Outlook, Vol. 14*, 16-27.

Arnold, J. (2004). Why rural tourism is no picnic, BBC News.

Baldock, B., and Beaufoy, G. (1993). *Nature Conservation and New Directions in the EC Common Agricultural Policy*. London, UK: Institute for European Environmental Policy.

Barke, M., and Newton, M. (1994). A new rural development initiative in Spain: the European Community's Plan LEADER, *Geography, Vol. 79*, 366-371.

Bates, and Wacker, S.C. (1996). *Tourism and the European Union: A Practical Guide. EU Funding, Other Support, EU Policy and Tourism,* Luxembourg: European Commission, Directorate—General III Tourism Unit.

Beeton, S. (1999). Rural tourism policy: cross-sectional land-use regulation and government policy in Australia. In Daugherty, C.M. (Ed.), *Proceedings of Sustaining Rural Environments: Issues in Globalization, Migration and Tourism.* Department of Geography and Public Planning. Flagstaff, AZ: Northern Arizona University.

Berry, S. (1994). Estimating discrete-choice models of product differentiation, *Rand Journal of Economics, Vol. 25*, 334-347.

Bollman, R. (2005). Tourism employment in rural Canada. *Rural and Small Town Canada Analysis Bulletin, Vol. 5*(8).

Bowen, J.T. (1998). Market segmentation in hospitality research: no longer a sequential process. *International Journal of Contemporary Hospitality Management, Vol.10* (7), 289-296.

Bowler, I.R. (1985). Some consequences of the industrialization of agriculture in the EEC. In Healey, M.J., and Ilbery, B.W. (Eds.), *Industrialization of the Countryside* (pp. 75-98), Norwich: GeoBooks.

Brown, D. (2005). *Rural Tourism: an Annotated Bibliography*. Technical report, Economic Research Service, U.S. Dept. of Agriculture.

Busby, G., and Rendle, S. (2000). The transition from tourism on farms to farm tourism, *Tourism Management, Vol. 21*(8), 635-642.

Calatrava, R.J., and Aviles, P. (1993). Tourism: an opportunity of disadvantaged rural areas? *Leader Magazine, Vol. 4*, 6-9.

Cardell, S.N. (1997). Variance components structures for the extreme-value and logistic distributions with application to models of heterogeneity. *Economic Theory, Vol. 13* (2), 185-213.

Clarke, J. (1996). Farm accommodation and the communication mix. *Tourism Management, Vol. 17* (8), 611-620.

Cloke, P. (1993). The countryside as commodity: new rural spaces for leisure. In, Glyptis, S. (Ed.), *Leisure and the Environment* (pp. 53-67). London: Belhaven Press.

Clough, M. (1997). Profiting from farm tourism. *Western Morning News*, 11 June.

Commission of the European Communities. (1986). Action in the field of tourism. *Bulletin of the European Communities*, Supplement 4/86, European Commission, Brussels.

Cox, L.J., and Fox, M. (1992). Linkages between agriculture and tourism. In, Khan, M. A. et al. (Eds.), *VNR'S Encyclopedia of Hospitality and Tourism*. New York, NY: Van Nostrand Reinhold.

Denman, R. (1994b). The farm tourism market. *Insights*, 49-64.

Dernoi, L. (1983). Farm tourism in Europe. *Tourism Management, Vol. 4*, 155-166.

Dernoi, L. (1991). Prospects of rural tourism: needs and opportunities. *Tourism Recreation Research, Vol.16* (1), 89-94.

Dower, M. (1980). *Jobs in the Countryside*. London: National Council for Voluntary Organization.

Edgell, D.L. (1999). *Tourism Policy: the Next Millennium*, Champaign, IL: Sagamore Publishing.

English Tourist Board (1991). *Tourism and the Environment—Maintaining the Balance*, Report of the Countryside Working Group, London.

Ervin, D.E. (1988). Set-aside programs: using U.S. experience to evaluate U.K. proposals. *Journal of Rural Studies, Vol. 4*, 181-189.

Evens, N.J., and Ilbery, B.W. (1989). A conceptual framework for investigating farm-based accommodation and tourism in Britain. *Journal of Rural Studies, Vol. 5*, 257-266.

Evens, N.J., and Ilbery, B.W. (1992). The distribution of farm-based accommodation in England. *The Journal of Royal Agricultural Society of England, Vol. 153*, 67-80.

Fershtman, C., Gandal, N., and Markovich, S. (1999). Estimating the effect of tax reform in differentiated product oligopolistic markets. *Journal of Public Economics, Vol. 74*, 151-170.

Fleischer, A., and Pizam, A. (1997). Rural tourism in Israel. *Tourism Management, Vol. 18*(6), 367-372.

Fleischer, A., and Tchetchik, A. (2005). Does rural tourism benefit from agriculture? *Tourism Management, Vol. 26*, 493-528.

Fleischer, A., Engel, Y., and Tchetchik, A. (2005). *Rural Tourism in Israel 2004*. Technical report. Jerusalem, Israel: The Hebrew University of Jerusalem.

Flint, D. (1992). *Tourism in Europe*. Hove, E. Sussex: Hodder Wayland.

Forsyth, T. (1995). Tourism and agricultural development in Thailand. *Annals of Tourism Research, Vol. 22*(4), 877-900.

Frater, J.M. (1982). Farm tourism in England: planning, funding, promotion and some lessons from Europe. *Tourism Management, Vol. 4* (3), 167-179.

Freshwater, D. (1991). The historical context of federal rural development policy. *Western Wire*, 1-12.

Galston, A., and Baehler, K.J. (1995). *Rural Development in the United States. Connecting Theory, Practice and Possibilities*. Washington D.C.: Island Press.

Gasson, R., and Potter, C. (1988). Farmer participation in voluntary land diversification scheme: some restriction from a survey. *Journal of Rural Studies, Vol. 4*, 365-375.

Hauber, B.A., and Parsons, G. (2000). The effect of nesting structure specification on welfare estimation in random utility model of recreation demand: an application to the demand for recreational fishing. *American Journal of Agricultural Economics, Vol. 82* (3), 501-514.

Healey, M.J., and Ilbery, B.W. (1985). *The Industrialization of the Countryside*, Norwich Norfolk: Geo Books.

Hewison, R. (1987). *The Heritage Industry: Britain in a Climate of Decline*. London: Methuen.

Hjalager, A. (1996). Agricultural diversification into tourism- evidence of a European Community development program. *Tourism Management, Vol. 17* (2), 103-111.

Ilbery, B.W. (1990). The challenge of land redundancy. In, Pinder, D. (Ed.), *Western Europe: Challenge and Change* (pp. 211-225). London: Belhaven Press.

Ilbery, B.W. (1992). State-assisted farm diversification in the United Kingdom. In Bowler, I.R., Brynt, C.R., and Nellis, M.D. (Eds), *Contemporary Rural Systems in Transition. Vol. 1: Agriculture and Environment* (pp. 100–118). Melksham, Wiltshire: Redwood Press.

Ilbery, B.W., Bowler, I., Clark, G., Crockett, A., and Shaw, A. (1998). Farm-based tourism as an alternative farm enterprise: a case study from the Northern Pennies, England. *Regional Studies*, Vol. 32 (4), 355-364.

Jenkins, J.M., Hall, C.M., and Troughton, M. (1998). The restructuring of rural economies: rural tourism and recreation as a government response. In Butler, R, Hall, C. M., and Jenkins, J. (Eds.), *Tourism and Recreation in Rural Areas* (pp. 43-68). Chichester, W. Sussex: John Wiley.

Ladki, S.M. (1993). Evaluation of tourists' experience in rural Northern West Virginia. *Proceeding of the Society of Travel And Tourism Educators Conference, Vol. 5*, 90-102.

Lane, B. (1994). What is rural tourism? In, Bramwell, B., and Lane. B. (Eds.), *Rural Tourism and Sustainable Rural Development*. Clevedon, England: Channel View Publications.

Latimer, H. (1985). Developing island economies—tourism vs. agriculture. *Tourism Management*, Vol. 16, 32-42.

Le Goffe, P., and Delache, X. (1997). Impacts de l'agriculture sur le tourisme, une application des prix hedonists. *Economie rurale, Vol. 239*, 3-10.

Luloff, A.E., Bridger, J.C., Graefe, A.R., and Saylor, M. (1994). Assessing rural tourism efforts in the United States. *Annals of Tourism Research, Vol. 21*(1), 46-64.

MAFF (Ministry of Agriculture, Fisheries and Food). (1995). *Success with Farm-Based Tourist Accommodation*. London: MAFF Publications.

McFadden, D. (1978). Modeling the choice of residential location. In Karlqvist, A., Lundquist, L., Snickars, F., and Weibull, J. (Eds.), *Special Interaction Theory and Planning Models* (pp. 75-96). Amsterdam, North Holland. Reprinted in J. Quigley (Ed.). (1997). *The Economics of Housing*, 1 (pp. 531-552). London: Edward Elgar.

Nitsch, B., and Straaten, J. (1995). Rural tourism development: using a sustainable tourism development approach. In, Coccossis, H., and Nijkamp, P. (Eds.), *Sustainable Tourism Development* (pp. 169-185). Avebury, Wiltshire: Aldershot.

Oppermann, M. (1996). Rural tourism in South Germany. *Annals of Tourism Research, Vol. 23*, 86-102.

Owens, P.L. (1984). Rural leisure and recreation research. *Progress in Human Geography, Vol. 8*, 158-188.

Shaw, G., and Williams, A. (1994). *Critical Issues in Tourism: A Geographical Perspective*, Oxford, UK: Blackwell.

Slee, B., Farr, H., and Snowdon, P. (1997). The economic impact of alternative types of rural tourism. *Journal of Agricultural Economics, Vol. 48* (2), 179-192.

Smith, V., and Wylde, P. (1977). The multiplier impact of tourism in Tasmania. In Mercer, D. (Ed.), *Leisure and Recreation in Australia* (pp. 165-172). Melbourne: Sorrett Publishing.

Tchetchik, A. (2006). *Rural Tourism in Israel: Structure Analysis and Policy Implications*. Ph.D. Dissertation. Jerusalem: The Hebrew University.

Tchetchik, A., Fleischer, A., and Finkelshtain I. (2008). Differentiation and Synergies in Rural Tourism: Estimation and Simulation of the Israeli Market. *American Journal of Agricultural Economics, Vol. 90* (2), 553-570.

Browne A. (2001). Now our tourist industry faces ruin, all because of farming. *The Observer*, 11 March.

Vanslembrouck, I., Huylenbroeck, G.V., and Meensel, J.V. (2005). Impact of agriculture on rural tourism: a hedonic pricing approach. *Journal of Agricultural Economics, Vol. 56* (1), 17-30.

Wanhill, S. (1997). Peripheral area tourism: a European perspective. *Progress in Tourism and Hospitality Research, Vol. 3*, 47-70.

Weaver, D.A., and Fennel, D.A. (1997). The vacation farm sector in Saskatchewan: a profile of operations. *Tourism Management, Vol. 18* (6), 357-365.

Windhorst, H.W. (1989). Industrialization of agricultural production and the role of large-scale farms in U.S. agriculture. *Geography, Vol. 80*, 270-282.

INDEX

E

F

G

H

M

Q

R

S

T

U

Y

Z